Machzor: Challenge and Change Volume 2

PREPARING FOR
MISHKAN HANEFESH
AND THE
HIGH HOLY DAYS

Machzor:
Challenge and Change
Volume 2

PREPARING FOR
MISHKAN HANEFESH
AND THE
HIGH HOLY DAYS

Central Conference of American Rabbis
5774   New York   2014

Edited by Rabbi Hara E. Person, Adena Kemper, and
Liz Piper-Goldberg

Discussion Questions by Adena Kemper and
Liz Piper-Goldberg

The Central Conference of American Rabbis would like
to thank everyone who participated in the Continuing
Conversations about the *Machzor* conference calls and
allowed their presentations to be used in this format.

Library of Congress Cataloging-in-Publication Data

Machzor : challenge and change : preparing for
Mishkan HaNefesh and the High Holy Days /
edited by Rabbi Hara E. Person, Adena Kemper,
and Liz Piper-Goldberg.
   volumes cm
  Includes bibliographical references and index.
  ISBN 978-0-88123-216-5 (v. 2., pbk. : alk. paper) 1.
Mahzor. High Holidays. 2. High Holidays--Liturgy.
I. Person, Hara, editor. II. Kemper, Adena, editor. III.
Piper-Goldberg, Liz, editor. IV. Central Conference of
American Rabbis, issuing body.

  BM675.H5Z777 2014

  296.4′531046—dc23

                                        2014007652

10 9 8 7 6 5 4 3 2 1

CCAR Press, 355 Lexington Avenue,
New York, NY 10017
(212) 972-3636
www.ccarpress.org

CONTENTS

Hin'ni: Liturgical and Homiletic Approaches

PART 2. BETWEEN FAITH AND PROTEST: BRINGING BACK TO LIFE THE CHALLENGING METAPHORS IN THE *MACHZOR*

Machzor Presentations from the CCAR Convention, 2013, Long Beach

PART 3. RELATED ARTICLES AND POEMS FROM *CCAR JOURNAL: THE REFORM JEWISH QUARTERLY,* SUMMER 2013

Acknowledgments

Thanks first of all to the many colleagues and scholars who agreed to participate in the CCAR's long-distance learning programs related to *Mishkan HaNefesh*, the new CCAR *machzor*. Long before the *machzor* even had a name, all these wonderful minds generously lent their time and expertise so that CCAR members could become engaged in this process of *machzor*-making. We are also appreciative that they have agreed to let their oral presentations be preserved, typed up, and used in this collection. Huge thanks also to Rabbi Debbie Prinz of the CCAR, who planned and organized all these calls, with help from Ivette Ruiz.

Tremendous thanks to Rabbi Elaine Zecher, who helped imagine this collection of presentations and essays, who served as the guest editor for the *machzor*-themed *CCAR Journal* issue that is included within the covers of this volume, and who has spear-headed the CCAR's *machzor*-making process from the start. Thanks also to Rabbi Joseph Skloot, incoming Chair of the CCAR Worship and Practice Committee, and Rabbi Don Goor, Chair of the CCAR Press Council. And of course, no CCAR publication could ever see the light of day without the support of Rabbi Steven A. Fox, CCAR Chief Executive.

Many others have been integral parts of the making of the book, including our two wonderful HUC-JIR interns, Adena Kemper Blum and Liz Piper-Goldberg, and our in-house team of staff members: Deborah Smilow, Ortal Bensky, Rabbi Dan Medwin, and Cori Carl. Thanks to Rabbi Susan Laemmle, immediate Past Chair of the *CCAR Journal*, under whose guidance the *Journal* issue included here was developed. Thanks also to copy-editors and proofreaders Debra Hirsch Corman and Michael Isralewitz, and the compositors from Publishing Synthesis.

Finally, a special thanks to the devoted colleagues who make up the *Machzor* Editorial Team, including Rabbis Edwin Goldberg, Janet Marder, Sheldon Marder, and Leon Morris, as well as Rabbi Peter Berg, CCAR Member Liaison, Rabbi Elaine Zecher, *Machzor* Advisory Group Chair, and Cantor Evan Kent, ACC Representative.

Rabbi Hara Person
Publisher, CCAR Press

Preface

We live in a magnificent time of innovative liturgical development and creative application of Jewish tradition. In the Diaspora and around the world, thoughtful rabbis, cantors, lay leaders, scholars, and educators have woven and continue to weave a varied tapestry of progressive liberal Judaism in the realm of the spirit. Consider the pages before you a collective toolbox filled with intellectual and spiritual resources. We hope you will find insights and conduits for learning, for discovery, and even for surprise.

It is possible to see the *machzor* in a similar way—it too is a tool kit for the soul. Though it is only one facet of the High Holy Day experience, it certainly plays a key role. We chose to name the *machzor Mishkan HaNefesh* because our focus during these Holy Days centers on the place of the soul in one's life and community. How we nurture it, ensure its strength, and guarantee its sacred purpose embodied in each person depends on the spiritual work we do during the High Holy Day season. As Martin Buber wrote in *Way of Man*, we need to start with ourselves but not end with ourselves. The introspection, self-accountability, and recognition of our transgressions must lead us outward to be active players in the world in which we live. Jewish tradition offers us the chance to repair ourselves, our relationships, and our communities. We have striven to ensure *Mishkan HaNefesh* can serve as a catalyst for such endeavors.

This publication joins the first in this series of *Machzor: Challenge and Change*, both of which are meant to help bring deeper reflection and consideration to the process of preparing for a new *machzor*. We have been planning for the arrival of *Mishkan HaNefesh* for many years. Congregations have used pilot services during the High Holy Days and even at other times during the year in order to experience its content and what it elicits. At the same time, the CCAR has held a series of phone seminars on different topics related to the *machzor*, invited dialogue and discussion at CCAR Conventions, and published a second *CCAR Journal* dedicated to the *machzor*. We are eager to share these conversations and teachings. Their topics reveal the kind of thoughtful innovation the editors of the *machzor* have considered as they create *Mishkan HaNefesh*. Many ideas emerge from these presentations and articles such as theology, concepts around sin and transgression, challenges to some of the key prayers and components of the High Holy Day liturgy, and much more. Prepare yourself to find a treasure trove for thoughtful consideration.

We live in a time of bold transformation made possible because our worship experience and the presentation of prayer challenge us to rise to new levels and to delve deep into our souls. What lies before you on the following pages is a wonderful complement to the liturgical experience. We hope you are enriched not only in what you learn but also by the path you take toward your own spiritual fulfillment around, during, and because of the High Holy Days.

Rabbi Elaine Zecher
Chair, *Machzor* Advisory Group
Chair, Worship and Practices Committee

Opening Questions

1. What do you value about the *Yamim Noraim*? What do you hope to experience on a personal, spiritual level during these days? What impact would you like to have on your community?
2. How do your actions on these days, including preparation during Elul, services, study sessions, and sermons, help to achieve these goals? What, if anything, are the shortcomings of these actions?
3. How might our values of preserving tradition and acting as part of *K'lal Yisrael* on these holy days come into conflict with our personal search for meaning and spiritual elevation?
4. On what different levels do you experience prayer? How would you define those levels? How can you make the best use of these different entry points?
5. What are your personal boundaries concerning making changes to the liturgical text? How do we best communally set boundaries?
6. How important is it to follow the "traditional" liturgy?
7. How do you define "traditional," in light of the complex process of liturgical change that occurs over time?
8. What options do you use to deal with difficult text?
9. What changes do you permit yourself to make in order to pray using liturgy that is in line with our values and/or our theology?
10. What is the process for making change?

11. How do you balance individual and communal needs in prayer?
12. What is the role of the clergy in making decisions, changes, explanations, *kavanot*, teaching, and so on?
13. What is the value of adding new voices to this process, and how can they take a part?

PART 1

CONTINUING CONVERSATIONS ABOUT THE *MACHZOR*

Presentations from CCAR Continuing Professional Education Phone Seminars

Editor's Note

The following are transcripts of oral presentations made during a series of Continuing Professional Education conference calls offered by the CCAR for its members over three years.

Each set of presentations generally covers some of the following:

1. The origin of the text and its development over time
2. The Reform Jewish approach to this text, both in content and form
3. The theological contributions of each text
4. Ways to reframe the text to highlight its various dimensions of meaning
5. Questions, *d'rashot*, *kavanot*, and creative ways to experience the liturgy in preparation for the *Yamim Noraim* and during services

In the sidebars are discussion questions and additional background information where relevant. Refer to the glossary in the back for translations and explanations of key terms, texts, and personages.

Traditional Torah Readings Reconsidered Session 1: *Akeidah*

Akeidah: Historical Background

Dr. Richard S. Sarason

I want to discuss two things in this presentation. One is the history and the theological rationales that undergird the traditional Torah readings for Rosh HaShanah. The other is a brief account of the history of Reform practice in this area, from the nineteenth century onward.

The earliest sources that we have about Torah readings for all of the festivals are in the Mishnah, *M'gilah* 3:5. This is then supplemented by the *Tosefta*, *M'gilah* 3:5, and then the *Tosefta* materials are supplemented in *Bavli, M'gilah* 31a. We also learn a bit about the Torah-reading customs in the Land of Israel in *P'sikta D'Rav Kahana*, which is a homiletical midrash on the Torah and haftarah readings for the Festivals and special Shabbatot in the Land of Israel (which differ from the Babylonian readings that became the basis for the medieval traditional readings; these are listed first in *Seder Rav Amram*, a liturgical-halachic composition from the late ninth century).

It is interesting, in the light of subsequent custom, to note that although there is a theoretical discussion in the Mishnah of a second day of Rosh HaShanah on account of ambiguity as to when the new moon actually occurs, the evidence of all of the *Eretz Yisraeli* sources (Mishnah, *Tosefta*, *Y'rushalmi*, midrashim) suggests that only one day was actually observed in the Land of Israel at that time. None of the sources from the Land of Israel list Torah readings for two days of Rosh HaShanah; these only appear in Babylonian sources. And, interestingly enough, in the Mishnah, the Torah reading for Rosh HaShanah is not either of the Genesis passages that we know today, but is Leviticus 23:23ff., the portion of the priestly festival calendar that deals with the observance on the first day of the seventh month (it is not yet the beginning of the new year): *Bachodesh hashvi-i b'echad lachodesh* ("In the seventh month, on the first day of the month"). This is also the Torah reading for Rosh HaShanah in *P'sikta D'Rav Kahana.*

Do you find it surprising that only the Babylonian sources cite Torah readings for two days of Rosh HaShanah? Why or why not?

The *Tosefta* gives an elaboration of the brief ruling that appears in the Mishnah. We don't know whether the *Tosefta* represents an earlier version of the tradition that is more extensive and of which the Mishnah represents an epitome, or the other way around. The *Tosefta* version of the tradition that deals with the Torah reading for Rosh HaShanah adds the following to the Mishnah's version: "And there are those who say [that the reading for Rosh HaShanah is] *V'Adonai pakad et Sarah* ["And God took note of Sarah"] (Genesis 21:1ff)." This may originally have been a variant, parallel custom, but it becomes the traditional reading for the first day of Rosh HaShanah from the *Bavli* onward. The rationale for reading this text on Rosh HaShanah is likely to be as follows: One of the themes of

Rosh HaShanah is *Zichronot*, which is not initially about our act of remembering on Rosh HaShanah, but God's. Rosh HaShanah is the day on which we are calling upon God to take providential notice of us, to pay attention to the needs of the Jewish people. In Genesis 21, God pays providential attention to Sarah. There is an aggadic tradition that on Rosh HaShanah, the wombs of four barren matriarchs (Sarah, Rebekah, Rachel, and Hannah) were opened, and they conceived. And that is the thematic and theological association of Genesis 21 with Rosh HaShanah. It adumbrates the theme of *Zichronot*. That is also the basis for the association of the story of Hannah's barrenness and the miraculous birth of Samuel with Rosh HaShanah and its selection as the haftarah for this day. Both stories instantiate God's *Zichronot*—providential attention.

The Babylonian Talmud (*M'gilah* 31a) cites the version of the tradition found in the *Tosefta*, but interestingly enough, the tradition now is glossed with information about the haftarot, and someone, probably at a slightly later time, has also indicated what the Torah and haftarah readings are for the second day. The *Bavli* text reads as follows: "On Rosh HaShanah [we read] *In the seventh month* (Leviticus 23:23ff.) and conclude with [= and the haftarah is] *Truly Ephraim is a dear son to me* (Jeremiah 31:20ff.)." Nowadays this is the traditional haftarah reading for the second day that is paired with the *Akeidah*. (The reason for the association of the Jeremiah passage with Rosh HaShanah is, again, the *Zichronot* theme, which appears in Jeremiah 31:20, *Zachor ezk'renu od*, "My thoughts would dwell on him [= Ephraim] still.")

The Talmud continues by relating the *Tosefta*'s alternative tradition, "There are those who say [that we read on Rosh HaShanah] *And God took*

> Which do you think would be an appropriate reading on Rosh HaShanah: Leviticus 23 or Genesis 21? Why?
>
> Remembrance is a central theme of the High Holy Days. Why is remembering and being remembered so important, especially at this time in the Jewish calendar?

providential note of Sarah (Genesis 21:1ff.) and conclude with [the story of] Hannah (I Samuel 1:1ff.)."
Following this is a gloss that says, "And nowadays,
since we observe two days, on the first day we follow the custom of the alternative opinion [that is to
say, we read *And God took providential note of Sarah*
(Genesis 21)] and the haftarah is Hannah. On the
next day, [we read] *And God put Abraham to the test*
(Genesis 22, the *Akeidah*), and we conclude with
Truly Ephraim is a dear son to me (Jeremiah 31:20ff.)."
And that is the reading custom that is indicated in
Seder Rav Amram, the first post-Talmudic liturgical-
halachic compendium (ca. 870), and it becomes the
traditional custom. The only new information that
Amram gives is that there is an additional reading on both days of Rosh HaShanah from a second
scroll, from the festival calendar in Numbers 29,
where we read about the offerings in the Temple
and the Tabernacle for the first day of the seventh
month. This, too, becomes traditional in medieval
Jewish practice.

We may well ask about the rationale for reading the *Akeidah* on Rosh HaShanah. Here, too, we
find an adumbration of the *Zichronot* theme, since
there are appeals in the traditional liturgy for God
to remember—to be mindful—on our behalf of the
merit of the Binding of Isaac. In a midrashic interpretation of the *Akeidah* that appears in *Midrash
Tanchuma,* Abraham, after passing the test, says to
God, "Look, I'm not leaving this place until You
make me a promise. I could have protested against
what You were asking me to do, but I didn't protest,
and now You owe me one. So this is what I want
You to do: in the future, when my children sin, and
You judge them on Rosh HaShanah, I want You to
be filled with compassion for them for the sake of
what Isaac and I did today, and to account on their

behalf the merit of the Binding of Isaac." And God replies, "Fine. All they need to do in order to remind me is to blow on the horn of that ram caught in the thicket behind you over there. See him? And I will be mindful of your merit in this regard." That is the thematic association for classical Rabbinic culture between the *Akeidah* and Rosh HaShanah, and that is why the story is read on Rosh HaShanah.

Let us now turn to the history of Reform practice with respect to the Torah and haftarah readings for Rosh HaShanah. In fact, Reform practice has been quite varied since the time of the first congregational prayer book of the Hamburg Temple in 1819. Hamburg maintained the tradition of two days of Rosh HaShanah, and they kept the traditional Torah readings, although, interestingly enough, they did not read the haftarah. The *machzor* of the first Reform congregation in Great Britain, the West London Synagogue, dates from 1843. They also observed only one day of Rosh HaShanah (under the influence of their Anglican neighbors, they saw themselves as "biblicists"and observed only the biblical dates for the Festivals). Their reading for the single day of Rosh HaShanah is the *Akeidah*, Genesis 22. But they continue to read the Numbers passage on the sacrificial offerings for the day, from the second scroll. They also do not read a haftarah. Because Abraham Geiger's 1854 Breslau prayer book was written for the entire community (not just for the supporters of Reform), he tends to be a bit more traditional with regard to hallowed customs, so he gives the traditional Torah readings for both days. Interestingly enough, the last German Reform prayer book before the Hitler era, the so-called *Einheitsgebetbuch*, or "Union Prayer Book" of 1929, gives either Genesis 21 or Deuteronomy 33 for the first day of Rosh HaShanah, followed by Num-

Is this rationale for reading the *Akeidah* on Rosh HaShanah compelling for us today? Why or why not?

How many days of Rosh HaShanah does your community observe?

bers 29 from the second scroll, and then gives the traditional readings for everything else.

On the North American continent, the first major Reform prayer book was that of Temple Emanu-El in New York, edited by Leo Merzbacher, published in 1855. They observed only one day of Rosh HaShanah; they read Genesis 22 and apparently did not read a haftarah, since none is listed. David Einhorn's *Olath Tamid,* published in 1858, also observes only one day of Rosh HaShanah. He gives the Torah reading as the *Akeidah,* and the haftarah is the story of Hannah, which both thematically and traditionally goes instead with Genesis 21. Einhorn's readings were to become the custom of the *Union Prayer Book* (1894, 1918, 1940). Isaac Mayer Wise's High Holy Day volumes of *Minhag America* (1866) also observe only one day of Rosh Ha-Shanah. The Torah reading is Genesis 22, the *Akeidah,* but the haftarah is Jeremiah 30. The custom of the *Union Prayer Book,* volume 2 (*UPB-2*), which again, observes only one day, is to read the *Akeidah,* but there are a lot of variations regarding the haftarah. The earliest *UPB-2,* Isaac Moses's draft of 1893 that was never published, gives three options: Isaiah 61, Jeremiah 31, or the story of Hannah in I Samuel. The original *UPB-2* that was published in 1894 gives as haftarah options either I Samuel or Nehemiah 8, the rededication ceremony among the returnees to Jerusalem, at which the Torah was read. The revised version of 1922 gives Isaiah 55 as the second option, while the newly revised version of 1945 reverts to Nehemiah 8 as the second option. *Gates of Repentance* is the first North American Reform *machzor* that makes provision for two days of Rosh HaShanah, in that it gives two services. The first Torah reading, of course, is the *Akeidah,* and the second, in keeping with the theme of *hayom*

Chaim Stern, ed., *Gates of Repentance: The New Union Prayerbook for the Days of Awe* (New York: CCAR Press, 1978; rev. ed. 1996).

harat olam ("Today is the birthday of the world"), is the Creation story in Genesis 1, which for some of us may be a little bit problematic because we will be reading it again just three weeks later. Those are the reading options that are given historically, traditionally, and also in the Reform Movement.

An interesting question that we might pose is why, when the North American Reform Movement moved to a one-day observance of Rosh HaShanah, the traditional reading for the second day, Genesis 22, was retained instead of the reading for the first day, Genesis 21. This might have been done, in part, because the Reformers weren't happy with the traditional rationale for *And God remembered Sarah*, but I'm also inclined to think that the reason might be more sociological, since everybody is impressed by, and remembers, the *Akeidah* story, which also deals with the power of faith.

Why else might reading Genesis 1 be problematic in this context?

If you could choose only one, which would you rather read on Rosh HaShanah: Genesis 21 or Genesis 22? Why?

High Holy Day Traditional Torah Readings: Sources

משנה מסכת מגילה פרק ג משנה ה

בפסח קורין בפרשת מועדות של תורת כהנים. בעצרת, שבעה שבועות. **בראש השנה, בחדש השביעי באחד לחדש. ביום הכפורים, אחרי מות.** ביום טוב הראשון של חג קורין בפרשת מועדות שבתורת כהנים, ובשאר כל ימות החג בקרבנות החג:

Mishnah M'gilah 3:5

On [the first festival day of] Pesach one reads from the section in Leviticus dealing with the festivals (Lev. 23); on Shavuot, *Seven weeks* (Deut. 16:9–12); on Rosh HaShanah, *In the seventh month on the first day of the month* (Lev. 23:23–25); on Yom Kippur, *After the death* (Lev. 16); on the first festival day of Sukkot one reads from the section in Leviticus dealing with the festivals (Lev. 23), while on the rest of the days of Sukkot one reads about the sacrifices during the festival [of Sukkot] (Num. 29:17ff).

תוספתא מסכת מגילה (ליברמן) פרק ג

...יום טוב הראשון של פסח קורין בפרשת הנף שבתורת כהנים ושאר כל מות היפסח מדלגין הלכה ה-ח מעניינות הפסח הכתובין בתורה בעצרת שבעה שבועות ויש אומ' בחדש השלישי
בראש שנה דבר אל בני ישראל בחדש השביעי באחד לחדש יהיה לכם שבתון ויש או' וה' פקד את שרה
ביום הכפורים קורין אחרי מות ומפטירין בעשור שבחומש הפקודים ביום טוב הראשון של חג קורין דבר אל בני ישראל לאמר בחמשה עשר יום לחדש הזה חג הסוכות וגו' בשני ביום השני בשלישי וביום השלישי ברביעי ביום הרביעי בחמשי וביום החמשי בששי וביום הששי בשביעי וביום השביעי בשמיני וביום השמיני

Tosefta M'gilah (Lieberman), Chapter 3, Halachah 5–8

On the first festival day of Pesach, one reads the section concerning the waving [of the omer] in Leviticus (Lev. 23:4ff.), and on all other days of Pesach one skips around among the various passages throughout the

Torah that deal with Pesach. On Shavuot one reads *Seven weeks* (Deut. 16:9-12), and some say, *In the third month* (Ex. 19:1ff.). On Rosh HaShanah, *In the seventh month on the first day of the month you shall observe a day of solemn rest* (Lev. 23:23-25), and some say, *And Adonai remembered Sarah* (Gen. 21). On Yom Kippur, *After the death* (Lev. 16), and concludes with *On the tenth day* in the Book of Numbers (Num. 27:7ff.). On the first festival day of Sukkot one reads, *Speak to the Israelites, saying: On the fifteenth day of this month is the festival of Sukkot* (Lev. 23:34ff.); on the second day, *On the second day* (Num. 29:17); on the third day, *And on the third day* (Num 29:20); on the fourth day, *And on the fourth day* (Num. 29:23); on the fifth day, *And on the fifth day* (Num. 29:26); on the sixth day, *And on the sixth day* (Num 29:29); on the seventh day, *And on the seventh day* (Num 29:32); on the eighth day, *And on the eighth day* (Num. 29:35).

תלמוד בבלי מסכת מגילה דף לא עמוד א

תנו רבנן: בפסח קורין בפרשת מועדות, מפטירין בפסח ו(יהושע ה') גלגל.
והאידנא דאיכא תרי יומי, יומא קמא בפסח גלגל, ולמחר בפסח (מלכים ב' כ"ג)
יאשיהו. ושאר ימות הפסח מלקט וקורא מעניינו של פסח. מאי היא? אמר רב
פפא: מאפ"ו סימן. יום טוב האחרון של פסח קורין (שמות י"ג) ויהי בשלח
מפטירין ו(שמואל ב' כ"ב) וידבר דוד, ולמחר (דברים ט"ו) כל הבכור, ומפטירין
(ישעיהו י') עוד היום. אמר אביי: האידנא נהוג עלמא למיקרי: משך תורא קדש
בכספא פסל במדברא שלח בוכרא. בעצרת (דברים ט"ז) שבעה שבועות ומפטירין
(חבקוק ג') בחבקוק, אחרים אומרים: (שמות י"ט) בחדש השלישי, ומפטירין
(יחזקאל א') במרכבה. והאידנא דאיכא תרי יומי עבדינן כתרוייהו, ואיפכא. **בראש
השנה** (במדבר כ"ט) **בחדש השביעי, ומפטירין** (ירמיהו ל"א) **הבן יקיר לי אפרים,
ויש אומרים** (בראשית כ"א) וה' פקד את שרה, ומפטירין **(שמואל א' ב') בחנה.
והאידנא דאיכא תרי יומי, יומא קמא כיש אומרים, למחר (בראשית כ"ב)
והאלהים נסה את אברהם, ומפטירין הבן יקיר. ביום הכפורים קורין (ויקרא ט"ז)
אחרי מות ומפטירין** (ישעיהו נ"ז) **כי כה אמר רם ונשא, ובמנחה
קורין בעריות ומפטירין ביונה.**
יום טוב הראשון של חג קורין בפרשת מועדות שבתורת כהנים, ומפטירין
(זכריה י"ד) הנה יום בא לה', והאידנא דאיכא תרי יומי, למחר מיקרא הכי
נמי קרינן, אפטורי מאי מפטירין? (מלכים א' ח') ויקהלו אל המלך שלמה,
ושאר כל ימות החג קורין בקרבנות החג. יום טוב האחרון קורין כל הבכור
מצות וחוקים ובכור, ומפטירין (מלכים א' ח') ויהי ככלות שלמה. למחר קורין וזאת
הברכה ומפטירין (מלכים א' ח') ויעמד שלמה. אמר רב הונא אמר רב: שבת שחל
להיות בחולו של מועד, בין בפסח בין בסוכות, מקרא קרינן (שמות ל"ג) ראה
אתה, אפטורי, בפסח (יחזקאל ל"ז) העצמות היבשות, ובסוכות (יחזקאל ל"ח)

ביום בוא גוג.

Babylonian Talmud, *M'gilah* 31a

Our Rabbis taught: On Passover we read from the section of the festivals and for haftarah the account of the Passover of Gilgal. Now that we keep two days of Passover, the haftarah of the first day is the account of the Passover in Gilgal and of the second day that of the Passover of Josiah. On the other days of the Passover the various passages in the Torah relating to Passover are read. What are these? Rav Papa said: The mnemonic is M'A'P'U. On the last day of Passover we say *And it came to pass when God sent,* and as haftarah *And David spoke.* On the next day we read *All the firstborn,* and for haftarah *This very day.* Abaye said: Nowadays the communities are accustomed to read *Draw the ox, Sanctify with money, Hew in the wilderness,* and *Send the firstborn.* On Pentecost, we read *Seven weeks,* and for haftarah a chapter from Habakkuk. According to others, we read *In the third month,* and for haftarah the account of the Divine Chariot. Nowadays that we keep two days, we follow both courses, but in the reverse order. **On the New Year we read *On the seventh month,* and for haftarah *Is Ephraim a darling son unto me.* According to others, we read *And the Lord remembered Sarah,* and for haftarah the story of Hannah. Nowadays that we keep two days, on the first day we follow the ruling of the other authority, and on the next day we say *And God tried Abraham,* with *Is Ephraim a darling son to me* for haftarah. On the Day of Atonement we read *After the death,* and for haftarah *For thus saith the high and lofty one.* At *Minchah* we read the section of forbidden marriages, and for haftarah the Book of Jonah.**

On the first day of Tabernacles we read the section of the festivals in Leviticus, and for haftarah *Behold a day cometh for the Lord.* Nowadays that we keep two days, on the next day we read the same section from the Torah, but what do we read for haftarah: *And all the men of Israel assembled unto King Solomon.* On the other days of the festival we read the section of the offerings of the festival. On the last festival day we read *All the firstlings,* with the commandments and statutes [which precede it], and for haftarah *And it was so that when Solomon had made an end.* On the next day we read *And this is the blessing,* and for haftarah *And Solomon stood.* Rav Huna said in the name of Rav Sheishet: On the Sabbath which falls during the intermediate days of the festival, whether Passover or Tabernacles, the passage we read from the Torah is *See, Thou [sayest unto me]*, and for haftarah on Passover the passage of the dry bones, and on Tabernacles *In that day when Gog shall come.*

High Holy Day Torah Readings

	M. *M'gilah* 3:5	T. *M'gilah* 3:5	BT *M'gilah* 31a	Alt there	P'sikta D'Rav Kahana	Amram
RH 1	Lev. 23:23ff.	alt. Gen. 21	same as M,T	Gen. 21	Lev. 23:23/ Gen. 1	Gen. 21, Num. 29
Haftarah	not listed	not listed	Jer. 31:20ff.	I Sam. 1–2	not listed	I Sam. 1–2
RH 2	not listed N/A	not listed N/A		Gen. 22	N/A	Gen. 22, Num. 29
Haftarah	not listed N/A	not listed N/A		Jer. 31:1ff.	N/A	Jer. 31:1–20
YK A.M.	Lev. 16	and Num. 29:17ff.	same as M,T		Lev. 16	Lev. 16, Num. 29
Haftarah	not listed	not listed	Isaiah 57		not listed	Isa. 57:14–58:14
YK P.M.	not listed	not listed	Lev. 18		not listed	Lev. 18
Haftarah	not listed	not listed	Jonah		not listed	Jonah

European Reform High Holy Day Readings

	Hamburg 1819	Hamburg 1841	London 1843	Geiger 1854, 1871	*Einheitsgebetbuch* 1929
RH 1	Gen. 21, Num. 29	same	Gen. 22, Num. 29	Gen. 21, Num. 29	Gen. 21 or Deut. 33, Num. 29
Haftarah	none	none	none	I Sam. 2:1–10	I Sam. 1–2
RH 2	Gen. 22, Num. 29	same	not observed	Gen. 22, Num. 29	Gen. 22, Num. 29
Haftarah	none	none	none	Jer. 31:1–20	Jer. 31:1–20
YK A.M.	Lev. 16, Num. 29	same	same	same	same or Exod. 33:12–34:1
Haftarah	Isa. 57:14–58:14	none	same	same	same
YK P.M.	Lev. 16, 17, 18 sel	none	Deut. 30	Lev. 19:1–18	Lev. 19
Haftarah	Jonah	none	Jonah, Micah vv.	Jonah 2:2–4, 2:11	Jonah, Micah vv.

North American Reform High Holy Day Scriptural Readings

	Merzbacher 1855	Adler 1860	Einhorn 1858	Wise 1866	*UPB* Moses 1892–93	*UPB* 1894–95	*UPB* 1918/24; 1940/45
RH	Gen. 22	same	Gen. 22:1–20	Gen. 22, Num. 29	Gen. 22	Gen. 22	same
Haftarah	not listed	same	I Sam. 1:1–2:10	Jer. 31:2–21	Isa. 61 or Jer. 31 or I Sam.	I Sam. 2:1–10/ Neh. 8	or Isa. 55
YK A.M.	Lev. 16	same	Lev. 16	Lev. 16, Num. 29	Lev. 16	Deut. 29:10–30:6	Deut. 29:9–14, 30:11–20
Haftarah	Isa. 58	same	Jer. 57:14–21, 58	Isa. 57:14–58:14	Isa. 58	Isa. 57:14–58:14	same
YK P.M.	Exod. 33:12ff.	same	Lev. 19:1–37	Exod. 32–34 excerpts	Lev. 19:1–18	Exod. 33:12–34:10	1945: Lev. 19 excerpts
Haftarah	Jonah (all)	Jonah 3–4 (all)	Jonah (all)	Jonah, Micah 7:18–20	Jonah 3–4	Jonah 3–4	1945: Jonah 1, 3–4

Akeidah: From a Poetic Perspective

Jessica Greenbaum

I want to speak freely about the relationship between my love of metaphor and my search for
meaningful metaphor in structures in Jewish text,
and what it is I seek from sermons, and especially
in relation to, of course, the *Akeidah*. Here's my con-
ceit: If I was in a dialogue with rabbis, I would say,
"I want to understand Torah as deeply as I am able.
As a member of your congregation, this is what I'm
hoping you will investigate in the text." I come to
a sermon hoping to be offered much of what the
study of poetry offers, the beauty of the lyric, and
the relationship of lyric to meaning, and the revelation and resolution of life's complexities within
those metaphors.

> What do you come to a sermon hoping? What do you want to ask of your rabbi(s)? How does your answer differ depending on the time of year (i.e., High Holy Days versus the average Shabbat)?

"After these things, God tested Abraham, saying to him, 'Abraham,' and he said, 'Here I am.'
'Take your son, your only one, the one you love,
Isaac, and go forth to the land of Moriah.'" The sud-
denness with which the story takes up is like the
excitement of a line break. The passages, cadences,
and its haunting mix of beauty and sorrow are like
an inverted lullaby. The lines seem to play an ex-
isting cut on our mind, but rarely do those lines
carry the very same resonance from one year to the
next. As a congregant, I hope the rabbi is going to
explicate the text, as she would a classic piece of
literature. I love clarification through close observations and contrasts, because meaning through
metaphor is my stock in trade. In a recent book of
poems, Connie Wanek describes the head of garlic as a "hobo's bundle." If this strikes you as truly
as it struck Wanek, the association of garlic with

> Have you ever read a book over and over again? If so, why? How can this literary practice help us to understand the Jewish ritual of reading the same Torah and haftarah portions every year?

17

the humble seasoned traveler will stay with you, and hobos and garlic will forever have a mutually enriched relationship in your mind. Similarly, when you look at the little space taken by the *Akeidah* in Genesis, it's not unlike looking at a famous sonnet that has moved through time and fourteen lines and has proved to contain volumes of thought, revelations, ironies, and paradoxes, which deepen our understanding of this very mysterious life. The *Akeidah's* dominant phrase, "*Hineini,* Here I am," and the plot's suspense, "who will be left?" echo what Wallace Stevens tagged the naming of parts: the very naming in Genesis, which brings the world into being, and the poet's impulse to name parts, as well. The phrase "here I am" could encapsulate our metaphorical annual rebirth as Jews, at the head of year, but it's a difficult rebirth. We have to travel through this terrifying story and come out saying, "Here I am." This is one metaphor we find by looking at the text.

I once had the pleasure of hearing a Rosh HaShanah sermon by Rabbi Rick Jacobs, where he spoke of guided meditation that led the congregation back before *alef,* before the first letter. The meditation offered the experience of beginning at the beginning of the world. It helped me leave my accumulated mental clutter, and to the extent that I was able to do that, I could approach the *Akeidah* relatively free of anxiety, exhaustion, and preconceptions. I remember that sermon above most others, so I am eager to let you know that however you help yourself focus on the oft-revisited conundrum of Isaac's finding, this may help your congregants, too.

What is the larger metaphor, the relationship between an off-putting story like the *Akeidah* and personal commitment to *t'shuvah,* asked of us on the High Holy Days? The *Akeidah* forces a complex

response to the Torah as authority, and never being very good with authority figures, I greatly appreciate that. Isaac's binding, not being a loaves
and fishes homily, binds us in an engagement with
difficulty, as many great pieces of literature do.
The happy families are all alike, supposedly, so
we don't care to read about them. And neither do
we look repeatedly at poems that merely describe
beauty or peace. Such portraits do not fully engage.
I prize the fact that the Torah is not dogma. It's not
static to me in the least. And I look to the rabbis to
see its liveliness, to look beneath the rock of this
ancient foundation, to the darting lizard of its cha-
meleon nature, to grant us access to the conversations of the rabbis over the centuries and to offer
us, also, the newer directions in which contemporary minds might assay.

I hope rabbis listen for, and convey to us congregants, their own intuitive response. Like Connie
Wanek's hobo bundle of garlic, our intuition makes
the best connection to genuine lasting meaning,
regardless of prevailing concepts. The practice of
respectful listening for the mind's innate sublimi-
nal associations is the poet's best tool. We have our
ear against the wall of the heart and the mind. As a
congregant, I listen for the concept that feels true to
the speaker, because then I know it might feel true
for me. Who has not been thrilled by a sermon that
pulled authentic meaning from a passage, as a ma-
gician pulls real handkerchiefs from a pocket? One
of the more evocative sermons I've heard simply
proposed that the serpent in the Garden of Eden
was not being punished but rewarded by being
commanded to crawl on its belly, eating dust all the
days of its life. Although this state is explicitly cited
as a curse, the sermon asserted that it is, in fact,
a gift to have a niche among the living and know

> What do you think
> the presenter means
> when she says that
> Isaac's binding is
> not "a loaves and
> fishes homily"?

which food is your food. And how do we square that metaphor with the notion of a curse? Was this public cursing of the serpent just a show? Had God meant all along for Adam and Eve to move on?

What new understandings of the *Akeidah* have you gained over time?

What might the *Akeidah* reflect if you turned the text once again, at another angle? If you pulled for the truth coming from your own deep well of associations, and pulled that association up like an apple, dripping wet, the same way that metaphor uses the second image to sharpen the first, sometimes the second text can bring Torah to life. For instance, I've forged an easy, ongoing relationship between the *Akeidah* and S. Y. Agnon's great anthology *Days of Awe,* whose treasury of legends and commentaries I generally find myself consulting as the holidays draw near.

Shmuel Yosef Agnon, *Days of Awe: A Treasury of Jewish Wisdom for Reflection, Repentance, and Renewal on the High Holy Days* (New York: Schocken Books, 1995).

In one example, Agnon cites a nineteenth-century prayer book as noting that the word "Elul" has the numerical value of the word for understanding, "*binah.*" To understanding, it says in Isaiah, comes *t'shuvah,* "an understanding with their heart, return and be healed" (6:10). Is there something here for us to consider when considering the story of the *Akeidah?* What is the numerical value hidden inside the shell of the *Akeidah* for you as rabbis? What metaphor do we understand from the *Akeidah* that brings us *t'shuvah?* What is the posture of the congregants who distance themselves from the *Akeidah* altogether? Is it possible that the objectionable nature of the story acts as its own sacrificial lamb for the year? Is it our annual pest? Might it be saying, "If you want to reject one story, reject this one, because if you can reject this one, if you can sacrifice the most important story of the year and still be Jewish, then you're really in like Flynn, or Horowitz." Is that what we need to understand?

How would you respond to these questions posed by the presenter?

Also, in *Days of Awe*, Agnon retells the Chasidic homiletic called "Secret Language," which reads:

> The reason for the blowing of the ram's horn was revealed to me in a dream. It is as though two friends or a father and son, who do not wish that what the one writes to the other should be known to others, were to have a secret language known to no one but themselves. So it is on Rosh Ha-Shanah. It was not the will of the Omnipresent that the accuser should know of our pleas. Therefore, he made up a language for us. That is the ram's horn, which is only understood by him.

Agnon, *Days of Awe*, 73–74

Maybe for some of you this homily is the starting point. Maybe "Secret Language" is a metaphor that allows you to enlarge on the story of Isaac's binding. For instance, could this story be God's concession of insecurity in a secret language that we are privileged to share? In a midrash I wrote about the *Akeidah* in a class taught by Rabbi Ellen Lippmann, I surmised that Abraham always knew he was performing a pantomime for the ages. He knew he was being chosen to play out a dark skit about faith, and he never thought for a moment he was going to kill his son. Maybe the secret language he shared with God allowed him to know that.

Finally, I'll just mention a tale in Agnon's anthology about the Baal Shem Tov that ends, "When a man truthfully breaks his heart before God, he can enter into all the gates of the apartments of the king above all kings, the Holy One, blessed be He." That metaphor of the brokenhearted Jew having broken all of the locks and having access to Juda-

Agnon, *Days of Awe*, 74

How does this metaphor of the brokenhearted Jew speak to you? What other metaphors help you to grapple with the *Akeidah*?

ism's innermost rooms seems important to me because who would not be brokenhearted to have a
God who would demand, "Take your son, your
only one, the one you love, Isaac, and go forth to
the land of Moriah"?

Akeidah: Contemporary Challenges and Innovations

Rabbi Ellen Lippmann

I am not entirely certain at this moment of where I'm standing in relation to the *Akeidah*, but I am here to talk about a sermon that I gave a couple of years ago and what has transpired since then in our congregation. Related to that experience, I will offer some thoughts on the possibility of making change, or perhaps about going back to the earliest days of our tradition when there were a variety of choices. First, let me just say a word or two about our High Holy Day services in my congregation, especially about our encounters with the *Akeidah*, which we have read at various times on the first day of Rosh HaShanah, on the second day of Rosh HaShanah, and almost always, for at least ten years, we have had the extraordinary body of modern interpretive midrashim presented by Arthur Strimling, a member of my congregation and an actor, a theater director, and our *magid hamakom*. Arthur has drashed the *Akeidah* in every imaginable way, becoming, in turn, each of the characters in the story, including sometimes the knife, and given us a whole range of possibilities on how to, as Jessica said, turn it again. So that was the reality in our community a couple of years ago when I decided, for a number of reasons, to suggest that we not read the *Akeidah* anymore on Rosh HaShanah. It was, for some, a shocking suggestion; for some, a very welcome suggestion, and I will just tell you a little bit about that sermon, and then a little bit about what transpired afterward then, and, as I say, where I am now in this less certain place.

How can we use modern midrash to grapple with troubling texts?

23

I became interested in the possibility of making change, probably because it was the fall of 2008, and change, "Yes We Can," was in the air, and I also was very much of the mind that we, in our nation—to some extent, in our Jewish communities—were bereft of a kind of moral leadership that we desperately needed in our world. And, because I felt that our stories, both personal and collective, shape our lives, I felt that the power of the *Akeidah* that has been evoked here was power that was presenting us a model that perhaps was not the model we wanted at that moment in our world. I did not suggest change just to have change, although sometimes that can be enlivening. I suggested that we leave out the *Akeidah* because what we need now, to face the terrifying world, is a story of moral courage, of protest, and of hope, not one of submission to God, who lays down an impossible command. And so, I spoke a little bit about how the *Akeidah* had come to be the story that we read, not quite to the extent that Rick has given us here so helpfully, and I suggested in a number of ways that we really needed to think about our moral development, the development of moral leadership, and to try to find another text for this moment, not that we never read the *Akeidah*—for instance, not that we not read *Vayeira* in its turn in the annual Torah reading cycle—but that for Rosh HaShanah, we choose something else. One of the things that I did was to ask two people, in addition to myself, to suggest alternate texts. One was a fifteen-year-old girl in our congregation who spoke very beautifully about the possibility of reading the story of Noah, and suggesting that perhaps at this moment in time, we wanted a universal tale of new covenant. I also asked our friend and teacher Peter Pitzele, the biblio-dramatist par excellence, who was not able

What aspects of your High Holy Day worship would you like to change this year? Is there any aspect of High Holy Day worship that should absolutely not be changed for any reason? Why should that aspect not be changed?

How are the High Holy Days the perfect opportunity to address morality in a communal setting? How might we do so outside of the classical sermon?

Parashat Vayeira can be found in Genesis 18:1–22:24.

What is the difference between reading the *Akeidah* as part of the annual Torah reading cycle and as the primary Torah reading for Rosh HaShanah?

to be with us, but whose words were read, and he suggested that we might read the Dance of Miriam, on the other side of the Sea of Reeds; her celebration fits the occasion of the New Year. Her drumming and her lost song can be re-created communally in our own version, and the dance of the women and the men who join in, as a glorious image of community and joy, and more than sacrifice or wrestling offers me a glimpse of the world-to-come. He had started with the possibility that we read Jacob wrestling with whoever it is. And I, myself, suggested that we read Genesis 18, Abraham arguing with God, even though ultimately his arguments are not successful; the presentation of our founder, as it were, being an example that we might prefer to live with and aspire to called to me at that time. I also looked at the story of Rabbi Akiva in the Babylonian Talmud, *Taanit* 25b, for an example of the possibility of change. Akiva responds to a drought, as so much of *Taanit* shows us, and kind of busts through the expected and normal order of prayer in order to give us a prayer that might have an effect with God as the text says it does. And, he said, "Our Father, our King, we have no king, but You are Father, our King, have mercy upon us for Your own sake," whereupon the rain fell. And so, I was inspired by Akiva's example to say, "You know, we too can bust through what has so long been expected and find other possibilities in the many, many possible texts that we might turn to." And at the very least, that we might read more than one text at a time—I had an idea at one point that we might read the *Akeidah*, but read another text at the very same moment, so that there was a kind of cacophony of text reading to indicate the confusion and obfuscation of the message that I was hoping to hear.

Which of these suggested alternatives to reading the *Akeidah* on Rosh HaShanah appeal to you and why?

So, I gave the sermon. I will say it produced a kind of wildness in the congregation at that moment. It was followed by a very wild, jazzy version of *Avinu Malkeinu,* going back to the Akiva text, and the whole place kind of erupted, so there was sort of joy and wildness, and then, we sat on that for a little while. What followed was Arthur Strimling and I, who are long-time midrashists on the *Akeidah,* had a public conversation about the *Akeidah.* He argued very strenuously that we needed to keep the *Akeidah,* that it was the perfect text, and as many, many years as the selection, was not just a random turn of the scroll, as Larry Hoffman at one point suggested. We also taught a class together on many, many kinds of interpretations of the *Akeidah,* before the holidays last year. What we did in the year that I gave this sermon is we read the traditional text selections. We read the Sarah and Hagar text on the first day of Rosh HaShanah, and we read the *Akeidah* on the second day, with minimal spoken midrash and primarily musical midrash, a father and son playing saxophone and clarinet, who played all of the pretty minimal conversation between Abraham and Isaac in the *Akeidah,* not spoken, but musically, and their appearance as father and son, and the sounds of their instruments, one lower pitch, one higher pitch, were an incredibly moving accompaniment to this text, which I read. I don't always read the text on the holidays, but I wanted to read it that day to kind of complete my encounter with it, and I was deeply moved by this musical midrash.

Since then, we have been a little bit up in the air. We have not gotten rid of the *Akeidah* altogether. We have done a number of other things and have yet many more choices. One of our choices that we may do this year is to read it, but to read it in a different way, like the very quiet way that certain problematic texts are traditionally read. We may read another text; we may read another text in addition. We don't have a decision yet for this year, but I just want to offer, I guess, in closing, the possibility that we might. And, certainly, I think that the possibility that a new *machzor* that comes out from our movement might present more than two textual choices, whether they present the text in full or the suggestions of them, that other moments of change, of argument, of leadership, of covenant, of approach to God, might be suggested, if not presented. And finally, I hope that we can have a text that will be as rich as the *Akeidah*, but with some moral standing that I continue to feel we need now.

What are the moral messages of our time? What lessons on morality do we need to hear right now?

Akeidah End-of-Call Discussion

Rabbi Elaine Zecher, Rabbi Deborah Prinz, Dr. Richard S. Sarason, Rabbi Ellen Lippmann

Rabbi Elaine Zecher

As we embark on the process of putting together *Mishkan HaNefesh*, all of the different ideas and views in understanding how to go forward are very much part of the thinking of the editorial group. I would like to take a moment to lift up what I think is a key word from each of the presentations. Dr. Sarason spoke about *zichronot*. His concern has been very much part of our concern. What is necessary to take note of and what role the theme of remembrance plays in directing us need to inform how we go forward. So even as we recognize this is the way it might have been done it in the past, we have a number of options the past gives us.

As Reform Jews, we're always balancing authority and autonomy in thinking about how the text and how the particular Torah readings and haftarah readings help guide us. In terms of metaphor, I love how Jessica Greenbaum spoke about going further in, and even as we take these ideas, whether it is the secret language or the idea of *binah*, they allow us to go deeper into what the readings are, particularly the *Akeidah*. So, we want to make sure, as we put together the *machzor*, there is opportunity to go deeper, not just to have a variety of choices. And last, as Rabbi Lippmann spoke about so beautifully, this text is a very challenging text when we look at the *Akeidah*. The other challenge we have, certainly in our congregations, is how people who come every week or many weeks find the High Holy Days either serve as a pinnacle, a dénouement, or a distraction from their weekly practice. For those who don't come very often, this is our one- or two-time chance to get to them, and how they receive the text and how they receive what we offer are very important. I'll just end by telling this brief story. I was speaking with one of the editors about something we do in our congregation for our family service. We actually act out the story, and our editor said, "You even have Abraham with a knife over his son?" And I said, "Well, we know the end of the story. We know that he doesn't kill his son," Somehow in this family service, it works by watching how this story plays out. So, there are many opportunities and many ways we have in taking the text and making it come alive. As we move forward in thinking about the *machzor*, we recognize that it is the text we have in front of us, and the power of the text will come from how we bring it to life with our words, with our enactments, with our teaching.

Rabbi Deborah Prinz

Dr. Sarason, we do have one question for you, and then I would like to give the panelists an opportunity to comment. This is the question: It has been suggested that the choice of the readings for the two days of Rosh HaShanah was a response to the Christian narrative—the faith of the Jewish masses that we have both miraculous birth, as well as resurrection, with the understanding that Isaac was sacrificed and was resurrected. Do we have anything that would indicate that this was the case, either in the choice of the readings, or later years as a polemic?

How would the answer to this question affect your approach to the Torah texts we read on Rosh HaShanah?

Dr. Richard S. Sarason

In terms of the choice of the Torah readings for Rosh HaShanah, no, there is no evidence for this at all. The explicit thematic connections between these Torah narratives and Rosh HaShanah that are made in Talmudic literature are simply the ones that I have discussed above. In terms of later polemical treatments of the *Akeidah* vis-à-vis the Christian narrative (and the Christian typological interpretation of the *Akeidah*), these certainly appear in some of the *Akeidah piyutim* that were written in response to the Crusades in Germany, and about which Shalom Spiegel writes in *The Last Trial.* Here the motif of vicarious sacrifice, either the actual sacrifice of Isaac (and his resurrection), or the very-near sacrifice of Isaac, is surely polemical vis-à-vis Christianity in the context of Rhineland culture (but—and this is crucial—it is not *only* polemical). To be sure, the earlier classical midrashim originated in the context of Byzantine culture. But it's not so clear that the motifs were generated through a polemical interaction with Christian religious thought and practice. I think these themes are sufficiently resonant internal to the Jewish historical experience, certainly internal to the classical Rabbinic experience, that one need not appeal to anti-Christian polemics to make sense of them. For the record, I'm not trying to be polemical here myself vis-à-vis a kind of scholarship for which anti-Christian polemics seem to be the default mode of (over-)explaining most things. Rather, I think that the structure of Rabbinic thought as it responds to Scripture in the Greco-Roman period often has its own cultural logic, and we don't constantly need to invoke Jewish-Christian polemics to account for the origin of certain midrashic treatments of

Shalom Spiegel, The Last Trial (Woodstock, VT: Jewish Lights Publishing, 1993).

Scripture. (Parenthetically, anti-Gnostic polemic figures much more heavily in this literature than anti-Christian polemic.) I think that, obviously, in a Christian context, these treatments often take on certain kinds of coloration that they wouldn't have otherwise, and that's one of the interesting things about a rich historical tradition. It changes and becomes even richer as the cultural context in which it is enacted changes, but I don't see this, certainly in terms of the Rosh HaShanah observances, as being primary.

Rabbi Ellen Lippman

I have to confess, I think, that having raised the possibility of getting rid of the *Akeidah,* I have spent a great deal of time reading and thinking about it since, and I am now finding new possibilities in it, which is why I said originally that I am not entirely sure where I'm standing now, but I so appreciate the possibility of hearing about it with new ears and new potential ways of exploring it from both of these wonderful presenters.

Dr. Richard S. Sarason

Yes, I want to underscore and endorse some things that all of my colleagues have said. As we move forward toward a new *machzor,* we have the opportunity to use the *Mishkan T'filah*–type format (two-page spread) to include a formidable range of options in the book, and I totally endorse that, just as I endorse what Rabbi Zecher was saying about commentary and going deeper. I think it would be possible to have some commentary in the *machzor* text itself, perhaps around the page, as we present the text, obviously not limited to what's on the

Elyse D. Frishman, ed., *Mishkan T'filah: A Reform Siddur* (New York: CCAR Press, 2007).

What kind of commentary would you want to see around the Torah readings in the new *machzor?*

page in terms of what we want the experience to be. As for metaphor, that's the name of the game when dealing with religious language, the importance of language, and delving deeply into the language. I think we have an opportunity, with the new *machzor,* to open up all of these things, and I fully endorse that.

Akeidah **Wrap-Up**

1. How does the history behind the selection of the *Akeidah* help us to make decisions today about what Torah text to read on Rosh HaShanah?
2. How do you utilize metaphor and midrash within worship?
3. What did you learn from these presentations on the *Akeidah* that you would like to implement in your community's High Holy Day worship?
4. What are some ideas you have about addressing the concerns around the *Akeidah*?

Traditional Torah Readings Reconsidered Session 2: *Nitzavim*

Nitzavim: Historical Background

Dr. Richard S. Sarason

What is interesting about the traditional Torah readings for Yom Kippur is that unlike those for Rosh HaShanah, there is, for all intents and purposes, no variation in the sources and no change over time. The morning Torah reading has always been Leviticus 16, as listed initially in *Mishnah M'gilah* 3:5. And that makes a certain amount of sense because, from a Rabbinic perspective, Yom Kippur is the Temple-centered annual observance par excellence. It is only discussed in the priestly calendars in Leviticus and Numbers, where its rites are centered on the Temple (indeed, they have to do with the purification of the sanctuary). So, for both the biblical authors and their Rabbinic heirs, the rites in the Temple are central to the observance of the day. And when those rites could no longer be performed in the Temple, the Rabbis ordained the recitation/performance/enactment of those Torah *texts* and those Mishnah *texts* that describe the rites in the Temple, on the theory that the verbal performance substitutes for the physical performance. That is why the Torah reading for Yom Kippur morning is always Leviticus 16, and why the crucial portions of *Mishnah Yoma* form the centerpiece of the traditional *Seder HaAvodah,* which initially, before the addition of poetic elaborations, was simply a recitation of those Mishnah texts.

Tosefta M'gilah 3:7 adds the information that we "conclude" (*maftirin*) the Torah reading with Numbers 29:7ff., the enumeration of the sacrifices that were to be offered on the tenth day of the seventh month (this is read from a second scroll). The same information is also found in *Mishnah Yoma* 7:1 and *Sotah* 7:7, both of which specify what the High Priest reads from the Torah scroll on the Day of Atonement. The word *maftirin,* "and one concludes with," in the Mishnah and *Tosefta,* does not refer to a reading from the Prophets, what we today call the haftarah, but rather to a concluding Torah portion from a separate scroll. Prophetic readings/haftarot for the Festivals and High Holy Days are not listed in the Tractate *M'gilah* traditions until we get to the Babylonian Talmud.

The *Bavli's* tradition expands that of the *Tosefta.* It now uses the term *maftirim* to refer to "the haftarah," a reading from the Prophets, and lists Isaiah 57:15 as the reading for the morning service. This passage, which includes the section *Is not this the fast that I have chosen? . . . ,* becomes the traditional (and, with some abbreviation, the Reform) morning haftarah reading.

Mishnah and *Tosefta* do not mention a Torah reading for Yom Kippur afternoon. This first appears in the *Bavli,* which lists the afternoon Torah reading as Leviticus 18, and the afternoon haftarah as the Book of Jonah. And those remain the traditional afternoon readings.

How could the "traditional" Torah readings for Yom Kippur enhance worship? How could they detract from it?

As for Reform treatments of these readings, it is noteworthy that all nineteenth-century European Reform prayer books retain Leviticus 16 as the morning reading. And, interestingly enough, so do the early Reform liturgies in North America: the prayer book edited by Leo Merzbacher for Temple Emanu-El in New York (1855) as well as its subsequent 1860 revision by Samuel Adler, David Einhorn's *Olath Tamid* (1858), Isaac Mayer Wise's High Holy Day volumes of *Minhag America* (1866), and the very first *Union Prayer Book*, volume 2 (*UPB-2*), edited by Isaac S. Moses (circulated as a draft in 1893, but never published) all give Leviticus 16 as the morning Torah reading for Yom Kippur. It is only in the officially published *UPB-2* of 1894 that Leviticus 16 is dropped. In its place, *UPB-2* 1894 gives Deuteronomy 29:9–36 (*Nitzavim*). This reading remains in the two subsequent revisions of *UPB-2* (1922 and 1945), with some minor adjustments in extent: instead of 29:9–36, we find in both revisions 29:9–14, followed by 30:11–20. This adjusted reading is retained in *Gates of Repentance* (1978). The reason why the Torah portion was changed in the *Union Prayer Book* is clear: in place of the traditional reading's focus on priestly Temple rituals of a somewhat magical cast, *Nitzavim* focuses on the existential, spiritual, and ethical choices—for life and death, for good and bad—that we are divinely commanded to make on "this day," construed of course as *yoma*, "The Day" par excellence—Yom Kippur.

The haftarah from Isaiah is sometimes shortened in Reform prayer books, but given the fact that it addresses the issue of fasting from the spiritual and ethical perspective of social justice—"Is not this rather the fast that I have chosen? To break every yoke, to give the poor their bread, to let the

> Why do you think the editors of *UPB II* of 1894 dropped Leviticus 16 as the Torah reading for Yom Kippur when their Reform predecessors did not?

> Does the rationale behind reading *Nitzavim* on Yom Kippur still resonate? Why or why not?

oppressed go free?"—one could not ask for a better Reform reading for the Day of Atonement. (What is noteworthy, of course, is that the same is true from a classical Rabbinic perspective—the Rabbis here balance the ritual/cultic with the spiritual/ethical, accepting both.)

The traditional Torah reading for the afternoon is Leviticus 18, which catalogues permitted and forbidden sexual relations, the latter deemed to cause impurity. The rationale for this reading is that all impurities and sins are to be cast out of the congregation on the Day of Atonement, including sexual improprieties. This comports, then, with the theme of purification on Yom Kippur. Needless to say, Reform prayer books, almost without exception, drop this reading. The first Reform congregational prayer book, that of the Hamburg Tempelverein (1819), gives selections from Leviticus 16, 17, and 18. The 1843 High Holy Day prayer book of the West London Synagogue gives Deuteronomy 29–30 as the Torah reading for the afternoon service, since they retain Leviticus 16 in the morning service. Leviticus 19 (*You shall be holy*) appears for the first time as the afternoon Torah reading in Abraham Geiger's prayer books of 1854 and 1871. Interestingly enough, that choice does not carry forward in all of the North American Reform prayer books. Merzbacher, for his afternoon service, instead gives Exodus 33–34, where Moses asks to behold God's face, and God responds instead by passing before him and calling out the divine attributes (which come to function as the centerpiece of the *S'lichot* penitential liturgy on Yom Kippur). Einhorn, however, carries forward Geiger's use of Leviticus 19 here. Wise carries forward the thematic logic of Merzbacher and gives excerpts from Exodus 32–34. While the 1893 draft of *UPB-2* gives Leviticus 19 as the afternoon Torah reading (following Einhorn), the "official" *UPB-2* of 1894 instead follows Wise and Merzbacher, giving Exodus 33–34. It is only in 1945 that the *UPB-2* reverts to excerpts from Leviticus 19, which are carried forward in *Gates of Repentance*.

The Book of Jonah as the afternoon haftarah is not at all controversial in the Reform context and is universally found. Some Reform prayer books also give the Micah verses, Micah 7:18–20, that conclude the traditional haftarah (in Europe: London 1843 and Berlin 1929; in North America: Wise 1866). The *UPB-2*, in all three editions, abbreviates the reading from Jonah to chapters 3 and 4. *Gates of Repentance* gives the entire text in Hebrew but omits the psalm (chapter 2) in English. And, of course, the rationale for reading Jonah on Yom Kippur is that it is all about *t'shuvah*: if the people of Nineveh can do it, then surely the people of Israel can. If God is quick to accept the repentance even of the Ninevites, Israel's traditional enemies, then certainly God will hasten to accept the true repentance of Israel.

What do you think about the various Reform adaptations made to the Yom Kippur Torah readings? What would you choose to do today?

For more on *Nitzavim*, see "Yom Kippur in Moab" by Dr. Elsie S. Stern, page 439.

Nitzavim End-of-Call Discussion
Rabbi Elaine Zecher,
Dr. Richard S. Sarason, Dr. Elsie Stern

Rabbi Elaine Zecher

Based on your perspective and what you spoke about, and also what you heard from each other, what do you think the editors of the *machzor* should know and should be thinking about regarding the Torah portions: what to keep, what to add, what to readjust in the new Reform *machzor*?

Dr. Richard S. Sarason

I'll state at the outset the point of view from which I approach this. I think the *Mishkan T'filah* format of the two-page spread, which I imagine will go forward in some way in the new *machzor*, allows us multiple options. I think in some respects we can do a "both/and" rather than "either/or" here, although obviously we cannot print too many options on the page, since it gets to be too expensive. But I think that we may wish to consider readmitting Leviticus 16 to the *machzor* without necessarily dispensing with Deuteronomy 29–30. I think there's room for both. I think that dialectic actually would be very strong. Another thing I will say on the basis of what Dr. Stern was saying: I think Elsie makes a wonderful case for the re-inclusion of the entire traditional haftarah, beginning with Isaiah 57:14. As it turns out, in looking through some prayer books while Dr. Stern was talking, I found that the decision to lop off the Isaiah 57 portion that she was talking about was made by

Refer to a later version of Dr. Elsie Stern's article on *Nitzavim*, "Yom Kippur in Moab," page 439.

Chaim Stern for *Gates of Repentance*. It's actually all there in all three versions of the *Union Prayer Book* (in English of course, not in Hebrew). But I think Dr. Stern makes a great case for restoring the whole thing, and that's what I would urge going forward. Also, I think Dr. Stern just gave us a wonderful set of sermonic ideas for Yom Kippur, and the Ruth and Boaz turn even takes us back to the haftarah from Isaiah, where we are the ones who essentially bring the Messiah by doing what we should be doing, from the perspective of social justice, in our everyday lives.

Dr. Elsie Stern

I'm with Dr. Sarason that to put the Leviticus back in acknowledges that for many contemporary liberal Jews there is something about religious mystery that is interesting again. And something about the numinous is interesting again. There is something just really modernist about Deuteronomy 29 and 30. If you put the Leviticus back in, you are also incorporating kind of our earlier sensibilities, but also our postmodernist sensibilities in some way, and it feels that that combination would be contemporary in a way that having just Deuteronomy 29 and 30 feels modern, really mid-twentieth century rather than early twenty-first century.

Do you agree with this presenter that we need more options for High Holy Day Torah readings? When is more options too many and therefore confusing or overwhelming? What is the right balance?

Nitzavim **Wrap-Up**

1. How do we balance our often dueling heritages of "traditional" Judaism and Reform Judaism?
2. Background and context are often necessary for a full understanding of our liturgy. How could we incorporate some of the learning from this presentation into our High Holy Day worship to make it more robust and accessible without lecturing?
3. How do our choices of Torah readings reflect our values and goals in High Holy Day worship?
4. What did you learn from these presentations on *Nitzavim* that you would like to implement in your community's High Holy Day worship?

Traditional Torah Readings Reconsidered Session 3: Creative Reclamation of Leviticus 16

Creative Reclamation of Leviticus 16: Introduction

Rabbi Leon A. Morris

I suggested this topic, both because of my own work on how liberal Jews can make sense out of text related to sacrifice in Temple, and also out of my own experience of reintroducing Leviticus 16 in my congregation for the morning reading of Yom Kippur. The replacement of another Torah reading for traditional reading of Leviticus 16 reflects, of course, a larger ambivalence of how we should relate to text about sacrifice. And while it may be obvious that prayers for restoring the sacrificial system would be problematic in a Reform context, it does not necessarily follow that references to the Temple and to the sacrificial system as history and memory have no place in the Reform synagogue. And so as we look at Leviticus 16 this afternoon, lurking in the background of our discussions are questions about other references to sacrifice. The big questions for which Leviticus 16 is one site are things like: Might

How do you relate to text about sacrifice?

there be ways of referencing the sacrificial system that could be useful for us in terms of providing a historical context and in presenting the origins for the religious life we now practice? And I use the term "ambivalence" to describe our relationship with the sacrificial system quite deliberately, rather than use the word "opposition" or "rejection." There are inescapable allusions to sacrifice in our daily religious life and numerous practices that only make sense in light of their sacrificial origins, one example being the very notion of morning and afternoon prayer. Might we need to creatively retrieve text about sacrifice in order to more fully develop a narrative in which prayer is understood as a substitute for and an evolution from sacrifices, in which our study is seen as a worthy substitute for sacrifice, in which *tzedakah* is seen as a form of sacrifice, etc. So, it would seem to me that with Yom Kippur as the sacrificial ritual par excellence, described in Leviticus 16, we have an opportunity to connect our contemporary observance of Yom Kippur with its historical origins. And it seems to me that much of this language of Yom Kippur, in terms of reference, concepts, and vocabulary, that could lend itself so easily to metaphor and poetry has been lost in our Reform communities by separating ourselves so decisively from the story of the *Kohein Gadol* and the *se'ir laAzazel*, as described in Leviticus 16. The questions that I've been thinking about are: How might Leviticus 16 facilitate a reinsertion of ourselves into the mythical historical narrative of the Jewish people? How might the national and communal *kaparah* experience as described in Leviticus 16 serve as a counterweight to the more personalized and individualistic work of *t'shuvah*? And in thinking about Jacob Milgrom's work on the Book of Leviticus, we might ask ourselves:

Jacob Milgrom, *Leviticus: A Book of Ritual and Ethics* (Minneapolis: Fortress Press, 2004).

How would Leviticus 16 present us with new ways of speaking or old/new ways of speaking about how our actions have the power of either allowing God to continue to dwell among us or the power to drive God away? The questions that anchor our conversation today are: What might be gained by reclaiming Leviticus 16 in the Reform synagogue? And how might we go about reclaiming it?

How would you respond to the questions posed by the presenter before reading ahead? Then compare your answers with those suggested by the following presenters.

Creative Retrieval and Reclamation of the *Avodah* Service

Rabbi Herbert Bronstein

Refer to Herbert Bronstein's article "Yom Kippur Worship: A Missing Center?" in *CCAR Journal: A Reform Jewish Quarterly,* Summer 2004, 7–15. This article can also be found with discussion questions in *Machzor: Challenge and Change* (New York: CCAR Press, 2009), 197–205, 208, or "Yom Kippur Worship: A Missing Center?" at http://www.ccarnet. org/lifelong-learning/ teleconferences- webinars/session-iii- creative-reclamation- leviticus-16.

What liturgy do you consider to be at the center of Yom Kippur worship?

In the spirit of creative retrieval, a sensible and imaginative restoration of the *Avodah* service would be a substantial contribution to our liturgy. Its classical themes are in fact central to the very themes of Yom Kippur observance: renewal and restoration through acts of atonement and God's mercy, grace and forgiveness. It has the potential of powerful experiential mimesis of ancient Temple worship rooted in Scripture.

Further, practically speaking, in terms of our mission as rabbis, at a time when so many people are in synagogue, a time as open as any to Torah teaching, the *Avodah, authentically* rendered would provide a greater awareness and comprehension of the narrative structure of Judaism revealed in our liturgy; its very design: **From** God's Creation, **Through** Israel's Covenant Service, **To** a Culmination of God's Sovereign teaching in the world (see diagram in Appendix I).

Consider, too, the importance of the *Avodah* service in our long history. The Tannaitic/Amoratic/ Geonic Liturgical "project" assigned the *Avodah* to the *middle* section, literally the *emtza,* or central section of the *Musaf* service; virtually, its theme--statement. From Talmudic texts we know that the *Musaf* was meant to be a replacement for the sacrifices in the Temple. Representing almost every period and geographic location of Jewish history, there are at least seventy renditions of the *Avodah* all following a similar design from creation through Israel's Covenant Service, (sometimes including martyrdom) to a culmination of both particular and universal restoration.

For its afternoon service *Gates of Repentance* undertook a more diffuse, generalized (and longer) *Avodah*: a "snapshot" idea of Jewish history, a long distance from the original intent, role and purpose of the *Avodah*. The 1945 *Union Prayer Book*, volume 2 preserved, under scholarly supervision, a more exacting and authentic version of the *Avodah* with interpretative prayers to be sure; but at the same time, in the absence of a *Musaf* service, relegating it to the marginal location of the afternoon service, during which far fewer people are present.

The potential today of communicating the genius of Judaism enlarged by the knowledge given to us by modern critical studies in the History and Phenomenology of Religions enhances both our understanding and the potential of the *Avodah*. We know that all of the Axial ("High") religions were developed out of the prior sacrificial systems of the great river valley agricultural empires based in the center-ideology of Sacral Kingship and the renewal of cyclicity in Nature and order in Society. The central person, at the central time, at the central place of the world (each of these empires consider themselves the center of the world), performed complex sacrificial rites of renovation/renewal of Nature of "Seed Time and Harvest", to ensure perenniality and, at the same time, to reinstitute caste or social systems apexing in a Divine King; social systems considered to be integral with Nature. These rites focused on minutely performed ritual observances to the utmost detail. It was generally believed that if they were not performed with punctual detail, catastrophes in Nature such as drought, plague, floods or rains out of season, and conquest by enemies, and like calamities, could result.

The genius of Judaism was to spiritualize and moralize observance whether outright, through prophecy, or spiritualize through inwardness, repentance and the reestablishment of the moral order through communal practice of both ritual acts and justice and mercy on which the order of the world does in fact depend.

The *Avodah,* the covenant service leading to culmination, includes, in many renditions, in the absence of the Temple, the rabbinic replacements and martyrdom (*Kiddush HaShem*).

Center symbolism (Land of Israel, Jerusalem, Temple, Holy of Holies, and on a personal level the High Priest) remain in Judaic motifs. Another theme, on which all of the Axial Religions at least to some degree converge, appears prominently in Jewish tradition: The transcendence of the ego (of self-worship, the origin of all forms of idolatry). According to Jewish tradition, the culminating moment was when the High Priest entered the Holy of Holies and there, at the center of the world, at the central moment, recited the otherwise ineffable Name of God. But this had to be done with utter *kavanah,* with utter self forgetfulness. For, if an unworthy self-regarding thought should enter the mind of the High Priest at the moment of its expression, the ruin of worlds could result (see Appendix II, the meditation of Rabbi Azrael found by S. Ansky during his research into folklore of Ukrainian Jewry after World War I and used in his classic drama, "The Dybbuk").

This brings us to the "Broken Center" symbolism expressed in the *Avodah* service (cf. the prayers expressing loss, absence, negation, void, etc.), and which has been analyzed also by recent studies in the fields of modern literature and the History of Religion and is expressed *par excellence* in Judaism

> What might it mean for our communities to put "Jerusalem as the spiritual center of the world "? What would that look like?

> S. Ansky, *The Dybbuk and Other Writings* by S. Ansky, ed. David G. Roskies (New Haven, CT: Yale University Press, 2002).

by the destruction of the Temple at the Center. [An attempt was made to express these themes in the Tishah B'Av service found in the CCAR's *Gates of Prayer*, a few aspects of which could be adapted for the *Avodah* service]. Broken-Center mentalities such as radical ambiguity and anomie are common in the literature and arts of post-modernity. This is prophetically expressed in his poem, "The Second Coming", written after World War I (1919) by William Butler Yeats.

> Things fall apart; the centre cannot hold;
> Mere anarchy is loosed upon the world,
> The blood-dimmed tide is loosed, and
>   everywhere
> The ceremony of innocence is drowned . . .

As to the Scripture Reading from Leviticus 16: If the *Avodah* could be restored to a more central location in the Morning service, then the question arises as to whether Leviticus 16 should at least be an alternative reading for Yom Kippur morning along with, quite properly, Isaiah 58.

When one reads the biblical text, *mikot chatoteichem . . . tit'haru* ("From all your sins . . . you shall be cleansed" Leviticus 16:30), the sense of fulfillment and renewal from sin and from breakdown come into being. Since then the job is to find some way to communicate that culmination of the ability to get beyond regrets, beyond what we have done wrong, and to renew ourselves from the spiritual center and outward from that center and into the world.

Appendix I

Narrative Structure of *T'filat Musaf*

FROM ----------------------->THROUGH ---------------------> TO		
God	*Emtzai*	**Culmination**
of ancestors	Israel's Covenant Service	Acceptance
of powers	*Avodah*	Thanksgiving
natural and	The service of the day	Peace; symbolism
Supernatural	*K'dushat HaYom, Atah*	of culmination
of holiness	*B'chartanu, Yaaleh V'yavo*, etc.	
	Emtzai (*Avodah*) of	
	T'filat Musaf Yom Kippur	
	[Restoration of moral order]	
Frames:		
Aleinu	From Creation through	Purification
Heyeh im Pipiyot	Priestly Service at the	Restoration
Achilah LaEl	Temple Purification	
Acclamation and Pleas	(*Amitz Koach/Atah Konanta*)	
For Adequacy	*Avodah* proper (service	
	of the High Priest)	
	The Glories of the rites	
	The Broken Center and	
	Ritual Void	

Appendix II

Rabbi Azrael's Discourse from "The Dybbuk"

The world of God is great and holy. In all the world the holiest land is the Land of Israel. In the Land of Israel the holiest city is Jerusalem; in Jerusalem the holiest place was the Holy Temple and the holiest spot in the Temple was the Holy of Holies. (*He pauses.*) In the world there are seventy nations, and of them the holiest is Israel. The holiest of the people of Israel is the tribe of the Levites. The holiest of the Levites are the priests, and amongst the priests, the holiest is the High Priest. (*Pause.*) The year has three hundred and fifty-four days. Of these the holidays are the holiest. Holier than the holidays are the Sabbaths and the holiest of the Sabbaths is the Day of Atonement, Sabbath of Sabbaths. (*Pause.*) There are in the world seventy tongues. The holiest of all things written in this tongue is the Holy Torah; of the Torah the holiest part is the Ten Commandments, and the holiest of all the words in the Ten Commandments is the Name of the Lord. (*Pause.*) At a certain hour, on a certain day of the year, all these four supreme holinesses met together. This took place on the Day of Atonement, at the hour when the High Priest entered the Holy of Holies and there revealed the Divine Name. And as this hour was holy and terrible beyond words, so also was it the hour of utmost peril for the High Priest, and for the entire commonweal of Israel. For if, in that hour (which God forbid), a sinful or a wayward thought had entered the mind of the High Priest, it would have brought the destruction of the world. (*Pause.*) Wherever a man stand to lift his eyes to heaven, that place is a Holy of Holies. Every human being created by God in His own image and likeness is a High Priest. Each day of a man's life is the Day of Atonement; and every word he speaks from his heart is the name of the Lord. Therefore the sin of any man, whether of commission or of omission, brings the ruin of a whole world in its train.

Creative Reclamation of Leviticus 16: The Yom Kippur *Avodah* within the Female Enclosure

Dr. Bonna Devora Haberman

Bonna Devora Haberman, "The Yom Kippur *Avoda* within the Female Enclosure," in *Beginning Anew: A Woman's Companion to the High Holy Days*, ed. Gail Twersky Reimer and Judith A. Kates (New York: Touchstone, 1997), 243–57. This essay can also be found as "The Yom Kippur *Avoda* with the Female Enclosure" at http://www.ccarnet.org/lifelong-learning/teleconferences-webinars/session-iii-creative-reclamation-leviticus-16.

I'll be brief and say a few words about the essay "The Yom Kippur *Avoda* within the Female Enclosure," and I'd be very delighted to answer and discuss and engage with others. I suggest that the act of entering deeply into sacred space is both metaphoric and a very physical, material process. The metaphor compares the *Mishkan* or *Mikdash*, the Temple, to a woman's physiology whereby the *Kodesh HaKodashim*, the Holy of Holies, is the inner room, the sanctum. The enclosed passageway through which the *Kohein Gadol* enters and exits and the innermost space in which s/he enacts the most sacred ritual of the Jewish year is equivalent to the vagina and womb. This image describes not only a physiological alignment with the topography of the Temple, but also a functional equivalence. The Temple ritual replicates the cycle of potency, of life and death, of renewal and loss. As Rabbi Bronstein so beautifully stated it, the *Mikdash* motif is the activity of renewing the cycle of Creation, where brokenness is at the core and the fulfillment of a ritual has the effect of renewing, not only at the individual level, but also at a national level. In some respect, there is even a larger vision—without being territorial or ethnocentric—that also affects the entire cosmos.

Every person, man and woman, participates in the activity and enactment of the sacred service. This is a very personal embodied experience that connects prayer with fertile renewing cycles. These cycles are not only in a woman's body, but also the interaction between women, between a man and a woman, in a cycle of sexuality and love. This relates to another question, and also the Reform context, the relevance of Leviticus altogether and sacrifices as one of the motifs in a Reform setting. How do the concepts of *tumah* and *taharah*—words that don't translate well into English because the connotation of purity and impurity refer much more to detergents and soap rather than to the imminence of mortality—apply? I propose that they refer to the quest for *k'dushah*, for holiness. In any case, *tumah* and *taharah* arise here along with sacrifice. I'm so delighted, as someone who's not part of the Reform community, to engage with you and see you all taking this with such seriousness and honor, *kavod*, in your hearts and in your prayers and in your learning; I'm really touched by this.

> The Hebrew word *k'dushah* means "holiness," but it also has the connotation of separation, setting aside. How do we separate ourselves or aspects of our lives during the High Holy Days?

In any case, the central idea is that the personal being—body, mind, and soul—and also the national being are both partaking of a sacred process. The liturgy engages the congregation in an enactment of the sacred *Avodah* of Yom Kippur. The larger frame of the *Avodah* is easier to speak about in *Y'rushalayim*, where throngs of people have come today to be present in this place to which we attribute *k'dushah*. There we reactivate a national experience of fulfilling our desire for the sacred, our body moving toward higher being, and entering as close as possible into the sacred domain—at the Temple retaining walls that still stand today, just a few kilometers from where I live. So, we can consider the entire Yom Kippur experience and its expression as very close to ourselves and our intimate lives— where intimacy is understood in both spiritual as well as in bodily terms. I think that's enough to open, and I'm happy to engage with you all.

Rabbi Leon A. Morris

In addition, your essay highlights several themes that are of particular interest to us; the first, embodiment and intimacy. I want to ask about two other themes that I think are particularly relevant for us: the connection between the *Mishkan* and our own synagogues, and the reciprocity between the priests who serve as a kind of paradigm for the religious leadership and the people. Would you say more about those two themes—the connection between the *Mishkan* and our synagogues as it plays out in Leviticus 16 and in *Seder HaAvodah*, and this relationship of reciprocity between the priest and the people.

Dr. Bonna Devora Haberman

I describe the structure of the *Mishkan* and the synagogue and also, of course, the *Beit HaMikdash* according to this very potent metaphor of human bodies. I give examples in the essay and in other places of how there's almost a one-to-one connection between not only the physiology of the body, but also the function of the body in the sacred service of the *Mishkan* and the *Mikdash*. Now, the synagogue is a further displacement—I discuss in the essay about how cleaned up it is, how tidy it is, how less full the experience is. There's so much verbiage and so few smells and sounds and feelings, and there's no goat, right? There's no blood; there's no material. The materials we have are muted and impoverished compared with the immediacy of the experience with life, with mortality that sacrifice represents. Of course, I can identify with not sharing the desire to reinstate sacrifice. The purpose here is not to mourn the passing of sacrifice from our lives, but to look for ways that we can experience the freshness and, in a certain way, totality of human awareness that comes from the embodied material contact, the engagement with life and death. The *Avodah* is a paradigm.

I'd like to be more direct about your first question concerning the connection. There is a displacement in the move to the synagogue from the *Mikdash* and from the *Mishkan*; however, there's also tremendous democratization that synagogues represent. It says in Leviticus 16 that there's only one person who has the possibility of touching that most sacred endeavor, and of course, we're reminded of this because of Nadav and Avihu. The chapter begins *Acharei Mot*, after the death of two of Aaron's children. And so with the displacement, there's also less danger. If we think of all of this having something to do with coming into closer contact, into greater intimacy with the *kodesh* (holy), with *k'dushah* (holiness), then the synagogue is a further displacement, on the one hand. And also the topography of the synagogue is more muted. There's usually one main enclosure. There are corridors and halls and outer spaces, and there are often doorways that mark the one sanctuary. We could interpret this topography also with *Keilim* in the discussion in the Mishnah, the ten *k'dushot*, the ten layers of holinesses. And in the synagogue, there's less definition; there's less exclusion and more openness, which is a very great opportunity for more people to participate and have more access and at the same time less intensity.

I would like to suggest a couple of things in that domain about how it's possible to enable people to feel more proximity and more material arousal, even in a synagogue setting. One of the practices that I've initiated when I lead the *Musaf Avodah* is to bring essential oils from the ingredients of the *k'toret*, the incense, and invite members of the community to go under a simple tent where all of these aromas are infused into the air. Each congregant, alone for a moment, enclosed in the tent, inhales, fills her/his being with the ancient sacred aroma. This is at least a hint of the kind of sensory experience of the *Avodah*. If we start to think creatively, there might be other ways that we could bring more tactile aspects into our very neat and tidy spaces. In general, we need to better face the challenges generated by the separation from the more rugged, more material, more palpable experiences of the *Avodah*.

How can High Holy Day worship appeal to all the senses? What would an experiential service look like? Refer to Evan Kent's article "When I Hear the Shofar I Taste Chocolate," page 327.

On the second question about reciprocity, there are multiple layers that every member of a congregation experiences in the *Avodah* on Yom Kippur, both the leader and the members of the congregation. During the reenactment—recitation of the *Avodah* in the *Musaf*—the community performs full prostrations (though this may not be practiced in Reform congregations). Each time the prayer leader mentions how the *kohein* pronounces the divine name, the congregation traditionally prostrates fully onto the ground. In some communities, only the leader does this, but it has become more and more popular in more communities to actually enact the full prostration. Another place is in the counting of the blood, *achat achat v'achat*, and the reproduction of that recitation by the community answering to the prayer leader. So, these are some places where the actual members of the community participate as if s/he is the *kohein/et*. And so the prayer leader enables each member of the congregation to feel him/herself a *kohein/et*. With the conclusion of the period of the sacrifices, *chazal* reinterpreted the mitzvot and the obligation of *talmud Torah* and *Avodah* as being applicable to every single member of the Jewish people at all times. In a certain way, every person became *kohein/et* in that structure through the sacred service of prayer and study. So, in terms of reciprocity, there are opportunities in the liturgy for the community to participate and even more so—for each member to feel prompted by the liturgy to see him/herself as actually, in some sense, entering the *kodesh*.

Creative Reclamation of Leviticus 16:
Storahtellings Approach

Amichai Lau-Lavie

I've been working through Storahtelling to rein-
vent what we do with Yom Kippur for the last six
years, leading services for primarily unaffiliated
Jews and various mixed-faith communities, families, and in some cases, children. It's a very mixed
crowd. And we've been struggling with how to
make both the liturgy and the Torah story of Yom
Kippur really relevant to the very open new public.
One of the things we've done in the last few years
is looking at *k'riat haTorah* for Yom Kippur as a way
to position every single person there as the High
Priest and inviting everyone to reimagine what it's
like to understand this metaphor for entering the
innermost, before really entering what is most sacred within each one of us. By doing that, we've
gone to metaphor, we've gone to what mystics and
darshanim have done of reinterpreting *Seder Avodah*
and the geography and the sacred geometry of the
Temple as an inner experience, which may have
once served the ancestors of the actual live theater
of ritual, and for us is now being redefined.

Several years ago we created a Storahtelling for
Yom Kippur focusing on the scapegoat and com-
paring the story of the two goats as the two sons
of Aaron. And the story for the people present and
for the audience was really looking at the anguish
of the father, of Aaron and what would it mean to
officiate and be involved in religious life when your
heart is broken and when your faith is not something that you can rely on. We went to the questions of faith and faithfulness in the face of having

Is it easy or
difficult to have
faith in today's
world? Why?

58

to enter the sacred and moving along a very powerful theme where a person, the maven who translated and acted as Aaron, broke out in tears the
moment before entering the Holy of Holies crying,
"How can I enter my heart? My heart is not open
for this moment of faith." So, that was one version
that we've tried a few times.

When do you "enter the sacred"? How does it feel?

Last year, and this is the text included here,
again inspired by some of the texts mentioned earlier, we're looking at *The Dybbuk,* and we're looking at this notion of entering the Holy of Holies or
the innermost as a psycho-spiritual invitation. We
created a retelling of the *k'riah* in which the people
doing the "mavening," the translation that Storahtelling does, are a woman playing a bride and a
woman playing a mourning mother. And what we
worked, based on *The Dybbuk* monologue, was that
entering the chuppah or sitting down for shivah
are moments of entering the innermost. It's about
intimacy, it's about eye-to-eye, face-to-face; what
do life and death have to offer. And that each and
every single person with us on this day is invited
to take the time to enter the innermost. And following in the footsteps of the High Priest and replicating those steps and those procedures, but in a
way that's emotional, psychological, personal, and
ritualistic. In the monologue, we took some of the
text from *The Dybbuk* and really focused on this notion of the Holy of Holies. The bride walked in and
said, "I'm about to enter the Holy of Holies. Am I
ready? What do I leave behind before I enter?" The
mourning mother delivered a similar text. The
emcee addressed the audience, the *kahal,* and said,
"The High Priest of Israel is about to enter the Holy
of Holies. Is he ready? What will he have to leave
behind before the great intimacy of God? Are you
ready? You are the High Priest. You're about to en-

See page 62.

What does it mean to be ready to enter the Holy of Holies, the inner sanctum, sacred space?

ter the Holy of Holies. What do you leave behind?" and so on. The actual verses of the difficult *p'sukim* were translated with that notion of personalizing it today. Was everybody able to understand this procedure that was once a reality and now simply a metaphor?

I want to mention one last thing. In the middle of the *k'riat haTorah* and between the second and the third *aliyot,* as we do it, we paused and there was the notion of the scapegoat ritual. What do we do with that today? We created something very strange last year that actually, I think, was very powerful. We handed out, together with the programs and the books people got when they got in, blank sheets of paper and little golf pencils, and at some point, one of us addressed the *kahal* and said, "Well, we don't have a scapegoat, but we can take all the collective transgressions and all the 'oops' moments and put them somewhere together." People were inspired and invited to write on a piece of paper what is it that they want to get rid of, and we collected it all together. It was kind of a drama of the bride saying, "I will take this," loosely based on the *bedeken* ritual where a bride when unveiled takes upon herself all the blessings and the prayers of people coming to her. So, the bride went around collecting five hundred notes from people while music was playing the *Ashamnu* in between the *aliyot,* and then when she had this big basket of notes, she actually broke down crying and said, "You know what? I can't do this. I can't take this." And that became a great discussion: What do we do with this? How does the community deal with this collective angst? And what do we do with this basket of notes? There's no scapegoat. No one's going to take care of this for us. We ended up collecting all the notes in a big white manila envelope and put it in the ark until

Do you think asking people to record their transgressions would be an effective element to include in Yom Kippur services? Why or why not?

How would you respond to the questions posed by the presenter? How does dealing with collective transgressions factor into your services on Yom Kippur?

N'ilah. The day after *N'ilah* there was a survey that went around to everybody online with five options of what to do with it, and the option that was chosen was to take all these notes, plant them in the ground as compost, and then the flowers that will grow in someone's backyard will be used next Yom Kippur. So, that was one way of taking the narrative and transferring it, as some of you have said, to a personal introspective metaphor, and we found it extremely powerful, especially to people for whom the *Avodah* at face value means absolutely nothing.

How do you balance the roles of collective prayer and individual introspection in your Yom Kippur worship?

ST⊙RAHTELLING

INNERMOST: Upon Entering the Holy of Holies

Excerpts from YOM KIPPUR STORAH
SERVICE 5770,
New York City/*Acharei Mot,*
Leviticus 16:1–13

Opening (*before taking the Torah out of ark*)

(**Bride** *enters slowly, in white, from the back of the sanctuary, climbs stage, and faces the audience. Mourning mother, in black, comes out from the back of the house and stands next to her on stage. She helps the bride veil herself.*)

Bride: I am about to enter the Holy of Holies. Am I ready? What do I leave behind before I enter?

MC/Maven: The High Priest of Israel prepares to enter the Holy of Holies. Is he ready? What will he have to leave behind before the great intimacy of God?

Are you ready?

(**Bride and Mourning Mother** *deliver
this next text, in turns.*)

Every piece of ground on which a person stands when she raises her eyes to heaven is a Holy of Holies; everyone created in the image of God is a High Priest; every day in a person's life is Yom Kippur; and every word which a person speaks from her heart is God's name.

Some say: God's world is holy and great. The holiest land in the world is the Land of Israel. The holiest place in Israel is Jerusalem. The holiest place in Jerusalem was the Temple, and the holiest spot in the temple was the HOLY OF HOLIES.

There are 354 days in the year, and among them the holy days are sacred. And the Sabbath is holier than the holy days. The holiest of all holy days, the Sabbath of Sabbaths, is Yom Kippur, which is the Day of Atonement.

There are seventy nations in the world, and among them, some say, the people of Israel is the holiest. And the tribe of Levi is the holiest of all twelve tribes of Israel, and among the Levites the holiest are the priests. And among the priests the holiest is the High Priest.

There are seventy languages in the world, and the holiest among them is Hebrew. And the holiest words in the Hebrew language are the words of the Torah, and its holiest part is the Ten Commandments, and the holiest word in the Ten Commandments is the name of God.

Once a year, on Yom Kippur, the four holiest sanctities gather together precisely when the High Priest enters the Holy of Holies in order to pronounce the ineffable name of God. And at that immeasurably holy and awesome moment the High Priest and the people of Israel are in the utmost peril, for even a single sinful or wayward thought in the High Priest's mind at that instant might, God forbid, destroy the entire world.

Therefore every sin and every wrong committed by humans brings the world to destruction.

Therefore, every second of sacred intention, of truth, of love, brings the world to life.

Every piece of ground on which a person stands when he raises his eyes to heaven is a Holy of Holies; everyone created in the image of God is a High Priest; every day in a person's life is Yom Kippur; and every word which a person speaks from his heart is God's name.

Bride: I am ready to enter the Holy of Holies. (*Walks off stage.*)

Mourning Mother: I have entered the innermost. I am here now.

MC/Maven: Are we ready to enter? (*Lead into taking out the Torah.*)

(Based on a text from S. Ansky's *The Dybbuk*, edited by Amichai Lau-Lavie)

Sample Storah Translations: Leviticus 16:3–4
(Hebrew verse is chanted, followed by the Mavens in English.)

3 Herewith shall Aaron come into the holy place: with a young bullock for a sin-offering, and a ram for a burnt-offering. (JPS)

Maven: Aaron must prepare. He brings with him a live ox, it will be killed and offered as a sin sacrifice.

Mourner: My sacrifice.

Maven: He must also bring a live ram, a sacrifice to the flames.

Mourner: The ox, reminder of the golden calf. The ram, just like the one that Abraham sacrificed, instead of his son, Isaac. My son.

4 He shall put on the holy linen tunic, and he shall have the linen breeches upon his flesh, and shall be girded with the linen girdle, and with the linen mitre shall he be attired; they are the holy garments; and he shall bathe his flesh in water, and put them on. (JPS)

MC/Maven: Ready? To enter the Holy of Holies Aaron wears a special uniform: linen tunic, linen pants, linen belt, linen hat. Sacred vestments. All white. Before dressing, he will wash his flesh with water, then dress.

Bride: I dressed slowly this morning. Item by item I become more than my name, other than my usual self. I am dressed up for the part I am about to play, the new me I about to become.

"**W**e will offer the words of our lips instead of bulls" (Hosea 14:3). What shall we say instead of bulls and in place of the scapegoat? We will offer the words of our lips.
A crimson thread was tied to the horns of the scapegoat. Israel said to the Holy One: We have no crimson thread now that the Temple is destroyed and we have no scapegoat. God replied: Your lips are like a thread of scarlet, and the utterance of your lips as beloved to me as the strip of crimson. (*Midrash Shir HaShirim Rabbah* 4:9)

Creative Reclamation of Leviticus 16
End-of-Call Discussion

Rabbi Leon A. Morris, Rabbi Herbert
Bronstein, Rabbi Elaine Zecher,
Dr. Bonna Devora Haberman,
Amichai Lau-Lavie

Rabbi Leon A. Morris

I would love to invite the three of you to make a very brief comment that might be inspired by one of the other comments.

Rabbi Herbert Bronstein

I appreciate your use, Amichai, of the word "metaphor," but the service is meant to be a re-actualization, through memory, a re-dramatization of the *Avodah*, of the service of the High Priest, an opportunity to actually experience it. In the seder, every person is supposed to feel as if he or she went forth from Egypt and was experiencing the redemption in the process of the seder itself going from *g'nut* (defamation) to *shevach* (praise), from *shibud* (slavery) to *Avodah*, service of God. Likewise, *Avodah* is supposed to re-dramatize the move from Temple to synagogue. Look at that *Avodah* in the afternoon service of the *Union Prayer Book*, volume 2, of 1945, in which there is congregational participation. We would want much more. But I think the goal should be not only recollection. Yes, recollection and what it means, an interpretative text of what that means at the center, reordering the order, the moral order of the world, reminding us that it's up to us to maintain that moral order, that we are part of the law that broke this, but we can repent and start again. And this service is meant to let us enter the Holy of Holies because we've purified ourselves, we are purified in some sense. There should be some catharsis of that kind, something to lead us toward the actual experience, and even the scapegoat can be used. But we can't leave it to goats. There were barbarians, according to the Mishnah, they called them barbarians, who actually grabbed the goat to lay their hands on it to get rid of their sins, but that wasn't the point. I can't go into all the details as described in the Mishnah, but we could even do something with the scapegoat of taking it back on to our own responsibility and so forth as a move ahead. I think we're in the right direction of re-actualizing the experience of entering the holy, of renewing through our *Avodah* service, and I think that is the goal we should at least agree to, more engagement of the congregation in an old pattern. It's right there in Leviticus 16 that it moves from the work of the priest into the work of the people and goes much further in Rabbinic literature. As to the synagogue, the synagogue is the center. Each synagogue, depending on the spirit of the people and their reach, becomes that connection between down here and up there that the center represented in the renewal ceremonies of sacrifice. And the rabbi, in a way, is leading the service, or whoever is leading the service, or the *chazan*, does take on a tremendous responsibility.

Rabbi Elaine Zecher

Is there anything you wanted to say to those of us who are working on *Mishkan HaNefesh*: what do you think we should be considering based on this conversation?

Dr. Bonna Devora Haberman,

I affirm that the *Avodah* is a very, very important element of Yom Kippur that needs to be appropriately adapted to the context of the Reform liturgy that you use. It needs the fullest possible expression in a way that can be meaningful to your congregations. You might choose units or pieces. I am contributing this reading of Leviticus 16, emphasizing that these materials are not in any way neutral. The *Avodah* is an erotic process, profoundly connected to our hearts beating, to our grasp of mortality, to our desire, to our embodied experience. Having burned the incense and aroused our lover, our partner, we then move carefully forward delicately and with gentleness. Entering deeper inside, we open ourselves. Within the inner enclosure, we replicate an erotic, intimate encounter. Then, carefully, we retreat backward, always facing face-to-face, preserving our attentiveness and arousal. We retreat, wash, dress, and reenter, going in and out. Whatever liturgical expression you find should protect that very delicate intimate process of love and passion that the *Avodah* communicates.

What might it mean to approach Yom Kippur, or at least elements of its liturgy, in an erotic way?

Amichai Lau-Lavie

I would say less is more as you are going to think of using these verses in this liturgy in ways that are compelling to this very modern audience; less is more as far as the verses. Maybe getting creative with using this metaphor does not necessitate working with all of the text, really with just highlights. I feel like I've done work in the last few years with several rabbis and leaders, helping them with some creative ways to enliven this liturgy and the

Torah, and I'll be happy to continue this conversation with anybody else who wants to and come up with creative ways that can possibly be replicated on a larger scale.

Creative Reclamation of Leviticus 16 Wrap-Up

1. What is the difference between reading Leviticus 16 on Yom Kippur morning and reading it as part of the annual Torah reading cycle in *Parashat Acharei Mot*?
2. What would need to happen first with our overall approach to sacrificial texts in order to support the re-inclusion of Leviticus 16 on Yom Kippur?
3. What are the stories that Leviticus 16 tells? What are the teachings worth gleaning from these stories?
4. What did you learn from these presentations on Leviticus 16 that you would like to implement in your community's High Holy Day worship?

Shofar Service

Shofar Service: Historical Background

Dr. Richard S. Sarason

In this presentation, I want first to discuss the original context of this material and then what has been done with it in various Reform contexts. At the outset, it is worth noting that what we call the Shofar Service is actually a creation of Reform prayer-book editors. It is a combination of two elements in the traditional liturgies for the High Holy Days: (1) the shofar blowing, together with a blessing, that takes place after the reading of the haftarah, while the Torah scrolls are still out, and (2) the shofar blowings that accompany the verses and prayers of *Malchuyot, Zichronot,* and *Shofarot* in the *Musaf Amidah.*

The Reform Shofar Service with which we are familiar basically was framed as a creative response to the elimination of *Musaf* in most Reform prayer books, particularly in North America. As noted above, it takes two elements from the traditional service and combines them into a separate entity. The oldest of these elements is the *Malchuyot, Zichronot,* and *Shofarot* insertions in the *Musaf Amidah.* Each of these is composed of ten verses dealing with the appropriate theme, preceded by a poetic introduction, and followed by a petitionary prayer that concludes with a *b'rachah.* The shofar was to be sounded at the conclusion of each of these *b'rachot.* Momentarily, we will look at a Mishnaic text that is our earliest evidence for this custom. *Malchuyot-*

Mishnah Rosh HaShanah 4:5–6 uses the form Malchiyot instead of Malchuyot, but we use the latter variant today.

Why might it be advantageous to reincorporate Musaf back into the High Holy Day liturgy? Why might it be advantageous to continue to leave it out?

Zichronot-Shofarot were always considered to be part of the Rosh HaShanah *Amidah*. The second element in the Reform Shofar Service is the shofar blessings and the blowing of the shofar that was done in the morning service, while the Torah was out of the ark, before communal announcements and the prayer for the congregation.

I want to discuss what these ritual actions and recitations initially signify. In the Torah itself (Leviticus 23:24ff., Numbers 29:1ff.), there is, of course, no Rosh HaShanah in Tishrei—there is no Tishrei. There is, instead, the first day of the seventh month, which is known as Yom T'ruah or Yom Zichron T'ruah, on which a lot of noise is made. The noise that is made, the *t'ruah*, is intended to get God's attention, because this is a crucial time of year. We're bringing in the summer crops that will sustain us over the long winter. We need rain for the new season's crops, and we're looking forward with some trepidation to the beginning of the rainy season in the hope that the rains will come at the right time and in the proper amount. At this time of transition, we particularly need God's protection and blessings. So it's clear that the purpose of the *t'ruah*, the loud noise-making, is to attract God's attention. We want God to *zachor*—not simply to remember, but to take note, to pay attention to the needs of God's people. And that is, in fact, the core of *Yaaleh V'yavo* in the festival liturgy: May our notice come before you. Pay attention to us. We need your assistance.

What is the psychological import of asking God to pay attention to us?

See Shofar Service: Sources 1, page 78.

Turning now to the relevant Mishnah texts: The second chapter of Tractate *Taanit* gives us the liturgical ritual for occasional fast days proclaimed on account of drought. The ark is brought out into the open, public space, and it is covered with ashes so that its penitential garb is clearly visible to all (and to God). The prayer leader recites twenty-four *b'rachot*, the daily *Sh'moneh Esreih* plus six: *Zichronot, Shofarot,* and four psalms of need. Rabbi Y'hudah dissents, maintaining that it is not necessary to recite *Zichronot* and *Shofarot*, only two other passages from Scripture that deal with the situation of need.

What we learn from this, first of all, is that *Zichronot* and *Shofarot* are also associated with fast days. This means that they, too, are intended to draw God's attention to the needs of the people. We learn, too, that, as far as the Mishnah is concerned, these are nothing more than a series of biblical verses that one recites—voices, if you will—with the intent of invoking God's providential attention. One of the reasons why there is a fair amount of scriptural texts in rabbinic liturgy is that these are deemed to be powerful words, words that we know have worked in the past, so we'll use them again. Scripture is where God says "this," and we're reminding God of that, and so we are merely asking God to do what God has promised to do! To summarize so far: *Zichronot/Shofarot* are associated with fast-day liturgies, as well as with Rosh HaShanah, because on all of these occasions the community is in need and trying to get God's attention.

The second text is from *Mishnah Rosh HaShanah*, chapter 4, paragraphs 5 and 6. This, by the way, is the earliest text to mention the names of the *Amidah* benedictions. What appear here, of course, are the Seven Benedictions for festivals, rather than the Eighteen Benedictions for weekdays. The text articulates the order of the benedictions as follows: *Avot* (Ancestors), *G'vurot* (God's Power), *K'dushat HaShem* (God's Sanctity), then indicates that *Malchuyot* is to be included in *K'dushat HaShem*, after which there is to be no shofar blowing. Then follows *K'dushat HaYom* (Sanctity of the Day), after which the shofar is to be blown. This in turn is followed by *Zichronot*, after which the shofar is to be blown. Then follows *Shofarot*, after which the shofar is to be blown again. Then the *Amidah* concludes, as on all other days, with *Avodah* (For the Acceptance of Our Worship), *Hodaah* (Thanksgiving), and *Birkat Kohanim* (Priestly Blessing).

This is the opinion of Rabbi Yochanan ben Nuri. According to his opinion, *Malchuyot*, which voices the theme of God's kingship and the renewal of that kingship at the beginning of the year, belongs thematically in *K'dushat HaShem*, which also deals with God's majesty. But the shofar is not to be blown until after *K'dushat HaYom*, presumably because that is the special *b'rachah* of the day. This then is to be followed by *Zichronot* and *Shofarot*, after each of which the shofar is to be blown.

Rabbi Akiva, who has the last halachic word in this dispute, raises a trenchant objection: If you're not going to blow the shofar over *Malchuyot*, then why do you even bother to recite these verses? Rather, you recite *Avot, G'vurot, K'dushat HaShem*, and include *Malchuyot* in *K'dushat HaYom* and then blow the shofar. Then you recite *Zichronot* and blow the shofar, recite *Shofarot* and blow the shofar, and then finish up with the three concluding blessings.

What precisely constitute *Malchuyot, Zichronot*, and *Shofarot*? According to the Mishnah, these are each a series of scriptural verses. As mandated in paragraph 6, we voice no fewer than ten *Malchuyot* verses, ten *Zichronot* verses, and ten *Shofarot* verses. And that is indeed the halachah to this day and what is found in the traditional liturgy. These sets of verses form the centerpiece of these rubrics, which together are referred to in the Babylonian Talmud as the *T'kiata D'vei Rav* (whether *Rav* refers to the Babylonian Amora Rav or, more likely, whether *d'vei rav* is simply the commonplace expression for a house of study). In the liturgy that has come down to us, these verses are surrounded fore and aft by Rabbinic *b'rachah* material: poetic introductions (*Aleinu l'shabei-ach* for *Malchuyot*, *Atah zocheir maaseih olam* for *Zichronot*, and *Atah nigleita b'anan k'vodecha* for *Shofarot*) and petitionary conclusions that end with a *chatimah*. Each is followed by shofar blasts.

Rabbi Yochanan ben Nuri holds that the obligation may be fulfilled by reciting even as few as three verses in each section. The Mishnah also holds that we should not recite any verse, for any of the sections, that mentions divine retribution and punishment of Israel, since we do not want thereby to call down punishment on ourselves. The Mishnah states that we should begin with verses from the Torah and conclude with verses from the Prophets (the latter containing divine promises of consolation and restoration). Rabbi Yosei holds that it is good to conclude with a Torah verse. That is why, to this day, the custom is to recite three, three, and three, plus one—three verses from Torah, three from the Prophets, and three from the Writings (usually psalm verses), and then one at the end from the Torah. My colleague, Professor Debra Reed Blank, will deal in more detail with the thematic issues of these texts.

What might be the symbolism behind this structure? How might you use or adapt this rubric for your community?

What is interesting, of course, is how Reform prayer books have dealt with this, in light of (a) the issue of abbreviation, which includes the elimination of *Musaf,* and (b) the fact that there is another shofar blowing with *b'rachot* after the reading of the haftarah. The *b'rachah* for blowing the shofar (actually for *hearing* the shofar blast, since that is what is deemed to be the mitzvah) traditionally is not recited during the *Musaf Amidah* because the mitzvah has already been fulfilled.

Why do you think
these radical
Reformers refrained
from blowing the
shofar altogether?

Interestingly enough, most of the Reform
prayer books in Germany kept the *Musaf* service,
and that is true to this day. The radical Berlin Re-
formgemeinde, which did away with *Musaf* and
did away with most of the Hebrew liturgy, didn't
blow the shofar at all, so the issue was moot for
them. But in the United States, the very first major
Reform prayer book, which was edited for Temple
Emanu-El in New York by Leo Merzbacher in 1855,
did away with *Musaf*. And while it kept the shofar
blowing with the *b'rachot* separate from *Malchuyot,
Zichronot,* and *Shofarot,* Merzbacher had to decide
how formally to structure this material without
a *Musaf Amidah*. He gives the first shofar blowing
with benedictions during the Torah service, and
then, after *Ashrei,* gives *Malchuyot, Zichronot,* and
Shofarot by themselves, independent of any *Amidah*
framework, and followed simply by *Kaddish,* the
end of the service. This prayer book was revised
in 1860 by Samuel Adler, who was far more radical than Merzbacher. He eliminated *Malchuyot, Zichronot,* and *Shofarot* altogether. He simply gives
a shofar blowing at the end of the Torah service,
followed by the standard concluding *Aleinu* (which
had been eliminated by Merzbacher because it otherwise would have duplicated the beginning of
Malchuyot).

Most interesting in this regard is David Einhorn's treatment in *Olat Tamid* (1858). He includes
Malchuyot, in German, in the *K'dushat HaYom* benediction of the *Amidah* (its traditional location, but in
the morning service, since there is no *Musaf*), followed immediately by *Zichronot,* in German. Both
of these are creative renderings and they dispense
with the verses (although some are incorporated
paraphrastically into the German paragraphs). They
also are not followed by any shofar blasts. *Zichronot*

here has been incorporated as well into the *K'dushat HaYom* benediction. It is thus followed by the rest of the benediction—*kadsheinu b'mitzvotecha* and *Yaaleh V'yavo*—and the three concluding *Amidah* benedictions. *Shofarot* appears after the haftarah reading, the traditional place for the shofar blessings, and that is where the shofar now is blown.

The *Union Prayer Book*, volume 2, of 1894 gives a Shofar Service, after the haftarah reading, with no shofar blessings and an interpretative *Malchuyot, Zichronot, Shofarot* in English with a shofar blowing after each. This remained the pattern in all the revisions of the *Union Prayer Book*. The shofar blessings are not included until 1945. Some of the British and German liberal prayer books that were published after the *Union Prayer Book* of 1894 followed its lead to some extent in compressing and reshaping these elements.

The treatment in *Gates of Repentance* is modeled on that of the *Union Prayer Book*, with a separate Shofar Service after the haftarah reading, which now includes a blessing for the shofar blowing incorporated into *Malchuyot*. Since there is no *Amidah* framework, we have only *Malchuyot* with a shofar blowing, *Zichronot* with a shofar blowing, and *Shofarot* with a shofar blowing.

Which Reform practice regarding *Malchuyot, Zichronot,* and *Shofarot* resonates the most for you? Is there a possibility you would like to add?

Shofar Service: Sources I

Mishnah Taanit 2:1–3

(א) סדר תעניות כיצד... (ב) עמדו בתפלה, מורידין לפני התיבה
זקן ורגיל...ואומר לפניהם עשרים וארבעה ברכות, שמונה
עשרה שבכל יום, ומוסיף עליהן עוד שש: (ג) ואלו הן, **זכרונות,**
ושופרות, אל יי בצרתה לי קראתי ויענני, אשא עיני אל ההרים
וגו', ממעמקים קראתיך ה', תפלה לעני כי יעטוף. ר' יהודה אומר,
לא היה צריך לומר זכרונות ושופרות, אלא אומר תחתיהן,
רעב כי יהיה בארץ, דבר כי יהיה וגו', אשר היה דבר ה' אל
ירמיהו על דברי הבצרות. ואומר חותמיהן:

What is the order [of service] for fast days? . . . When they stand up
to pray they place [as reader] before the ark an old man conversant
[with the prayers], who has children and whose house is empty [of
food], so that his heart is concentrated on his prayer; he recites before
them twenty-four benedictions, the eighteen recited daily, to which
he adds six as follows: ***Zichronot, Shofarot,*** and [these psalms]: *in
my distress I called unto the Eternal* (Psalm 120); *I will lift up mine eyes
unto the mountains, etc.* (Psalm 121); *out of the depths have I called Thee,
O Eternal* (Psalm 130); *a prayer of the afflicted when he faints* (Psalm 102).
Rabbi Y'hudah says: **He need not recite the *Zichronot* and *Shofarot*,**
but instead he should recite the following scriptural passages: *if there
be in the land famine, if there be pestilence* (I Kings 8:37–41); *the word of the
Eternal that came to Jeremiah concerning the droughts* (Jeremiah 14:1–10);
and he ends each [of the additional six] sections with its appropriate
concluding benediction.

Mishnah Rosh HaShanah 4:5–6

(ה) סדר ברכות, אומר אבות וגבורות וקדושת השם, וכולל
מלכיות עמהן, ואינו תוקע. קדושת היום, ותוקע. זכרונות, ותוקע.
שופרות, ותוקע. ואומר עבודה והודאה וברכת כהנים, דברי רבי
יוחנן בן נורי. אמר ליה רבי עקיבא, אם אינו תוקע למלכיות,
למה הוא מזכיר אלא אומר אבות וגבורות וקדושת השם, וכולל
מלכיות עם קדושת היום, ותוקע. זכרונות, ותוקע. שופרות,
ותוקע. ואומר עבודה והודאה וברכת כהנים: (ו) אין פוחתין
מעשרה מלכיות, מעשרה זכרונות, מעשרה שופרות. רבי יוחנן בן

נורי אומר, אם אמר שלש שלש מכולן, יצא. אין מזכירין זכרון
מלכות ושופר של פורענות. מתחיל בתורה ומשלים בנביא.
רבי יוסי אומר, אם השלים בתורה, יצא:

The order of benedictions [is as follows]: [The prayer-leader recites
the benedictions dealing with] the Ancestors, God's Power, and God's
Sanctity [literally, "the Sanctity of the Name"] and includes the Sovereignty verses with them and does not blow the shofar. He then recites
the Sanctity of the Day and blows, the Remembrance verses and blows,
and the Shofar verses and blows; he then recites [the benediction for
the restoration of] the Temple service, the Thanksgiving Benediction,
and the Priestly Benediction. This is the view of Rabbi Yochanan ben
Nuri. Said Rabbi Akiva to him: If he does not blow the shofar for the
Sovereignty verses, why should he recite them? No; [the rule is as follows:] he recites [the benedictions about] the Ancestors, God's Power,
and God's Sanctity, and recites the Sovereignty verses along with the
Sanctification of the Day and blows the shofar, then he recites the Remembrance verses and blows, and the Shofar verses and blows; then
he recites [the benediction for the restoration of] the Temple service,
the Thanksgiving Benediction, and the Priestly Benediction. No fewer
than ten Sovereignty verses, ten Remembrance verses, and ten Shofar
verses should be recited. Rabbi Yochanan ben Nuri says: If the prayer-
leader recites three from each set, he has fulfilled his obligation. One
does not mention Sovereignty, Remembrance, and Shofar verses that
signify punishment. It is proper to begin with the Torah and conclude
with the Prophets. Rabbi Yosei said: If one concludes with the Torah, he
has fulfilled his obligation.

Shofar Service: Shofar as Symbol
Dr. Debra Reed Blank

I want to probe some of the implications of the shofar and the liturgy that's grown up around the blowing of the shofar, as having become the climax of the Rosh HaShanah service.

See Shofar Service: Sources II on page 86.
The first text is Leviticus 23, where you see that, in fact, the shofar is the only distinctive mitzvah of Rosh HaShanah. It's our only calendar occasion that has the physical symbol of the shofar that's associated particularly with it.

In Psalm 47 and Numbers 10, you see that the two liturgical themes of *malchut* and *zikaron* are already biblically associated with the shofar. In Psalm 47, one of the numerous kingship psalms, you see the thematic and linguistic connections between *t'ruah* or *t'kiah* (= shofar) and *malchut*. In Numbers 10, particularly in verses 9 and 10, you have the connection between blowing the shofar and the effect of *zikaron*. These three themes, *malchut* and *zikaron* and shofar, constitute the unique liturgical material of the Rosh HaShanah service. The point here is: shofar was already key on Rosh HaShanah in the biblical period and already linked to these other two themes.

In the traditional rendering of the liturgy, the shofar is blown during the *Musaf Amidah*. Rosh Ha-Shanah 32b asks, "Why do we blow it at *Musaf*?" and the answer is, because most people are in the synagogue at *Musaf*—just like today in a Conservative or Orthodox synagogue! (Reform doesn't have this attendance problem.)

The shofar blowing, the liturgical climax of Rosh HaShanah, is couched within the central three *b'rachot* of the nine *b'rachot Amidah* for the *Musaf.* There are the first three introductory *b'rachot,* the last three closing *b'rachot,* as you do with all *Amidot* (in traditional liturgy), and in the middle are the three climactic *b'rachot* of *Malchuyot, Zichronot,* and *Shofarot* as the apex. The Reform liturgy, despite all its vicissitudes and changes that Dr. Sarason summarized, has always remained true to the understanding that the shofar and the liturgy around it need to have climactic placement. But in the absence of *Musaf,* the shofar blasts and the liturgical material around shofar get clustered at the Torah service.

To return to *Mishnah Rosh HaShanah* 4:5 that Dr. Sarason taught, Akiva is saying there that the shofar blowing is *the reason* the three unique Rosh HaShanah *b'rachot* exist. In other words, the three special *b'rachot* are the handmaidens of the shofar blowing. This results from the fact that the shofar is the only physical object associated with Rosh Ha-Shanah. *Malchut* doesn't lend itself to symbolic portrayal: there's nothing you can do ritually to symbolize God's sovereignty. There's nothing you can do physically to indicate God's *zikaron*-ing, God's act of taking note of us. But the shofar sound does have a physical manifestation, and because it is biblically linked to the other two themes, the shofar comes to represents all three themes, and the shofar blast becomes the whole point of the liturgy.

A further reason for shofar's prominence: elsewhere in the liturgy, including in *Untaneh Tokef,* shofar is understood to be symbolic of the messianic age, and that is underscored in the verses traditionally contained within the *b'rachah* of *Shofarot.* Those verses from Isaiah and Zachariah emphasize that the shofar is going to be blown in the messianic age.

Why the shofar? Why is the shofar "it"? Why not another object? Numbers 10 lists all the occasions on which a shofar was blown in the biblical period (see verses 1–8). Verses 9 and 10 indicate that the shofar is blown on occasions of celebration. Because it makes noise, as Dr. Sarason pointed out, it can be used to express celebration.

The second reason (according to this biblical text) that the shofar is blown is that it ensures the efficacy of the *korbanot*. That is key, when you think about how, in the Rabbinic period, the *avodah* of *korbanot* becomes reinterpreted as *avodah shebalev*. So blowing the shofar also makes the *t'filot* effective.

The third reason (again in verses 9 and 10) we blow the shofar is for apotropaic purposes. When you go to war, you blow the shofar, because it will ensure victory. How does it ensure victory? Because shofar blasts ward off evil.

Fourth, to echo what Dr. Sarason said, the shofar ensures that the *korbanot* will cause God to take note (*zachar*) of us, pay attention, remember the covenantal agreement—the Hebrew root *zayin-kaf-reish* is connected in the text with the offering of sacrifices over which one blows the shofar. This is called theurgy—believing that doing something (blowing the shofar while offering a sacrifice) has a positive effect on the Divinity, can positively influence the Divine.

In sum, the biblical text understands shofar blasts to be powerful. They express celebration, but also ensure the efficacy of *korbanot*, ward off evil, and have theurgical value. In other words, blow the shofar and you are guaranteed that all will go well.

The Rabbis elaborate on why we blow the shofar: in the Babylonian Talmud, *Rosh HaShanah* 16a–b, they further "rationalize" the shofar. The shofar effects the crowning of God. It causes God

---

Why do you think human beings are compelled to make noise when celebrating?

Does the sound and symbol of the shofar continue to add to the efficacy of our prayers today?

Apotropaic: intended to ward off evil.

to remember us. The shofar has a theurgical effect (Abahu) because when God hears the blasts, God's attitude toward us becomes *k'ilu* (as if) we bound ourselves on the *mizbei-ach* (sacrificial altar) like Isaac. Shofar's apotropaic qualities (Rabbi Yitzchak) are explained as causing Satan to become confused. Rashi and the *Tosafot* on that same page elaborate on this point: the *Tosafot* say that the shofar increases everyone's *kavanah*, which then effects the efficacy of *t'filot*. But then, the reason it confuses Satan is because he thinks he is hearing the *Shofar Gadol*. In other words, we're back to the messianic age.

What this all boils down to is that the sound of the shofar is very potent. Shofar is a game changer. Shofar changes things for the better. It causes things to happen. It has apotropaic qualities, it has theurgical qualities, it wards off evil, it makes *korbanot* and *t'filot* effective, and it effects the sovereignty of the Deity. And all of these are things that will happen in the messianic age: a salutary effect on the Deity, the ultimate crowning of the Deity as sovereign, the triumph of good over evil, and the efficacy of the *korbanot*—because of course, in the messianic age, the Temple is going to be rebuilt and the sacrificial cult will be reestablished.

Thanks to the Bible and Rabbinic texts, we've explained shofar—or have we? I personally think that all of this textual analysis misses the point. We blow the shofar because of that inexplicable, ineffable response we have to hearing it. You can't explain how it makes you feel, and the reason you can't quite verbalize that thrill, the burst inside of you, is because shofar is a symbol. When the shofar is blown, you are witnessing a symbol in action, you are coming into contact with the power of a symbol. Symbols can't be explained intellec-

What other symbols or rituals are similar to the shofar in this way?

tually. A symbol is, by definition, an object that is objectively without meaning, like a ram's horn or a piece of bread or a cup—objectively it has no meaning other than its functional purpose. But subjectively, the object carries great significance, and the significance is obvious to the members of a particular group. In other words, Jews understand that a shofar has tremendous symbolic resonance—a non-Jew likely won't. To the members of the group for whom the symbol is evidentially important and significant, there is tremendous emotion attached to it, yet no one can adequately describe it. The more they try to explain why the symbol is important, the more inadequate words become. Victor Turner showed some fifty years ago that symbols are powerful precisely because they can't be explained. Furthermore, they are ambiguous. For Sally, it means one thing, and for Jon, it means something else. If you don't believe me, just sit down with an adult education group sometime and ask, "What does the shofar mean?" You'll get different explanations from everyone there.

If you take shofar's symbolic quality, and you overlay it with the biblical and Rabbinic reasons, the result is that when we hear the shofar blown, we are given the opportunity to give up that rational and intellectual side of ourselves that usually dominates and to embrace the irrational. I don't mean "irrational" negatively. Embrace the emotional. Embrace the spiritual. Embrace the ineffable. Let the spiritual and the religious impulse triumph over the intellectual for a brief time. *That's* what blowing the shofar means on an experiential or symbolic level. It invites us to stop being so intellectually rational for a little while. It invites us to believe, at least for a fleeting

Victor Turner, *The Forest of Symbols: Aspects of Ndembu Ritual* (Ithaca, NY: Cornell University Press, 1967).

What does the shofar mean to you?

moment, that all our *t'filot* have a positive effect on the Divine. It invites us to believe, for a second anyway, that ultimately good will triumph over evil. Shofar invites us to get a little glimpse of the messianic age.

Shofar Service: Sources II

Numbers 10:1–10

במדבר פרק י

(א) וַיְדַבֵּר יְהֹוָה אֶל מֹשֶׁה לֵּאמֹר:
(ב) עֲשֵׂה לְךָ שְׁתֵּי חֲצוֹצְרֹת כֶּסֶף מִקְשָׁה
תַּעֲשֶׂה אֹתָם וְהָיוּ לְךָ לְמִקְרָא הָעֵדָה
וּלְמַסַּע אֶת הַמַּחֲנוֹת:
(ג) וְתָקְעוּ בָּהֵן וְנוֹעֲדוּ אֵלֶיךָ כָּל הָעֵדָה
אֶל פֶּתַח אֹהֶל מוֹעֵד:
(ד) וְאִם בְּאַחַת יִתְקָעוּ וְנוֹעֲדוּ אֵלֶיךָ
הַנְּשִׂיאִים רָאשֵׁי אַלְפֵי יִשְׂרָאֵל:
(ה) וּתְקַעְתֶּם תְּרוּעָה וְנָסְעוּ הַמַּחֲנוֹת
הַחֹנִים קֵדְמָה:
(ו) וּתְקַעְתֶּם תְּרוּעָה שֵׁנִית וְנָסְעוּ הַמַּחֲנוֹת
הַחֹנִים תֵּימָנָה תְּרוּעָה יִתְקְעוּ לְמַסְעֵיהֶם:
(ז) וּבְהַקְהִיל אֶת הַקָּהָל תִּתְקְעוּ וְלֹא תָרִיעוּ:
(ח) וּבְנֵי אַהֲרֹן הַכֹּהֲנִים יִתְקְעוּ בַּחֲצֹצְרוֹת
וְהָיוּ לָכֶם לְחֻקַּת עוֹלָם לְדֹרֹתֵיכֶם:
(ט) וְכִי תָבֹאוּ מִלְחָמָה בְּאַרְצְכֶם עַל הַצַּר
הַצֹּרֵר אֶתְכֶם וַהֲרֵעֹתֶם בַּחֲצֹצְרוֹת וְנִזְכַּרְתֶּם
לִפְנֵי יְהֹוָה
אֱלֹהֵיכֶם וְנוֹשַׁעְתֶּם מֵאֹיְבֵיכֶם:
(י) וּבְיוֹם שִׂמְחַתְכֶם וּבְמוֹעֲדֵיכֶם וּבְרָאשֵׁי
חָדְשֵׁיכֶם וּתְקַעְתֶּם בַּחֲצֹצְרֹת עַל עֹלֹתֵיכֶם
וְעַל זִבְחֵי שַׁלְמֵיכֶם
וְהָיוּ לָכֶם לְזִכָּרוֹן לִפְנֵי אֱלֹהֵיכֶם אֲנִי
יְהֹוָה אֱלֹהֵיכֶם:

The Eternal One spoke to Moses, saying: Have two silver trumpets made; make them of hammered work. They shall serve you to summon [military bodies of] the community and to set the divisions in motion. When both are blown in long blasts, the whole company [of fighters] shall assemble before you at the entrance of the Tent of Meeting; and if only one is blown, the chieftains, heads of Israel's contingents, shall assemble before you. But when you sound short blasts, the divisions encamped on the east shall move forward; and when you sound short blasts a second time, those encamped on the south shall move forward. Thus short blasts shall be blown for setting them in motion, while to convoke [military bodies of] the congregation you shall blow long blasts, not short ones. The trumpets shall be blown by Aaron's sons, the priests; they shall be for you an institution for all time throughout the ages. When you are at war in your land against an aggressor who attacks you, you shall sound short blasts on the trumpets, that you may be remembered before the Eternal your God and be delivered from your enemies. And on your joyous occasions—your fixed festivals and new moon days—you shall sound the trumpets over your burnt offerings and your sacrifices of well-being. They shall be a reminder of you before your God: I, the Eternal, am your God.

Psalm 47:1–10

To the chief Musician, A Psalm for the sons of Korach. O clap your hands, all you peoples; shout to God with the voice of triumph. For the Lord most High is terrible; He is a great King over all the earth. He subdues peoples under us, and nations under our feet. He chooses our inheritance for us, the pride of Yaakov whom he loves. (Sela.) God is gone up with a shout, the Lord with the sound of a shofar. Sing praises to God, sing praises: sing praises to our King, sing praises. For God is the King of all the earth: sing a Maskil psalm. God reigns over the nations: God sits upon the throne of His holiness. The nobles of the peoples are gathered together, the people of the God of Avraham: for the shields of the earth belong to God: He is greatly exalted.

מז פרק תהלים

(א) לַמְנַצֵּחַ לִבְנֵי קֹרַח מִזְמוֹר:
(ב) כָּל הָעַמִּים תִּקְעוּ כָף הָרִיעוּ לֵאלֹהִים בְּקוֹל רִנָּה:
(ג) כִּי יְהֹוָה עֶלְיוֹן נוֹרָא מֶלֶךְ גָּדוֹל עַל כָּל הָאָרֶץ:
(ד) יַדְבֵּר עַמִּים תַּחְתֵּינוּ וּלְאֻמִּים תַּחַת רַגְלֵינוּ:
(ה) יִבְחַר לָנוּ אֶת נַחֲלָתֵנוּ אֶת גְּאוֹן יַעֲקֹב אֲשֶׁר אָהֵב סֶלָה:
(ו) עָלָה אֱלֹהִים בִּתְרוּעָה יְהֹוָה בְּקוֹל שׁוֹפָר:
(ז) זַמְּרוּ אֱלֹהִים זַמֵּרוּ זַמְּרוּ לְמַלְכֵּנוּ זַמֵּרוּ:
(ח) כִּי מֶלֶךְ כָּל הָאָרֶץ אֱלֹהִים זַמְּרוּ מַשְׂכִּיל:
(ט) מָלַךְ אֱלֹהִים עַל גּוֹיִם אֱלֹהִים יָשַׁב עַל כִּסֵּא קָדְשׁוֹ:
(י) נְדִיבֵי עַמִּים נֶאֱסָפוּ עַם אֱלֹהֵי אַבְרָהָם כִּי לֵאלֹהִים מָגִנֵּי אֶרֶץ מְאֹד נַעֲלָה:

ויקרא כג:כג-כה

וַיְדַבֵּר ה' אֶל מֹשֶׁה לֵּאמֹר: דַּבֵּר אֶל בְּנֵי-יִשְׂרָאֵל לֵאמֹר, בַּחֹדֶשׁ הַשְּׁבִיעִי בְּאֶחָד לַחֹדֶשׁ יִהְיֶה לָכֶם שַׁבָּתוֹן זִכְרוֹן תְּרוּעָה מִקְרָא קֹדֶשׁ, כָּל מְלֶאכֶת עֲבֹדָה לֹא תַעֲשׂוּ, וְהִקְרַבְתֶּם אִשֶּׁה לַה'.

Leviticus 23:23–25

The Eternal One spoke to Moses, saying: Speak to the Israelite people thus: In the seventh month, on the first day of the month, you shall observe complete rest, a sacred occasion commemorated with loud blasts. You shall not work at your occupations; and you shall bring an offering by fire to the Eternal.

תוספתא ראש השנה א:יב

אמרו לפניו מלכיות, זכרונות, ושופרות. מלכיות, כדי שתמליכוהו עליהם; זכרונות, כדי שיבא זכרונכם לטובה לפניו; שופרות, כדי שתעלה תפלתכם בתרועה לפניו.

Tosefta, Rosh HaShanah 1:12

Recite [texts mentioning] kingship, remembrance, and the shofar. Kingship, in order that they will make God king over them; remembrance, in order that your remembrance will be favorable before God; shofar, in order that your prayer will rise before God on the *t'ruah.*

תלמוד בבלי ראש השנה טז:א-ב

ואמרו לפני בראש השנה מלכיות, זכרונות, ושופרות; מלכיות, כדי שתמליכוני עליכם; זכרונות, כדי שיעלה זכרוניכם לפני לטובה, ובמה? בשופר.

Babylonian Talmud, *Rosh HaShanah* **16a–b**

Recite before Me on the New Year [texts mentioning] kingship, remembrance, and the shofar. Kingship, so that you may proclaim Me king over you; remembrance, so that your remembrance may rise favorably before Me; and through what? The shofar.

אמר רבי אבהו: למה תוקעין בשופר של איל? אמר הקדוש ברוך הוא: תקעו לפני בשופר של איל, כדי שאזכור לכם עקידת יצחק בן אברהם, ומעלה אני עליכם כאילו עקדתם עצמכם לפני.

Rabbi Abahu said: Why do we blow on a ram's horn? The Holy One said: Sound before Me a ram's horn so that I may remember on your behalf the Binding of Isaac, and account it to you as if you had bound yourselves before Me.

למה תוקעין ומריעין כשהן יושבין, ותוקעין ומריעין כשהן
עומדין? כדי לערבב השטן. ואמר רבי יצחק: כל שנה שאין
תוקעין לה בתחלתה, מריעין לה בסופה. מאי טעמא? דלא
איערבב שטן.

Why do we sound *t'kiah* and *t'ruah* sitting and then again sound *t'kiah*
and *t'ruah* standing? In order to confuse Satan. Rabbi Yitzchak said further: If the shofar is not sounded at the beginning of the year, evil will
befall at the end of it. Why so? Because Satan has not been confused.

רש"י, תראש השנה טז:ב, ד"ה: בדי לערבב

שלא ישטין, כשישמע ישראל מחבבין את המצוות, מסתתמין דבריו.

Rashi on Babylonian Talmud, *Rosh HaShanah* 16b, "In order to confuse"

So that he will not [be able to] accuse [Israel]; when he hears that Israel
is so devoted to the mitzvot, his accusations will be stopped up.

Shofar Service: Zero-Based *Machzor* Building

Rabbi Edwin C. Goldberg

What I would like to do is take you through a process that we call "zero-based *machzor* building," so you'll understand where we're coming from in the larger picture. This is a glimpse inside what we as a core committee of the *machzor* team have been thinking about in terms of the bigger picture, and I'll explain zero-based *machzor* building in a moment. But I want to start by pointing out that the very first prayer book published by the CCAR was not, in fact, *Union Prayer Book*, volume 1, although one would think that would be the case, but for various reasons, I believe it had to do in part with the fact that the prayer book committee wasn't satisfied with the *UPB-1*, so they waited. So actually, the first book published was *Union Prayer Book*, volume 2, in 1894, and at the CCAR convention in New Orleans, I mentioned this fact—I actually put up on a PowerPoint slide, which you also have available today for you on the website, a picture of this first *Union Prayer Book*. What I didn't realize until I got back to Miami, looking at the copy that I had stored away somewhere, was that this copy belonged to my great-grandfather, Louis Wessel, who I won't say davened with this book, but certainly used this book at Shaaray T'filah in the Upper East Side of New York. So, it's very gratifying for me to be working on a new *machzor*, knowing that my great-grandfather prayed from the first one. But why I'm bringing all of this up is that this really is the last one that Reform rabbis as a committee put together from scratch. In other words, the other

The PowerPoint "CCAR Presentation Goldberg" can be found at http://www.ccarnet.org/lifelong-learning/teleconferences-webinars/continuing-conversations-about-machzor-session-1-shofarot-service.

UPB-2s were obviously based on UPB-2, the first one published in 1894. Then the *Gates of Repentance*, which we have used for many, many years, is actually more or less taken from the British Liberal Movement's version, and in fact, when we buy a copy, we are still giving some of our funds to them as a royalty. Not that it's not a wonderful work, it is. But it doesn't reflect, we'll say, a completely home-grown effort. So, I think that the fact that we're doing it now is very significant. It's been a long time.

One of the things we, the *Machzor* Editorial Team, talked about was to say, just philosophically, what if we were starting from scratch? What if we had a blank page, and we really weren't going to automatically assume the inclusion of anything, not as radical Reformers, or out of disrespect, but just from the point of view of process. Now, if you're familiar with zero-based budgeting, what we tend to do, of course, is we take the budget we have from last year and decide if we want to spend more or less, and go from there. It makes perfect sense. Zero-based budgeting is when you really say, "No, we are not going to do that. We are going to start from scratch. What are our priorities, what's important to us, what are our resources?" and move forward. It is a very difficult thing, but it can be a very useful thing. The only time it usually happens, of course, is when you're starting something from scratch. Another example, if you have an iPhone or an Android phone, every now and then, at least with my Android phone, it doesn't work so well, so I hard reset it, which basically returns it to its pristine state, and then I have to decide which apps I want to reload or not. So, in a way, that's what we're doing here. We've done a hard reset, not in the final product, of course, but for purposes of philosophical discussion, we've done a hard reset and decided from the beginning what we want to include in our *machzor.* When it comes to the final goal, we have to think about what is the ultimate outcome that we want. And we have stressed this in our vision statement that we put together—we want to create a *machzor* based on providing the best experience for the worshiper. In other words, although it's impossible to measure this, because it's really something that is more existential or affective, that's really what our goal is. It's not to create the best *machzor* ever created, or anything like that, because that would be impossible, but to create a wonderful, ultimate experience for people. That's really the goal. Once we've decided that's the goal, then it's clear, from the beginning, that this is the Reform Jewish High Holy Day prayer book, so there are certain things that we're going to put right back in, just as you would on your smartphone, right? You need a calendar, you need e-mail, the basics. So, we're going to look at the traditions, Jewish tradition in general. What does our Jewish heritage suggest? Secondly, we're going to look at *Gates of Repentance.* What does *Gates of Repentance* suggest? It is the book that most of our movement has used for decades. And third, we are going to look at what *Mishkan T'filah* suggests. Our congregations are more and more comfortable with *Mishkan T'filah,* and that's a wonderful thing. I think one of the reasons why we're moving forward with our *machzor* is because *Mishkan T'filah* has impressed us, and we want a *machzor* that has some similarity. So, those are really the building blocks, as we build our new *machzor.*

For more information on understanding by design, see the writings of Grant Wiggins and Jay McTighe, as well as http://www.ascd .org/research-a-topic/ understanding- by-design- resources.aspx.

I want to point out something that most educators, certainly Jewish educators, know about, this idea of understanding by design, which teaches us that you begin with the end in mind. So, again, the end is a meaningful *machzor* experience. I use the word "experience" very widely, because I think in our society, today, experience is such a vital part of people's authenticity or sense of meaning. There is a book that was published a few years ago, called *The Experience Economy,* which has the subtitle *Work Is Theatre and Every Business a Stage,* and I mean no disrespect to apply secular business ideas to our worship, but I think we certainly should at least look at them for some framing.

So, what do we mean by an experience economy? We mean that if you take coffee beans and sell them, you're selling coffee beans. It you take the coffee beans and package them, then you are already moving one step up, as far as the kind of experience you provide. When I go in the grocery store, I only see Peet's Coffee—it's already a different experience for me. Then, of course, if you actually brew the coffee for people, then you're giving them another kind of experience, and then you get to something like Starbucks where the actual visit to the store is part of the experience. And from our point of view, we want to have our *machzor* be simply a very, very important tool in that. So, once again, the goal of our *machzor* team is not just to create a *machzor,* but to create a tool that will help in this bigger experience of the High Holy Days. As our vision statement says, we want to inspire "Reform Jews to participate in the multi-faceted experience of the *Yamim Noraim*—from feelings of awe to moments of solace, from the solitude of contemplation to the solidarity of song and worship." And, of course, we know that that is not easy to do. We're also concerned that we don't want to make things too complicated. You can do everything you want, but at the end of the day, you have someone sound the shofar, and if you don't, it's not going

B. Joseph Pine II and James H. Gilmore, *The Experience Economy,* updated ed. (Boston: Harvard Business School Publishing, 2011).

See pages 277–79 below in Edwin C. Goldberg's article "The New Reform *Machzor* Is a Solution, but What Is the Problem?" for the complete text of the vision statement.

to feel like it's Rosh HaShanah. I was just speaking with an eighty-year-old congregant who talked about the seder he just led, and he kept getting interrupted from his four-year-old granddaughter, who kept wanting to chant the Four Questions and sing songs, and he didn't realize that she could do it, so he was humoring her, and then she stood on a chair and started doing it, and there wasn't anyone who wasn't completely moved. That's the symbolic moment for a seder.

So, what is a symbolic moment for Rosh HaShanah? Now, I want to get to two examples, and one in particular, the Shofar Service. About a year ago, our team decided that the Shofar Service was symbolic, the sounding of the shofar, rather, and to use the marketing strategy, which again, is just an exercise; it doesn't mean we're trying to put worship on that level. But if we were marketing Rosh HaShanah morning, what is the brand? In other words, what is the symbol? What would be the logo? And, for us, it's the shofar, for all of the reasons we've talked about. You can't really have a Rosh HaShanah experience without the shofar. So, on that level, we decided that the way the Shofar Service is presented in Reform congregations, it's what I would call in the journalistic world, burying the lead. In other words, it's so important, and yet, it's placed toward the very end. And if you have two double services as we have in so many congregations, by the time you get to the end of the first service, the cantor is getting ready for the shofar, the executive director is standing there looking at his or her watch, saying, "We've got to move the parking lot." It just doesn't seem like the best place for it, if we were starting from scratch. So, what we decided to do for the pilot was to divide up a Shofar Service and spread it throughout. And one of the reasons why we wanted to do this was we knew our musical history, and we know that if you look at the classic first movement of an early symphony, not of course the later, more romantic ones, you have in that classic first movement a sonata structure, which Rabbi Lawrence A. Hoffman also speaks about in *Gates of Understanding 2*, and we thought, what if we had some kind of way that we could make the shofar reflect that in the sense that *Malchuyot* is one theme, and *Zichronot* a second theme, and *Shofarot* the third theme, that not only are they three different themes, but that they move in an i-axis. In other words, we're moving from one place to a different place throughout the service. So that's what we've done, and those of you who have graciously piloted know what of which I speak. We put *Malchuyot* tied in with *HaMelech* as it is recited at the end of *P'sukei D'zimrah* or at the beginning of the *Sh'ma Uvirchoteha*. Then we put *Zichronot* tied in as close as we could to the Torah service, with the idea of Rosh HaShanah and God remembering Sarah, etc., etc. And then, *Shofarot* is more or less where it's been all along. Some people have thought it's wonderful. Some people have been upset for various reasons. My favorite reason that some colleagues are upset is, as someone said, "If we put it toward the beginning, people will have their fill of shofar and they'll leave." I'm hoping that we'll have other ways to make our worship engaging besides that. But we certainly are taking seriously everything that people are saying.

This is an example where we can find certainly some support from the Reform tradition. After all, once *Musaf* is gone, then one can argue that there's a lot of room for originality. But at this point, I hope we're not focusing on the finished product so much as the process, and that's the last point I wanted to make. We are experimenting, as well, with the different theologies that, of course, *Mishkan T'filah* integrates, and I think that the bar is even higher when it comes to the *Yamim Noraim* because if we don't address different theologies, including the more challenging theology of Deuteronomy, then are we really presenting a High Holy Day experience? At the same time, if that's really what we present, are we going to lose a good deal of people? To put it another way, we have theology, and we have therapy, and there's a spectrum. And we want to make sure that the *nefesh* is a focus, as well as hoping that God hears our shofar and pays attention to us.

So, this is what we're all working through, and when I say all, we have a wonderful core editorial team: myself, Rabbis Janet Marder, Sheldon Marder, Leon A. Morris, working very closely with Rabbi Hara E. Person and from the *Machzor* Advisory Group, Rabbi Elaine Zecher, Cantor Evan Kent representing the American Conference of Cantors, and many, many others who are consulting and advising.

Shofar Service End-of-Call Discussion

Dr. Richard S. Sarason,
Dr. Debra Reed Blank,
Rabbi Edwin C. Goldberg

Dr. Richard S. Sarason

Just a small footnote: in 1892, the CCAR did publish a *Union Prayer Book,* volume 1. For various political reasons, it was recalled for revision in 1893. A draft text of volume 2 in fact had been circulated to the membership in 1893. But the reconstituted Liturgy Committee decided that they would revise that before going back and revising volume 1. That's why in 1894, the first "official" *UPB* volume was actually volume 2. They finished the revisions of volume 1 in 1895.

Dr. Debra Reed Blank

As Rabbi Goldberg was describing the placement of the shofar blows in the new *machzor,* I was reflecting upon my comments about shofar always being placed at the liturgical climactic point, both in the traditional *Musaf* and in the Reform *machzorim* (that I've looked at). Rabbi Goldberg summed up the thinking of the committee and the possible problems with the new placement of the shofar blasts. But as I think about it now, I don't see that the new placement violates the principle of keeping the shofar blows at climactic points, because even when it's done traditionally, as part of the *Musaf Amidah,* you still have liturgical downswings among the three points at which the shofar is blown. I think that what the committee has done is actually quite creative and true to the thematic development of both the liturgy, traditionally, as well as the service as a whole—moving from *HaMelech,* then to the idea of the *zikaron* being connected to the Torah reading, and then followed by the *Shofarot* section. I don't see that there's a conflict there. I thought that there was, but now that I think about it, I don't think that there is.

Rabbi Edwin C. Goldberg

One of the questions that I have for Dr. Sarason is, after looking at Rabbi Y'hudah's comments in the first text, this idea that the shofar is associated with famine and things like that, if that's an opportunity that we have missed in the past for, in fact, bringing to the shofar blasts yet another kind of relevance on Rosh HaShanah or Yom Kippur. In other words, even if it's a poetic treatment of that theme, the shofar is a warning, not to God, but to us, or something like that. I don't know if there might be room for some more, what we call in the *machzor* or *Mishkan T'filah,* "left sides."

Dr. Richard S. Sarason

I agree. One of the things that Dr. Reed Blank brought up in this call is the multiple associations throughout Jewish tradition with the shofar, and because it is symbolic, and symbols convey multiple meanings, I think it would be wonderful for the left side of the page to focus on some of those meanings, and that could even be throughout the service.

Shofar Service Wrap-Up

1. The presenters all seem to agree that we need a Shofar Service, a premise that some of our classical forebears rejected. To what extent is Rosh HaShanah defined by the blowing of the shofar?
2. Where would you put the shofar blasts and why?
3. How do you understand the themes of *Malchuyot*, *Zichronot*, and *Shofarot*? How can we translate these ideas for a contemporary audience?
4. What did you learn from these presentations on the Shofar Service that you would like to implement in your community's High Holy Day worship?

Seder HaAvodah: Its Structure and Contemporary Possibilities

Seder HaAvodah: Introduction
Rabbi Leon A. Morris

The words of *Seder HaAvodah* recall the approach of the High Priest into the Holy of Holies and the sending off of the scapegoat into the wilderness. With the destruction of the Temple, sacrifices ceased, and the ancient rite of Yom Kippur came to an end. The sole means for effectuating national atonement—and ensuring that God's presence would remain with the people—was suddenly gone. The Rabbis responded by building new religious paradigms: repentance (*t'shuvah*), prayer (*t'filah*), and charity (*tzedakah*)—all of them dependent on human initiative—were the substitution for achieving atonement. Yet, the original ritual of Yom Kippur, with its religious drama culminating in national atonement, could not be entirely consigned to ancient history. *Seder HaAvodah* as liturgy is one example among many of how the Rabbis adapted to their new and radically different reality and how words came to replace the very acts they described. Drawing heavily from the Mishnah's detailed description of the Yom Kippur ritual, the editors of the *machzor* shaped a liturgical substitution for the actual performance of the ritual.

For about fifteen hundred years, the *Avodah* service of Yom Kippur has provided a historical link between the most ancient elements of Yom Kippur and our contemporary post-Temple observance. Recited in synagogues that replaced the service of the ancient Temple, the *Avodah* service provides a window into the past. It reminds worshipers of the origins of this most sacred day and serves to underscore both elements of continuity and discontinuity between that time and our contemporary practice. The creative genius of the Jewish people is evident in the various *piyutim* (liturgical poems) that were written over the centuries to frame the narrative of the High Priest's preparations and entrance into the Holy of Holies. These powerful ceremonies of Yom Kippur loomed large in the imagination of the Jewish people. While the experience of praying in our synagogues is vastly different from the Temple rites of Yom Kippur, this liturgy links these two experiences across time and space.

Seder HaAvodah:
Background and Application

Rabbi Leon A. Morris

The context for this discussion is that the highlight of the traditional Yom Kippur liturgy has historically been *Seder HaAvodah*. It is, of course, a poetic recollection and a kind of literary re-creation of the ceremony of Yom Kippur as it was performed in the days of the Temples, the First and Second Temples. And, as we know, after the destruction of the Temple, the Rabbis responded by building new religious paradigms that would also achieve atonement, things like *t'shuvah, t'filah, tzedakah,* as well as some others. And yet the original ritual of Yom Kippur with all of its powerful drama was, in some ways, a bit too powerful in the Jewish imagination just to be consigned to the realm of ancient history. And so *Seder HaAvodah* emerged as a liturgy in a way that allowed the Rabbis to adapt this ancient practice and to turn it into liturgy to show how words could come to replace the very things that the words themselves describe. And it's that very idea that is one of the reasons that reworking this in some way might be very exciting for liberal Jews, this notion that words come to replace the very acts that they describe. The literary genius of the Jewish people is evidenced throughout this liturgy in terms of various *piyutim* that were written over the centuries to kind of frame the narrative of everything that took place, the High Priest's preparations and his entrance into the Holy of Holies on this one day a year.

Largely, we could say that the liturgy is an expansion of *Mishnah Yoma.* That tractate is an unusual

What is the relationship between words and action?

tractate because it's really distinguished by a narrative style, and most likely, our first *Avodah* service was simply a reading of selections from *Mishnah Yoma*. In fact, there are two sources in the *Talmud Bavli* that describe prayer leaders on Yom Kippur reading their version of the Mishnah before Rava in the fourth century. And as that Mishnah became adapted through the years to make it more compatible with the synagogue service, we have the origins of the *Avodah* service, so that by the fourth or fifth century, there emerges a kind of a classic style of the *Avodah* service. That structure takes the following form: First, it begins with an introductory *piyut* that provides a context for the Yom Kippur ritual, and these introductory *piyutim* are usually acrostics that start with the creation of the world and then culminate in the appointment of Aaron as the High Priest and Aaron and his sons performing this Yom Kippur ritual. There are a variety of different *piyutim* that do this, but they almost all have the same form in terms of beginning with Creation and working up to Aaron and his sons. The most common one in Ashkenazic communities is *Atah Yatzarta,* and the most common in Sephardic is *Atah Konanta.* Chaim Stern, *alav hashalom,* took his inspiration for the way that *Gates of Repentance* reinterpreted the *Avodah* from this introductory *piyut* of the *Avodah* service, and then rather than have it conclude with the establishment of the Yom Kippur ritual by Aaron and his sons, he had the poem continue through the Shoah, through immigration to America, the reestablishment of the State of Israel. It's probably one of the most interesting and creative parts of *Gates of Repentance,* but it's also interesting to note that it wasn't used to lead up to the ancient ritual of Yom Kippur, but was inspired by this introductory *piyut.* So, that's the very first piece.

If we were to write a similar *piyut* today, in what would the creation of the world culminate and why?

The second piece of the *Avodah* service is the narrative of the Yom Kippur ritual itself, the expansion of *Mishnah Yoma*, including the three confessions made by the *Kohein Gadol*. Much of this is also poetic. There are different versions. Much of it draws not just from Rabbinic text, but from the Apocrypha, like Ben Sira, and from other Second Temple texts, and it's a mix of dramatic reading and ritual wherein traditionally the congregation prostrates themselves each time and reciting *Baruch shem k'vod malchuto l'olam va-ed*. Each time they recall the High Priest saying the name of God in the Temple. This narrative section concludes with the successful exit of the High Priest and the idea that atonement has been achieved for Israel. And then there is also a blessing that the High Priest would say upon exiting safely the Holy of Holies, and sometimes that blessing is moved in the services to the end of the narrative or even to the end of the whole *Avodah* service. So, we have the introductory *piyut*, the narrative of the Yom Kippur ritual itself, and then finally there's a prayer acknowledging that we can't perform these acts any longer. And this is part of the *Avodah* service that attempts to bridge the gap between then and now, and particularly for non-Orthodox liturgies, this is an opportunity to make the case for the validity of what practices emerged instead of this ancient Yom Kippur ritual.

Seder HaAvodah has within it some profound ideas that can be easily translated to a contemporary context, and I want to highlight just seven of these themes. One is that our need to give is even greater than our desire to receive. That the *Avodah* service inspires us to rethink sacrifice as a form of gift-giving where the desire to give back to God is paramount and where, because of the tremendous

How does the experience of giving a gift differ from that of receiving one?

gap that exists between us and God, there's a real uncertainty about whether our gift will be accepted. And this is an idea that I have really learned to appreciate through the work of Moshe Halbertal.

The second idea is there's something exceptional and maybe even unjust about the nature of Yom Kippur where even sins committed *b'meizid*, deliberately, can be forgiven. And it seems to run against the prophetic impulse for justice, contracted, for example, with Jeremiah, chapter 7. This is an idea I was introduced to by Rabbi Yoel Bin-Nun in Israel, and the *Avodah* service emphasizes and even intensifies an already radical idea that Yom Kippur, the day itself, can erase deliberate sin, and the Rabbis take it even further in saying it can turn sins into merits.

The third idea is about God's proximity. Jacob Milgrom, *alav hashalom*, wrote and taught about the way in which the pagan understanding that Judaism adapted and changed was that the gods could be driven out of their houses by demons and that Judaism said the demon that can drive our single God out of God's house is human sin. And so we need this one day a year to cleanse the sanctuary so that God won't be driven out of God's house. There was a kind of an understanding of almost a magnetic force that drew human sin to the Temple. So, this theme in which human sin polluted the Temple is really demonstrative of the way in which human action can drive God away from our world.

The fourth idea is the aspirational and the real aspects of the Temple service. There are numerous stories to draw upon from Rabbinic literature that emphasize the gap between what we wanted the Temple to be and what it actually was.

The fifth idea is a proper balance between ritual and the ethics that they're intended to bolster.

Sidebar notes:

Moshe Halbertal, *On Sacrifice* (Princeton, NJ: Princeton University Press, 2012).

Rabbi Yoel Bin-Nun is an Israeli educator and *rosh yeshivah* who has spearheaded the revolution in *Tanach* study in Israel, primarily at Yeshivat Har Etzion and the Herzog Teachers' College in Alon Shevut. He has written numerous articles and books on *Tanach*, Jewish history, Jewish thought, and halachah.

How could this concept be relevant for High Holy Day worship?

What ideas are at stake in the detailed ritual of the *Avodah* service, and what ideas are at stake in the rituals that we still affirm? So, this is a kind of way of rethinking ritual, not necessarily as empty, but thinking about how ritual can be a kind of performance that embeds a set of ideas.

The sixth idea is that each of us today is a *Kohein Gadol*. What are the implications of now saying that every person is a High Priest?

How would you respond to the questions posed by the presenter?

And finally, this whole *Avodah* ritual emphasizes the communal nature of seeking atonement, that the fate of the entire nation is in the balance. And so, in a way, the *Avodah* service can be a kind of corrective to an increasingly individualistic form of spirituality. The *Avodah* reminds us that the experience of Yom Kippur is communal, not just in the sense that many separate individuals come together to do *t'shuvah*, but that we're seeking also a *kaparah*, an atonement, as an entire nation.

For further information on this subject by this presenter, see the following resources posted at http://www.ccarnet.org/lifelong-learning/teleconferences-webinars/continuing-conversations-about-machzor-session-2-avodah-service:

- Rabbi Leon A. Morris, "The Imaginative Power of Sacrifice," *Sh'ma* (September 2008): 13–14.
- Rabbi Leon A. Morris, *Seder HaAvodah (the Avodah Service): Working Out the Origins and Contemporary Meaning of Yom Kippur: A Six-Session Study Guide*, 71 pages.

Seder HaAvodah: Piyutim

Yair Harel

I'm glad to be part of this conversation to share with you my work, my interpretation of the *Seder Avodah* and how we can also preserve it. I'm going to focus on the *piyutim* that I've sung, as an introduction to the introduction. I'm going to take an example of *piyutim* that were written for the moment before the official *Seder Avodah* service starts off. And basically the essence of that purpose, the purpose of those *piyutim,* are to take all the points that Rabbi Morris just spoke about and to meld them into one song, to have them expressed in the form of a song. Of course, they are not only spoken, but sung with music. That way can prepare us before we enter the more official prayer, and basically, that is historically one of the basic purposes of the *piyutim.* The *piyutim* are like contemporary prayers that have always been written and formed as an introduction where the conversations are more contemporary preparation into the more official prayer, which basically doesn't change so much. Now, as we see it today, the *piyutim* also became something that is fixed; there haven't been a lot of new *piyutim* in the last several hundred years. And after Sepharad and maybe after also in the time of Tz'fat, but basically after Sepharad, the siddur more or less, the Orthodox siddur anyway, was closed. And those *piyutim,* which basically were contemporary and were written, a *chazan* (cantor) could come with a new *piyut* before *Seder HaAvodah* and introduce it, and that *piyut* will be written in a way that we can try to focus on his time and his congregation. These piyyutim can help us communicate or inter-

How does music differ from the spoken word in a liturgical setting?

Why do you think the Orthodox siddur "closed" at a certain point? What challenges and opportunities does this create for the development of new liturgy?

pret or prepare ourselves to be closer to the ideas of the service, and to find our own midrash or our connection to those words that are being passed on in tradition.

So, that was to connect with Rabbi Morris, and before I go to the specific views I wanted to share with you and also sing with you, I wanted to say a word about the *piyut* website and also about Invitation to Piyut North America, the project we just recently launched in the United States. The *piyut* website holds at the moment around eight hundred songs, *piyutim*, with a lot of information about every *piyut*: the content, introductions about the poet, etc. And on those eight hundred songs, the site holds around four thousand recordings of different tunes, different traditional tunes, to the *piyutim*. For example, *Y'did Nefesh* has maybe forty different recordings and *L'chah Dodi* probably even more, so you can really get a picture of the depth of Jewish tradition or interpretation. These are different emotional interpretations of the same words. They have been created around the last thousand or at least hundreds of years around the Jewish world. And this is a very, very powerful resource, and it's part of the website, the idea of which is basically to make these resources available, take them out of the archive and make them accessible. This is part of quite a powerful movement that is happening around Israel in the last ten years. It is connected, of course, to many things that happened before, but I think the need for more meaningful connection and feeling with Jewish practice, with Jewish identity, particularly step forward into something that touches also the heart, not only the intellectual part, is something that has many dimensions now in Israel. There's also a *Piyut* Festival in Jerusalem now, and there are singing communities and things that

http://
piyutnorthamerica.org

http://
www.piyut.org.il

are going on that are influencing at lot of different projects around Israel. Recently last year, after several years of preparation, we launched Invitation to Piyut North America in partnership with the B'nai Jeshurun community in New York, and I'm co-directing it with my very close friend, brother, and rabbi, Roly Matalon; we had a very exciting retreat last November where eighty people—rabbis, cantors, educators, and musicians—came from around the States and Canada for four days in Baltimore, and we explored together how these resources can be relevant for Jewish communities, synagogues, and schools around the States. Of course, there is the language, and there is the music, which is quite different from what American ears and eyes are used to. And we found that very interesting and there's a lot of potential for that.

So now let's get into the *piyut* that I'd love to share with you today. What happens before the official start of *Seder HaAvodah* is a bit different in Sephardic and Ashkenazic; I'm referring to *piyutim* that are sung in the Sephardic tradition and appear in most of the Sephardic *machzorim*, and those *piyutim* again are performed before *Seder HaAvodah* and help prepare us in an emotional way, in a meditative way. The words help us connect to *Seder HaAvodah* at a time that is far removed from the days when what is described was happening. So, let's jump into hearing the *piyut*. The words were written by Rabbi Shlomo ibn Gabirol in Spain, in the eleventh century, and the tune that you're going to hear is from the Tunisian tradition sung by

http://www.piyut.org
.il/textual/799.html

Youssef Balesh. I'll just say the first words; you can go on the site for the full text. The first words that are sung are: *Aromimcha chizki v'chelki, b'vo-i b'rov dovki v'dofki, gam b'shofchi zaaki v'tzaaki, b'kor'i aneini Elohei tzidki*, which is a general introduction. *Seder*

HaAvodah is still not mentioned there but soon, after that we're getting more specific into the idea of *Seder HaAvodah*. How can we transform the practice of the *Kohein Gadol*, how we can put our words into a context that is meaningful for us today? So, *Aromimcha chizki v'chelki*, basically, "I praise the Eternal." *B'vo-i b'rov dovki v'dofki*, "coming and wanting to get closer to you in the time that I'm knocking on your doors." This is a very basic translation, of course. *Gam b'shofchi zaaki v'tzaaki*, "When I pour out, I scream out, I shout out my need." *B'kor'i aneini Elohei tzidki*. Let's listen to the voice of Youssef Balesh.

It's a simple melody and it's repetitive, like a meditative form of melody that allows you to imagine yourself singing before entering *Seder HaAvodah*. You can even take the time to imagine yourself singing something else to that tune or translating the song into English in order for that to have better meaning. But I'll leave that for your imagination, for your work. So, again, I'll remind you of the tune: *Aromimcha chizki v'chelki, b'vo-i b'rov dovki v'dofki, gam b'shofchi zaaki v'tzaaki, b'kor'i aneini Elohei tzidki.*

How do we balance the desire for elaborant and elegant music on the High Holy Days with a need for accessible simple melodies that can be easily learned?

The Accommodation of the Yom Kippur *Seder Avodah* to Modernity

Dr. Rhoda J. H. Silverman, PhD

Allow me to share briefly how I got interested in the *Avodah* liturgy. When I was reviewing scholarly literature in order to find a topic for my dissertation, all of the literature that I encountered on the *Seder Avodah* repeatedly stated, "No *Avodah* poems, save for one by Samuel David Luzzatto written in the nineteenth century, have been written since Meshullam ben Kalonymos's *Amitz Koach*." What a striking and disturbing statement to be, again, repeatedly stated throughout the scholarly literature! If there were no "new *Avodah*s," what was I praying in the *Seder Avodah* section of *Gates of Repentance* every Yom Kippur afternoon? So, this has now occupied me for the last two years, and while it may seem at first glance removed from the practical realities of creating and leading modern-day worship—really, what does it matter what academics think of our worship?—it has significant ramifications.

How would you respond to the questions posed by the presenter?

A larger issue that extends well beyond the scope for this conversation is who gets to define Jewish worship, and what are the boundaries of that definition? I believe that the post-Luzzatto *Avodah* literature has been ignored primarily because it has veered away from using Hebrew. The vernacular is simply not understood as a legitimate form of Jewish worship. There was, for example, a compilation of *Avodah* poems published in 2005, which ignores everything written in this genre after Luzzatto. The authors, contemporary scholars, continue to forward the notion that nothing new has been written. More to the point of this conversation, however, is that the qualification of what is or isn't a legitimate *Avodah* poem forces us, and particularly the editors of a new *machzor*, to thoughtfully consider our relationship as progressive Jews to this liturgical rubric. Does this reflection on the sacrificial atonement ritual of the ancient Temple have a place in our *machzor*? If so, what should it look like?

This rubric, as Rabbi Morris already mentioned, has always been viewed as essential and central to the Yom Kippur liturgy. Historically, the confessional ritual of the *Avodah* was a high point of the year in the Temple period, and despite our own movement's uneasiness with all things related to the cult, has remained highlighted in our prayer book. It's never really been completely excised from any prayer book, even in the Reform Movement. So, though, in this limited amount of time, it is impossible to go through every version of the *Avodah* that has appeared in the nineteenth and twentieth centuries (if you are interested, look up my dissertation), allow me to quickly offer an overview of the history of the *Avodah* in the modern period.

First, Samuel David Luzzatto's work. This was written very early. Though there's no publication of it until as late as 1879, evidence points to it being authored in 1815. It was never intended for us as a liturgy. It was a poetic exercise for Luzzatto, and as such, it has never been found in any prayer book and no prayer-book editors or writers refer back to it. But it is highly significant in that it's the first known attempt at authoring a completely innovative *Avodah* text since the medieval period. It is highly innovative. Luzzatto completely rewrites the *Avodah*. He stays true to its traditional themes but changes the language—even of the well-known thrice-repeated confession. The only thing traditional about it is that it was written entirely in Hebrew with no accompanying vernacular. Sadly, still to date no translation of it has been published.

As Rabbi Morris mentioned, there are in essence two major rubrics to the *Avodah*: a historical preamble that was initially a separate literary poem, and the Mishnaic narrative of a confessional text to which this historical narrative in time gets attached. Luzzatto gets rid of that historical preamble completely. In its place, he writes an introduction that is similar to the *r'shut piyut* that we just listened to, a plea for praising of God and a plea for God's attention to our prayers, not our sacrifices, but the words from our lips. It references the House of Levi but never builds up to it in any sort of historical fashion as a traditional introduction to the *Avodah* does. Luzzatto's confessional narrative as well is striking because the Hebrew is entirely original. In every *Avodah* text that has appeared, even through today, the confessional narrative quotes the Mishnah. Luzzatto completely rewrites the Hebrew. For example:

What can we learn from Luzzatto about adapting traditional liturgy for our contemporary communities?

אנא יהוה! חטאתי, אף-עויתי,
ולפניך הרבה פשעתי אני,
ובני ביתי.

Ana Adonai! Chatati, af aviti, u'lifanecha harbeh pashati ani, u'vnei beiti.
Please, O God! I have sinned, even I transgressed, before you I have sinned greatly, [I] and the children of my house.

No other *Avodah* liturgy has done that since. Even our nineteenth-century liturgical innovators, such as Geiger, left the Hebrew of the confession alone.

Let's to jump to Geiger. Luzzatto was working in Italy, of course. In Germany, while we think of the Hamburg siddur as the first innovative Reform prayer book, in terms of the *Avodah*, Abraham Geiger can be attributed with compiling the first innovative vernacular *Seder Avodah*. In the Hamburg siddur, the *Atah Konanta* text is used, which is the normative Sephardic text, and by the way, the earliest known text to put together the historical preamble along with the narrative derived from the Mishnah. But Geiger is the first to rewrite the *Avodah* completely in the vernacular. He also removed a great deal of the sacrificial language. The only things he leaves in Hebrew are, not surprisingly, the threefold confessional, the three confession texts of the High Priest, which we still recite today in our Reform *machzor*, and one account of the High Priest blood-sprinkling ritual, a ritual that is detailed in the traditional *Avodah*. Everything else is in German, and here too, he removes most of the sacrificial language. The other thing that is significant about Geiger's work that influenced all later liberal examples of the *Avodah* is he, like Luzzato, although it's clear he was not influenced by Luzzatto, removed the historical preamble that culminates in the House of Aaron. Instead, he includes that statement of humility and that plea, that petition, for continued grace and acceptance of prayer. This becomes a prototype for all future liberal, particularly Reform, attempts at re-visioning the *Avodah*.

In America, liturgists also took a stab: Merzbacher, Szold, Isaac Mayer Wise, Einhorn, they all made significant contributions. Most wrote in the vernacular; however, there is innovation in the Hebrew. Wise offers a fully original Hebrew *Avodah* with accompanying translation, and he introduces his with the *piyut* that we just sang a moment ago, *Aromimcha chizki v'chelki.* Like the example of Geiger, Wise introduces his original *Avodah* with a focus on petition, not history. The history that he does provide, instead of culminating in the House of Aaron, culminates at the moment at Sinai, of revelation, which remains significant in Stern's *Avodah* used in *Gates of Repentance.* In contrast, Einhorn writes completely in the vernacular. He, along with other of his contemporaries, introduced the idea of *mamlechet kohanim* into the *Avodah* to replace the idea of the selection of the House of Levi.

Mordecai Kaplan, Eugene Kohn, and Ira Eisenstein, eds., *High Holiday Prayer Book* (New York: Jewish Reconstructionist Foundation, 1948).

Jumping to the twentieth century, the most significant and most influential *Avodah* that was written appeared in 1948. It is found in the Reconstructionist *machzor,* by Kaplan, Eisenstein, and Kohn. This *Avodah* is the prototype, the model upon which Chaim Stern based his *Avodah,* first with John Rayner when they formulated the British *Petach Teshuvah* and then later alone when he revised it for *Shaarei Teshuvah.* It's an interesting *Avodah* to look at and will look familiar to all of us well versed in the Reform *machzor.* Chaim Stern reduces verbiage and updates the narrative to reflect the founding of Israel (recall, Kaplan's book was published just in 1948), but generally speaking, the texts are the same. Interestingly, the *Avodah* text in the current Reconstructionist *machzor* is completely revised. Time does not allow for discussion of that text, but I encourage a look at it. It is highly innovative and creative, and in my opinion, extremely relevant to the discussion of creating new liturgies.

Do these approaches to *Seder HaAvodah* speak to you? Why or why not?

After reviewing all of the texts published since Luzzatto, I see two major trends. One is to treat the *Avodah* rubric as primarily a historical reflection of the Temple period's atonement ritual. This is the traditional way into the *Avodah.* In other words, understanding the ancient ritual as a history lesson in order to motivate us to the proper repentance. It's not our *Vidui*—it's the *Vidui* of the High Priest that should motivate us to be sincere in ours, which soon follows in the traditional *machzor*. A beautiful and modern example of such an *Avodah* is found in the Conservative Movement's new *machzor, Lev Shalem*. This *Avodah* pulls together pieces of various medieval examples to create a new *Avodah* presentation. The second approach, which I think is a little more interesting for contemporary worshipers, is to re-contextualize the *Avodah* to modernity, so that the confessional texts themselves, assuming they are quoted in the *Avodah* (as they have been to date), become our own personal *Vidui*. We model the priests in that moment of recitation. The focus becomes less on remembering the Temple ritual per se, but on how we can use the High Priest's ancient words in our own day in order to enact atonement. Both of these approaches are valid, and often a single *Avodah* text draws on both, with the focus leaning in one direction. The struggle between reflection on our history and using the text as a vehicle for active atonement appears to be the primary motivation in the creation of new *Avodah* liturgies. I expect it will be the challenge in the creation of an *Avodah* for the Reform Movement's new *machzor*.

Seder HaAvodah:
A Contemporary Model
Rabbi Richard N. Levy

Richard N. Levy, ed., *On Wings of Awe: A Fully Transliterated Machzor for Rosh Hashanah and Yom Kippur,* rev. ed. (Brooklyn: Ktav, 2011).

The Pittsburgh Platform of 1885: http://ccarnet .org/rabbis-speak/ platforms/declaration-principles/.

Refer to "Rabbi Azrael's Discourse" and "The Avodah Service" at http:// www.ccarnet.org/ lifelong-learning/ teleconferences-webinars/continuing-conversations-about-machzor-session-2-avodah-service.

Some of you may know that KTAV Publishing Company has recently reissued *On Wings of Awe* in an expanded, revised edition. My disucssion of the *Avodah* service will be informed by the *Avodah* service in this book and maybe expanding beyond it. Cantor Silverman mentioned Einhorn's classic Reform notion that we should see ourselves as a priest people bringing the nations close to God, as the *kohein* brought an individual close to God. And this is not only Einhorn, but in all sorts of the early Reformers. It's in the Pittsburgh Platform of 1885. I think that this is a very important sort of *asmachtah* (proof) for this service, and what I tried to do is to combine the sense that this was a historical event into which we could enter, but it's also a spiritual event into which we could enter as well. Another text, which Rabbi Herbert Bronstein recommended to me, is the well-known text from S. Ansky's *The Dybbuk,* "The world of God is great and holy and going from the holiest land, the holiest city," and then ending, "Whenever a person stands to lift one's eyes to the heavens, that place is the Holy of Holies." That also relates the historical event very much to the individual. So, I would recommend those two texts to us as *kavanot* in a sense for the *Avodah.*

If you look at the text of the *Avodah* service from the new *On Wings of Awe,* it begins with an introduction that talks about connecting the physical offering with the offerings of words. So, when the physical animal or grain was placed on the fire of the altar, the fire changed its physical form into smoke, essentially invisible, a form in which it mingled with the invisible places where God dwells. And later on, when talking about prayer, it connects to the idea that prayers are words, that as they too are quite invisible, they can easily mingle with the invisible places where God dwells. In recalling the animal sacrifices people can imagine that they themselves were entering their presence, feeling themselves lifted up along with their gift before the very throne of glory. Whereas, prayers say it is as though we ourselves were entering the presence of God, and we can feel ourselves lifted up along with our gift before the very throne of glory, suggesting that people look at the High Priest ritual as one that is for them. Then *On Wings of Awe* continues with what really is a *piyut* just before the *Avodah* service and the traditional *machzor Achilah LaEl*, which is a prayer that God might give us eloquent speech to sing of God's power amidst the congregation, and it ends with *Yih'yu L'ratzon*. I put it there in the hope that that would seem to be the words of the High Priest, but also the words of us as we conflate this experience. Then there follows a wonderful *kavanah* that Rachel and Moshe Adler included in the *machzor* that they did some years ago using the story of the Baal Shem Tov, who, when misfortune was threatening the Jews, would go to a certain part of a forest to meditate, light a fire, say a prayer, the miracle would be accomplished, and gradually people forgot how to light the fire but could say the prayer, didn't know the prayer, but knew the place, and then finally Israel of Ruzhin, who says, "I don't know the fire, the prayer, or the place. All I can do is tell the story, and this must be sufficient." And it was sufficient, and the Adlers added, "Listen, God, we are going to tell the story," which again

How does this rendering of *Seder HaAvodah* in the form of a dramatic dialogue speak to you?

emphasizes that this is a drama acting out by our telling of it what was done in fact. Then after a brief introduction of the *Amitz Koach* version of the introductory *piyut*, the rest is in English, and then with the three statements of the High Priest, I included footnotes, noted in the Hebrew and English text, where people are encouraged to put themselves in the place of the worshipers in the Temple court and saying when to get down on your knees, when to bow, and when to prostrate. I think that by our encouraging people to do that, and particularly now since prostration during the Great *Aleinu* is becoming more and more the practice, it will enable people to conflate the High Priest's actions and their own during these three times in the service. Prostration can make one tired, but when one reads the conclusion, "the High Priest was elated, his face shone like the sun, the clouds distilled their dew, the land rang with song. How fortunate the people are whose God is *Adonai!*" It might be interesting to create a contemporary version of *Mareih Kohein,* the *piyut* that is included in this section, and to sing it or to sing some other triumphant melody.

And then I included some questions for reflection after the *Avodah* service. This is not a time in the service where there are a lot of people usually, and some people could turn to each in *chevruta* and talk about these questions:

How would you respond to the questions posed by the presenter? Could you implement this *chevruta* discussion in your High Holy Day services?

1. If you were the High *Kohein,* whom would you like to bring close, *karov,* to God? How? How might you do it through the life you live now?

2. If you were entrusted with knowledge of words as powerful as the intimate name of God, what other words would you like to know? How might you use the power of those words to bring good things to the world?

3. If you were the High *Kohein* prostrating yourself in submission to the most powerful being imaginable (which people will have just done), what would you pray for in that moment? What is the most important prayer for you now?

And then the last one:

4. When the Israelites were on the way to the Promised Land, they built a prototype of the Temple called the *Mishkan*, a structure that helped them experience the holy in their midst. The process of building that structure was called *m'lachah*, literally "work," the same word that describes the work we do every weekday. What is holy about your work? What can you identify about your work that contributes to the building of a *mishkan*, a center for holiness? In what ways do you, might you, act as a *kohein* in that *mishkan*?

I would recommend that questions like that, and others that you all might think of, might help to inform a rewriting of the *Avodah* section, but using the historical event as a way of letting people act it out and then to reflect on it, might be one way of re-elevating this central part of the service to a central part of our own Yom Kippur experience.

Seder HaAvodah
End-of-Call Discussion

Rabbi Elaine Zecher,
Rabbi Leon A. Morris,
Dr. Rhoda J. H. Silverman, PhD,
Rabbi Richard N. Levy, Yair Harel

Rabbi Elaine Zecher

As we're moving in the development of the *machzor* for the Reform Movement, though we have not yet arrived at the work on the *Avodah* service, I am struck today how the presence of Yair Harel from Israel turned our attention to the Land of Israel. Certainly this part of the service focuses not only the sacred ritual and the sacred moment, but also a sacred place. And I wonder if our speakers could just give a few comments to that idea of the incorporation of Jerusalem and the Land of Israel in this sacred ritual.

Rabbi Leon A. Morris

I think you raise a wonderful idea in terms of allowing this to be yet another place in the liturgy where our focus can turn to Israel. One of the associations that I have with that suggestion is maybe to weave together this notion of the Temple as this ideal institution that the Rabbis themselves reflect on—its lack of ideal, its realness, its gap between the ideal and the real—and that's an idea that also applies to our relationship with Israel. So what does it mean to have divine aspirations but human institutions?

Dr. Rhoda J. H. Silverman, PhD

What first comes to mind is Max Klein, who was a rabbi in Philadelphia. He wrote a *machzor* called *Seder Avodah* that has a wonderful *Avodah* in it that starts out based on Kaplan's, so it looks a little bit like what we have in *Gates of Repentance*. But he does deal with Israel in a wonderful way. I think it's a model because at the end of a traditional *Avodah*, as Leon mentioned, the Temple period has ended, but there's also a tendency in a traditional *Avodah* to almost be sad about that and to want to look toward one that is rebuilt. Klein beautifully turns that on its head and says, look toward modern Israel and the institutions that people have made. He interprets the entire idea of the House of Levi, the priesthood, to be those who teach, those who lead, those who serve as leaders of the Jewish community and how they have helped to build Israel. So, I think that's a wonderful model to look toward and like that. So that's what first came to my mind, the idea that Israel can be part of the culmination of where a modern-day *Avodah* goes, forcing us to struggle with what's really happening there in modern-day Israel—reality versus vision.

Max D. Klein, *Seder Avodah: Service Book for Rosh Hashanah and Yom Kippur* (Philadelphia: Maurice Jacobs, 1960).

Rabbi Richard N. Levy

I think the danger of secularizing this is huge, so what comes to my mind that if we want to have some focus on the notion of a holy place being *Har HaBayit*, to be faithful to our Reform roots, which said that we want to build places where *k'dushah* could be felt everywhere, that we would have to ask, what would a messianic house of worship be? What would be the worship that took place in the ultimate holy place in a messianic age? And I think that kind of question might be more faithful to the

How is secularization "dangerous"? What might a useful or "safe" blend of the religious and the secular look like?

How would you respond to the questions posed by the presenter?

Reform notion of what the destruction of the Temple meant in terms of bringing on the ideal time closer.

Yair Harel

As someone living in Jerusalem, very connected to Jerusalem, let me take the other side in contrast to Rabbi Levy and say that one of the interpretations of the *Rabbanim* (Rabbinic sages) who stayed in *Bavel* (Babylonia) in the time of the Second Temple, most of them didn't come back to Israel, and one of their interpretations of the word *Tzion* means a place, *makom sheYisrael m'tzuyanim sham. Tzion* again is not necessarily a specific geographical place, but to build on what Rabbi Levy said, a place where you can establish *mashehu m'tzuyan,* and going on in terms of holiness, the central place that you can, after the destruction of the Temple, transform into a place where you can hold deep meaning of what is Judaism.

How does this conceptualization of Zion speak to you?

Seder HaAvodah Wrap-Up

1. Which elements of *Seder HaAvodah* could be incorporated into a new version of the service?
2. What are the main messages of *Seder HaAvodah* that you would want to convey? What is still meaningful in this ancient liturgical unit?
3. What role does music play in High Holy Day worship in general and in engaging with challenging liturgical texts in particular?
4. What did you learn from these presentations on *Seder HaAvodah* that you would like to implement in your community's High Holy Day worship?

Eileh Ezkerah

Eileh Ezkerah: Introduction

Rabbi Leon A. Morris

This is a great opportunity to study one rubric of the Yom Kippur service that we editors of the *machzor* haven't yet tackled, and to do so with colleagues joining us on the phone and with three very gifted scholars who will be teaching us today. And it seems especially appropriate to be doing this on Yom HaZikaron.

When we think about *Eileh Ezkerah*, it raises many questions for us, and in addition to the very concrete questions that we may have about its origins and its function, there's also a great deal of conceptual questions that we bring to the table, conceptual in the sense of exploring really what's the meaning of the link between Yom Kippur and remembering the rabbis who were martyred in Roman times. In what ways is this an expression of *z'chut avot*, meant to elicit God's compassion for us? In what ways is recalling the courage of these rabbis meant to be an inspiration or a model to us? And in what ways does the martyrdom of our sages represent a kind of substitution for the sacrifices that existed in the days of the Temple, the most important one, of course, on Yom Kippur itself, as part of the *Avodah*?

There will be two parts to this call, an initial presentation on a different facet of *Eileh Ezkerah* by each of our three teachers, and then we'll do a second round in which we'd like to provide an opportunity for each of our three teachers to share how they might approach this liturgy for a twenty-first-century *machzor*.

Eileh Ezkerah: Overview of the Liturgy

Dr. Ruth Langer

I want to invite all of you to look at a document that is titled "Langer Musaf for Yom Kippur." I didn't write this, but it is the text that we're looking at in its traditional context. I apologize for using the ArtScroll *machzor*, but it was the best way out and the clearest to use. Where I started this file is actually at the end of the *Seder Avodah*. Now the *Seder Avodah* requires a word of explanation, in that this is one of the earliest known *piyutim* for Yom Kippur. The *piyut*, the *Seder Avodah*, begins with the story of Creation, and like several other genres of *piyut*, it moves from the story of Creation to its high point and end point, which is the thing that is relevant to that day. In the case of the *Seder Avodah*, this is obviously the ceremonies of Yom Kippur in the Temple in the days when the Temple stood. Where I've started this handout is with the end of that, that is, when the High Priest is done with this all, he does this great big sigh of relief and has a great big party for everybody.

Then there is this wonderful prayer that we should have a nice, a great year, and then a contemplative *piyut* at the bottom of page 570/571 on how wonderful the *Kohein Gadol* looked at this point, so the community is really joining in in this sense of rejoicing. But at the end of it, on page 572, all of a sudden you have, "This is all what it was when there was a Temple and we could be joyful then but, boy, now are we sad," that then moves—I'm running very fast through this—to, at page 574, this happened because of our sins. This is the transition into what is really ten pages or five pages—

Refer to "Mussaf for Yom Kippur" in Rabbi Meir Zlotowitz and Rabbi Avie Gold, eds., *The Complete ArtScroll Machzor Yom Kippur* (Brooklyn: Mesorah, 1986), 570–97, or "Mussaf for Yom Kippur" at http://www.ccarnet.org/lifelong-learning/teleconferences-webinars/machzor-eileh-ezkerah.

Usually we think of Yom Kippur as a sad holiday. Where is there room for joy on this day?

actually, it's double numbered—that I've skipped here, of saying, "Boy, did we do badly; boy, have we sinned."

That then leads to a formal beginning on page 584, which is the next page in the handout, of what are now the *S'lichot*, the penitential prayers that are going to lead up to the *Vidui*, and that, the context of the *Eileh Ezkerah*, is penitential liturgy. So it's quite different from the way that it gets laid out in the *Gates of Repentance*, even though the basic structure is maintained.

I want to just draw your attention on page 584 to this paragraph, which sets up the penitential theme by saying, *zachor, zachor, zachor, tizkor*—remember, remember, remember and, of course, *zachor rachamecha*—remember God's mercy. The other word that is echoing through again and again in this is this theme of God's mercy. So God, remember to be merciful to us. God, remember to be merciful for us. That theme—if you've printed this out, you can flip with me to the very end of the handout, to page 592—gets picked up again after *Eileh Ezkerah*, where all of a sudden you have, again, *zachor lanu b'rit avot*—"remember for us the covenant of the ancestors."

This idea of *z'chut avot*, of remembering the context, remembering us, and remembering us because of something that's happened, is very, very important, and that's the context in which *Eileh Ezkerah* then comes in. In some ways, it's not so different from another genre of *piyut* for Yom Kippur, the *Akeidah*, which doesn't appear in what remains of the Ashkenazi liturgy, but it certainly did use to be there.

If we take a look at the *piyut*, the transition into *Eileh Ezkerah* itself is the very bottom line on page 584, which is this line *chatanu tzureinu s'lach*

What does God's mercy look like? What does it mean for God "to be merciful to us"?

lanu yotzreinu—"we have erred, our Rock, please forgive us, our Creator" (and note that I'm not using the ArtScroll translation when I say that). That line itself tells us that we are in the context of the genre that's known as a *s'lichah*. According to Ezra Fleischer, we don't know the origin of the use of this line as a refrain, but he says that it appears very early (that is in terms of *piyut*) in six texts that are leading up to the *Vidui*, or perhaps in texts that are replacing *Vidui*; and it's also then found as a refrain, both in *piyutim*, where it reflects the content of the *piyut*, and also as here, where it doesn't really reflect the content of the *piyut*, but it tells us that the penitential context exists.

Fleischer says that early on in the classic period of *piyut*—that would be the late Byzantine period just before the Arab conquest in the seventh century and through that a little bit—there are lots of *piyutim* at that point that tell the story of the Ten Martyrs. So he dates the origin of this genre of *piyut*, although not necessarily this particular one, to that period. We don't really know when this particular *piyut* comes from. It's very classic in its structure. It's signed by the name Yehudah, but we have a whole handful of *pay'tanim* who go by that name, so that doesn't help us very much.

The *Eileh Ezkerah*, then, is a *piyut* that has as its refrain, in the better versions of the text, this *chatanu tzureinu s'lach lanu yotzreinu*—"please remember us, God, we've sinned," and that's its purpose: to ask God to recall the merit of these martyrdoms to our benefit. In terms of the structure of the *piyut*, we know also—and this is very clear in this particular printout or this particular setting—that it's an alphabetic acrostic, going all the way through the *alef-bet*, ending on page 592, and then, as I said, it has the signature of the

Ezra Fleischer (1928–2006) was a Romanian-Israeli Hebrew-language poet and philologist who served as a professor of Hebrew literature, specializing in medieval Hebrew poetry and Jewish liturgy, at the Hebrew University of Jerusalem.

author in the last stanza, or the second to last stanza.

If you look on page 592, you can see how this was written to lead into the *S'lichot* liturgy, because the third line up from the bottom of the *piyut* ends *Hashem Hashem El rachum v'chanun*, which, of course, is a lead-in to the thirteen qualities of God's mercy, and then the last line ends *El melech yosheiv al kisei rachamim*, which is the text that is the transition into the recitation of those thirteen qualities of mercy in a traditional liturgy. Those used to be part of this liturgy in *Musaf*—at some point, they dropped out of Ashkenazi liturgy except for in *Kol Nidrei* and *N'ilah*, where, in a traditional liturgy, they bang on the doors of heaven, I like to say, by being repeated many, many times over.

How can we reconcile this liturgical tradition of repetition with Reform Judaism's tradition of eliminating liturgical repetition?

The *piyut* itself mourns over the death of the ten sages. It's got a parallel that's recited—or this particular version is recited also some places on Tishah B'Av—but there is a different version of it that's recited in the western Ashkenazi tradition. This one is from the eastern Ashkenazi tradition for Yom Kippur, and it sets up the martyrdom as a sort of a trap that's set by the Roman ruler. He asks these rabbis what happens (this is in the *dalet* stanza), "What's the law if a man is found to have kidnapped a member of his Jewish brethren and he enslaved and sold him?" The rabbis say, "That kidnapper has to die," and then he replies, "That's what your ancestors did to Joseph when they sold him to a caravan of Ishmaelites and so, therefore, now you have to accept that judgment and you must bear the sin of your ancestors." I think that that line, which is the bottom line on page 586/587, is particularly powerful here, as it is telling us what's setting up this whole sense of the *piyut*. Do we bear the sin of our ancestors, or does the martyrdom of these ancestors, these people who died even though they were, according to Jewish view, blameless, does that somehow stand in the place of our sins?

If we turn to page 590—I'm not going to go through the names of the individual rabbis and what happens to them, that you can do yourself—but note the *samech* and *ayin* stanzas: the angels don't understand this and the voice from heaven responds, "Yup, this is what needs to happen, this is what you need to accept in spite of all this." There's enormous pain and enormous struggle and confusion that is deeply, deeply embedded in this *piyut*. That's where this leads us going into the *Vidui*, is with this pain and this struggle with the martyrdom of these rabbis who stood up for Torah, stood up for what they believed in, in spite of everything else. That then, I want to really emphasize, is setting the stage for a *Vidui*. That *Vidui* is missing in the afternoon service in the *Gates of Repentance*, but that's where this service is supposed to be keeping us, is in that penitential mode, and that's really the purpose of this *piyut*, is to be struggling with these themes of penitence.

How would you respond to the challenging questions posed by the presenter?

As an exercise, read about these martyr rabbis in the original *piyut*. How do we relate to their stories today?

How can we set the stage for *Vidui* in a Reform liturgical context?

Eileh Ezkerah: **Historical Background**

Dr. Richard S. Sarason

It is worth pointing out that while we indeed cannot date the poem on the basis of either the name of the poet or the formal literary characteristics of the poem, we can locate it chronologically a bit better on the basis of its content and its relationship to other sources. Max Arzt, in his commentary on the *machzor* entitled *Justice and Mercy*, provides good reasons for concluding that this poem was composed in Ashkenaz soon after the First Crusade. There are many such poems written in Ashkenaz that deal with issues of martyrdom in the wake of the Crusades. Artzt writes:

See the excerpts in *Eileh Ezkerah: Aggadic Sources and Interactions,* on page 140.

> This dirge is a reflection of the utter bewilderment of that generation in their inability to understand the meaning of the martyred deaths of countless innocents. *Eleh Ezkerah* is an expression of their pathetic search for an explanation of the absence of supernatural intervention on behalf of those done to death by the crusading mobs that invaded the Rhineland. Such unspeakable tragedies had to be explained without impugning the purity and the nobility of character of the victims, and without accusing God of abandoning His hunted and tormented people. For this reason, they resorted to the tradition of the Ten Martyrs, which told of a previous instance of martyrs suffering death, not for their own sins but in expiation of the sins of previous generations. (Arzt, *Justice and Mercy*, 253–54)

How could we respond theologically and liturgically to the unspeakable tragedies of our generation?

There are approximately ten different recensions of the legend of the Ten Martyrs in prose form, and this one is the eleventh, in poetic form. There are other versions in poetic form, too, as Dr. Langer indicated. I've supplied a brief bibliography at the end of the presentation. Adolph Jellinek, in *Beit Hamidrash*, published three versions of the text. Gottfried Reeg published a critical synoptic edition of all ten versions, with an introduction and German translation, and Joseph Dan has discussed the versions at length in a fine Hebrew article, "The Development and Purposes of the Story of the Ten Martyrs." Much, though not all, of what I'm going to discuss is based heavily on these materials.

See page 140.

What is interesting is that the legend of the Ten Martyrs is actually post-Talmudic. It begins, to be sure, in Talmudic legends about various rabbis who were executed during the era of the Hadrianic persecutions, particularly the well-known story of the execution of Rabbi Akiva, which, by the way, only appears in amoraic literature, in *Bavli, B'rachot* 61b, with a parallel in *Y'rushalmi*. The story of the execution of Rabbi Chanina ben Teradion (the rabbi who is wrapped up in the Torah scroll and talks about the letters flying heavenward when the parchment burns) is in *Bavli, Avodah Zarah* 18a. The story of the executions of Rabbi Shimon ben Gamliel and Rabbi Yishmael, each trying to be the first, is in *Avot D'Rabbi Natan*, in both of its recensions.

But the motif of specifically *ten* martyrs is later; it appears with a list of names in *Midrash T'hillim* (Midrash on Psalms) and in *Midrash Eichah Rabbati* (Midrash on Lamentations). There are some variations in the names. The final editing of these midrashim is relatively late, and as Dan points out, they may already know one of the aggadic versions of the story of the Ten Martyrs rather than being a source for it.

The motif of collective atonement for the guilt of the ten brothers in selling Joseph into slavery is found in *Midrash Mishlei* (Midrash on Proverbs), which is also relatively late. There is an interesting observation in the Book of Jubilees, which dates from the late Second Commonwealth period, that the fast of the tenth day of the seventh month, what we now call Yom Kippur, commemorates the sale of Joseph by his brothers, which took place on this day. Now, that tradition does not appear in Rabbinic literature and so does not provide an association with Yom Kippur for liturgical purposes.

The text that is called both *Midrash Eileh Ezkerah* and *Maaseh Asarah Harugei Malchut* dates from the geonic period at the very earliest, but it clearly develops in medieval Ashkenaz. The narrative itself has a distinctively Ashkenazi style and cast, and it corresponds to a lot of the other martyrological writings from the period of the Crusades. It is also closely related to the mystical *heichalot* literature (which tells, among other things, how esoterically knowledgeable rabbis ascended above the seven heavens to attain a vision of God seated on the divine throne). Some of this material occurs in *Sefer Heichalot Rabbati.* We also know that the *heichalot* literature was well known and continued to develop in medieval Ashkenaz, particularly, though not exclusively, in the circles of the *Chasidei Ashkenaz.*

The prose narrative mentions the ascent to heaven of Rabbi Yishmael the High Priest to find out whether or not the death sentence against the martyrs is really a decree directly from God. (The same motif is alluded to in the poem.) The designation of the tannaitic Rabbi Yishmael as Rabbi Yishmael the High Priest (*Kohein Gadol*) already

> Within the framework of this theology, at what point will the Jewish people no longer be deserving of punishment for Joseph's brothers' sin?

indicates the specific provenance of this material, because it only occurs in the *heichalot* literature. Some of the prose versions of this legend contain a lengthy description of Yishmael's pronouncing the divine name, ascending to heaven, and having a conversation with the angel Gabriel—that is *heichalot* material. And, interestingly enough, in the rudimentary version that appears in *Heichalot Rabbati*, chapters 4 and 5, only four sages are named.

The main theological points of the story, according to Joseph Dan, are two. One is that the death of the ten righteous, pious martyrs effects atonement for a past sin of the people, the ten tribes who sold Joseph into slavery, as Dr. Langer mentioned. It is a theodicy for the martyrdom of the righteous. The second point is that the death of those righteous ones now provides an ironclad guarantee that, in the future, the wicked kingdom of Rome will be destroyed and Israel redeemed. This is expressed through the narrative motif that when Samael, the guardian angel of the Roman Empire, exalts that these ten rabbis are going to be executed, God says to him, "Now if you agree that these ten are to be executed, then in the future, at the time of judgment, you too will be judged and will suffer all the degradations of the curses of Deuteronomy," and Samael assents to this. Dan underscores this point.

That motif is found also in *Heichalot Rabbati*, so there is an eschatological thrust to this legend. The death of the martyrs is understood to be in some measure vicarious: it guarantees that Israel will triumph in the end and that Rome will be vanquished. The death of these ten righteous and pious martyrs not only atones for the sin of the selling of Joseph into slavery by his ten brothers (ten for ten), but also guarantees that in the future Israel will triumph over Rome. And in the narrative, these theodicies are imparted by the angel Gabriel to Rabbi Yishmael the High Priest during his ascent to heaven.

The ten different versions of the narrative have different introductions. The one that is called *Eileh Ezkerah* has an introduction that doesn't figure in the *piyut* at all. It states that the tall trees were inappropriately proud before God created iron to cut them down: corresponding to this was the inappropriate pride of some Jews in their Sages after the destruction of the Temple before God condemned the Sages to be slaughtered by the Roman Empire. Dan understands this as an indictment of those Jews who have lost a fervent eschatological faith in the speedy rebuilding of the Temple. Many late aggadot have an eschatological flavor to them; this one does as well.

Since this appears in greater detail in the material that follows, I will be brief. Most of the narrative details deal with how the Roman emperor arrives at the idea of studying Torah and why he then sentences the ten rabbis to be executed. This is found in both the *piyut* and the prose versions. Regarding the narrative of the ten executions themselves, it is interesting to note that the first four, which also occur in the Talmudic literature, are deployed in a similar fashion in both the prose and the poetic versions, and they share certain motifs that are not in the Talmudic material. But from this point on, after the death of the fourth sage, none of the narratives that appear in the prose version appear in the *piyut*. The *piyut* at this point becomes much more compact, in part because it is an acrostic that will otherwise run out of letters. For whatever reason, the names also occur in a different order.

Dan points out, fascinatingly, that it is not always clear whether the prose versions are sources for the poetic version or whether, in at least some cases, the poetic version is the source for the prose versions, or whether these are all coming to artic- ulation at approximately the same time. But Dan thinks that the poem itself has had some influence on how the prose materials develop.

How does the history of the development of *Eileh Ezkerah* help us when crafting High Holy Day worship?

Eileh Ezkerah: Aggadic Sources and Interactions

Max Arzt, *Justice and Mercy: Commentary on the Liturgy of the New Year and the Day of Atonement* (New York: Holt, Rinehart and Winston, 1963):

In reading of these Ten Martyrs, we of this generation cannot help but direct our thoughts to the six million of our people who were slaughtered during World War II. . . . Composed soon after the First Crusade (1096 c.e.), this dirge is a reflection of the utter bewilderment of that generation in their inability to understand the meaning of the martyred death of countless innocents. *Eleh Ezkerah* is an expression of their pathetic search for an explanation of the absence of supernatural intervention in behalf of those done to death by the crusading mobs that invaded the Rhineland. . . . Such unspeakable tragedies had to be explained without impugning the purity and the nobility of character of the victims, and without accusing God of abandoning His hunted and tormented people. For this reason, they resorted to the tradition of the Ten Martyrs, which told of a previous instance of martyrs suffering death, not for their own sins, but in expiation of the sins of previous generations. (253–54)

Basic Bibliography

Joseph Dan, "The Development and Purposes of the Story of the Ten Martyrs" (Hebrew), in *Simon Halkin Festschrift*, ed. Ezra Fleischer (Jerusalem: Magnes Press, 1973), 15–22 [= Dan, *The Hebrew Story in the Middle Ages* (Jerusalem: Keter, 1974), 62–68].

Adolph Jellinek, Bet Hamidrash (6 vols.; Leipzig: Friedrich Niese, 1853-77; reprint in 2 vols., Jerusalem: Wahrmann Books, 1967. The relevant texts are in vols. 2, pp. 46–72, and 6, pp. 19–30 and 31–35.

Gottfried Reeg, ed., *Die Geschichte von den Zehn Martyrern/Ma'aseh Asarah Harugei Malkhut* (Mohr-Siebeck, 1985)—a critical synoptic edition of all the versions, with introduction and German translation.

Narrative Elements in the Aggadic Tradition and Their Relationship to the *Piyut*

- Introduction: Inappropriate pride of the tall trees before God creates iron to cut them down = inappropriate pride of some Jews in their Sages after destruction of the Temple before God condemns them to be slaughtered by the Roman emperor; Joseph Dan understands this as an indictment of those Jews who have lost a fervent eschatological faith in the speedy rebuilding of the Temple (not in all recensions and <u>not in the *piyut*</u>).

- Roman emperor (Hadrian) gets it into his head (from God) to study the Torah of the Jews; when he gets as far as Exodus 21:16 ("He who kidnaps a man—whether he has sold him or still holds him—shall be put to death"), he sees that this applies to Joseph's sale into Egyptian slavery by his ten brothers and determines to avenge this with the execution of the ten most distinguished Torah scholars of the generation (since the brothers of Joseph are no longer alive and cannot be punished): **"You will bear the sin of your ancestors"** (<u>all of this in *piyut*</u>).

- Sages ask Rabbi Yishmael the High Priest to pronounce the divine name and ascend to heaven to ascertain whether or not this is a divine decree, to which they must submit (<u>all of this in *piyut*</u>).

- Description (in some recensions, quite lengthy) of Yishmael's heavenly ascent and his conversation with the angel Gabriel: if the decree is not sealed on high, Yishmael has the power to annul it (a power that even the angels don't have)—this is the *Heichalot*-related material (<u>these details not in *piyut*</u>)—[miraculous birth of Rabbi Yishmael and his extreme good looks].

- Gabriel informs Yishmael that the divine decree has been sealed (<u>in *piyut*</u>), since **God has not found a more perfect generation of righteous Sages to atone for the sin of the ten brothers until now** (<u>explicit theodicy not in *piyut*</u>).

- Samael, the Guardian Angel of Rome, rejoices at this news; God gives him a choice: either to release the Sages from their martyrdom or to suffer plague and destruction in the future; Samael chooses the latter course—**thus the martyrdom of the ten righteous Sages will be avenged by God in the messianic era through the destruction** of Rome; their martyrdom now ensures Rome's destruction in the future. This motif also appears in *Heichalot Rabbati* (not in *piyut*).

- Gabriel shows Yishmael an altar next to God's throne on which **sacrifices are offered daily by Michael; these are the souls of the righteous** (not in *piyut*).
- Yishmael tells his fellow Rabbis, who accept the decree (in *piyut*).
- Narrative of executions:
  1) Shimon ben Gamliel and Yishmael—elaboration of the story in *Avot D'Rabbi Natan* (each wants to die first; they draw lots, Shimon goes first; his head is cut off, and Yishmael mourns over the head); new motif: the emperor's daughter is attracted by Yishmael's beauty, futilely attempts to save him, has his face peeled off to keep and look at, he dies when the peeling reaches his *t'fillin* (all of these details in the *piyut*); refrain after each death: **Is this the reward for studying and observing the Torah?** God's response: **His merit will stand for the generations to come** (a version of this in the *piyut*).
  2) Rabbi Akiva—elaboration of the story in Babylonian Talmud, *B'rachot* 61b; flayed to death [very briefly in *piyut*] (here, he dies reciting *Tzidduk HaDin* instead of *Sh'ma*); Elijah the Prophet attends to his burial, brings his soul to heaven, where he teaches Torah to the souls of the righteous.
  3) Rabbi Chanina ben Teradion—elaboration of the story in Babylonian Talmud, *Avodah Zarah* 18a—burned to death wrapped in a *sefer Torah*: "The parchment burns but the letters ascend to heaven" (brief version in *piyut*).

  From this point, none of the narratives appear in the *piyut*; only the names, together with exhortations to mourn, occur in the following order: Rabbi Hutzpit the Meturgeman, Rabbi Eleazar ben Shamua, Rabbi Chanina ben Hakinai, Rabbi Yesheivav the Scribe, Rabbi Y'hudah ben Dama, Rabbi Y'hudah ben Bava.

  4) Rabbi Y'hudah ben Bava—original (formulaic) story, modeled somewhat on martyrologies in Books of Maccabees: to be executed on Erev Shabbat; still has faith, allowed to perform mitzvah

of *Kabbalat Shabbat* (*K'dushat HaYom*), expires on last word (patterned on Akiva story).

5) Rabbi Y'hudah ben Dama—to be executed on Erev Shavuot, still has faith, not allowed to perform mitzvah of *kabbalat hechag*; dragged by his hair by a horse through the streets of Rome; limbs chopped off, buried by Elijah (patterned on Akiva story); Roman sage tells off the Emperor, affirms that God will requite on Rome the murder of Israel's Sages; the sage then becomes a Jew.

6) Rabbi Hutzpit the Meturgeman—130 years old less one day; dialogue between rabbi and emperor about God's providence (Maccabees model); stoned and impaled/hung.

7) Rabbi Chanina ben Hakinai—fasts on Erev Shabbat (patterned on Y'hudah ben Bava, Akiva), recites *Kiddush*, expires on "holiness."

8) Rabbi Yesheivav the Scribe—tells his students that Rome is destined to be destroyed, while Israel's Torah will be praised by all; tells emperor that God will avenge on him the blood of his servants; he is burned.

9) Rabbi Eleazar ben Shamua—executed on Yom Kippur; tells his students that he sees Rabbi Akiva and Rabbi Y'hudah ben Bava arguing halachah in heaven, with Rabbi Yishmael deciding between them; all the souls of the righteous and all the angels gather to learn Torah from Rabbi Akiva; his soul expires in purity.

Eileh Ezkerah in *Gates of Repentance*

Rabbi Neil Gillman, PhD

I have to say from the outset that I have not been identified with the Reform Movement, and I have rarely worshiped in a Reform synagogue or used Reform prayer books. I have on Shabbatot but never on *Yamim Noraim*. So my first exposure to *Shaarei Teshuvah* (*Gates of Repentance*) and to that version of *Eileh Ezkerah* found within it was in preparation for this call, and I sat down and read it very, very thoroughly and carefully and slowly a number of times since then, but I have not read it as a davening Jew, in a davening context. I've read it as a student of the liturgy and someone who is extraordinarily concerned with the whole idea of what's the relationship between liturgy and prayer and what's left to happen when we're confronted with the text of this kind and we're sitting in the synagogue on Yom Kippur and we are exposed to this material and to these issues.

So my first impression was that what we have in *Shaarei Teshuvah* is an anthology—and I've counted them a number of times—of twenty-four texts, ranging all the way back from biblical sources, Rabbinic material, to almost contemporary or even contemporary texts, mostly dealing with Jewish martyrdom or Jewish suffering, but with some universal texts that have a more universal application, and also near the end, with an eschatological theme, mainly that the restoration of Israel and the prayers for the messianic era mean that all of this suffering and martyrdom will be behind us.

Now, this is what I discovered in the *machzor*. I don't know how this *machzor* is used in a syna-

Refer to Chaim Stern, ed., *Gates of Repentance: The New Union Prayerbook* for the Days of Awe (New York: CCAR Press, 1978), 429–49, or *"Eileh Ezkerah* from *Gates of Repentance"* at http://www.ccarnet.org/lifelong-learning/teleconferences-webinars/machzor-eileh-ezkerah.

gogue context. I know I should say I'm not a pulpit rabbi, but I have for some forty-five to fifty years officiated on Rosh HaShanah and Yom Kippur as an overflow rabbi in congregations all around the country, and therefore, for some forty-five years, I've had to deal with *Eileh Ezkerah* using the various *machzorim* produced by the Conservative Movement.

So two things. I don't know, but I suspect that the *Eileh Ezkerah* in *Shaarei Teshuvah* was viewed as an anthology, where the officiating rabbi/cantor selected passages, and it's possible that there are additional liturgical passages that didn't make it into the book. We found material—Anne Frank, some Holocaust memories, and possibly some Holocaust theology—and used these scattered references. The material, which has struck me very quickly, is all over the place and most strikingly and most disturbingly, to me at least, there is no bridge material in which the editors of the *machzor* tell us what it all means: How does it all fit together? Why these texts and not others? What are these texts saying? What are they saying individually, but much more importantly, what are they saying comprehensively? At the very end of this, after some twenty-five pages of text, what are we supposed to walk away with on Yom Kippur as worshiping Jews dealing with these issues or this issue?

This led me to recall what I did for forty-five years when I was dealing with *Eileh Ezkerah,* and I did a variety of things. Most notably, I let the congregation read the text in the *machzor* itself, which was the traditional text, and while this was going on or before or after, each year, I selected three or four—not twenty-four—three or four very selected texts sometimes from the classical martyrdom literature or sometimes from Holocaust literature,

How has your community utilized the lengthy *Eileh Ezkerah* anthology in *Gates of Repentance?*

How would you respond to the questions posed by the presenter?

and either I copied them and had them distributed or, more likely, I invited them, the congregation, to get up and to read these texts. But they were not short snippets. They could have been, you know, three- to four-page extracts that I felt had a theological message.

But what was most important, to me at least, was that I provided bridge comments on whatever was going on in the worship service, and what I felt all of this related to, to the traditional text of the *Eileh Ezkerah,* which was in front of them. And at the end, suggesting in relatively five minutes, not much more, this is what it means to me, and this is what I think the whole thing means to you, this is why it's here, this is how it's related to the *Avodah,* this is how it's related to the *Vidui,* which is what we're going into. I have to add to you that at most of the synagogues where I've done this, the *Eileh Ezkerah* was part of *Musaf,* not part of *Minchah,* as it is in *Shaarei Teshuvah.* And then we went on to the *Avodah* service.

I then discovered that there is a book called *Gates of Understanding 2,* and after having gone through the *Shaarei Teshuvah* material, I was struck by the fact that I didn't see an order, I missed the bridge passages, I missed the coherence including messages as to what it all means, and I didn't know how it all fit together. It did not seem clear to me that it fit together, and then I discovered that in the *Gates of Understanding 2,* there is an attempt at least to identify the sources, which are not identified in *Gates of Repentance* but they are in *Gates of Understanding 2,* to identify the sources and to provide at least a hint as to what the message is and why they were included here. But this is in a separate book, and I said to myself, "So what? Does the worshiper have *Gates of Understanding* next to the *machzor*?" I

Would this or a similar approach to *Eileh Ezkerah* work in your community? Why or why not?

See Lawrence A. Hoffman, ed., *Gates of Understanding 2 (Shaarei Binah): Appreciating the Days of Awe* (New York: CCAR Press, 1983).

doubted that, and you confirmed that this has not been the case.

So the very fact is that the material needed to make sense of what is in *Gates of Repentance* was, by and large, inaccessible. If there was a copy in the synagogue library, the library was closed and locked on Yom Kippur, one of the great tragedies of American Jewish synagogue life. On a day when people are in the synagogue, the books they need are often inaccessible. And educationally, how would *Gates of Understanding 2* help the worshiper in the synagogue, even if it had accessible the bridge passages? The bridge passages are much more important to me than the footnotes telling me that this passage was originally a passage from Chaim Stern or that this is a poem by Shlonsky or this is a historical reference. I'm interested in these things, but I'm much more interested in why is it there in the first place and what is it saying and how does it fit into the other passages. And all of this was possibly in the *Gates of Understanding* but the worshiper must have sat there and felt absolutely totally bereft unless the *machzor* itself was used in a way that the rabbi was an actively involved teacher of the material on all these issues throughout this portion of the service.

Now, this is a multi-layered problem and it goes far beyond *Eileh Ezkerah* because there are half a dozen questions you have to ask and, I suspect, that the editors of the new *machzor* will have to deal with. First of all, why is there an *Eileh Ezkerah* in Yom Kippur in the first place? Why was it there traditionally and do we still need it? Do we want it? And if you do want it, how do we justify its use on Yom Kippur? By trying to extract some of the traditional text, it gives us meaning. What does it say to us? What are we walking away with? How

Mishkan HaNefesh continues the approach used in *Mishkan T'filah* of putting commentary and explanation directly on the page. How does that change the experience described here?

Abraham Shlonsky (1900–1973) was a Hebrew poet, editor, and translator born in Ukraine, although he spent much of his life in the Land of Israel.

does that help us as religious Jews deal with Yom Kippur or deal with our lives in general? What's the message if we want the text of Israel? If it's martyrdom, then how do we feel about martyrdom as a theological issue? And how do we feel about a God who welcomes martyrs or who meets martyrs? So what do we want this liturgy to say? Finally, how then should the *machzor* deal with this particular issue? *Gates of Repentance* doesn't deal with it. It provides a dozen possible ways of dealing with it, but then I don't know what the rabbi does with all of this material from the pulpit while this is being prayed. How does the rabbi use the anthology?

And then the editors of this new *machzor*, I believe, have to ask themselves, what is it that we have to provide the rabbi and the congregation if we decide that we want to include *Eileh Ezkerah* traditionally in some form, and there are a dozen theological issues—issues of theodicy, issues of repentance, issues of what kind of a God are we davening to? How does this relate to Yom Kippur in general? How does this relate to my life when I walk out of the synagogue? All possible issues that *Eileh Ezkerah* could raise. What do we mean by redemption? Why do we end this whole thing with a reference to the return to Zion and all of that? In other words, what's the religious message that we want to convey? My sense is, in fact, *Shaarei Teshuvah* does not convey a clear, coherent religious message, and even if *Shaarei Binah* were available, it would not help much on the issues. *Shaarei Binah* is scholarly; it is scholarship, and scholarship, as we know, is not worshiping. They're two different things, two different models.

How would you respond to the questions posed by the presenter?

Scholarship and worship are two different models, but are they mutually exclusive? How might we bridge these two fields in order to create worship that appeals to more than one kind of worshiper?

Eileh Ezkerah End-of-Call Discussion

Rabbi Leon A. Morris,
Dr. Ruth Langer,
Dr. Richard S. Sarason,
Dr. Neil Gillman

Rabbi Leon A. Morris

Your teachings have presented us with a great deal that needs to be considered as we think about *Eileh Ezkerah,* and you've raised some really crucial questions for us. I want to take some of Dr. Gillman's closing questions and ask you to respond briefly: What your approach to a new *machzor* might be and what should the conceptual takeaways be for a twenty-first-century *machzor?* How do we treat concepts like *z'chut avot,* our expiation of sins of a previous generation; what do we do with an eschatological vision of how, in the end, our world will be redeemed? Should this be a way of trying to make sense of our own experience of suffering?

These are huge questions but I'd like to ask you to just respond to a piece of that as a way of sharing with us what your approach to a new *machzor* might be given some of these questions.

Dr. Ruth Langer

I will start with something structural, which is to say, in the *Gates of Repentance,* the section "From Creation to Redemption" sort of hangs out there in nowhere, in that the afternoon service has sort of ended, but it's not ended. You have had even *Aleinu,* and then you have this "From Creation to

Redemption," and then you have a Torah service. *Eilah Ezkerah* belongs in the midst of the *Amidah* of what is called the afternoon service, or if there is some reintroduction of *Musaf*, you've got to fill in the hours of the day somehow, but make this integral to the day.

At the same time, this day should not become the Ninth of Av, so I have some problems with expanding the *Eileh Ezkerah* to include all aspects of Jewish mourning. There's something else, there's something quite specific here that's going on, setting up the *Vidui*, and I think that that should be important and should be held onto. We *are* talking about a context of *z'chut avot*, and that is not always entirely comfortable, but it's talking about the crisis aspect of Yom Kippur. How do we hit people in their guts with this day? It's not a day to be all intellectual, but it's a day to be feeling like, gosh, we're standing before God and what we're doing is really important. And so this is part of building up that sort of emotional tension about the day.

So moving to redemption at the end is not what the *piyut* is doing here. To do something that takes the idea of people being willing to give their all for God and that somehow or other standing for the benefit of the community might be a creative way of moving the message and contextualizing it, as Dr. Gillman was saying, in a way that will communicate to contemporary people.

What is the difference between recalling Jewish martyrs and mourning national Jewish tragedies?

Dr. Richard S. Sarason

I have a huge problem with this, along the same lines that Dr. Gillman does. I understand the history of what's going on here and that needs to be stated. It's worth pointing out that none of this appeared in any North American Reform liturgy until *Gates of Repentance.* The material actually derives from the British *Gate of Repentance* (1973) and was written for that volume by Chaim Stern and Albert Friedlander. It addresses a particular, local (Diaspora) Jewish sensibility during the late 1960s and 1970s. The subtext of "From Creation to Redemption" is the experience of that generation that lived through the Second World War, the Holocaust, the founding of the State of Israel, and had to reexamine these wounds after the shocks of the Six-Day War and the Yom Kippur War—both the fears and the victories of 1967 and 1973 allowed Diaspora Jews to see the State of Israel and its recent victories as somehow a consolation for the Holocaust, a redemption following a cataclysm, providing a mythic narrative that made some sense of the tragedies. This was put into the *Avodah* service as a way of broadening it out, as a way of bringing its mythic narrative down to our day, of collectively owning the experience. And also, in some respects, it is a kind of a counterpoise to what David Einhorn and then David Philipson and Kaufmann Kohler did with the *Seder HaAvodah* in *Olath Tamid* and the *Union Prayer Book*, where the valorizing of the Temple's destruction and the cessation of the sacrificial cult was completely turned on its head.

I think this has to be part of a much larger and more radical discussion of what *Mishkan HaNefesh* is going to do with *Seder HaAvodah* as a whole. Interestingly enough, in the British *Gate of Repentance*, it actually appears in a *Musaf* service. In the American *Gates of Repentance*, as well as in the *Union Prayer Book*, it appears in the afternoon service because there is no *Musaf* service. But the larger question is this: How do we craft an afternoon service that is meaningful and that does not

For further discussion on this subject, see the presentations on *Seder HaAvodah*, pages 101–125.

feel like it is simply marking time until *N'ilah?* What do we want any *Seder HaAvodah* to mean, to accomplish? "From Creation to Redemption" goes on forever, and when I conduct services, I radically prune large portions of it because it's too dense, belabored, and repetitious. It feels like we're just marking time—and that needs to be avoided at all costs in a new *machzor.* Also, the cultural moment that it celebrates is, unfortunately, past.

The reason why *Eileh Ezkarah* appears there is all about subtext, subtext, subtext—and the *piyut* itself really isn't there. The very beginning of it is quoted, and then it's alluded to in a prose narrative.

How can we present *Eileh Ezkerah* for a twenty-first-century community without turning it into Tishah B'Av or Yom HaShoah liturgy?

I agree with Dr. Langer. I think the Ninth of Av and Yom HaShoah are the appropriate times to memorialize and reflect upon the traumatic catastrophes in Jewish history. But we don't need to do that on Yom Kippur in a new *machzor* for the twenty-first century—even if that is the only time of year when most of the community is in the synagogue. This is a very, very 1970s' text, which addresses the sensibilities and traumas of the American Jewish community at that time. It's not where the community is now, so in some respects, I have no problem omitting *Eileh Ezkerah* entirely, because the *piyut* itself raises huge theological difficulties in terms of its theodicies, and I think the whole thing needs to be rethought.

Rabbi Leon A. Morris

I'd just point out that we've had a previous conversation just focusing on *Seder HaAvodah* (see pages 101–125). It sounds like part of what you're saying is that if it were to be included that there is some kind of integral connection that should be maintained between *Seder HaAvodah* and *Eileh Ezkerah.*

Dr. Richard S. Sarason

There is absolutely *no* instrinsic connection between *Seder HaAvodah* and *Eileh Ezkerah* and none in the traditional liturgy. *Eileh Ezkerah* **follows** *Seder HaAvodah* (it is not a part of it), because the latter ends on a note of desolation, mourning for the destroyed Temple and its rites, concluding with a penitential plea that God not punish us for our folly and our sins. This leads into the *S'lichot*. In this context, the *piyut* gives yet another example of divine punishment—in this case, the martyrs' vicarious sufferings for the people's sins. Nice theology for the twenty-first century, no?

Dr. Neil Gillman

Dr. Langer made that connection, and I must tell you, it's the first time I saw that. I've always taken these two units as separate units, individual units. I've never felt the need to mark a liturgical connection that they would do. But it's there, obviously, and I feel very grateful to Dr. Langer for having pointed this out.

I also want to just vociferously agree with everybody else that you can't do a mishmash of Yom HaShoah, Tishah B'Av, *Yizkor*, and *Eileh Ezkerah*, which I have, unfortunately, had to participate in once and I will never do again—I just would bow out or walk out at that. This is a real failure—it's educational malpractice. It's because we don't know what to do with Temple. We don't know what to do with martyrdom. We don't know what to do with the Shoah, theologically, we don't know what to do with it, or ritually or liturgically; and therefore, we mush it all together into one panorama of Jewish disasters and tragedies and martyrs and everything like that, and what we've done, basically, is obliterated certain very distinctive and very important parts of our tradition—we've just erased them from our communal memory.

So I think that the answer is not to mush it all together, but the answer is concentrate very clearly—and I think both Dr. Langer's and Dr. Sarason's contributions here are important—concentrate very clearly on what is it that we want *Eileh Ezkerah* to say. And it should not be saying the same thing as Yom HaShoah or Tishah B'Av. It's a whole—the larger question, of course, is well, how far do you want to expand it? What is it that they want our people to walk out of shul with at the end of Yom Kippur? What's the comprehensive message, religious message, religious meaning? And, of course, the much broader question that we're all struggling with is what are we supposed to walk out of shul with and feel? You know, what's the relationship between synagogue worship and our own personal religious lives?

How would you respond to the questions posed by the presenter?

Eileh Ezkarah **Wrap-Up**

1. How are the Ten Martyrs from Roman times still relevant for contemporary Jews?
2. To what degree should we incorporate the Shoah and those who died for the founding and in defense of the State of Israel?
3. What are the connections and distinctions to be made between *Eileh Ezkarah* and *Yizkor*?
4. How do we feel about the theological implications of reciting *Eileh Ezkarah* on Yom Kippur, namely, that we are asking God to have compassion on us because of those who died to sanctify the divine name?
5. How do we explain the notion of martyrology in light of the contemporary appropriation of martyrdom by Islamic extremists?
6. What did you learn from these presentations on *Eileh Ezkerah* that you would like to implement in your community's High Holy Day worship?

Yizkor

Yizkor: Historical Background

Dr. Richard S. Sarason

Ivan Marcus, *The Jewish Life Cycle: Rites of Passage from Biblical to Modern Times* (Seattle: University of Washington Press, 2004), 221–43.

Solomon B. Freehof's article, "Hazkarath Neshamoth," in *Hebrew Union College Annual* 36 (1965): 179–89.

The basic sources of information on *Yizkor* have been usefully sythesized and interpreted most recently by Ivan Marcus in his book *The Jewish Life Cycle: Rites of Passage from Biblical to Modern Times.* Also helpful is Solomon B. Freehof's article, "Hazkarath Neshamoth," in *Hebrew Union College Annual.*

The *Yizkor* prayers for family members originated in the Rhineland during the era of the Crusades, together with many other Jewish mourning and memorialization practices: the prayer *Av HaRachamim* that is recited every Shabbat; the liturgical poem *Eileh Ezkerah*, which is discussed elsewhere in this volume; the custom of *yahrzeit*, observing the anniversary of a death; and even the recitation of *Kaddish* by mourners, *Kaddish Yatom.* One of the noteworthy aspects of Marcus's treatment is his contextualization of Ashkenazic practices, noting the ways in which they in fact interacted with those of German Christian society. He points out, for example, that the development of Jewish mourning and memorialization practices, although sparked obviously by the trauma of the Crusades, also relates to Christian memorialization practices in the surrounding culture (think of All Saints' Day, All Souls' Day, candles lit in churches, and similar observances). The Jewish mourning customs developed at this time eventually spread from Germany to the rest of the Jewish world. *Yizkor*, in particular, is found also in the Spanish-Portuguese and the Italian rites, but not elsewhere. Marcus elegantly summarizes,

> [These customs] developed there [in the Rhineland] because that is where a cult of the local Jewish martyrs of 1096 emerged as a coherent set of practices that became part of a regional Jewish collective memory. The rites designed to remember the special martyrs of Germany developed in central and Eastern Europe into broader memorializations of the dead of every family. The relative absence of this cult and memory of the dead among Jews from Muslim lands points to the regional origins of these rites and prayers.

Ivan Marcus,
*The Jewish Life
Cycle*, 227–28.

Yizkor/Hazkarat N'shamot (both names are used) is the memorialization of one's dead relatives as opposed to the memorialization of the martyrs, and it included donating charity on behalf of the souls of the dead, who also need atonement and deliverance and who might be able to intercede on behalf of their living relatives. This donation of charity was called *matnat yad*. Initially the memorialization of family members was recited only on Yom Kippur after the Torah reading, but it spread to the three festivals by the early fifteenth century. Maharil mentions this in his discussion of Sh'mini Atzeret in *Sefer HaMaharil*.

In Eastern Europe, this custom was not popularized until the seventeenth century. It is first mentioned there by Mordecai Jaffe in his *Levush*. *El Malei Rachamim*, which for us is perhaps the most iconic memorial text, actually is relatively late. It originated in Eastern Europe in the seventeenth century, following the Chmielnicki massacres. It contains phraseology that is similar to the Sephardic *Hashkavah* prayer, which is recited at funerals and has also been taken over into the Shabbat liturgy in the Spanish-Portuguese rite. *Hashkavah* begins with the words *M'nuchah n'chonah tachat kanfei haShechinah* ("Perfect rest under the wings of the Divine Presence"). It is noteworthy that this version was taken over into some of the early Reform rites in place of the Ashkenazic one. (It was not uncommon among the early Reform liturgists to substitute Spanish-Portuguese Sephardic formulas for Ashkenazic ones that, for various reasons, were deemed to be problematic.)

There is variation among the traditional rites regarding what the *Yizkor* rite includes, but most of them contain what we would consider to be the core *Yizkor* prayers: the paragraphs *Yizkor Elohim nishmat* _____, for father, mother, and also usually one for the martyrs. In some of the later prayer books, we also find *Yizkor* formulae for husband, wife, or (more recently) generic man/woman if there are yet other people one desires to memorialize. Some rites additionally incude the text *Adonai Mah Adam* ("O Lord, what is man?"), which is a series of psalm verses from all over the Book of Psalms. Some, but not all, rites include *El Malei Rachamim*, and *Av Ha-Rachamim*, which is the text for the martyrs that is recited every Shabbat.

Reform treatments of *Yizkor* from the very outset (which is to say from the very first Reform congregational prayer book, that of the Hamburg Tempelverein in 1819) have been made more elaborate by the inclusion of vernacular prayers and meditations, as well as additional psalm texts and choral settings, which add heft to this section of the service. As we noted, many of the early Reform prayer books omit

Refer to "*Yizkor* From 1819 Hamburg Temple pb," "*Yizkor* in Geiger pb 1854," "*Yizkor* in Wise 1866," "*Yizkor* in *UPB* 1894," "*Yizkor* in *UPB II* Revised," "*Yizkor* in Einhorn 1958," and "Memorial of Departed Souls" at http://www .ccarnet.org/ lifelong-learning/ teleconferences- webinars/ machzor-yizkor.

El Malei Rachamim and use in its stead the Sephardic *Hashkavah* prayer. Most of these prayer books do not mention the donation of charity for the benefit of the soul of the departed, although Rabbi Don Rossoff has called to my attention that the prayer book edited in 1855 by Rabbi Leo Merzbacher for New York's Temple Emanu-El includes a *Mi Shebeirach* prayer that mentions that the congregation has donated money in memorialization of the dead (this was deleted in the later revisions of that prayer book by Rabbi Samuel Adler).

Why do you think donations in memorialization of the dead were deleted from early Reform prayer books? What would be an argument for including them again?

Unusual for contemporary sensibilities is the fact that *Kaddish Yatom* is not included in the traditional *Yizkor*. This is because the traditional *Yizkor* is recited at the end of the Torah service, as part of the community "good and welfare" blessings recited on behalf of the congregation while the Torah scrolls are out. However, in all of the Reform prayer books, *Kaddish Yatom* forms part of *Hazkarat N'shamot*. Generally, the version of the prayer that appears at this point is the elaborated one that originated in the Hamburg Temple prayer book, which actually includes paragraphs about "the departed whom we now remember."

A fuller, freestanding *Yizkor* service was fashioned in most Reform prayer books by the addition of psalm texts: Psalm 90, for example, *Adonai maon atah hayita lanu* ("O God, You have been our refuge in all generations"); Psalm 16, *Shiviti* ("I have set God before me at all times"); later in the 1940 *UPB* in English, Psalm 23 ("The Lord is my shepherd"), and then in *Gates of Repentance* in Hebrew, *Adonai ro-i*; in *Gates of Repentance*, Psalm 121, *Esa Einai* ("I lift up my eyes to the hills"), Psalm 63, *Elohim Eili Atah* ("O God, You are my God"). The 1945 *UPB-2* actually even includes an excerpt here from *Eileh Ezkarah* and responds in English with an original

Why are psalm texts an appropriate choice for this liturgical unit?

passage to the events that were unfolding in Europe at that time.

What is interesting also is the placement of *Yizkor* in the Reform prayer books. The German prayer books all keep the traditional placement, that is to say, as part of *Seder K'riat HaTorah*, after the haftarah reading, before the Torah is returned to the ark. The first prayer book to create a separate memorial service, designated as "Memorial of Departed Souls," is the one edited by Leo Merzbacher for Temple Emanu-El in 1855. Merzbacher puts this memorial liturgy in the afternoon between the "vespers" service and the concluding service, that is to say, between *Minchah* and *N'ilah*. This is the only Reform prayer book before the *Union Prayer Book*, volume 2 (1894) to locate the memorial liturgy at this point during the day.

David Einhorn, in his 1858 prayer book *Olath Tamid*, places the memorial liturgy within the afternoon service after the *S'lichot* and before the Torah is removed from the ark for the afternoon reading. Interestingly, when his son-in-law, Emil G. Hirsch, in 1886 produced a new, adapted English edition of Einhorn's prayer book for Sinai Temple in Chicago, he put the memorial liturgy after the afternoon service and before the concluding service, just like the *UPB* that had been published two years earlier and that was heavily edited by his brother-in-law, Kaufmann Kohler.

Also noteworthy, Isaac M. Wise, in his 1866 High Holy Day volume of *Minhag America*, places the memorial liturgy in the Yom Kippur evening service before *Aleinu*, following Spanish-Portuguese custom. The custom of the *Union Prayer Book* to recite *Yizkor* prayers in the afternoon right before *N'ilah* (with the hope that people who come for *Yizkor* will stay for *N'ilah*) has effectively become the North American Reform tradition.

Yizkor: Sources

Historical Origins

Yizkor prayers for family members originated in the Rhineland during the era of the Crusades, together with many other Jewish mourning and memorialization practices (*Av HaRachamim, Eileh Ezkerah, Yahrzeit, Kaddish Yatom*)—in context of Rhineland Christian memorial practices (All Souls' Day, All Saints' Day, with memorial candles); they eventually spread from Germany to the rest of the Jewish world:

> They developed there because that is where a cult of the local Jewish martyrs of 1096 emerged as a coherent set of practices that became part of a regional Jewish collective memory. The rites designed to remember the special martyrs of Germany developed in central and eastern Europe into broader memorializations of the dead of every Jewish family. The relative absence of this cult in memory of the dead among Jews from Muslim lands points to the regional origins of these rites and prayers. (Marcus, 227–28)

Yizkor: family memorial (included donating charity—*matnat yad*—on behalf of the souls of the dead, who also need atonement and deliverance) initially recited only on Yom Kippur after the Torah reading; spread to three festivals by the early fifteenth century (Maharil); Eastern Europe by the seventeenth century (mentioned by Mordecai Jaffe in *Levush*); *El Malei Rachamim* following Chmielnicki massacres.

Reform Development of *Yizkor*

The Memorial Service is distinctively ours. . . . Though rooted in memorial prayers that reach back a few centuries, "Yizkor" (as it was known) was at best a tiny interlude at the end of the Morning Service, by the time the Reform Movement was born. But Reform Jews were convinced of the merit of a deeper experience of memorializing the dead on Yom Kippur. So they granted the Memorial Service its own structural autonomy, an idea that has since been adopted by Conservative and Orthodox Jews as well. (Hoffman, 147)

Reform Belief in Immortality

We reassert the doctrine of Judaism that the soul is immortal, grounding the belief on the divine nature of human spirit, which forever finds bliss in righteousness and misery in wickedness. We reject as ideas not rooted in Judaism, the beliefs both in bodily resurrection and in Gehenna and Eden (Hell and Paradise) as abodes for everlasting punishment and reward. (Pittsburgh Platform, 1885) (The full text of the CCAR Platforms can be found at http://www.ccarnet.org/rabbis-speak/platforms/.)

Judaism affirms that man is created in the Divine image. His spirit is immortal. He is an active co-worker with God. As a child of God, he is endowed with moral freedom and is charged with the responsibility of overcoming evil and striving after ideal ends. (The Guiding Principles for Reform Judaism, 1937)

Amid the mystery we call life, we affirm that human beings, created in God's image, share in God's eternality despite the mystery we call death. (Reform Judaism: A Centenary Perspective, 1976)

We trust in our tradition's promise that, although God created us as finite beings, the spirit within us is eternal. (A Statement of Principles for Reform Judaism, 1999)

The Dead Need Kaparah

כַּפֵּר לְעַמְּךָ יִשְׂרָאֵל אֲשֶׁר פָּדִיתָ (דברים כא:ח)
כפר לעמך: אלו החיים.
אשר פדית: אלו המתים מלמד שהמתי' צריכי' כפרה.
-ספרי פרשת שופטים פיסקא סז

Absolve your people Israel whom You have redeemed (Deuteronomy 21:8).
Absolve your people Israel: these are the living . . .
Whom You have redeemed: these are the dead, which teaches that the dead need atonement. (*Sifrei, Shof'tim 67*)

Pledging צדקה/גמילות חסדים in Memory of the Dead

נהגו לידור צדקות ביום הכיפורים בעד המתים
ומזכירין נשמותיהם דהמתים ג"כ יש להם כפרה ביה"כ (מרדכי):
-שולחן ערוך אורח חיים סימן תרכא:ו

It was customary to contribute charity on Yom Kippur on behalf of the departed. [Isserles, quoting the Mordechai, adds the comment:] And we make mention of the names of the departed souls, since they also obtain atonement [absolution?] on the Day of Atonement. (*Shulchan Aruch, Orach Chayim* 621:6)

Yizkor as Catharsis

A swift comparison between the nineteenth-century American prayerbooks and their European correlates shows the former by and large to be on a somewhat grander scale, and more involved and imposing. The suggestion might be ventured that the elaborateness of the American *Yizkor* Service stems from an implicit wish to ward off or cleanse oneself of guilt, [satisfying] a felt need for a *kippur* or *kaparah* between the generations. . . . The role of the Yom Kippur *Yizkor* Service as an occasion for catharsis was to last a fairly long time, if not at least an entire century, chiefly because of the two major waves of immigration and their overlap. (Friedland, 277)

Basic Bibliography

Jeffrey M. Cohen, *Understanding the High Holyday Services* (London: Routledge & Kegan Paul, 1983).

Solomon B. Freehof, "Hazkarath Neshamoth," *Hebrew Union College Annual* 36 (1965): 179–89.

Eric L. Friedland, "The Atonement Memorial Service in the American Machzor," *Hebrew Union College Annual*, vol. LV (Cincinnati: HUC, 1984).

Daniel Goldschmidt, *Machzor l'Yamim HaNora-im* (Jerusalem: Koren, 1970).

Lawrence A. Hoffman, ed., *Gates of Understanding 2: Appreciating the Days of Awe* (New York: CCAR, 1984).

Ivan R. Marcus, *The Jewish Life Cycle: Rites of Passage from Biblical to Modern Times* (Seattle: University of Washington Press, 2004), 227–55.

Yizkor: Guided Meditations and Other Creative Approaches

Rabbi Elie Kaplan Spitz

The bulk of this presentation is guided meditation. To enact the presenter's words, have someone read this piece aloud to you.

I have done a setup for *Yizkor* in many different ways. The basic goal is to provide a pause before beginning the liturgy to enable people to shift and go inward. My goal is before people recite words, to draw to mind the person or people that they are seeking to remember, and even to connect on some emotional level with them. Now, there are different ways of doing this, depending on the time that I want to allocate to the setup and to the nature of the service.

The simplest is simply to acknowledge a need for a pause and to say to people: This is *Yizkor*, the opportunity to remember, the opportunity to bring to mind our loved ones who are in many ways responsible for our being here, and to recall them as people of flesh and blood who touched us and whose memory endures in us. Please take a moment before you recite the words to close your eyes and to bring to mind an image of the person whom you wish to remember. See the color of their hair, the color of their eyes. Bring an image, a picture, a hologram of them before you, and feel their presence and their love. And feeling that presence, now recite these words in their honor.

Now, that's the simplest way to begin, but there is a more invested way that I often do as well that creates a more profound experience, an experience that can surprise people in terms of feeling the presence of a departed loved one. It would go something as follows, and you might even consider rather than taking notes, if you are, to just allow

165

yourself to have an experience and in doing so to be able to potentially use something like this as a setup.

It would be as follows, a more developed imagery. Please for those who would wish to participate, close your eyes and place your feet flat on the ground, and allow yourself to relax. Breathe out all tension and breathe in calm. Breathe out judgment and breathe in trust. See yourself sitting in a room, feeling deep calm. The room is bare except for the chair in which you are seated. The door opens and your loved one or loved ones for whom you will remember enter into your presence. Pause and look at your loved one, see his or her physical appearance, the color of her hair, perhaps even a smell, and rise from your chair and reach out and take her hand in yours. Feel the goodness of her presence. Allow yourself to feel the goodness of what was your many encounters.

And now, pause and listen as your loved one shares a word with you expressing a blessing. Allow yourself to listen to this loved one bless you. And now hold onto that blessing as a gift and express in your own words a blessing of love to this person—"Dear God, thank You for the blessing of . . ."—and begin to share how this person was a blessing in your life. And remember the words that you shared, and now embrace this loved one and pause, feeling the goodness of her love. Let go of the embrace, and if there is another person there for whom you would say *Yizkor,* likewise go over and take his or her hands in yours and listen. Listen as this second loved one blesses you, and now share your words of blessing in return. Pause, and if there are others, let them together bless you. And now bless those who have spoken last and pause.

Remember the words that have been shared, and more, feel the goodness of your loved ones, knowing that in their life and in their deeds, they left you feeling loved, they left you with a legacy, a legacy of blessing. Thank them for their presence in your life. And now, they begin to leave the room, walking toward the door, opening the door, leaving one by one. As the door closes, take a seat again in the chair, breathe out any tension and breathe in the feeling of love and goodness. Remember the words of blessing and hold them close to you.

In a moment you will recite the *Yizkor*, and when you do, know that those whom you just shared time with endure for you, always near you, always close to you. You are in the land of the living and yet your loved ones continue to be a source of love and nurturing. Their words continue to endure as blessing. We'll count from three to one, and at one you will return fully to this space, yet feeling calm, feeling blessed, feeling ready to rise to honor your loved ones with *Yizkor*, with words of remembrance, words that draw you toward them, knowing that their presence endures for you. Three, two, one.

Slowly opening your eyes and adjusting to this space, the space of community, allowing yourself to be of clarity of mind and wholeness of spirit as we as a community engage in *Yizkor*, words of memory. If you participated, I encourage you to again know that you return to this place of awareness with the recognition of the power of the mind to transport us to other places while simultaneously being present fully in the moment too.

I close with that because it's silent on the other end. I don't know how the impact has been for you, but I will say just a few words to pull this together. As a pulpit rabbi, just completing my twenty-fourth year in my community, more and more I'm aware that my opportunity is to create religious experiences for people, that the words are, to quote Reb Zalman Schachter-Shalomi, like freeze-dried coffee. They are crystals that need juices, that need the hot water to make them an uplifting brew, and that the words alone without imagination often don't touch, don't elevate, don't uplift. So in my preaching as well as in my liturgy, I try to enable my community to bring themselves, including their imagination, into the experience, thereby being touched and elevated. And *Yizkor* in particular, which touches people so emotionally by virtue of who they are seeking to remember, is an opportunity to make it real.

For more on contemplative High Holy Day worship, see Rabbi Laura Geller's presentation "Who Shall I Say Is Calling?" on metaphors in the *machzor* on page 231.

I just did it in the moment, and I tend to do my guided meditations in the moment. I focused it on the exchange of blessing. Sometimes it might have a sentence to share with you. It needs to be brief. It might simply be without words. It might simply be to hold hands and feel their presence, to feel an awareness of the incompleteness of the relationship and yet the wholeness that is also part of the gift of connection. So what takes place in that moment may differ. There's no hard and fast one way to do it, and I like to change it so there's an element of surprise; but in sum, my goal is to create a pause to engage the imagination in order to enable an experience that creates a context for *Yizkor* to be more impactful, more real, and a source of healing, wholeness, and even holiness.

Yizkor End-of-Call Discussion

Rabbi Deborah Prinz, Dr. Richard S. Sarason, Rabbi Donald B. Rossoff, Rabbi Elie Kaplan Spitz

Rabbi Deborah Prinz

I'm going to ask Rabbi Rossoff and Dr. Sarason a very general question. What do you think congregants are looking for in a *Yizkor* service? What do you think rabbis might be looking for in a *Yizkor* service? Could you help us think about that?

Dr. Richard S. Sarason

Beyond the sorts of issues that Don raised in his presentation, it's very significant that one of the early Reform innovations was to enlarge this service in recognition, I think, of what congregants really are looking for. We've all, or will at some point, suffer loss. How we deal with matters of life and death, how we remember on the Day of Atonement our parents, our loved ones, who have died, is extremely important. I think that both congregants and rabbis are looking for and appreciate a time and a space to enact these kinds of memorializations. That's why everybody, whatever else they may or may not do on Yom Kippur, comes to the memorial service—because it addresses something that is real in all of our lives: loss and death. Everybody knows and loves somebody and has lost somebody. Opportunities to reflect on this, on the meaning of life and death and love and loss, and—

as Don has said—ways by which we may find hope to move beyond despair, to move on and move forward with these people whom we love and we have lost, ways in which we carry them forward—this is what *Yizkor* provides. Here is an opportunity to think about these big human issues, through insightful meditations, and to express our feelings through prayers. I think it's hugely important.

Rabbi Donald B. Rossoff

I think Dr. Sarason hit the nail on the head. There's one other element that we didn't talk about so much, which especially our Reform forebears put in the service, which was a recognition of our own finitude. I think in the back of our minds, all of us know that at any moment we or a loved one could be taken from us without warning. We are all here for just a short time, and I think if we dwelled on that, if we kept that in mind as real as it is every moment of our day, we would go crazy. So I think *Yizkor* allows us moments to look that in the face. I know Rabbi Yitz Greenberg talks about Yom Kippur in total as a time that we rehearse our own deaths, we see our own finitude.

How does it feel for you to contemplate your own finitude? How do you (or might you) talk about it with your family or friends?

One of my favorite parts of Reform *Yizkor* liturgy is the reading actually originally written by Rabbi Isaac Mayer Wise that talks about how each one of us is subject to the same end, and all of us, like Moses on Mount Nebo, can see the promised land but we'll never get there. We lose our hold on life as a child lets go of its toys—I mean, that's real stuff and it's stuff that, as he said—actually, this was added later—makes the whole world kin. And so looking, in a sense, death in the face hopefully helps us understand the preciousness of every moment that we have in our lives and every moment that we have with our loved ones.

Dr. Richard S. Sarason

Yes, that's hugely important. In every death we encounter, we ultimately see our own.

Rabbi Elie Kaplan Spitz

As an extension of the words that Don was sharing, I find that in my own education, I never had a conversation with my teachers as to whether they personally believed in the survival of the soul. That kind of agnosticism or at least silence on that topic led me to write a book for Jewish Lights called *Does the Soul Survive?: A Jewish Journey to Belief in Afterlife, Past Lives, and Living with Purpose*. And colleagues have shared that that book, too, with a kind of personal approach to the questions of what do I believe about the survival of the soul and what does the Jewish tradition as a whole teach, as also an opportunity before *Yizkor* to answer a question that is on most people's minds by virtue of being human that all too often has been ignored from the pulpit.

Elie Kaplan Spitz, *Does the Soul Survive?: A Jewish Journey to Belief in Afterlife, Past Lives, and Living with Purpose* (Woodstock, VT: Jewish Lights Publishing, 2000).

Rabbi Deborah Prinz

I'm now going to pose a question to our speakers from a colleague who asks about the basic assumption that *Yizkor* still has the power it once had, that, whatever other services people might or might not attend, they still come to *Yizkor*. That's true for a certain generation, writes this colleague, but this colleague is not so sure that it's as true as it once was. So I'm wondering about your thoughts with regard to that.

Rabbi Elie Kaplan Spitz

I find that there is less compulsion to attend *Yizkor* than in the past. There isn't the same sense of responsibility and attendant guilt to attend *Yizkor* as previous generations, and yet I do find it's still widely attended and is for rabbis and community an opportunity for powerful connection.

Rabbi Donald B. Rossoff

I would second that. I think we all know that our people are losing the sense of obligation and are looking for meaning and community and connectedness, and so certainly will not have that same baggage—people won't be bringing that same baggage of obligation to the moment, which means many who might be there won't be. But I think we have the potential to create the meaningful moments that will make that happen, and then of course I know many of us experience the post-*Yizkor* exodus, and I think we can try to address that as well going forward.

Dr. Richard S. Sarason

I would second that, too. I do think that for psychodynamic and life-cycle reasons, yes, there is a group of people at a certain age that may not be coming now; but I think that, as people get older, these things tend to resonate more and more.

Yizkor **Wrap-Up**

1. Since the separate *Yizkor* service is a Reform creation, can we rewind the clock and simply reinsert this ritual into the Yom Kippur Torah service, or is it too late to put the *Yizkor* genie back in the bottle?

2. Why do or don't members of your community attend *Yizkor*? How can answering this question help us to craft a more meaningful *Yizkor* experience for them?

3. How can the other opportunities for *Yizkor* in the Jewish calendar, on the three festivals, influence our approach to *Yizkor* on Yom Kippur?

4. What did you learn from these presentations on *Yizkor* that you would like to implement in your community's High Holy Day worship?

N'ilah

Text, Context, and History:
A Background of N'ilah

Rabbi Richard N. Levy

There's a custom that when *Kol Nidrei* gets under way, with people on the pulpit holding the *sifrei Torah*, the ark is empty. And there's a stark symbolism there, for it becomes a reminder of another kind of *aron*, namely that in which we are buried at the end of our life. But it's also a reminder of our life at the time. How are we going to fill the *aron* that is our life? And as the day waxes and wanes, there are many opportunities for that filling, so that by *N'ilah*, we are standing before an ark that is filled with *sifrei Torah*. And there is something about the *N'ilah* service that brings that realization that we are facing our own mortality.

What choreographic or dramatic elements do you incorporate into your High Holy Day worship? What is the emotional impact of these elements?

Originally, *N'ilah* was offered daily in the time of the *Maamad*, where groups from the community whose priests were serving at the Temple would gather. *N'ilah* was offered by them, and it was called *N'ilat Sh'arim*, the drawing close of the gates. The name comes from that period because it marked the time when the gates of the Temple were closed. But later, outside the Temple precinct, it was said only on public fast days. So the closing service, certainly after the Temple was destroyed, disappeared from every other part of the liturgy. It was retained on Yom Kippur, where it came at the exact time of the forgiveness of sins. The sense was that when the sun set, it took our sins with it.

The time of the end of Yom Kippur was extended. Some, like Maimonides, didn't like that idea. He and others felt that it should end at nightfall. But that sense that *N'ilah* corresponded with a time when our sins were forgiven led to several changes in the Yom Kippur liturgy. As you know, *kotveinu* (may we be written) was changed to *chotmeinu* (may we be sealed) in the Book, in the High Holy Day inclusions in *Avot*. In *Sim Shalom* also, *kotveinu* was changed to *chotmeinu*. It's there in a whole section of *Avinu Malkeinu* and in *Sim Shalom*, it's in the *nizacheir v'neichateim*, "may we be remembered or may we be preserved and sealed." Other changes were the addition of a prayer that begins *Atah notein yad l'foshim*. And particularly the middle of it, which says to God, You know that our end is *rimah v'tolei-ah*, that our end is worms and maggots—and that's why You increase our *s'lichah. Mah anu? Meh chayeinu? Meh chasdeinu? Mah tzidkeinu?* Those are quite some questions to ask after we have been praying and reviewing our sins all day and all night long. But it emphasizes the sense that *the* time is coming when sins will be forgiven. After the *Amidah* comes, of course, in *N'ilah*, the major conclusions, and they also build. So, we say the *Sh'ma* once, as you know, and there's one understanding that in that single saying, we take upon ourselves the *ol malchut shamayim* and the *ol mitzvot* just in saying the words of the *Sh'ma* itself. We respond then by saying *Baruch shem k'vod malchuto l'olam va-ed* three times. One interpretation is that it reminds us of the statement *Adonai melech*, God was the ruler before Creation, *Adonai malach*, God has been ruling until now and thereafter, *Adonai yimloch l'olam va-ed*, that God will reign in the world-to-come. And as difficult as the notion of *malchut* is for us, we are brought back to it in *N'ilah* at the very end to recall and to experience God's eternal sovereignty over our life and over the world. Then we say *Adonai hu haElohim* seven times. That is an allusion to I Kings 19, particularly verse 39, when Elijah engages the Baal priests in the great contest, and God defeats them by sending down fire upon Elijah's offering. Elijah says twice *Adonai hu haElohim*. And so that casts *N'ilah* in the sense of another grand cosmic battle between God's sovereignty and all the other things in the world that on other days we make sovereign in place of God. But at this time, we remember no, it's not power, it's not titles, it's not what we own, it's *Adonai hu haElohim*.

Another interpretation for saying it seven times, which may appeal to some of you and not others, is that after the *Shechinah* has been with us, has sojourned with us during Yom Kippur, we escort the *Shechinah* back up through the seven firmaments of heaven, so that with each saying we help God's *Shechinah*, God's earth-dwelling presence, to return and unite with the godhead. And that implies some sadness. It's a little like *Havdalah* when we say good-bye to the *n'shamah y'teirah*, the extra Shabbat soul we say farewell to, God's *Shechinah*, which has been with us, and at this moment when our sins are being forgiven, God is going to take God's earthbound presence back for renewal itself. And then, after that there is the shofar blast, a single blast in the Diaspora, traditionally three in *Eretz Yisrael*. And there too this sense of escorting the *Shechinah* back through the seven realms of heaven is suggested; perhaps this shofar blast may have been inspired by Psalm 47:6: *alah Elohim bit'ruah*—God has ascended with the sound of a *t'ruah*. Some people like to think that it recalls the blast when Moses first ascended Mount Sinai on Rosh Chodesh Elul to receive the second tablets

What is the significance of maintaining a sense of humility and awe before God?

How do you often feel at the close of Yom Kippur? Which is a more appropriate emotional response to *N'ilah*—sadness or joy (or another emotion)? Why?

and sounded again when he descended. And other people like to think that perhaps it is a reminder of the *Yovel*, whose name means "shofar blast," and which took place on Yom Kippur. And, of course, it brings together not only the themes of *malchut* from earlier on, but also the sound of the shofar. And it helps in that remarkable feeling that the gates leading us to sin are closed.

What is the difference between conceptualizing *N'ilah* as the gates leading us to sin are closing as opposed to the gates of repentance are closing?

Another of the liturgical changes is that we don't say the full *Al Cheit*, we only say the brief *Ashamnu*, and so we don't want God to remember at that moment of forgiveness all the things that we have done but only the short symbolic one of *Ashamnu*. And one might even say that one might hear in that final shofar blast, the ascendance not only of God's *Shechinah* into the highest heavens, but the descent of our pure clean-washed soul, where perhaps it has also taken refuge during Yom Kippur, as God in the seven heavens has cleansed it and purified it so that, as on Sinai, God ascends and we descend, rather the opposite of what happened with Moses and God at Sinai. And we feel cleansed, and we feel ready to start living again as we see the sun descend, carrying our sins into the ocean with it.

How do you relate to this mystical interpretation of *N'ilah*? Does this teaching help or hinder how you approach this liturgical unit?

And some of us are near one of those oceans, so it's easy to imagine that, with the shofar sound, we are cleansed once more, and the gates have closed, and we literally fly out of the synagogue with our own seven heavens before us to ascend.

N'ilah: **Contemporary Challenges**
Rabbi Edwin C. Goldberg

I'm going to be speaking on the challenge of *N'ilah*, and I want to start by sharing with you a memory that I have when I grew up in Kansas City at Congregation B'nai Jehudah, often just called "The Temple." And what I remember is sitting in the sanctuary, there would be some kind of afternoon service, when I was old enough to go to that I would remember that, and then we would have *N'ilah*. We would do the *N'ilah* service, and I was very hungry, and I was very excited because I could see we were three pages away from the finish, two pages away from the finish . . . And then all of a sudden, the rabbi would announce that we were continuing with *Yizkor*. We would turn back in the book, and for a hungry kid that was just very annoying. We would turn back in the book and we would do the full *Yizkor* service in *UPB-2*. And then, when that was finished and there was only one page left in *N'ilah*, we would do *N'ilah*. And when I was old enough to ask my dad, he simply said that this is the way that the rabbi ensured that people would stay for *N'ilah*, because they would stay for *Yizkor*. And I was young enough—or old enough, I guess— to know that that was a trick. It maybe was pragmatic and maybe it worked, but it seemed to me that if *N'ilah* is an important service, it shouldn't be something at which people are tricked into staying, especially hungry people and kids at that. And then it seemed like, at least for me, if we were going to do *N'ilah* because we had to do it and trick people into staying, wasn't that sort of like when my mom made me stay home an extra day of school

Does your community also struggle with retaining people for *N'ilah*? How do you navigate this situation?

because I was really feeling better, but just to make sure. You know, *N'ilah* is sort of like just to make sure you've got that *t'shuvah* thing going.

And I think there are some folks who still look at it that way. I know that many congregations seem to be making *N'ilah* end earlier and earlier because the break the fast in the suburbs is sometimes miles and miles away. So, one could argue that we're talking about something that we've got to do, but we're not real excited about it. Of course, that's ironic because the truth is, not only is *N'ilah* beautiful, but it's also not simply going through the motions one more time before we call it a day or a year. It is nuanced, however. So it does take, I think, a fair amount of effort for *amcha*, even colleagues, to understand how important it is. And I know there are certain things that can make it seem very important, like the shofar blast at the end, or for some congregations, the *aron hakodesh* open the whole time. But I also think that in the actual *t'filah* itself there are some very, very interesting things that, as far as confronting the challenge of *N'ilah*, offer solutions to explore.

I'm going to share a couple of those. But first, I think if we look at the bigger picture, we see that *N'ilah* really isn't just the end of Yom Kippur. It's the bridge for what happens next. Because if we think about it, *N'ilah* is about going back to the world, but hopefully we're going back to the world, as Rabbi Levy said so beautifully, with more Torah in our lives and directed in a new way. And if the last few weeks have been tearing us down, so to speak, to see who we really are, and now we're being built back up again, Sukkot comes as part of that, not just because we build the sukkah, but because that's about dealing with the truths we've learned and moving forward. There is an *aron* waiting for

How can we make this bridge more explicit?

us, and on Sukkot we're still thinking about that. I like to call sitting in my sukkah sitting in the truth booth. We're still dealing with that, but hopefully we're moving on to embrace life despite the truth that we know.

As I was looking through the traditional *N'ilah* service, and those of us editing the *machzor*, of course, will always begin with that, it seemed to be something very striking, especially if you think about we're just going through the motions one more time, which of course is not the case. But let's assume we were. We're doing *Ashamnu* and we're doing *Ashamnu* like we do *Ashamnu*. We get through it. And all of sudden, instead of the *Vidui Rabbah*, the *Al Cheit*—we're all ready for the *Al Cheit* because that's what happens after *Ashamnu*, we're on autopilot—they're not there. And I think that is a dramatic—it's nuanced, I suppose, because we're hungry and tried, but that's a dramatic—that's the dog that did not bark. I mean, what happened to the *Al Cheit*? Are we done sinning? Is that what's going on? That's hard to believe. So then, what is there instead? And there are two new paragraphs, only in *N'ilah*. *Atah notein* starts one and *Atah nivdalta*. And *Vidui* is—we call it the *Vidui Zuta* because of *Ashamnu*, but also because this is dealing with *Vidui* too.

And there's one verse that just struck me as very important: *l'maan nechdal mei-oshek yadeinu*. Translated many different ways, but one way is "to withdraw our hands from all that we have taken wrongfully." We want the strength, we're praying to God, to withdraw our hands from all that we've done deceitfully or all we have taken wrongfully. What is this about taking wrongfully? Well, to put it another way, of all the sins that we've listed in *Al Cheit*, thievery is not one of the most popular ones. In fact, if anything, *lashon hara* is, I think, the most quantitatively important one. So why thievery? If we're going to just put in one here, why thievery of all of them? What do we learn from that? Why do we single out the sin of theft to beg forgiveness for in the closing moments of Yom Kippur?

I have found two explanations to address *l'maan nechdal mei-oshek yadeinu*. One is from *Sefer HaTodaah* from Eliyahu Kitov—Rabbi Avraham Kitov, born in 1912 in Warsaw, moved to Palestine in the 1930s, was an educator. And he writes that the sin of theft must be here a representation of all the sins that are *bein adam l'chaveiro*. In other words, we're in *N'ilah*, *bein adam laMakom*, we're *yotzei*, we've done it, we can feel good, go have break fast. But, *bein adam l'chaveiro* is something else, you don't get off so easily. And so Yom Kippur reminds us we cannot atone for those sins that we've committed against other human beings until we've personally dealt with them. And thievery is, I suppose, as good as any.

By the way, just as an aside, this year for the first time, we really got into the different *midot* for each day of counting of the Omer. I know it's based on chapter 6 of *Pirkei Avot* and you can make your own *midot*, but I found a list, and so the last *midah* that we struggle with—and of course, I'm speaking about myself as well as my colleagues—the last *midah* we struggle with right before Shavuot, of all of them, what is it? *B'shem omro*, about proper attribution. So it's interesting that not only do we talk about thievery at the end of *N'ilah*, but also go ahead and take some stuff. Imitation is the sincerest form of flattery. But by taking care with *b'shem omro*, by attributing the sources of our material, another kind of thievery avoided.

I want to give you one other point of view as far as why we mentioned thievery here, *oshek*. This

Exercise: Compare the forty-eight *midot* listed in *Mishnah Avot* 6:6 to the litany of sins in the *Vidui Rabbah*. How are the two lists similar, and how are they different? How does each list teach us to be better (i.e., more ethical) people?

is from *Chidushei HaRim*, Yitzchak Meir Alter, the Gerer Rebbe, as he was often called. Born 1799, died 1866. First rebbe of the Ger Chasidic dynasty, and he, of course, is very well known. Now, according to the Gerer Rebbe, the theft refers to that which we steal from God when we do not use the powers God gave us for the purposes God intended. So this is very different. This isn't theft as representation of *bein adam l'chaveiro*, this is more like *bein adam l'atzmo* or *laMakom*. In other words, all that was taken wrongfully is that which we've taken from God because we haven't consecrated to God's purposes. In other words, I would argue that it's stealing away our potential, not living up to our potential. And it's really the consequence and effect of *Al Cheit*. As Rabbi Sidney Greenberg used to say, he always wanted to give a sermon about Nathaniel Hawthorne, who never wrote a particular story but he had his notes for it. The notes say: I want to write a story where the principal character never appears. So I think that might be certainly where the *Chidushei HaRim* is coming from. In other words, is that true of us? Have we not lived up to our potential and, therefore, are we guilty of theft because God gave us life and therefore we are indebted? And so, as the final moments of Yom Kippur slip away, we should think about the sins or the wrongdoings that have caused us to remain small, limited our potential, inhibited our relationship with God. And so, this is a form of *gozel*. We have not fulfilled our debt—that's thievery.

To go back to the challenge of *N'ilah*, on the one hand, it's to not just make it something where we have to trick people into staying or guilt people into staying. One year I was announcing, "Please stay for *N'ilah*," and the thunder clapped, and I had a few more people stay, so that was good. But you

Why do you think the sin of thievery is singled out in *N'ilah*?

can't count on that every year. So the challenge of *N'ilah* is not so much to find a trick, or to beg them, or to guilt them, but rather to find a way to make *N'ilah* speak to the people's soul work so they realize this is a very important way to end Yom Kippur. Last thought: the late Rabbi Alan Lew once wrote, "We all have a destiny, but we don't all get there," and maybe the end of *N'ilah* is to remind us that we have that destiny, we need to get there, or as Abraham Joshua Heschel said, "Let's not be the messenger who forgot the message."

Possibilities for Reconceptualizing *N'ilah*

Rabbi Leon A. Morris

I wanted to speak to two categories of ideas related to *N'ilah*, the first inside the *machzor* and then the second what operates beyond the *machzor*. First, in terms of inside the *machzor*, if you have the source sheet, this would be the first source. One of the central pieces of the liturgy for *N'ilah* is the centrality of the *Sh'losh-Esreih Midot*, the thirteen attributes of God. This creates a kind of bookend because it's also a central part of the *S'lichot* section of Yom Kippur evening, of *Kol Nidrei*. We begin with this recitation of the *Sh'losh-Esreih Midot*. We end Yom Kippur with the recitation of the *Sh'losh-Esreih Middot*. There's great variance over how many times it's chanted. In many traditions, whatever the number is that they were recited on *Kol Nidrei*, it's twice that number for *N'ilah*. So, in some traditions it's four times at *Kol Nidrei*, eight times at *N'ilah*. There are communities that recite it thirteen times.

See the sources on page 191.

I wanted to just look at the Talmudic source for that, which is the first source on the sheet from the *Bavli, Rosh HaShanah 17b*. And it's commenting on the verse from *Sh'mot*, from Exodus 34:6, of *vayaavor Adonai al panav vayikra*, "the Eternal passed in front of him," in front of Moses, "and called." And here, Rabbi Yochanan is reading it in a very literal way. Would it really? God passed in front of him and called? Rabbi Yochanan said, "Had the verse not been written, it would have been impossible to say such a thing." And then he goes on to say, "This teaches that the Almighty wrapped himself in a tallit as a *sh'liach tzibur* and showed Moses the order

Why do you think this piece of liturgy is so central to the High Holy Days?

185

of prayer. And God said to him, 'Any time Israel sins, let them perform this service—the recitation of the *Sh'losh-Esreih Midot*—before Me and I shall forgive them.'" So, it's loaded with this midrashic understanding that we have the power to remind God that God is *erech apayim v'rav chesed.* And this is explained beautifully in the Yom Kippur liturgy for the new *machzor, Mishkan HaNefesh,* it's kind of paraphrased—this is our second text—just by saying, "This portrait of an intimate relationship with God, the Holy One wrapped in a prayer shawl showing Moses how to pray conveys the spiritual promise of the songs of forgiveness, for this is the moment when the veil was lifted from our face. This is the moment when we are no longer hidden from our Maker. This is the precious moment of renewing the relationship." So that's some beautiful phrasing that tries to reclaim the centrality of this part of the liturgy.

There is also, in terms of creative possibilities then, there is a great deal that can be done with the *Sh'losh-Esreih Midot,* and that same Talmudic *sugya* that we spoke about a few minutes ago for *Rosh Ha-Shanah* 17b then tries to offer some kind of interpretation of each of the thirteen attributes. And just as an example of how much potential interpretive possibility there is with each of them, I wanted to just highlight the first: *Adonai, Adonai.* So, in that Talmudic passage in *Rosh HaShanah* 17b, the Gemara understands it as what's being said is God is God before a person sins and God is God after a person sins and does *t'shuvah.* And source number three is from a new book called *In His Mercy: Understanding the Thirteen Midot* by Ezra Bick, and he plays up on this little interpretive sentence from *Rosh HaShanah* in which he says that what this really tells us is—I love this quote—history is completely different af-

Ezra Bick, *In His Mercy: Understanding the Thirteen Midot,* trans. David Silverberg (New Milford, CT: Koren Publishers Jerusalem, 2011).

ter sin because amazingly, it continues. So here in the repetition of *Adonai, Adonai* with this Talmudic understanding that it's a reminder that God is our God before we sin and after we sin, and then *t'shuvah* is the possibility of allowing history to continue, that the world doesn't fall apart when we sin but that we have an opportunity to reconstruct it.

I want to pick up a little bit on some of the material that Rabbi Levy and Rabbi Goldberg mentioned about the distinctive liturgical additions in *N'ilah*. And here, if you have the source sheet, you can see all those parts that they were referring to that come as a substitution for the long confession. We have the *Ashamnu, Bagadnu, Gazalnu,* and then exactly when we expect, because we've done it so many times, to move on to the *Vidui Rabbah,* the long confession, instead we have the words that are distinctive to *N'ilah,* which I want to highlight, begin with *Mah nomar l'fanecha yosheiv marom*—"What can we say before You, You who dwell on high?" And I think that's a very deliberate introduction to the fact that we don't have the long *Vidui,* that we basically are saying, "What else can we say? We've said this *Vidui* so many times, and just a moment ago we said the short *Vidui,* and we're not going to go on with the long *Vidui,* because in truth, *mah nomar l'fanecha,* "what can we really say before You?" Both Rabbi Levy and Rabbi Goldberg mentioned just a sentence later what our teacher Rabbi Lawrence Hoffman indicated to us in some teaching that we did with him, and it seems to be borne out by a study of the liturgy itself, the key line of *N'ilah, Atah notein yad l'foshim*—"You stretch out a hand to those who sin." And having made our best attempt for twenty-five hours at this point, we now rely on God. Extend Your hand to us. And it's in that same paragraph, of course, that same section that we

How does the message of these texts impact your understanding of sin?

Do these questions to God reveal a defeatist attitude or a final attempt to appeal to God or something else altogether?

then move on to what Rabbi Levy mentioned, *Mah anu? Meh chayeinu? Meh chasdeinu? Mah tzidkeinu? Mah yisheinu?* "What are we? What are our lives? What is our kindness? What is our righteousness?"

I think a lot could be done with that. And one of the challenges, one of the challenges that we're wrestling with as editors of the new *machzor* is these few phrases that form the distinctive part of the *N'ilah* liturgy might be lost in the midst of all the other liturgy that traditionally occurs in this service, might be lost in the context of the larger *Amidah*. And that points us to source number five on the sheet, which is in the context of a Talmudic discussion about what *N'ilah* actually is. And there is an interesting Talmudic dispute between Rav and Sh'muel in which Rav says *N'ilah* is an extra *Amidah*. It's an *Amidah* followed by some other prayers, just as is the case for *Maariv* and *Shacharit* and *Musaf* and *Minchah*. And Sh'muel says no, *N'ilah* actually consists only of this distinctive stuff that begins with—well he kind of telegraphs it as *Mah anu? Meh chayeinu?*, but we can assume that it's all the stuff that begins with *Mah nomar l'fanecha yosheiv marom.* So, this is a very interesting, and I think for us, perhaps a very consequential Talmudic text in which Sh'muel floats the opinion that *N'ilah* may not actually be an *Amidah* but only these other key lines: *Mah nomar l'fanecha; Atah notein yad l'foshim; Mah anu? Meh chayeinu? Meh chasdeinu?*

Now, the Talmud seems to go on to refute Sh'muel's view that *N'ilah* is not an *Amidah* and ends up presenting what's traditionally done today, which is a combination of Rav and Sh'muel, which is yes, an extra *Amidah* for *N'ilah*, but also these special prayers about what can we say before You, extend a hand. But I think what's interesting to us is this minority opinion of Sh'muel, and it's something that we're thinking deeply about, that Sh'muel's view, that *N'ilah* may not consist of an *Amidah*, may allow some additional creative approaches that allow us to highlight these very distinctive parts of the liturgy for *N'ilah*. In other words, if we're concerned about these key lines of *N'ilah* being lost, we may have in Shmuel's Talmudic opinion a possibility of a different sort of approach, an approach that particularly highlights these key pieces.

So let me just offer a handful of ideas of things that go beyond the *machzor*. And a lot of these are things that many of us on the call are already doing. But I think it bears mentioning because although we have an awareness that the liturgy is an indispensable tool, there are many non-liturgical aspects that can enhance the experience. It was mentioned the custom of opening the ark—the ark is traditionally opened for the repetition of the *Amidah* in *N'ilah* and then it's kept open. And this idea of an open ark has, of course, resonances of the gates that are still open but about to close just as the ark is about to close, and it contributes to the drama of the moment. There are many of us who have our congregations invite them, those are able to physically, to stand for the entire service, to stand from the moment that the ark is opened for the *Amidah* to the very end.

Many of our congregations use *N'ilah* as an opportunity for everyone in the congregation to approach the ark, to come up on the bimah, either throughout the *N'ilah* service, or in my congregation we do it during a repetition of the *Sh'losh-Esreih Midot* that we're singing again, and again, and again, to come before the ark and to offer their final prayer before the closing of the gates.

Dr. Levy taught us beautifully about the ending of the *Sh'ma* one time, *Baruch shem* three times,

How could highlighting these key verses alter the tone of your *N'ilah* worship and the conclusion of Yom Kippur? How else could you utilize highlighting to emphasize certain aspects of High Holy Day liturgy?

and *Adonai hu haElohim* seven times. Many of us have found that rather than those being sort of very prescribed musical pieces, that inviting people to call them out, to shout them out, can be a very powerful experience, to have a congregation of people calling out in loud voices, *Adonai hu haElohim! Adonai hu haElohim!*

Many congregations invite children to come up to the bimah toward the end of *N'ilah*—for our children, sometimes dressed in white, to have front-row seats to enter the New Year with us for the final blast of the shofar. There is, in many congregations, a breaking out in song and dance with those children on the bimah to *L'shanah Habaah BiY'rushalayim* following the final blast. We have *Havdalah*, and if there are children on the bimah, I found that glow sticks kind of enhance the power of that moment.

How do these customs enhance the High Holy Day worship experience?

I just want to end with two final, sort of off the *machzor* page things. One is the greeting that is probably not well known by most of our communities, but the traditional greeting at the end of Yom Kippur, *Tizku l'shanim rabot*, that is part of the final stanza of the *piyut El Nora Alilah*. And I love what it represents, that we've had a day where we've felt so close to death—we've dressed in white, we've abstained from the most human aspects of our lives, from eating, from washing, from sexual relations—and now, having come so close to death, what we do, the very first thing, is we wish one another a long life, *Tizku l'shanim rabot*. And finally, I wonder if we might reconsider two rituals that are traditionally done before breaking the fast: *Kiddush L'vanah*, blessing the new moon, and putting the first screws in the sukkah.

How might we understand this greeting with the societal debate over quality versus quantity of life in the background?

N'ilah: Sources

1. Babylonian Talmud, *Rosh HaShanah* 17b

ויעבר ה' על פניו ויקרא, אמר רבי יוחנן: אלמלא מקרא כתוב אי
אפשר לאומרו, מלמד שנתעטף הקדוש ברוך הוא כשליח
צבור, והראה לו למשה סדר תפלה. אמר לו: כל זמן שישראל
חוטאין—יעשו לפני כסדר הזה, ואני מוחל להם. ה' ה'—אני
הוא קודם שיחטא האדם, ואני הוא לאחר שיחטא האדם
ויעשה תשובה.

"The Eternal passed in front of him and called . . ." (Exodus 34:6). Rabbi Yochanan said: Had the verse not been written, it would have been impossible to say [such a thing]—this teaches that the Almighty wrapped Himself in a tallit as a *sh'liach tzibur* and showed Moses the order of prayer. God said to him, "Any time Israel sins, let them perform this service before Me and I shall forgive them. *Adonai, Adonai*—I am the One before a person sins, and I am the One after a person sins and does *t'shuvah. . . .*"

2. *Mishkan HaNefesh* (Pilot Edition for Yom Kippur Evening)

In an astonishing midrash, the Talmudic sage Rabbi Yochanan imagined God majestically robed in tallit, teaching Moses the order of the prayers and saying to him: "Every time that Israel 'misses the mark,' let them read the Thirteen Attributes in My presence, and I will forgive them" (BT *Rosh HaShanah* 17b). This portrait of an intimate relationship with God—the Holy One wrapped in prayer shawl, showing Moses how to pray—conveys the spiritual promise of the Songs of Forgiveness. For this is the moment when the veil is lifted from our face; this is the moment when we are no longer hidden from our Maker. This is the precious moment of renewing the relationship.

3. Ezra Bick, *In His Mercy: Understanding the Thirteen Midot*

It is one thing for mortal beings to be the dwelling-place of God and the fountainhead of *kedusha* when they strive to serve God by accepting God's Torah and obeying God's laws. The sin of the golden calf logically destroys that dream. The same covenant must be recreated, but in radically new circumstances. How can corruption be the basis of sanctity? The answer is found in the mystery of the Thirteen Attributes—that God is the one who is *nesiat cheyt*—who bears sin. History is completely different after sin because, amazingly, it continues.

4. Excerpts from the *Vidui* for *N'ilah*

Short Confession (*Vidui Zuta*):

אשמנו, בגדנו, גזלנו, דברנו דופי. העוינו, והרשענו, זדנו, חמסנו, טפלנו שקר.
יעצנו רע, כזבנו, לצנו, מרדנו, נאצנו, סררנו, עוינו, פשענו, צררנו, קשינו עורף.
רשענו, שחתנו, תעבנו, תעתענו.

סרנו ממצותיך וממשפטיך הטובים ולא שוה לנו. ואתה צדיק על כל הבא עלינו,
כי אמת עשית ואנחנו הרשענו.

No Long Confession (*Vidui Rabbah*) for *N'ilah*. Instead the following appears:

מה נאמר לפניך יושב מרום, ומה נספר לפניך שוכן שחקים, הלא כל הנסתרות
והנגלות אתה יודע.

> **What can we say before You, You who dwell on high?**
> What can we declare before You, You who abide in heaven?
> Do You not know all, the hidden the revealed alike?

אתה נותן יד לפושעים, וימינך פשוטה לקבל שבים.
ותלמדינו יי אלהינו להתודות לפניך על כל עונותינו, **למען נחדל מעשק ידינו,**
ותקבלינו בתשובה שלמה לפניך כאשים וכניחוחים, למען דבריך ובעבור אשר
אמרת. אין קץ לאשי חובותינו, ואין מספר לניחוחי אשמתנו; ואתה יודע שאחריתנו
רמה ותולעה, לפיכך הרבית סליחתנו. **מה אנו, מה חיינו, מה חסדנו, מה צדקנו,**
מה ישועתנו, מה כחנו, מה גבורתנו. מה נאמר לפניך, יי אלהינו ואלהי אבותינו,
הלא כל הגבורים כאין לפניך, ואנשי השם כלא היו, וחכמים כבלי מדע,
ונבונים כבלי השכל, כי רוב מעשיהם תהו, וימי חייהם הבל לפניך; ומותר האדם
מן הבהמה אין, כי הכל הבל.

You extend Your hand to transgressors; Your right hand is outstretched to receive those who return, and You have taught us, Eternal our God, to confess before You all our iniquities, so that we may withdraw our hands from theft. . . .

5. Babylonian Talmud, *Yoma* 87b

מאי נעילת שערים? רב אמר: צלותא יתירתא, ושמואל אמר: מה אנו מה חיינו.
מיתיבי: אור יום הכפורים מתפלל שבע ומתודה, בשחרית מתפלל שבע ומתודה,
במוסף מתפלל שבע ומתודה, במנחה מתפלל שבע ומתודה, בנעילה מתפלל
שבע ומתודה—תנא היא, דתניא: יום הכפורים עם חשיכה מתפלל שבע ומתודה
וחותם בוידוי, דברי רבי מאיר, וחכמים אומרים: מתפלל שבע, ואם רצה
לחתום בוידוי—חותם. תיובתא דשמואל תיובתא. עולא בר רב נחית קמיה דרבא,
פתח באתה בחרתנו וסיים במה אנו מה חיינו ושבחיה.

What is *N'ilat Sh'arim?* Rav says: It is an extra *Amidah* prayer (i.e., the same seven blessings recited during the other *Amidah* prayers of Yom Kippur). But Sh'muel says: It consists only of the prayer, "What are we? What are our lives. . . ?" (i.e., it is not an *Amidah* prayer at all).

They challenged Sh'muel's view using the following *baraita:* On the night of Yom Kippur, one prays an *Amidah* consisting of seven blessings and confesses his sins. In *Shacharit,* one prays an *Amidah* consisting of seven blessings and confesses his sins. At *Musaf,* one prays an *Amidah* consisting of seven blessings and confesses his sins. At *Minchah,* one prays an *Amidah* consisting of seven blessings and confesses his sins. At *N'ilah,* one prays an *Amidah* consisting of seven blessings and confesses his sins, and he ends with a blessing about confession. This is the opinion of Rabbi Meir. But the Sages say: One prays an *Amidah* consisting of seven blessings and confesses his sins, and if he wants to end with a blessing about confession he may do so. This *baraita* represents a refutation of the view of Sh'muel. It is indeed a refutation.

Ulla the son of Rav went down to lead the prayers before Rava. He began the middle blessing of *N'ilah* with the words "You have chosen us . . ." and he ended that blessing with the words "What are we, what are our lives . . ." and Rav praised him (because he fulfilled the ruling of both Rav and Shmuel).

6. Rabbi Joseph B. Soloveitchik

Why is theft singled out with special emphasis in *Ne'ilah?* The reason is that theft actually covers every type of sin. With every sin a Jew commits, he or she forgoes their right to existence, as they violate the condition upon which their existence rests, thereby "stealing" from God. The significance of God's name as Adonai, which is derived from the word Adon, or Master, is that God is Master and Owner of the world by virtue of being its creator. All of a person's organs, talents, and capabilities belong to God and are only on loan to human beings. The very moment they are misused, the human being has violated his or her agreement with God. Living a life of sin is an act of theft and distortion.

N'ilah End-of-Call Discussion

Rabbi Deborah Prinz, Rabbi Edwin C. Goldberg, Rabbi Leon A. Morris, Rabbi Richard N. Levy

Rabbi Deborah Prinz

Before we turn to questions, I wonder if the presenters have anything that you want to share with each other or with the entire group based on what you've heard.

Rabbi Edwin C. Goldberg

I would ask Rabbi Morris to share his concerns or reflections based on the ancient Talmudic *machloket* whether *N'ilah* might or might not offer an *Amidah*.

Rabbi Leon A. Morris

I think that that Talmudic discussion informs a real challenge that we have, that if we have this beautiful distinctive *N'ilah* material that comes after the short confession in the midst of an *Amidah* that is also beautifully developed, it may be a case of the distinctive material being lost. So I think that position of Sh'muel, that kind of outlier position of Sh'muel that remained alive in some way on the books might be very informative to some choices that we'll have to make of how to retrieve and how to rescue the most powerful aspects of the *N'ilah* liturgy.

What do you consider to be "the most powerful aspects of the *N'ilah* liturgy"?

Rabbi Deborah Prinz

There is one question that's come in about the relationship between *Yizkor* and *N'ilah*. Would you all like to attempt to respond to that issue of the relationship between the two, perhaps about timing, perhaps about thematic placement?

Rabbi Richard N. Levy

Whether for the reasons that Rabbi Goldberg mentioned, traditionally, *Yizkor* comes in the midst of the Torah service. And like the *Mi Shebeirach*, it has great power there, that while the Torah is still opened before us, or at least not put away, we bring to mind the memory of people who have gone and ask them to say something good on our behalf before the throne of God. And I think by moving it so late, we run the risk of ending the service on a lugubrious note and lose the sense of bringing in the people whom we are remembering into the heart of the service itself. My understanding for the reasons was yes, it would bring people out to *N'ilah*, the people wouldn't stay if it was in the traditional place; we may have gained that, but we've lost something by moving it, I think.

Where does your community place *Yizkor* and why? What would the process be to move it?

Rabbi Edwin C. Goldberg

Many years ago, because we usually do it in the afternoon, but many years ago all the Miami synagogues, even the Orthodox, because of a coming hurricane, everyone was told to leave early. So, we ended up doing *Yizkor* also in the morning, and it felt great. The thing is, the way we're looking at Yom Kippur day with the *machzor*, it's like if some of you remember when you had to buy a stereo, do you buy components or you buy the whole thing together? This is like we're offering this as components. In other words, there are different modules. You can decide one year let's try *Yizkor* in the morning, or one year let's try *Yizkor* right before *N'ilah*, or after *N'ilah*. I mean, there are different modules, so the people, the team that creates the worship can decide what's best for them. If they're used to coming late afternoon, that's going to be a hard thing to break. But I think arguments could be made for any practice, and *Mishkan HaNefesh* is going to be, we hope, presented in a way that each congregation can decide what's best for them.

N'ilah **Wrap-Up**

1. To what extent should our liturgical choices behind *N'ilah* be guided by practicalities such as timing and attendance, and to what extent should they be guided by worship goals and values?
2. *N'ilah* contains the final moments of High Holy Day worship. What is the note on which you want to end? What is the best way to hit that note?
3. If the new Reform *machzor* were to reintroduce classical *N'ilah* liturgy that our forebears deleted, then what is the best method of teaching our communities this liturgy that is new to many or most of them?
4. What did you learn from these presentations on *N'ilah* that you would like to implement in your community's High Holy Day worship?

Hin'ni: Liturgical and Homiletic Approaches

Hin'ni He-ani Mimaas

To hear one example of *Hin'ni*, this one the Ashkenazi melody by Yossele Rosenblatt, refer to http://www.piyut .org.il/tradition/ english/1640.html? currPerformance =2149.

הִנְנִי הֶעָנִי מִמַּעַשׂ
נִרְעַשׁ וְנִפְחַד מִפַּחַד יוֹשֵׁב תְּהִלוֹת יִשְׂרָאֵל
בָּאתִי לַעֲמֹד וּלְהִתְחַנֵּן לְפָנֶיךָ
עַל עַמְּךָ יִשְׂרָאֵל אֲשֶׁר שְׁלָחוּנִי
וְאַף עַל פִּי שֶׁאֵינִי כְדַאי וְהָגוּן לְכַךְ
לָכֵן אֲבַקֵּשׁ מִמְּךָ
אֱלֹהֵי אַבְרָהָם אֱלֹהֵי יִצְחָק וֵאלֹהֵי יַעֲקֹב
אֵל רַחוּם וְחַנּוּן אֱלֹהֵי יִשְׂרָאֵל ה' ה'
שַׁדַּי אָיֹם וְנוֹרָא
הֱיֵה נָא מַצְלִיחַ דַּרְכִּי
אֲשֶׁר אָנֹכִי הוֹלֵךְ וְעוֹמֵד לְבַקֵּשׁ רַחֲמִים עָלַי וְעַל שׁוֹלְחַי
וְנָא אַל תַּפְשִׁיעֵם בְּחַטֹּאתַי
וְאַל תְּחַיְּבֵם בַּעֲוֹנוֹתַי
כִּי חוֹטֵא וּפוֹשֵׁעַ אָנִי
וְאַל יִכָּלְמוּ בִּפְשָׁעַי
וְאַל יֵבוֹשׁוּ בִי
וְאַל אֵבוֹשׁ בָּם
וְקַבֵּל תְּפִלָּתִי כִּתְפִלַּת זָקֵן וְרָגִיל
וּפִרְקוֹ נָאֶה וּזְקָנוֹ מְגֻדָּל וְקוֹלוֹ נָעִים
וּמְעוּרָב בְּדַעַת עִם הַבְּרִיּוֹת
וְתִגְעַר בְּשָׂטָן לְבַל יַשְׂטִינֵנִי
(נ"א דְּלוֹגְנוּ) עָלֶיךָ אַהֲבָה וִיהִי נָא דִגְלֵנוּ
וּפְשָׁעֵינוּ תְּכַסֶּה בְּאַהֲבָה
וְכָל צָרוֹת וְרָעוֹת
הֲפָךְ נָא לָנוּ וּלְכָל יִשְׂרָאֵל
לְשָׂשׂוֹן וּלְשִׂמְחָה לְחַיִּים וּלְשָׁלוֹם
וְהָאֱמֶת וְהַשָּׁלוֹם אֱהָבוּ
וְאַל יְהִי שׁוּם מִכְשׁוֹל בִּתְפִלָּתִי

וִיהִי רָצוֹן מִלְפָנֶיךָ

אֱלֹהֵי אַבְרָהָם אֱלֹהֵי יִצְחָק וֵאלֹהֵי יַעֲקֹב 'ה

הָאֵל הַגָּדוֹל הַגִּבּוֹר וְהַנּוֹרָא אֵל עֶלְיוֹן

אֶהְיֶה אֲשֶׁר אֶהְיֶה

שֶׁכָּל הַמַּלְאָכִים שֶׁהֵם פּוֹעֲלֵי תְּפִלּוֹת

יָבִיאוּ תְּפִלָּתִי לִפְנֵי כִסֵּא כְבוֹדֶךָ

וְיָפִיצוּ אוֹתָהּ לְפָנֶיךָ

בַּעֲבוּר כָּל הַצַּדִּיקִים וְהַחֲסִידִים וְהַתְּמִימִים וְהַיְשָׁרִים

וּבַעֲבוּר כְּבוֹד שִׁמְךָ הַגָּדוֹל וְהַנּוֹרָא

כִּי אַתָּה שׁוֹמֵעַ תְּפִלַּת עַמְּךָ יִשְׂרָאֵל בְּרַחֲמִים

בָּרוּךְ אַתָּה שׁוֹמֵעַ תְּפִלָּה

Hin'ni: Historical Background

Dr. Richard S. Sarason

I always associate the *Hin'ni* prayer with the well-known story about the rabbi, the cantor, and the *shamash* at prayer on Yom Kippur. The rabbi drops to the floor and beats his breast, saying, "*Chatati, aviti, pashati*: I have sinned, I have committed iniquity, I have transgressed. What am I? I'm a nothing. I'm a nobody." The cantor then does the same thing, and finally the *shamash* does the same thing. At this point, the rabbi turns to the cantor and, pointing to the *shamash*, says, "Look who thinks he's a nobody."

There is a danger in this prayer of putting on display what might be called "false humility." The prayer itself is a private meditation for the prayer leader. It uses the rhetorical vocabulary of a *r'shut*—the ritualized introduction to a series of liturgical poems, *piyutim*—in which the prayer leader asks permission from the congregation to interrupt the recitation of the *Amidah* to recite these poems. He represents himself rhetorically as being a nobody, a nothing, who stands in trepidation as he is about to take on the awesome responsibility of approaching God on behalf of the congregation. Traditionally, this prayer is recited before the *Musaf Amidah*, the most complex *Amidah* of the day, both on Rosh Ha-Shanah and Yom Kippur, because of the additions that are performed only once a year: *Malchuyot*, *Zichronot*, and *Shofarot* on Rosh HaShanah, and *Seder HaAvodah* on Yom Kippur.

In some synagogues, the performance practice of *Hin'ni*, rather than the meaning of the prayer itself, has become the focus. It is one of the cantorial highlights of the year, as the cantor enters dramatically from the back of the sanctuary. I have witnessed this dramatization of the ritual, and it has always struck me as being somewhat artificial. Once humility is put on display, it is no longer humility. When leading services, I prefer to retain the privacy of this prayer; I do not recite it aloud publicly for just those reasons.

How can the dramatization of a ritual detract from its meaning? How can dramatization add meaning and value to the worship experience?

The text itself nicely models the intended emotions of the *sh'liach tzibur*, but there is always, of course, the danger of routinizing those feelings. On the one hand, as a private *kavanah*, *Hin'ni* can be very powerful. However, as I have noted, it can be dangerous to put this prayer on display. *Gates of Repentance* situates the prayer at the very beginning of the Rosh HaShanah evening service, where it serves as a *kavanah*, or meditation, before all the prayers. The draft of the new *machzor, Mishkan HaNefesh*, follows the same practice. However, *Mishkan HaNefesh* also provides a *kavanah* for congregants to recite individually at this same time. It is contextualized with this note: "Ultimately, it is the merit and worthiness of the congregation, not the prayer leader's qualities, which gain God's attention and transform misfortune into renewed life." In this way, *Mishkan HaNefesh* democratizes the prayer activity and valorizes the individual congregant and community as much as, or even perhaps more than, the prayer leader—reflecting contemporary sensibilities.

What possibilities does this new format of *Mishkan HaNefesh* open for your worship experience?

Regarding the historical background of the prayer, we do not know who wrote it. However, its origins are certainly eastern Ashkenazic (Poland), probably in the seventeenth century. As it is not a statutory prayer, but rather a private *kavanah*, the benedictory formula with which the prayer ends does not include the divine name. It is simply *Ba-*

ruch atah, shomei-a t'filah, "Praised are You, who hearkens to prayer" (the second half being the generic formula concluding petitionary prayers).

Moving to the prayer's content: in it, the prayer leader expresses his (or, now, her) trepidation at the responsibility of coming before God bearing the prayers of the congregation, afraid of making a mistake, and thereby imperiling the fate of all those who sent him. There is a sense of unworthiness. "Help me," the prayer leader says, "to do this successfully. Accept my prayer as if I were totally qualified to do this." What is interesting is that the prayer now enumerates the qualifications of a prayer leader, thereby reflecting the cultural ideals of medieval Judaism. The prayer leader should be a *zakein,* somebody who is mature, fully formed. He should also be *ragil,* someone who is fully conversant with the material. *Pirko na-eh:* he should be learned, somebody who is a disciplined student. *Z'kano m'gudal* (an attribute that is omitted from the version in *Gates of Repentance*): literally, he should have a fully developed beard, that is, he should be of a certain age and be pious in bearing. *Kolo na-im:* he has a pleasant voice. He is *m'orav b'daat im kol hab'riyot:* he should be on good terms with, and well thought of, by everyone. Jonathan Sacks, in his edition of the *machzor,* translates: "whose mind is involved with the concerns of others."

The prayer then goes on to request that God rebuke *haSatan,* the adversary, so that he not prompt the prayer leader to error. This concept is not found in any Reform version. There is also a request that God pardon us and turn our sorrows into joy, followed by a request that the angels who bring our prayers before the divine throne may aid this prayer for the sake of all the pious and righteous ones, and for the sake of God's reputation, God's

Do you share the sentiments expressed by the *Hin'ni* prayer? How do you address this "sense of unworthiness"? How can these feelings lead to productive discomfort and, ultimately, more powerful worship experiences for the entire community?

shem. Again, the angelology is absent in the Reform versions.

Another very interesting aspect of this prayer (although not an atypical one) is that it contains multiple biblical references in its rhetoric, specifically in how God is invoked, and with which divine attributes God is described. For example, God is described as *Elohei Avraham, Yitzchak, v'Yaakov* (Exodus 3:15); *Adonai Adonai El rachum v'chanun* (Exodus 34:6); *Shaddai* (Exodus 6:3) *ayom v'nora* (Habakkuk 1:7); *El elyon* (Genesis 14:19); and *Ehyeh asher ehyeh* (Exodus 3:14).

Historically, this prayer did not appear in most Reform liturgies. Although there are other original personal meditations in virtually all Reform prayer books that appear in the vernacular, they are not usually intended for the prayer leader alone. Even in the European Reform prayer books, which generally do retain *Musaf,* this prayer does not appear. It also does not appear in any North American Reform prayer book that I am aware of prior to *Gates of Repentance.* There is a rabbi's prayer in English in the 1945 *UPB-2* before the Yom Kippur evening service, which reflects some of the same themes and the general rhetoric of *Hin'ni* and is clearly based on this prayer. In *Gates of Understanding 2,* Lawrence Hoffman writes, "We have no prayer for the cantor here, but we have a prayer for rabbis." In *UPB-2* 1945, the prayer appears accompanied by the following directive: "Immediately after the organ prelude, the Rabbi approaches the open Ark, the congregation standing, and prays:" The first paragraph reads as follows:

> Father of mercies, in awe and deep humility I stand before Thee on this Atonement Eve in the midst of Thy people who look to

me to lead them. I approach the holy Ark. I
have erred and sinned. Forgive me, I pray
Thee. May my people not be put to shame
because of me nor I because of them. (p. 168)

This is clearly derived directly from *Hin'ni*. *Gates of
Understanding* explains the liturgy that appears in
Gates of Repentance with the following notes about
the text:

Our text is abridged by A. Stanley Dreyfus
to blunt the impact of overly humiliating
language, which the medieval author applies to himself, and to avoid the theological notion of angels interceding between us
and God. (p. 165)

Otherwise, the text found in *Gates of Repentance* is
fully traditional. The text in the current draft of
Mishkan HaNefesh is identical to that in *Gates of Repentance*, except that it includes the Matriarchs as
well as the Patriarchs.

Hin'ni: For Myself and My Community
Rabbi Leon A. Morris

It will be helpful at the beginning to just look at the two texts of *Hin'ni* (see pages 226–227). These two versions of *Hin'ni* were provided in the *Mishkan HaNefesh* pilot for Rosh HaShanah evening. The first, which would go on the right side, is essentially just a new translation of the mostly traditional text, with some of the references that Dr. Sarason just pointed out as being absent in *Gates of Repentance* also absent here: including *satan* and the gendered language of what the prayer leader should look like. But it's a fresh, beautiful translation rendered by Rabbis Shelly and Janet Marder. The second piece, which would go on the left, allows each person, and not just the prayer leader, the opportunity to recite the *Hin'ni*. And there's a number of ways congregations could use this. It could be that the leader's reciting the right side and that the individual congregant is simultaneously reading the left side, or just providing a space for individuals to read the left side for individual reflection.

It's an interesting move to create a *Hin'ni* in which we really shift the role of leadership to each and every person, and we sort of play down the role of the rabbi, or the cantor, or the *sh'liach tzibur*. And I wanted to connect that move with a story. Rabbi Menachem Mendel of Rimanov turned to the congregation who had come to pray with him and he said, "You're a beautiful congregation but I cannot carry you on my shoulders. Each of you must exercise your own *t'shuvah*, your own *t'filah*, and your own *tzedakah*." So that's part of the kind of spirit or impetus that led to the creation of an individual reflective *Hin'ni* for the left side.

I want to just share a few thoughts about a few key lines that appear in the right-hand side version, and then I just wanted in the remaining time to point out a few other interesting links. The opening line, which we have here in English and in Hebrew is, *"hati laamod u'lchanein l'fanecha al amcha Yisrael asher sh'lachuni af al pi she-eini ch'dai v'hagun l'chach."* In some ways, this line really expresses the guiding spirit of the whole poem. This is a line, as Rick alluded to, that particularly at this time of year, we rabbis really feel. There's so much about the High Holy Days which is carefully scripted and choreographed, and yet this is a line that reminds us we have to cultivate in ourselves an awareness of what we're trying to do on the High Holy Days. What does it mean to facilitate *t'shuvah* and true *t'filah* for our communities when we may feel that we ourselves have not completed our personal work of *t'shuvah*? And on the one hand, it speaks of a need for modesty as a rabbi or cantor in stepping forward at all. But then at the end, we're drafted into service. It says, "I rise to pray and seek favor for Your people Israel because they have entrusted me with this task." And that balance is particularly striking and beautiful. It's the balance between the modesty and strength that's required of religious leadership.

There's a beautiful quote by Rabbi Jonathan Sacks, I think it is from his *machzor*, in which he says, "The paradox of spiritual leadership is that those who think they are great are small, those who think themselves small are great. In Judaism, all leadership, including leadership in prayer, is a form of service, not superiority or dominance, and cannot exist without humility." So that's one line I just wanted to offer reflection on. Another is just a little bit further down. We translated it here as, "I pray to you for success on my path. I pray for myself and my community." And I think it triggers us as *sh'lichei tzibur* to think about what really is a successful High Holy Days. There are so many other ideas about what a "successful" High Holy Days could be. "Everyone loved my sermon." "The new system of entrance cards worked really well." "The ushers did a great job." *Hin'ni* reminds us that the goal here is success on a path that has something to do with transformation, and change, and hope, and courage, something of alternate meaning.

I wanted to pick up, finally, just with this section that Rick mentioned, where the traditional text is not only as we have here that the leader be proficient in prayer, and unblemished in character, and pleasing in voice, but traditional text as, "*kabeil t'filati b'tifilat zakein v'ragil uz'kano m'gudal.*" So, putting aside the obvious problems that we would have with this and why we couldn't include this in *Mishkan HaNefesh*, the original context of this is from *Mishnah Taanit* 2:2 and it has to do with who is a fitting prayer leader for a time of drought, for a fast that has been established because of a drought. And that's a beautiful idea here. We aspire to be, in some sense, prayer leaders whose description fits the prayer leader in a time of drought. And I think it leads us to think about, well, what's the drought that we have? What's the spiritual drought in American Jewish life that we're trying to address? What do we ultimately want to do to bring rain to our community?

I wanted to highlight two links that are really worth checking out that are on the same homepage for this conversation. One is entitled 'Singing Leonard Cohen on Yom Kippur: Being an Angel or

See Rabbi Mishael Zion, "Singing Leonard Cohen on Yom Kippur: Being an Angel or a Broken Hill?". Huffington Post, 09/24/2012 (HuffPost Religion live-blog) http://www .huffingtonpost .com/rabbi-mishael-zion/leonard-cohen-on-yom-kippur-being-an-angel-or-a-broken-hill_b_ 1907516.html.

a Broken Hill?' This is an article for the Huffington Post that my friend and our colleague, Rabbi Mishael Zion, wrote about based on his experience growing up in Jerusalem in a particularly innovative minyan where, along with *Hin'ni*, Leonard Cohen's 'If It Be Your Will' would be sung. And this is his beautiful *d'rash* on the lines of Cohen's poem 'If It Be Your Will.' And there's also a link to the Webb Sisters and Leonard Cohen singing it in concert. My congregation actually used this on *Kol Nidrei*, at the very beginning of *Kol Nidrei* last year. Very, very powerful. There's also a link here from the great website, piyut.org.il, of Yossele Rosenblatt singing *Hin'ni* in all of its drama from the—as immodest as it may be, probably from the back of a sanctuary as Rick had mentioned. I hope all of these links are helpful.

Leonard Cohen—The Webb Sisters—If It Be Your Will—The Louisville Palace—30-03-2013" http://www.youtube.com/watch?v=xRhgaH-i-kOe4.

Hin'ni: A Pastoral Perspective
Rabbi Jo Hirschmann

I would like to begin with an image of the *chazan* chanting *Hin'ni*. As she recites *Hin'ni*, the *chazan* makes a lonely walk. She utters unflinching assertions of worthlessness and sinfulness. She is a lowly subject. She is a human being, a community member, a person painfully prone to making the same mistakes again and again. She walks in isolation. There is nobody to support her. She acknowledges *hotei u'foshei-a ani*, "a sinner and a transgressor am I." I believe that *Hin'ni* can be a tool for psycho-spiritual growth, and I am going to draw on Jung's notion of the Shadow to do so.

Hin'ni is an invitation to return to both ourselves and to God. As with so much of the liturgy of the High Holy Days, this prayer invites us to see God as compassionate and reminds us that forgiveness is within our reach. *Hin'ni* also invites us to acknowledge how flawed we are and how great is our capacity to hurt ourselves, others, and God. It invites us to look at the most damaged and damaging parts of ourselves and to continue the long hard work of personal change. These two themes that occur throughout *Hin'ni*—God's forgiveness and our capacity to make mistakes—are connected. God's capacity to hear prayer stands in direct relationship to our need to be heard, and God's capacity to forgive us stands in direct relationship to our need for forgiveness.

There is one sentence of the prayer that particularly encapsulates this dialectic. Here is an interpretive translation of this line: *V'tigar b'satan*, "may You nullify the hostile parts of myself." *L'val yastineini*,

In Jung's writing, and in subsequent psychological writing, "the Shadow" is treated as a proper noun.

Where else in our High Holy Day worship do we encounter these two themes? How can Hin'ni encapsulate and connect to the rest of the High Holy Day liturgy?

"and remove the parts of myself that cause me to damage, break, speak falsely, and do harm." *Vihi na dilugeinu alecha ahavah,* "may the parts of ourselves that we do not like to look at know Your love." *V'al kol p'sha-im t'chaseh b'ahavah,* "and may every transgression be covered with love."

Two caveats. First, in *Gates of Repentance* and I believe also in *Mishkan HaNefesh, dilugeinu* appears as *digleinu,* which *Gates of Repentance* places with *ahavah* and translates as "the banner of our love." The Reconstructionist *machzor* does something very similar, but some *machzorim,* including Birnbaum and ArtScroll, have the word *dilugeinu* instead, which is related to the verb *l'daleg,* "to skip." It is often translated as "fault" or "omission," or, as in my translation here, "the parts of ourselves that are the hardest to look at and that we wish to skip over."

Second, I have chosen the sentence that includes the references to Satan, which are removed in the Reform *machzor.* It is my understanding that they will not be in the new *machzor* either. There are many good liturgical and theological reasons for this choice, but I would like to explore what *haSatan* might mean if we looked further into this term. It is a theologically difficult concept. *HaSatan* is usually imagined as a rogue angel, and in my translation, I would like to suggest that it actually describes the parts of ourselves that are our own adversaries, our own worst enemies. These are the toxic voices that we might have carried with us since childhood, and these are our beliefs about the world that separate us from God, and from others, and from our own goodness.

In Jungian thought, this is the Shadow. For Jung, the Shadow encompasses the darkest parts of our personalities. Metaphorically, this casts a

What are the liturgical and theological reasons for this decision? Do you are agree with them?

How else could you reconceptualize *haSatan* for our current worship mentality?

shadow over how we see the world around us, it perverts our perception, and it causes us to project negative thoughts onto others. It is a personal *mitz-rayim*, which is described by Jung as, "a tight passage, a narrow door whose painful constriction no one is spared who goes down to the deep well." It is the part of ourselves that is the most painful to look at and the most gut-wrenching to name. *Vihi na dilugeinu alecha ahavah*, "may the parts of ourselves that we do not like to look at know Your love."

In his writings about the Shadow, Jung is clear about what we need to do. We need to face the Shadow, to name it, claim it as our own, and transform it into something else.

Rather than banishing it or pretending it does not exist, we might consider covering it in love. *V'al kol p'sha-im t'chaseh b'ahavah*, "and may every transgression be covered with love." It is unclear in the text of the prayer whose love this is. I would like to suggest that it might be a combination of God's love, our own love, and the love of the people in our lives. Many people have written and spoken about the ways in which Yom Kippur is about covering, and so here is another one. *Hin'ni* invites us to look at our own shadows with a loving gaze, to hold them with compassion, and to reintegrate them into ourselves in a new way.

This is especially important for those of us who are clergy, who are professional caregivers who take care of others. Henri Nouwen's model of the wounded healer is helpful here. He was a Dutch-born Catholic priest who died in 1996. He suggested that those who help others should make their own wounds into a source of healing and that these wounds might give us insight and compassion as we support congregants, patients, and clients. Our Shadow side gives us insight into the

How does a pastoral lens augment your understanding of *Hin'ni*?

areas of our life that most need our attention. They reflect our deepest longings, and they also give us insight into the contributions that we perhaps most need to make to the world.

I would like to conclude with some words from my chaplaincy colleague, Reverend Douglas Phillips, who has written about this. He is a Presbyterian pastor and a trauma chaplain at Westchester Medical Center, where he works on the burn unit. In an article that appeared in the *Journal of the Association of Professional Chaplains,* he described how when he was eleven years old he had an accident while using the stove in which he severely burned his torso. When he began doing clinical pastoral education at Westchester Medical Center, he would not enter the burn unit. In his words:

> Discovering the Shadow gift meant revisiting the walled-off shame and horror of my burn experience and reintegrating it into the rest of my psyche. It was facing down an old demon and transforming a weakness into a strength. On the day I finally worked up the courage to reenter this realm, my legs were shaking, mouth dry, and stomach churning. A colleague led me to the Burn Center, opened the door, and literally shoved me through the entry. Once I got my bearings, I noticed a weight falling away and I began to feel at home again.

Reverend Phillips describes an alchemical process in which transformation can happen, in which the Shadow becomes a gift. In a similar way, *Hin'ni* allows us to imagine God's sheltering love covering and soothing our most guilty places and creating a safe place in which this alchemical process can happen.

Our need to be heard is matched by the ability of *Shomei-a T'filah*, which is how God is addressed at the very end of this prayer, by the ability of *Shomei-a T'filah* to hear. Our need to evolve is matched by God's ever-changing, constantly evolving aspect. To me, it is no coincidence that *Ehyeh asher ehyeh* is one of the ways that God is named in *Hin'ni.* The prayer invites us to look with honesty and courage at how we function as adversaries to ourselves, our loved ones, and God. It invites us to embrace becoming and unfolding as holy processes. Change is welcome and it lives in the dialectic of humbly facing our own shadow while secure in God's compassion.

An Interpretive Translation

May you nullify the hostile parts of myself and remove the parts of myself that cause me to damage, break, speak falsely, and do harm; may the parts of ourselves that we do not like to look at know Your love and may every transgression be covered with love.	ותגער בשטן לבל ישטנני ויהי נא דליגנו* עליך אהבה ועל כל פשעים תכסה באהבא.

*In some *machzorim,* this appears as דגלינו.

Further Reading

Rev. Douglas Phillips, BCC, "Lessons Learned from Burns," *Chaplaincy Today* 26, no. 1 (Spring/Summer 2010).

Hin'ni: Creative Approaches
Rabbi Richard N. Levy

It seems almost counterintuitive to share creative approaches to *Hin'ni* because this is such a personal prayer, even though it is not always presented that way in traditional settings. In looking at the text of *Hin'ni*, one might in fact translate these ideas in many new ways. One of the practices that is important for rabbis to consider is to keep an Elul journal. If you do not already keep a spiritual journal, this is a wonderful year to start. Among the things that one might enter in such a journal is a response to this prayer. In what way am I *poor in deed*? Make some notes about that. *I am trembling and afraid.* Of what am I afraid? Sometimes we are afraid that people will not like our sermons or will not like us. Is there also a fear that God will find us wanting? Yet *I stand here to plead for your people.* What is our case for them?

How do you begin your preparation for the High Holy Days during Elul? Consider implementing the author's suggestions as one approach.

I think it is important to write out a case, a brief, for the people in our congregations and even to share it, and to make the presentation of that brief a part of your approach to *Hin'ni*. *Why* should they be able to live another year? What case would you make for God, for individuals, or for the whole congregation? It is important to write down how we are *chotim* and *posh'im* (sinners and wrongdoers), what marks we have missed, and how—even worse—we are *posh'im*, how we have knocked over the helpful barriers in our lives in the past year. We can respond to the sentence "Let them not be put to shame because of me." What shameful things have we done? Writing this in our journals is important as well. We all know an important part of journal

How would you respond to these questions posed by the presenter?

writing is not only the writing of it, but the reading of it as well. I would then move to encouraging the congregation to do some journal writing, too. If you have a chance to e-mail them before the High Holy Days, you might suggest that they also open a reflective journal then.

Hin'ni is also understood as the prayer to *change our afflictions to joy and gladness*. Here is another journal opportunity. What are our afflictions and how might they be changed to joy? Can physical pain, our own physical pain, be turned to joy by reaching out to others in pain? Can our loneliness be turned to gladness by paying a visit to a shut-in, starting a correspondence, by e-mail or real mail, with people who are confined to their homes, and doing a sort of congregational *cheshbon han'fashot*, an accounting of our souls, about how one might change one's affliction to joy and gladness, and perhaps publish for the congregation some specific suggestions. Similarly, the prayer "changes our misdeeds to active life." How might we do that? This suggests that in our misdeeds, in our sins, there are still some sparks of holiness that can be redeemed. I love the symbolism of *Tashlich*, when we throw crummy deeds that have gathered in our pockets into the sea for fish to be nurtured. What is there in our own misdeeds that can nurture other people? These are some of the questions that we might ask.

Regarding the traditional liturgical formulation of *Hin'ni*, I would not encourage reintroducing Satan. But perhaps we might put back the notion of angels. We sing *Shalom Aleichem* on Friday night, prompting us to wonder, who are our angels? Identifying our angels is an important way to recognize special individuals or forces in our lives.

Would you consider reintroducing angelology in your High Holy Day liturgy?

Finally, we can use *Hin'ni* to prompt everyone to consider, what is my own personal prayer today or tonight? *Hin'ni* could be used to allow each person to write a prayer and take it with them into the service and offer it. These are all ways of confession, of looking inside as a community and as individuals.

Hin'ni: I Am Here
Rabbi Zoe Klein

Hin'ni. I am here. I am ready. At one time, we were told on punishment of death to stay away. Do not touch the mountain or you will die. Moses climbed the mountain alone. The future is a mountain, its summit in the sky. *Hin'ni,* I am ready and I want you to come with me. I want you to touch the mountain and live, and leave the idols to sink in sand. I need your eyes to point out the subtleties of landscape, your hands when the path narrows. I need your strength to stake the tents along the way, your song when the way is wearisome. When we come face to face with the one who called us up, I want to witness with you. Not for you, beside you. Not on your behalf. To be here on the mountaintop with you, it is as if we are under a chuppah, creating a covenant, a communal renewal of vows, and it is time to lift the veil.

"Reading Torah in translation is like kissing your bride through a veil," so said Chayim Nachman Bialik. Some claim he originally said, "Reading poetry in translation is like kissing your bride through a veil." Either way, "through a veil" is not as good.

We have become so accustomed to veils. We see our friends' pictures on screens. We assume we know their lives, when in fact, pictures are just fictitious. "Selfies" are not a portrayal of how one sees oneself. They are a veil, a fantasy. They are not nearly as raw, wet, and messy as the tragic poetry that is our actual lives, lives of scratches and spills, cells and cesspools, broken pipes and bones. We are so used to living through a veil. We live our lives as virtual reality and convince ourselves that it is virtuous reality. Instead of experiencing, we are watching, recording, posting, judging, editing, nipping, tucking.

We are avatars of ourselves. Our true selves are ruptures, razor burns, and wrinkles. *Hin'ni*. I am here. I am really here to engage, to interact, to feel, to take off the veil, to witness not through a lens, to kiss the world. We are so accustomed to life in translation. We feel, but we do not even know what we are feeling. We are draped in a burqa.

Even our sympathy is a veil. As Susan Sontag wrote, "So far as we feel sympathy, we feel we are not accomplices to what caused the suffering. Our sympathy proclaims our innocence as well as our impotence. We need to set aside the sympathy we extend to others beset by war and murderous politics for a consideration of how our privileges are located on the same map as their suffering, and may—in ways we prefer not to imagine—be linked to their suffering." There is blood everywhere and we do not see it because of our filtering veil. We convince ourselves that we are witnesses, but we are not witnesses until we sweep aside the veil of tears that makes the world seem to move swimmingly.

In 1962, Martin Luther King preached, "The law court may force a man to provide bread for his family, but it cannot make him provide the bread of love." We do have our hands extended with the bread of love. Man does not live by bread alone, but man cannot live only by the bread of love we offer. All around us, there are people in need of actual bread. *Hin'ni* means I am really here and my hand is extended with real bread. *Hin'ni* means taking off the veil of fear. We support free speech, but we are afraid to speak because everyone and their cat is free to post a comment on what we say. We read op-eds, but we rarely write them. The story of the Exodus begins with the death of children and ends with the death of more children. It begins with a river turned to blood, ends with the blood in every home. How many children before we recognize they are ours? The children whose blood runs as a river and the child holding the gun that blew them all apart. The system into which they were all born, we parent it. We cry, we feel it, we hold out the bread of love. But *Hin'ni* is not about sympathy. Sympathy doesn't cut it. Sympathy is not so different from standing idly by the blood of our neighbor. We cry. The NRA organizes. *Hin'ni.* I am really here and I am rolling up my sleeves. *Hin'ni* means it is past the time to get mad or get sad. *Hin'ni* means it is time to get real and get busy.

The ninth plague was a darkness of which the Torah said, "A man saw not his fellow, nor rose any man from his place" (Exodus 10:23). We do see our fellow. We are so good at that. We see past racial lines, beneath dark hoodies. We believe in equality. We see the divine spark in every color. We integrate, elevate, celebrate. We have a rainbow coalition of friends and coworkers. Our hands are ever extending the bread of love. We do see our fellow, but we have too long been sitting in our place. *Hin'ni.* It is time to rise up from our place, to take off these thousand veils. We stand here on the mountaintop of the year on a communal renewal of vows, creating a covenant. This covenant is between you and the world. One day, you may make a covenant to another, but every day, we make a covenant to all others.

Do you take faith to be your partner and peace to be your guide? Do you, congregation of Israel, take a look outside of our chuppah's open walls to see all the people there looking to you? Do you care about treating them with kindness? Do you want to offer them real bread and say to them, *"Hin'ni,* here I am"? I do. By the power vested in me and by the states of Maine, New Hampshire, Vermont, Massachusetts, Rhode Island, Connecticut, Delaware, Maryland, Washington D.C., Minnesota, Iowa, Washington, and California, we now pronounce you helpers and healers, partners in Creation, stewards of the earth. Let's take off the veil and kiss the hurt and make it go away.

A reference to the states that had legalized gay marriage at the time of this presentation.

How does the imagery of the veil and the other images introduced by the author enhance your understanding of *Hin'ni*? What other imagery does *Hin'ni* evoke for you? How could you incorporate the author's imagery or your own images into your services?

Hin'ni: Sources

Notes on the *Hin'ni* Prayer in Erev Rosh HaShanah

Hebrew text differs slightly from traditional version:

a. We added the Matriarchs.
b. We omitted reference to Satan.
c. We omitted reference to angels.

We are following *Gates of Repentance* (Reform) tradition in placing this prayer in Erev Rosh HaShanah rather than as the introduction to *Musaf*. It sets an appropriate tone of humility to begin the service and emphasizes the partnership between prayer leader and congregation in creating meaningful worship.

As the opening of the High Holy Days it is a dramatic moment; we are transferring the drama from *Musaf* (recalling sacrifice) to the initial moment of the community's time together for the High Holy Days. For us the drama comes not from the historical memory of Temple sacrifice, but from communal gathering at the new year.

For the Prayer Leader

It's a faithful translation—we did our best to convey the meaning and spirit of the Hebrew original.

The prayer leader's version of this prayer is a "mini *cheshbon hanefesh*." It begins with the leader's personal confession of inadequacy ("so poor in deeds," etc.). Then it moves beyond the self to recognize the leader's connection to the congregation, then to all Israel ("May Israel's strife and misfortunes be turned into joy," etc.).

The prayer finally arrives at the leader's acknowledgment that God's reception of his/her prayer does not depend solely on the leader's own merits. The leader stands on the shoulders of those who came before, gains strength from the congregation, draws on the merits of the righteous, and speaks to a merciful God. In the course of reciting the prayer, the leader works through his/her personal sense of angst at bearing such overwhelming responsibility and realizes that "it's not all about me."

The prayer acknowledges the interdependence of leader and prayer community in creating powerful worship. It expresses the hope that the leader's flaws and failings (both moral and professional/technical) will not impede the congregation's prayer and recognizes that disunity and strife within the congregation could hamper the leader's own attempts to commune with God ("Let us love peace and truth—may they prevail among us. And may there be no impediment to my prayer.")

[Note: In the next version we are making a slight change in the translation: "Love peace and truth" will become "Let us love peace and truth."]

The prayer concludes by linking the leader of the congregation with Moses, the first to intercede with God on behalf of the people Israel— reminding the *sh'liach tzibur* that he/she now stands where Moses once stood, and recalling God's reassuring words to Moses: human strength waxes and wanes, but the Eternal is with us always.

As the prayer began tentatively, even fearfully—on a note of anxiety and uncertainty—it ends with quiet confidence in God's compassion and responsiveness to human need.

Hin'ni: For Individual Reflection

This prayer was developed on the model of the *Modim D'Rabanan*, the version of the *Modim* prayer created by the Sages to be said by the individual while the *sh'liach tzibur* is reciting the *Modim* aloud during the repetition of the *Amidah*. The *Modim D'Rabanan* was created, according to some, because you cannot have an agent offer thanks on your behalf; you must offer your own words of gratitude.

The concept for the individual *Hin'ni* is that, just as the prayer leader is recognizing his/her responsibility to the congregation, the individual worshiper should have an opportunity to articulate his/her own responsibility for meaningful prayer.

Purposes:

a. To prepare for prayer (and to introduce the idea that prayer requires preparation, focus, and proper intention).

b. To introduce the themes, vocabulary, and big questions that worshipers should be asking themselves during the High Holy Days.

c. To overcome the sense that worship is theater and the worshiper is a passive spectator, here to be entertained; to emphasize the need for the worshiper's own engagement and effort during the High Holy Days; to acknowledge that *t'shuvah* is a difficult task.

d. To focus on both a sense of personal solitude (necessary for introspection) and connection to others (necessary to maintain our sense of shared humanity and compassion). This double consciousness is captured in the first line, "Here I am, one soul within this prayer community," and throughout the prayer.

e. To acknowledge that we are given a "script" written by others ("the time-hallowed words of my people and the traditions cherished by generations before me") and challenged to find personal meaning in these inherited words and rituals ("I bring my own concerns and yearnings to this place, hoping they will find expression. . . .").

f. As the prayer leader works through his/her own anxieties in the leader's version of *Hin'ni*, in this version the individual worshiper first articulates the challenge before him/her—then focuses on what brings comfort, strength, and hope for the task ahead.

Hin'ni Wrap-Up

1. How do we balance the tension between the desire to recite the liturgy of *Hin'ni* beautifully and the desire to recite it humbly in keeping with the main message of the prayer?

2. These presentations offer ways in which *Hin'ni* can be used pastorally. How else might this piece of High Holy Day liturgy be used in the service of pastoral care?

3. What did you learn from these presentations on *Hin'ni* that you would like to implement in your community's High Holy Day worship?

From the RH Evening Draft of the New *Machzor, Mishkan HaNefesh*, pp. 7c–7d

Hin'ni: Here I Am

FOR THE PRAYER LEADER

Here I am.
So poor in deeds, I tremble in fear,
overwhelmed and apprehensive before You to whom Israel sings praise.
Although unworthy, I rise to pray and seek favor for Your people Israel,
for they have entrusted me with this task. Therefore —

God of Abraham, Isaac, and Jacob, God of Sarah, Rebekah, Leah, and Rachel...
Adonai, Adonai — merciful, gracious God of Israel, who inspires awe —
I pray to You for success on my path; I pray for myself and my community.
Do not hold them responsible for my wrongs and offenses.
May my deeds cause them no shame; and may their deeds cause me no shame.
Accept my prayer as though it were offered by one more worthy of this task:
a scholar — proficient in prayer; unblemished in character, pleasing in voice.

Let love be our banner; let it banish our wrongs.
May Israel's strife and misfortunes be turned into joy, renewed life, and peace.
Love peace and truth — may they prevail among us.
And may there be no impediment to my prayer.

Adonai —
God of Abraham, Isaac, and Jacob, God of Sarah, Rebekah, Leah, and Rachel...
great, mighty, awe-inspiring, God Most High,
who said to Moses "I Will Be What I Will Be"—
May it be Your will that my prayer reach Your Presence
for the sake of the righteous and blameless, the honest and pure of heart,
for the sake of Your glory.
You hear Your people's prayer with compassion.
Blessed are You, the One who hears prayer.

כַּוָנוֹת
Kavanot

הַדְלָקַת נֵרוֹת
Hadlakat Nerot

שָׁלוֹם עֲלֵיכֶם
Shalom Aleichem

מִזְמוֹר צ"ב
Mizmor tsadi-bet

שַׁעַר תְּפִלָּה
Shaar T'filah

תְּקִיעַת שׁוֹפָר
T'kiat Shofar

מִזְמוֹר ק"ג
Mizmor kuf-nun

הִנְנִי
Hin'ni

פִּיּוּט לְרֹאשׁ הַשָּׁנָה
Piyyut L'Rosh HaShanah

הַשָּׁנָה הַחֲדָשָׁה
HaShanah HaChadashah

HIN'NI: HERE I AM   This is the prayer-leader's confession. An admission of inadequacy and self-doubt in the face of a daunting responsibility, it simultaneously affirms traditional tenets of Jewish belief, especially the efficacy of prayer. Above all, *Hin'ni* reflects the humility and self-awareness necessary for approaching God during the Days of Awe and for the task of *cheshbon hanefesh* — taking an account of one's soul. Ultimately, it is the merit and worthiness of the congregation, not the prayer-leader's qualities, which gain God's attention and transform misfortune into renewed life.

Hin'ni: Here I Am

FOR INDIVIDUAL REFLECTION

Here I am,
one soul within this prayer community.

Like those around me, I bring my own concerns and yearnings to this place,
hoping they will find expression in the time-hallowed words of my people
and in the traditions cherished by generations before me.
May I bring the best of my energies to these Holy Days,
approaching this spiritual work with open heart and mind,
sincerity, and sustained focus on the deep questions of this season:
Who am I? How shall I live? Where have I fallen short — or failed?
This night I take up the challenge of the Days of Awe:
cheshbon hanefesh — a searching examination of my life,
a moral inventory of my deeds, words, and thoughts.
During the next ten days,
let me face the truth about myself and listen to Your still, small voice.
Taking comfort in Your promise that I am always free to change,
released from staleness and routine,
let me know the joy of beginning again.
May I gain strength as I share this task with those around me,
united by our common purpose:
tikkun middot (improving our characters)
    and *tikkun olam* (repairing the world).

I now prepare myself to pray — one soul amidst this holy congregation.

PART 2

BETWEEN FAITH AND PROTEST

Bringing Back to Life the Challenging Metaphors in the *Machzor*

Machzor Presentations from the CCAR Convention, 2013, Long Beach

Between Faith and Protest: Bringing Back to Life the Challenging Metaphors in the *Machzor*

Who Shall I Say Is Calling?

Rabbi Laura Geller

One of my teachers once said that each of us has only one or two sermons that we keep giving over and over.

Well, I've been giving the same sermon for years. It is about the *Untaneh Tokef.* I gave it when I was a Hillel rabbi at USC. I gave it when I first came to my congregation. I gave another version after the 1994 earthquake. I gave it after 9/11. Most recently I gave it through the midrash of Leonard

Cohen's "Who by Fire," with its haunting last line,
"And who shall I say is calling?"

> And who by fire, who by water,
> who in the sunshine, who in the night time,
> who by high ordeal, who by common trial,
> who in your merry merry month of May,
> who by very slow decay,
> and who shall I say is calling?
>
> And who in her lonely slip, who by
> barbiturate,
> who in these realms of love, who by some-
> thing blunt,
> and who by avalanche, who by powder,
> who for his greed, who for his hunger,
> and who shall I say is calling?
>
> And who by brave assent, who by accident,
> who in solitude, who in this mirror,
> who by his lady's command, who by his
> own hand,
> who in mortal chains, who in power,
> and who shall I say is calling?

These are the
line breaks and
punctuation
according to Cohen's
official website.

I have given this sermon in our main sanctuary; I have given it as a family sermon. I have written about the *Untaneh Tokef* in numerous temple
bulletin columns and in weekly messages from the
clergy. I have introduced it with poetic and powerful *kavanot* and *iyun t'filah*. I have taught it as text
study with *chevruta*. And while the details of each
are different (and beautifully crafted, of course),
the message is always the same:

- First, that it's an intentionally terrifying image. It's an image that is meant to grab us and

shake us, to wake us up to the reality of our mortality: some of us will live through this year and some of us will die.

- Second, that it is a metaphor, not an actual description of how God works in the world. The God I believe in is not the one described in the *Untaneh Tokef.* God is not responsible for what we do to each other. We are responsible. The God I believe in is a presence, not a person. The God I believe in is the power that makes it possible for us to feel connected to each other . . . the God I believe in doesn't write in a book of life or death, doesn't decree who will live and who will die. The God I believe in animates a material universe where everything that lives eventually dies, some by fire, some by water, some by sword, some by beast, some by earthquake, and some by epidemic. The God I believe in is the Divinity I experience in the gift of my life and my breath. It is . . . up to me to make something meaningful with that gift.
- Third, that the metaphor only works if you follow it along to the end: "But *t'filah, tzedakah,* and *t'shuvah* avert the severity of the decree." Whatever is going to happen is going to happen. People will get sick. People will get into accidents. People will die. We can't change the truth of our lives, but we can change how we experience what is happening, how we respond to what happens—through *t'filah, tzedakah,* and *t'shuvah.*

One year in a bulletin article I was determined to deliver the message clearly and directly. I wrote:

I don't like the metaphor because too many people take it literally. Too many people believe that God actually does write in some

big book . . . and that good people are supposed to be rewarded with another year
of life and bad people are supposed to be
punished by death. The problem with taking it literally is: it isn't true. Are we saying
that some consciousness actually predeter-
mines who will live and who will die? Not
me. If I were rewriting the High Holy Day
liturgy, I would get rid of that prayer.

I mean, how much clearer could I be?

I have written that and said that, but, even so,
I don't get rid of the prayer. I can't get rid of it because it moves people more than any of the other
liturgy; in some ways it captures the essence of the
Yamim Noraim. Some of us *will* die in the coming
year. The "decree" is that things we didn't plan will
happen. God does not issue the "decree"; what will
happen, will happen. People die because people
die . . . sometimes when they are young and still
full of potential; sometimes in old age after a well-
lived life. It is just the way things are. We can't completely control what will happen in our lives, but
we can control how we respond. That message is
the point of the High Holy Days.

But still I know that this is an image that wounds
people. And no sermon I have given seems to be
powerful enough to keep it from hurting. I meet a
congregant in a hospital room and they ask, "How
can God let this happen to me?" Or they say," This
is a punishment from God." Or they are just so angry at God that they pull away from Jewish tradition
and the synagogue. I know there is a time to be a
pastor and a time to be a teacher—the hospital room
isn't the time for a discussion about theology. And
the High Holy Days, or at least a sermon in the High
Holy Days, doesn't seem to be the right time either.

There are lots of metaphors that do work for me. *Kol Nidrei*, however bizarre, seems to me to be about imagining who I am without any of the promises I have made. Who am I if I am not a wife, a mother, a daughter, a sister, a friend, a teacher, a rabbi: who am I without my vows? And at the end of a long and exhausting day of reflection, which vows do I want to make again? *N'ilah*, then, is less about the closing of the gates than about the retying of the vows I want to make again.

Lately the most powerful image in the *machzor* for me comes from *Sh'ma Koleinu: Al tashlicheinu l'eit zikna*, "Listen to our voice; do not cast us aside when we are old." The metaphors and images don't change from year to year . . . but I do. And so I hear some of them differently now. I don't bring them back to life (as the title of our session implies)—they jump out and grab me because of what is going on in my life.

Like all of you, I work hard to prepare for the High Holy Days. But I also understand that the High Holy Days are not about my sermons or my ability to translate the metaphors of the *machzor*. I take comfort from a *kavanah* that Rabbi David Stern wrote:

I am Nachshon's swim instructor
And I am not happy.
We had trained so hard—
Breast stroke, crawl, butterfly
Ready to lead the swim to freedom.

And then, just as it was time to lift his feet
from the sea floor
For the first perfect flutter kick
The waters parted, and he walked his way
toward promise.

Just like a rabbi at the holidays
Impeccably prepared
Ready to lead our people's crossing
With thrash and splash
Or the precision of perfect strokes.

But then, in moments of unexpected grace
We sense the blessing that comes from
beyond ourselves
And the waters we had trained so hard to
master
Simply part
And we are crossing with them, jubilant
Without a flutter or a kick.

For the past few years, my colleagues and I have read this with each other prior to the beginning of services. It reminds us that the High Holy Days are not about us, not about the sermons, not even about the music, but about making the space for each one of our congregants and each one of us to open our hearts to the grace that makes spiritual transformation possible. I can't really protect my congregation from the metaphors that wound. I can't even adequately translate the ancient images of male hierarchical transcendence into what for me are empowering images of immanence. I suspect I can never adequately communicate why the images that work for me actually work. All I really can do is to prepare as best as I can, and then to try to share the Torah of my own life as a model for congregants to touch the Torah of their own lives. And then . . . to get out of the way.

The most powerful moment of our High Holy Day experience happens right before *N'ilah.* The sanctuary is full, over one thousand people. We ask the congregation to be completely silent. And then, in a tradition I learned from Rabbi Jack Riemer, we

invite people to come up to the open ark . . . in silence . . . to finish whatever work is left to do. The
first year—seventeen years ago—only a few people
came forward. Each year more people have come
forward. Now there are hundreds of them, quietly,
respectfully, gathering on the bimah and patiently
waiting their turn to stand for a moment in front of
the open ark. Many of them cry, their tears keeping the gates of repentance open. I sit in the first
row watching . . . and being reminded that it is not
about me. My role is to make space for them and to
do my own spiritual work.

The second most powerful moment happens
during the Torah service when we choreograph
group *aliyot*, a practice that began in our New
Emanuel Minyan weekly Shabbat morning service.
Each year we uncover a metaphor in the verses we
read and invite people who resonate with the metaphor to come forward. So, for example, one year
the first Rosh HaShanah *aliyah* was framed with
this introduction: "In this *aliyah*, God remembers
Sarah. Though both she and Abraham are very
old, she gets pregnant and their son Isaac is born.
Remember that Sarah had given up on the idea
of ever having a child—she believed that she and
Abraham were too old, that it would never happen.
Talk about surprise! This *aliyah* is for anyone who
had something to celebrate in this past year, some
joy, some achievement, some surprise, something
unexpected or something planned, but something
that makes you thankful to God." People come forward, more and more every year, chant the blessings together, and then often weep as I, or my
colleague Jonathan Aaron, reframe the invitation
into a *Mi Shebeirach*. Some years the invitation that
emerges out of the Torah reading is an intention for
the coming year; other years it is a reflection on the

year that is concluding. But it is always a moment when the Torah of their life is deepened through the Torah of tradition.

So, much of our High Holy Day experience does work for me. But much doesn't.

When I am no longer the rabbi at Temple Emanuel I doubt that I will go to our main sanctuary High Holy Day service. It is still too "high church" for me, too frontal even with all the innovations we have made over the years, too formal, too many people. No *machzor*, however beautifully constructed, however thoughtfully gendered, will make enough of a difference. So, although I wasn't part of it because I was in the main sanctuary or the family service, for the first time this past year we offered a contemplative service led by a rabbinic intern and a congregant, created by a group of congregants who have participated in the Institute for Jewish Spirituality's lay retreats. No formal prayer book . . . just chanting, meditation, one hundred blasts of the shofar on Rosh HaShanah, a focus on the *Al Cheit*s on Yom Kippur, some iconic liturgy, and mostly a lot of silence. There were thirty people there on Rosh HaShanah; sixty on Yom Kippur. It is obviously not for everyone. But I suspect that is where I will go. And perhaps the contemplative service, over time, will begin to have an impact on the main sanctuary service as well, making it possible to include more meditation and silence.

When I came to Temple Emanuel eighteen years ago, I decided that I would know I had succeeded if I would join Temple Emanuel when I was no longer the rabbi, that is, if Temple Emanuel was a place I could really pray. It already is on Shabbat, and I am hopeful we are on our way with the *Yamim Noraim*. And then I will know, to borrow the words from Leonard Cohen's midrash, "who is calling."

Machzor and *Malchut*

Rabbi David Stern

I do not call any of my children by their given names. Our daughter Lili is Billy, or Squib; our daughter Nina is Beans, or Boo; our twenty-year-old son Jacob still lets me call him Goosie in public.

It's my own parental version of negative theology. No single name could possibly capture or contain the richness of feeling I have for them: the depth of love, the horizon of hope, the judgment and frustration and wonder and glee. So meet Nancy's and my progeny: the Squib, the Bean, and the Goose.

So if you can't even figure out what to call your own kids—finite in body but reaching infinite depths in their parents' hearts—how in the world are we to figure out what to call God? Names delimit, and God is limitless. Naming gives power to the namer over the named—but to imply our power over the Holy One would be to un-God God. Some, like Marcia Falk, suggest that even to call God *Atah* posits a separation between subject and object, a segmentation of being that contradicts the notion of a God who fills all the earth. But even if *Atah* did not suggest such separation, "Hey You" does not seem to be the most intimate and tender form of address for the Source of all life and hope.

It seems that the Psalmist gives us a hushed and helpful path out of the thicket: *l'cha dumiyah t'hilah*—"to You, silence is praise" (Psalm 65:2). We will simply remain mum on the issue of divine naming. We won't cheapen the Holy One—or our relationship to every breathtaking sunset—by slathering it with words. We'll just sit up straight, plant our feet on the floor, and breathe.

All of which is good, until you have to write a *machzor.* Until you want to create communal norms, and language and ritual. Until you have to wrestle with the inspiring and vexing nature of naming the unnamable. When even images that feel just right—like *Ein Sof* or *YHVH*—endlessness and be-ing—still consist of finite letters in finite words on a finite page.

But we keep at it because we recognize that our own leap toward the ineffable requires some concrete springboard, some kind of image which—if we are at our best—will not limit our sacred imaginations, but launch them. It's how Marianne Moore famously described the poet's task: the pre-sentation of "imaginary gardens with real toads in them." You can't get to abstraction via abstraction. The word "God" might not get me thinking about the transcendent, but the word "sunset" just might.

The word "sunset," and maybe even the word "king." That's right—as if this whole enterprise of naming weren't challenging enough, we're now going to stir the contradictory brew of verbal ne-cessity and verbal inadequacy with a royal scepter. We're going to take our good twenty-first-century Jews—already struggling with the notion of God, or indifferent, or stuck in fairy-tale conceptions—already tending to be trapped within the confines of words on a page rather than using them as springboards to prayer or sacred imagination—and to that noble, struggling twenty-first-century Jew, we're going to give a bonus challenge: the notion of divine sovereignty.

If you thought addressing God as "Hey You" was bad, try saying "Hey You" to a God who hangs out on a throne. Try triggering every modern am-bivalence about authority, or zealousness about personal autonomy, or wariness of submission, or vigilance about the oppressive narrowness of gendered language. If our tradition had to go and name the unnamable, why did we have to pick a name that would end up being so damn complicated?

We're smart enough to know why the anthropomorphism of *melech* might have been valuable, and might be still: in conventional interpretation, it signifies protection, providential care, the assertion of order over chaos, a world governed by good. But we're also smart enough to be troubled by conventional images of royalty. There is an irony to using a human king as the *mashal* for noble divine sovereignty. The truth is, our tradition has been ambivalent about human kings from the start—worried about how they might render us powerless or demand too much. The modern Jew who wrestles with notions of divine sovereignty can sound a lot like the prophet Samuel warning the people about kings.

Now in the face of all these complexities, we have some options. We could decide to take an approach that is resigned or rejectionist. We could simply eliminate the term *melech* and thereby eliminate any sense of historical or theological continuity. Or, we can keep using it—not refute it, but give up on connecting to it. So that centuries from now, God could paraphrase God's self in *Parashat Va-eira* and say of us: *Ush'mi melech lo nodati lahem* (Exodus 6:3). Yes, the term *melech* was around, but those limited moderns were never able to grasp that dimension of My being.

Or we could maintain the imagery out of a sense of romance or nostalgia. When Rabbi David Hartman, *alav hashalom*, returned to his congregation in Montreal after visiting Jerusalem in the weeks following the Six-Day War, he walked into his shul on

Tishah B'Av to find his congregants sitting on the floor and mourning the destruction of Jerusalem. He stood before them and said, "The Jews in Jerusalem are presently jubilant!" He later compared his congregants' jarring chanting of *Eichah* to "the case of a parent who continues praying for a child to get well even after the child's recovery because [the parent] fell in love with the prayer." How could we keep using a term that smacks of gender and power, that all but undermines what our colleague Peter Knobel has called a "theology of human adequacy," that seems to fly in the face of modern need and modern truth? Maybe we're just in love with the prayer.

Maybe—or maybe *melech* still has something to teach me. So here are some things I believe. I believe *m'lo chol haaretz k'vodo,* that God is all-encompassing being: warp and woof and *din* and *rachamim* and sunset and baby's cry and the way you know your lover's fingerprints in the palm of your hand.

And I embrace (after a lot of struggle) even the hierarchy implied by *melech,* because it teaches me humility. In the immortal words of Mel Brooks's 2000-Year-Old Man, "There's something bigger than Phil." I am part of, and not greater than. And by learning and relearning humility, by practicing and re-practicing, I am able to connect anew to the all-encompassing presence that is also *melech.* It is for me a deeply sacred spiral when I can find the path: from wonder to humility to wonder again.

The challenge for a *machzor,* of course—and the reason I affirm the wisdom of counter-texts—is that those *machzorim* will be the onramps and springboards and portals of possibility for our spiritually diverse communities and for any one person's spiritually varied life. So one day I may enter the space of prayer as an overconfident Sovereign Self, in need of humbling. On another I might already be stricken with *kotzer ruach* and need all the bolstering and nurturing I can find. There may be moments when I need a God who is *melech*—when a sense of hierarchy or God's greater-than is healing and anchoring to me. Or moments too when I am already feeling so diminished that assertions of divine power and my own smallness may be the last alienating and discouraging straw. Counter-texts help the *machzor* stay true to our varied communities and our variegated selves.

I'd like to conclude with an excerpt from Moshe Cordovero's *Or Ne'erav* and an excerpt from *Untaneh Tokef.*

From Cordovero :

An impoverished person thinks that God is an old man with white hair, sitting on a wondrous throne of fire that glitters with countless sparks . . . .

But if you are enlightened, you know God's oneness; you know that the divine is devoid of bodily categories—these can never be applied to God. Then you wonder, astonished: Who am I? I am a mustard seed in the middle of the sphere of the moon, which itself is a mustard seed within the next sphere. So it is with that sphere and all it contains in relation to the next sphere. So it is with all the spheres—one inside the other—and all of them are a mustard seed within the further expanses. And all of these are a mustard seed within further expanses.

Your awe is invigorated, the love in your soul expands.

Translation from Daniel C. Matt, *The Essential Kabbalah: The Heart of Jewish Mysticism* (New York: HarperCollins, 1995), 22; italics added.

I believe that I am a mustard seed in the middle of the moon, which is itself but a mustard seed within the next sphere. The challenge is to get from that awareness to Cordovero's last sentence, about awe and love. How can I help myself—and help others—to see that being a mustard seed on the surface of the moon is in fact a source of awe and not diminution, of nobility and not dehumanizing distance?

One answer lies in the text of *Untaneh Tokef* as it appears in our new *machzor,* including the final passage *Ein Kitzvah,* omitted from *Gates of Repentance.* It describes God's unbounded presence, and then *Untaneh Tokef,* replete with its sometimes overwhelming juxtaposition of our mortality and God's eternity, ends with these three words: *ush'meinu karata vishmecha*—"And our name You have linked with Your own."

We are small, but never untethered from the One whose presence fills the earth. We are a seed-speck upon the moon, but never insignificant. *Ush'meinu karata vishmecha*—somehow, our name echoes within the name of God—subject and sovereign, sovereign and subject—in the call of a single breath.

God and the *Machzor*

Rabbi Ariana Silverman

I want to start tonight with words of gratitude. I am honored and humbled that Rabbi Hara Person asked me to be on this panel. Echoing the sentiments of our new president, Rabbi Richard Block, this morning Dr. Lewis Barth thanked Rabbi Jonathan Stein for inviting him to lead *Azkarah*, and I, in turn, thank Hara for including me on a panel of colleagues who are, truly, giants, not just in the movement, but for me personally. Perhaps one of the most profound things we do as rabbis is to challenge and support the next generation, and it is particularly poignant for me to be sitting on a panel with Rabbi Larry Kushner, who served with my childhood rabbi, mentor, and teacher Rabbi Arnold Jacob Wolf (z"l), whose memory is an eternal blessing. I am here tonight as Rabbi Wolf's student, and as a student of *his* student, and as a teacher concerned about the next generation of students.

One of my favorite parts of my rabbinate is the time I spend having one-on-one conversations with young Jewish adults in their twenties and thirties. Most of them, as you well know, don't come to synagogues, or if they do, it is only on the High Holy Days. There are many people here who are doing very important work with this population, but I want to speak for a moment about their struggles with God. Many of them are technologically proficient but feel theologically paralyzed. When they tell me they don't believe in God, I often ask them to tell me about the god they don't believe in. It is almost always the man on the throne ready to judge and punish them and their loved ones, and often

245

Joel Mosbacher, "Searching for God in the 7th Grade," *CCAR Journal: A Reform Jewish Quarterly*, Spring 2009, 39–51. This article can also be found with discussion questions in *Machzor: Challenge and Change Volume 1* (New York: CCAR Press, 2009), 95–107, 208.

seemingly unfairly. Rabbi Joel Mosbacher wrote a great article in the Spring 2009 *CCAR Journal* about "Searching for God in the 7th Grade," and I am similarly worried about how young adults search for God, particularly if they are only in our synagogues twice a year.

It was, in part, based on these conversations with young adults that this past Rosh HaShanah, and actually unbeknownst to Rabbi Person when she asked me to speak, I gave my sermon on God and the *machzor*.

I told my congregation that when I was an adolescent, Yom Kippur was my favorite Jewish holiday. Perhaps I should have known then that I would end up as a rabbi someday. But it wasn't just that I was in love with Judaism, it was that, frankly, as a teenager, there were many things about myself that I hated. I wasn't smart enough, cool enough, pretty enough, funny enough. I believed the words of the *machzor* when it said that we, that I, was of little merit. And what could be better for an insecure adolescent girl than a day in which we get to dwell on how inadequate we are? I sat there, hungry and guilty and afraid, before a God who seemed aloof and judgmental and waiting to strike me down.

But then I went to camp and I went to youth group events and I started to pray not just in synagogues but on mountaintops, and eventually I went to Jewish studies classes, and thank God, I came to understand that God was not just the God of the *machzor*.

But here is what worries me. Many Jewish young adults did not have those experiences. And so, for many of them, the last time they were really challenged about what they believe about God was at thirteen years old. And then, when they become adults, the words of the *machzor* become the primary, if not the only, Jewish language with which they interact with God. Not all, but many of them, don't engage with the Shabbat liturgy, or speak to God on mountaintops, or sit with other Jews to wrestle with who or what or where or how God is. And when they—when we—don't do those things, we do the seemingly impossible: we limit God.

And so in my sermon I said the following:

> Many of you know that my spouse, Justin, is a law professor. I once got to go with him to see him argue in appeals court. He was authoritative, assertive, spoke in legal jargon. He never smiled once. And then he came home, unfastened his bowtie, and made me dinner. He made me dinner and he laughed and made jokes and looked at me lovingly when he put the food on the table.
>
> During the High Holy Days, we meet a God that is judge. Authoritative, speaking in High Holy Day jargon, and not really smiling. But here's the thing: if Justin, who is only human, can be both a lawyer and a husband, a serious advocate and a smiling cook, don't we think God can transcend the limitations of these words and this space and this time?

My sermon was inspired by these young adults and spoke to many of them. But a sermon, while a powerful tool, does not suffice, and most of us do not have the time to sit and talk one-on-one with young adults and try to undo the damage of stunted theological growth. And so, when I looked at a draft of the new *machzor*, I felt an incredible sense that we are truly creating something that speaks to these challenges. While we work on the larger questions of engaging young Jewish adults, and, really, all Jews, in Jewish life, we can also work on a *machzor* that presents some of the depth and breadth of Jewish theology within its pages. Please don't misunderstand me—one book will not send young Jews flocking back to synagogues. But it can be a powerful tool, and I am looking forward to sharing it with my students, and for that, I turn to my teachers, on this panel and in this room, and I wish to express my gratitude.

Mystery and Liturgy
Rabbi Lawrence Kushner

Pacific Union Club

The Pacific Union Club is in the old Flood Mansion straddling the very top of Nob Hill. A few years ago, doubtless through some cosmic error, I got invited to give a luncheon talk. I chose what I thought was an easy way out: I told a story. But, when I was done some guy politely asked, "Rabbi, what does the story mean?"

I'd never thought about it. It was just a pretty good story: It left you with more questions than answers. "A story doesn't *mean* anything," I said. "It's just a story. If I could tell you what it meant, it'd just be another silly lesson."

I now believe it's like that with liturgical metaphors, too. They can only hint at some deeper, abiding mystery that can only be evoked but never told. *Duh*, that's the reason they're metaphors. If we connected all the dots to the *nimshal*, they'd all fall apart. The *reason for* the metaphor is exactly because *it cannot be told straight out*.

Reform Judaism learned this the hard way. Decoding religious language, distilling it down to linear logic, striking anything beyond rationality, does *not* make it more accessible; it only makes it sound dumb. Some things need to remain recondite.

A more contemporary, less draconian Reform solution is: multiple choice. You know, the left-hand page or services II through X. You don't believe this? Well, then, how 'bout that? Now there's nothing to disagree with, annoy, or, alas, evoke the Mystery.

When we deprive liturgy of its poetic, verbal clothing, we deprive it of the ability to open the other side of our brains. When we deprive it of mystery, we deprive it of being prayer.

Zohar, **Bialik, Dan, and Feld**

Zohar 3:152a.

The *Baal HaZohar* warns, "Woe to those who claim the Torah only comes to tell stories of this world in ordinary language. If that were so . . . we could . . . write a better Torah . . . !"

If you ask me, we need *more* metaphors, not less. I say: The more mystery, the better. Indeed, preserving The Mystery may be our most important task.

In his seminal essay "Revealment and Concealment in Language," Hayim Nahman Bialik reminds us that language protects us from the ultimate *tohu*, the primal Nothingness out of which we have all come and into which we will all dissolve. We are, at once, drawn to it and terrified of it. His words:

Haim Nahman Bialik, *Revealment and Concealment: Five Essays* (Jerusalem: Ibis Editions, 2000) [גילוי וכיסוי בלשון, Hebrew, 1915], p. 20, reprinted from "Revealment and Concealment in Language," trans. Jacob Sloan, *Commentary* 9, no. 2 (1950): 171–5.

We construct barriers: words upon words and systems upon systems, and place them in front of the darkness to conceal it; but then our nails immediately begin to dig at those barriers, in an attempt to open the smallest of windows, the tiniest of cracks, through which we may gaze for a single moment at that which is on the other side.

The language of prayer is designed to *scramble* language, *mess* with our brains, take us to rationality's *edge*, and then give a push. All the good stuff transcends language. Joseph Dan quipped that not *all* kabbalists were mystics. Mystics, he says, are only the trans-verbal ones . . . If you can talk, cautions Dan, you'll never make it as a mystic!

The editor of the new Conservative siddur, Rabbi Ed Feld, observes:

> Like poetry, liturgical prayer expresses that which is experienced by the listener as pre-verbal. It captures a feeling we only barely knew we felt. The words are not ours. We know that we would never have written this text. Yet, something of ourselves has been captured here. . . . It is not that we have affirmed a series of truths, but that something of ourselves may have been brought to light.

Edward Feld, "Poetry and Prayer," *CrossCurrents* 62, no. 1 (March 2012): 71–74.

For Feld, prayer is not so much rehearsing things we already believe, or even goose bumps on the shore of the lake, but a solitary walk in the woods.

Metaphor

Let's "walk in the woods" with a few of *yontif*'s monster metaphors: the Book of Life; who's gonna live and who's gonna die; written in pencil, not yet in ink; and our Father, our King. They're only problems if we insist on reading them literally and rationally. Indeed, one of the hidden themes of the High Holy Day experience may be our collective infantilization. Permit me to suggest how we might expand the four metaphors:

1. There really is a book *in heaven* but it's much bigger than you thought; this *ledger* extends from one end of the universe to the other. Like the light of dead stars or radio waves reverberating throughout all space, all our deeds are recorded in it, remembered by the universe. It's all about *how we have lived.*
2. The universe really knows *"who will live and who will die." Everything* we have done and *everything*

that might yet happen; all recorded. And on *yon-tif* we are lifted above the everyday static and glimpse a destiny and a future that have been patiently waiting for us all along. We have a brush with *bashert* and behold a higher form of our freedom.

3. All our deeds are recorded but only in pencil. *Whew!* There's still time. But beware, come the end of Yom Kippur, a hand will rewrite them all again in ink. You want, maybe, to reconsider or retract anything? It's up to you. Every sin can be transformed into a merit (Babylonian Talmud, *Yoma* 86b). It's not too late. Turning is always possible.

4. God really is *Avinu Malkeinu, our Father, our King;* but God is also *Imeinu M'rachmeinu,* our Mother and our Source. I suspect that we don't mind having a father in heaven as long as we have a mother there too.

And, of course, if all else fails, we can cash in on our illiteracy and simply leave it in Hebrew, which, since hardly anyone understands, conveniently permits us to supply our own meanings. I suspect that that's probably why our liturgy has been so resilient over the generations.

Kol D'mamah Dakah

Bialik again:

[There are . . .] languages without words: songs, tears, and laughter. . . . These languages begin where words leave off, and their purpose is not to close but to open. They rise from the void. They *are* the rising up of the void. . . . Every creation of the spirit which lacks an echo of one of these three

Bialik, *Revealment and Concealment,* 26.

> languages is not really alive, and it were best that it had never come into the world.

Sure, language tames reality. But the reality organized by languages is an illusion. As Daniel Matt says, "Just because we have names for all the parts of a tree doesn't mean a tree has all those parts." Nothing, in other words, changes because we can name it or describe it in a way that makes rational sense. Our anxiety is diminished. But beyond regular language there is only poetry, melody, and metaphor. They are doorways into the great silence, *kol d'mamah dakah*.

Between Faith and Protest: Bringing Back to Life the Challenging Metaphors in the *Machzor*
Discussion Questions

1. Is fear an appropriate emotion to evoke in our communities during High Holy Day worship? Why or why not? What other emotions are often associated with the *Yamim Noraim*?
2. What do you do with challenging High Holy Day liturgy? Do you resign yourself to it, reject it altogether, keep it for the sake of romance or nostalgia, or try to learn from it? Does your response depend on the prayer in question or your mood at the moment?
3. What are the challenges of reading liturgy literally? What are the challenges of reading liturgy metaphorically?
4. Which metaphors and images in the High Holy Day liturgy work for you and why?
5. How can the new *machzor* help to bridge our operational theology (the theology that influences how we operate) and our espoused theology (the theology we say we have)?
6. How can we use silence effectively in worship, especially on the High Holy Days?

7. How can we translate this conversation about metaphors in the *machzor* that is taking place among the elite for the folk in our communities, especially for our young people?
8. What did you learn from these presentations on metaphors in the *machzor* that you would like to implement in your community's High Holy Day worship?

Biographies of Presenters

Dr. Debra Reed Blank teaches the history and theology of Jewish liturgy at Hebrew College in Newton MA. Currently she is completing a book about Jewish-feminist rituals for newborn girls. From 1998–2009, she was a faculty member of the Jewish Theological Seminary (New York City), teaching liturgy and Talmud. She has also taught at the Academy for Jewish Religion (New York) and the Russian State University for the Humanities (Moscow). Her recent publications include "Reflections Upon Creating Innovative, Jewish Life-Cycle Ritual" (keshetonline.org) and her edited volume, *The Experience of Jewish Liturgy: Essays in Honor of Menahem Schmelzer* (Brill, 2011), which includes her article "The Curious Theological Grammar of *Ga'al Yisra'el.*" She received her PhD (Liturgy and Rabbinics) and ordination from the Jewish Theological Seminary.

Rabbi Herbert Bronstein is rabbi emeritus/senior scholar at North Shore Congregation Israel in Glencoe, Illinois, and serves on the faculty of Lake Forest College, teaching courses in the history of religions. He served as a member and then chairman of the Liturgy Committee of the CCAR and the Joint Commission on Worship of the CCAR and Union of American Hebrew Congregations; was editor of *A Passover Haggadah* (CCAR Press); and has written and lectured widely on the inner design of Jewish liturgy.

Rabbi Laura Geller is a senior rabbi at Temple Emanuel in Beverly Hills, California. She previously served as executive director of the American Jewish Congress, Pacific Southwest Region and as Hillel director at the University of Southern California and is a Fellow on the Corporation of Brown University. Rabbi Geller has been named one of *Newsweek's 50 Most Influential Rabbis in America*. An author of many articles in journals and books, she served on the Editorial Board of *The Torah: A Woman's Commentary*. She was ordained by the Hebrew Union College in 1976, the third woman in the Reform Movement to become a rabbi.

Rabbi Neil Gillman, PhD, is professor emeritus of Jewish thought at the Jewish Theological Society and is author of several books and essays, including *Sacred Fragments: Recovering Theology for the Modern Jew* (winner of the 1991 National Jewish Book Award in Jewish Thought); *Conservative Judaism: A New Century; The Way into Encountering God in Judaism; Gabriel Marcel on Religious Knowledge; The Death of Death: Resurrection and Immortality in Jewish Thought* (translated into Czech); *The Jewish Approach to God: A Brief Introduction for Christians;* and *Traces of God: Seeing God in Torah, History, and Everyday Life.*

Rabbi Edwin Goldberg holds a doctorate in Hebrew literature from Hebrew Union College-Jewish Institute of Religion. He is the senior rabbi of Temple Sholom of Chicago. He serves as the coordinating editor of the upcoming *Mishkan HaNefesh.* He has published five books, including his latest, *Saying No and Letting Go: Jewish Wisdom on Making Room for What Matters Most* (Jewish Lights, 2013).

Jessica Greenbaum is the author of *The Two Yvonnes*, a 2012 selection in the Princeton University Press Series of Contemporary Poets, and *Inventing Difficulty*, which won the Gerald Cable Prize in 2000. She is the poetry editor for the annual *upstreet*.

Dr. Bonna Devora Haberman is the Israeli founder of Women of the Wall. She is the author of National Jewish Book award finalist *ReReading Israel: The Spirit of the Matter* and *Israeli Feminism Liberating Judaism: Blood and Ink*. Among her projects in Jerusalem, she co-directs Israeli-Palestinian YTheater Project Jerusalem. Dr. Haberman has taught at Harvard, Brandeis and Hebrew Universities.

Yair Harel is director and editor-in-chief of the website "Invitation to *Piyut*," as well as artistic director of the Jerusalem *Piyut* Festival. He is a musician, singer and percussion player, and one of the founding members of the Ensembles *Tefillat & Haouman Hai*.

Rabbi Jo Hirschmann, BCC, is certified as a chaplain through the National Association of Jewish Chaplains. She currently serves as pastoral care coordinator at Phelps Hospice in Sleepy Hollow, New York. She writes and teaches on topics at the intersection of contemporary pastoral care and Jewish textual traditions.

Rabbi Elie Kaplan Spitz is rabbi of Congregation B'nai Israel in Tustin, California. A member of the Rabbinical Assembly Committee of Law and Standards and a graduate of the Jewish Theological Seminary and Boston University School of Law, he is the author of many articles dealing with spirituality and Jewish law and teaches the philosophy of Jewish law at the University of Judaism.

Rabbi Zoe Klein is rabbi of Temple Isaiah in Los Angeles. Rabbi Klein has written numerous articles, poems, and prayers which are used in houses of prayer all around the country. She has appeared as a commentator on the History Channel in *Digging for the Truth.*

Rabbi Lawrence Kushner is scholar-in-residence at Congregation Emanu-El, San Francisco. He teaches an annual, two-week seminar at the Hebrew Union College–Jewish Institute of Religion, Los Angeles campus. He has written eighteen books on spirituality and Kabbalah, and has oil paintings in two galleries in San Francisco.

Dr. Ruth Langer is professor of Jewish Studies at Boston College and associate director of its Center for Christian-Jewish Learning. She received her PhD in Jewish Liturgy in 1994 and her rabbinic ordination in 1986 from Hebrew Union College–Jewish Institute of Religion in Cincinnati. She is a graduate of Bryn Mawr College and a native of Pittsburgh, Pennsylvania. Her newest book, *Cursing the Christians?: A History of the Birkat HaMinim,* traces the history of a Jewish prayer that was, in its medieval forms, a curse of Christians. She is also author of *To Worship God Properly: Tensions between Liturgical Custom and Halakhah in Judaism,* and co-edited *Liturgy in the Life of the Synagogue* (Eisenbrauns, 2005).

Amichai Lau-Lavie is founding director of Storahtelling and spiritual leader of Lab/Shul. He is currently a rabbinical student at the Jewish Theological Seminary of America. Amichai was a Jerusalem Fellow at the Mandel Leadership Institute in Israel and is a consultant to the Reboot Network, a member of the URJ Faculty Team, and a fellow of the new Clergy Leadership Institute.

Rabbi Richard N. Levy is a former director of the school of Rabbinic Studies on the Los Angeles campus of HUC-JIR where he now serves as Director of Spiritual Growth. He is a past president of the Central Conference of American Rabbis. He is editor of *On Wings of Awe*, a High Holy Day *machzor*; *On Wings of Freedom*, a Passover Haggadah; and *On Wings of Light*, a Shabbat evening prayer book.

Rabbi Ellen Lippmann is founder and rabbi of Kolot Chayeinu/Voices of Our Lives. She is former East Coast director of Mazon: A Jewish Response to Hunger and former director of the Jewish Women's Program at the New 14th Street Y in Manhattan. She serves on the Executive Committee and board of The Shalom Center and chaired the first North American Rabbinic Conference on Judaism & Human Rights. Rabbi Lippmann was ordained in 1991 by Hebrew Union College–Jewish Institute of Religion.

Rabbi Leon A. Morris is rabbi of Temple Adas Israel in Sag Harbor, New York, and a member of the CCAR *Machzor* Editorial Committee. He was founding director of the Skirball Center for Adult Jewish Learning at Temple Emanu-El in Manhattan. Rabbi Morris was ordained by Hebrew Union College in 1997, where he was a Wexner Graduate Fellow. He has worked extensively as an educator with the Jewish community of India. He served as director of New York Kollel: A Center for Adult Jewish Study at HUC-JIR and was among the founders of Lishmash, a one-day festival of Jewish life and learning.

Rabbi Donald B. Rossoff is rabbi of Temple B'nai Or in Morristown, New Jersey. He is author of a book on spirituality, *The Perfect Prayer,* and contributed chapters to *The Jew in the Modern World: A Documentary History* and *Chosen Tales: Stories Told by Jewish Storytellers.* As a musician, he published *Adonai Li,* (with Cantor Bruce Benson) and the lyrics for "You Can Change the World" (with Cantor Jeff Klepper). As a flutist, he has performed and recorded with Kol Sasson and Kol B'seder and has performed on stage with Peter Yarrow, Debbie Friedman, and Craig Taubman.

Dr. Richard S. Sarason is professor of Rabbinic Literature and Thought at HUC-JIR, Cincinnati, where he has been a faculty member since 1979. Previously, he was assistant professor of Religious Studies at Brown University, where he received his PhD in 1977. He was ordained at HUC-JIR, Cincinnati, in 1974. He was a member of the Siddur Editorial Advisory Committee that worked on *Mishkan T'filah,* the new Reform prayer book. He serves as a vice-chair on the Joint Commission on Worship, Music, and Religious Living, and has been a regular contributor to "Ten Minutes of Torah: Delving Into T'filah."

Rabbi Ariana Silverman is a rabbi in Detroit, Michigan. She served as assistant rabbi at Temple Kol Ami in West Bloomfield, Michigan. She has worked for the Religious Action Center of Reform Judaism and the Coalition on the Environment and Jewish Life, and is a Wexner Graduate Fellowship alumna.

Dr. Rhoda J. H. Silverman, PhD, has served Temple Emanuel of Baltimore since 2000 and is currently filling the roles of both Rabbi and Cantor. She received her Doctorate in Jewish Studies from the Baltimore Hebrew Institute at Towson University (formally Baltimore Hebrew University) in May of 2012. She received her Masters of Sacred Music and cantorial ordination from HUC-DFSSM in 1993, and received independent Rabbinic s'michah concurrently with her doctoral studies in 2008 from The Rabbinical Academy.

Rabbi David Stern is senior rabbi of Temple Emanu-El, Dallas, Texas. He serves as Vice-President for Organizational Relationships of the Central Conference of American Rabbis, on the President's Rabbinic Council of Hebrew Union College-Jewish Institute of Religion, and as a Board Member of the Union for Reform Judaism. He is a former Vice-Chair of the Reform Movement's Joint Commission on Social Action. His poetry has been published in the *CCAR Journal*, and he has contributed essays to three volumes on Jewish High Holy Day liturgy published by Jewish Lights Press: *Who By Fire, Who By Water: Untaneh Tokef, All These Vows: Kol Nidre,* and *May God Remember: Yizkor*. He was ordained at the Hebrew Union College-Jewish Institute of Religion in 1989.

Rabbi Elaine Zecher is rabbi at Temple Israel of Boston, Massachusetts. She sits on the board of the Anti-Defamation League and has been instrumental in the development of *Mishkah T'filah*, the Reform Jewish Movement's new prayer book for Shabbat, weekdays, and festivals. She serves as the Chair of the Worship and Practices Committee of the Central Conference of American Rabbis, and also chairs the CCAR *Machzor* Advisory Group. She has also been one of the driving forces behind Synagogue 3000, a national project to revitalize the synagogue structure to support Jewish communities in engaging their congregants in new ways of meaning, spirituality, and connectedness.

PART 3

RELATED
ARTICLES AND POEMS
FROM *CCAR JOURNAL:*
THE REFORM
JEWISH QUARTERLY,
SUMMER 2013

Preparing for the New *Machzor* and the High Holy Days: An Integrated Approach

Elaine Zecher

In order to begin to speak about the new *machzor*, I first turn to the subject of medicine. Many years ago, I learned from my physician husband about a particular concept that I believe informs an approach to liturgy—especially *Mishkan T'filah* and the new *machzor*. It was and continues to be referred to as "integrative medicine."[1] The idea arose from the consistent and widespread use of medical approaches not widely practiced in established medical institutions like hospitals and doctors' offices. Common examples include acupuncture, herbal remedies, massage, and mindfulness-based meditation, to name a few. Their practice was widespread but they were deemed alternative or complementary as they were not part of the mainstream. Following a scientific survey documenting the widespread use of these practices[2] and continued studies of their safety and efficacies, the medical establishment slowly began to explore how best to incorporate them into medical settings like academic health centers and medical schools. Over the course of two decades, these modalities turned from having an exclusively complementary role in the practice of medicine to being more commonly integrated and part of routine treatment protocols. Side by side with traditional medical modalities like prescription drugs, surgery, radiation therapies, and other modern methods, the juxtaposition of these treatments created a potential synergistic relationship aimed at preventing, treating, and managing diseases. Each treatment method could stand on its own, but combined they could have a more powerful influence on the health

ELAINE ZECHER (NY83) has served as rabbi at Temple Israel, Boston, since 1990. She serves as chair of the Liturgy and Practices Committee of the CCAR. She also chairs the *Machzor* Advisory Group and is a vice president of the CCAR Board.

ELAINE ZECHER

and well-being of an individual. The goal wasn't necessarily to create a hybrid treatment but rather to apply these multiple medical
modalities in a coordinated fashion in conjunction with each other
so that a stronger result could potentially ensue.

Understanding the concept of integrative medicine has led me
to see parallels in the way we utilize a similar protocol through
Mishkan T'filah and the new *machzor*—though our intention is to
affect the soul more than the body. As a member of the Editorial Committee for the New Prayer Book, now called *Mishkan
T'filah*, I remember the conversation we had on how to arrange
a page of liturgy so that it contained multiple modalities of expression with traditional and other creative approaches. In the
beginning of putting together the prayer book, Elyse Frishman,
the editor, worked diligently to ensure each page could reflect
more than its traditional counterpart. She presented what has
become an integral part of the Reform liturgical experience: two
pages facing each other based on the theme of the prayer. In that
moment she opened up the possibility to enter different voices,
perspectives, and understanding into prayer. It was transformative. Poetry, psalms, creative interpretations, spiritual commentary, and source explanations could complement the traditional
prayer, the faithful translation, and transliteration.

Through organizing and reorganizing the two-page spread,
a design emerged, but something else happened as well. Most
of the historical, traditional prayers we use refer to God as omnipotent, omnipresent, and most often, in a hierarchical framework. With the advent of the two-page spread, we could also
include varied expressions of the Divine. In the same way that
integrative medicine seeks to combine different therapeutic approaches, both "conventional" and "complementary," to treat
an individual, we began to see how an individual could experience the sacred through the exposure and employment of
different approaches to God. Unlike *Gates of Prayer*, which has
different services each expressing a different theological view
of God, *Mishkan T'filah*, as designed by Elyse Frishman with the
Editorial Committee, could create a synergistic understanding
of God. I call this an integrated theology. As such, an integrated
theology juxtaposes and places different theological ideas in
close proximity allowing them to stand alone but also to combine for a stronger concept of God. Take most pages of *Mishkan*

T'filah and it is possible to find different voices rising from the page together.

The editors of the new *machzor* have taken the concept of an integrated theology but have applied it to the unique complexities of a High Holy Day prayer book. The new *machzor*, like *Mishkan T'filah*, will provide us new and innovative approaches and will certainly reflect the thoughtful work of these editors.

As we began to think about the introduction of the new *machzor*, we wanted to utilize this *CCAR Journal* symposium as a resource with which to consider new ideas and concepts, some of which will be reflected in our new High Holy Day prayer book. All of the articles, however, provide thoughtful consideration for this important season of the year. Whether we lead the prayers, offer words of Torah, interpret the liturgy through music, organize and administer all details, or find ourselves sitting among the community, this time of year calls upon us to prepare. Each year, the *machzor* invites us to plummet the depths of our souls, to be lost in the search, and then to find our way back.

It is an honor to introduce this symposium issue of the *CCAR Journal* focusing on the *machzor* and its myriad components. Though we may only use it during a brief time during the Jewish calendar year, its influence reaches much further beyond time and space. The articles that follow integrate many of the ideas that the *machzor* presents.

This issue is divided into three sections. The first one is made up of articles by the Editorial Core Team, whose efforts have helped to shape the new *machzor* in profound ways. Edwin Goldberg shares the *machzor* Vision Statement created by the editors as a vision to guide the process and provides commentary of it. Shelley Marder offers a beautiful understanding to the role of poetry not only in the new *machzor* but also its important place in liturgy as a whole. Leon Morris considers how to mine our traditional resources as a dynamic and vibrant process in creating innovative and meaningful worship. Although Janet Marder has not submitted her own essay, her influence is contained throughout.

We are grateful to have the voices of a professor of liturgy from each of the four HUC-JIR campuses, which make up the second section of the symposium. Whether through a personal experience with her Israeli students as Dalia Marx describes or Richard Sarason's wonderful concept of "music inside the text" or Richard

ELAINE ZECHER

Levy's analysis of the three major *machzorim* utilized by our movement or Larry Hoffman's foundational explication of the power
of liturgy done well, each of these professors continue to guide
us with their wisdom in order to increase and to deepen our own
understanding and thinking.

The third and final section's collection of articles by colleagues in
diverse Jewish settings further complements our preparation. We
begin on a conceptual level taking a broader and more general perspective and then move closer in to specific sections and prayers.
Cantor Evan Kent, whose contributions have been invaluable to
the Editorial Core Team, introduces the concept of synesthesia and
analyzes the importance of the senses to the liturgical experience.
Elyse Frishman beautifully synthesizes the role of the *machzor* as a
tool to the greater endeavor of High Holy Day worship. Lawrence
Englander explains his concept using concentric circles to describe
how relationships on multiple levels inform our understanding of
the *machzor*. Leon Morris offers an example of creative retrieval
and uses the "inescapable link between sacrifice and prayer" as an
example. Margaret Moers Wenig and Donald Rossoff help us make
the transition into specific sections of the *machzor* with a focus on
the *Yizkor* service. Wenig delves into the inherent significance of
the experience and Rossoff analyzes its structure and its impact,
presenting additional possibilities to be included. Donald Cashman demonstrates how *Kol Nidrei* can be offered through the involvement and direct participation of the congregation. Lindsay
Bat Joseph weaves a personal story around *Untaneh Tokef* and Amy
Scheinerman examines this same prayer through the lens of process theology.

This section and the symposium's concluding three articles
ground us with the influence of other important texts. Judith
Abrams exposes the *Y'rushalmi*'s mystical influence on the *machzor*.
Aaron Panken shares his scholarship of the Second Temple Period
and how texts from that time inform our understanding of the
machzor. And finally, Elsie Stern focuses her attention on the Deuteronomy sources that make up the Yom Kippur Morning Torah
Service as an intriguing perspective from Moab.

This year in particular, as 5773 turns to 5774, we want to help
position ourselves to enter into the Days of Awe with intention and
introspection. As we prepare to receive a new *machzor* in the near
future, we wanted to provide a forum to consider the many themes

PREPARING FOR THE NEW *MACHZOR* AND THE HIGH HOLY DAYS

and ideas provided by the worship experience itself, the liturgy, and the vast array of ideas and themes that stem from it to create an integrated and well-informed platform.

One more note: Many of us, as members of the Central Conference of American Rabbis, benefit in known and unknown ways from the work of the professionals at the CCAR. I want to express our profound gratitude to Hara Person, who works diligently on our behalf to develop, foster, and steward the many publications. Her contributions, in particular, to secure the strength and quality of the new *machzor* has enabled the kind of creative and innovative work being offered to produce this important piece of liturgy for our movement. We thank her immensely.

Notes

1. Ralph Snyderman and Andrew T. Weil, "Integrative Medicine: Bringing Medicine Back to Its Roots," *Archives of Internal Medicine* 162, no. 2 (2002): 395–97.
2. David M Eisenberg, Ronald Kessler, et al., "Unconventional Medicine in the United States—Prevalence, Costs, and Patterns of Use" *New England Journal of Medicine* 328 (1993): 246–52.

Section One: From the Editors of the New Machzor

The New Reform *Machzor* Is a Solution, but What Is the Problem?

Edwin C. Goldberg

Introduction

Creating a new *machzor* for the Reform Movement is a daunting task and, speaking on behalf of the editorial committee, we are humbled by the challenge. Effective worship is difficult enough to create under normal Shabbat circumstances. The theological, sociological, and logistical trials wrought by the Days of Awe (or Days of Fright, in Lawrence Hoffman's felicitous translation) are formidable. Of course, the challenge is a holy one, and a problem that reflects the greatest reason for our rabbinic *raison d'être*. Meeting this task head on, we are guided by a clear vision of what we wish to produce, as well as aided by the outstanding work of those who prepared earlier *machzorim* and siddurim. Indeed, we are honored by the position we have been given in the chain of American Reform Jewish continuity.

Shortly after beginning work on the *machzor* I came across an original 1895 *Union Prayer Book II*, which I had forgotten I owned. My great-grandfather's name is inscribed inside. I enjoy imagining Lewis Wessel praying with this book at Shaaray Tefila on the Upper West Side. Our new book will be quite different, of course, but if we succeed it will seek to solve the same essential problem: how do we help ourselves return to our sacred path, in a world that continually seduces us away from the work that we must do?

EDWIN C. GOLDBERG, D.H.L. (C89) is the incoming senior rabbi at Temple Shalom of Chicago.

THE NEW REFORM *MACHZOR* IS A SOLUTION, BUT WHAT IS THE PROBLEM?

This question has been at the forefront of the editorial team of the upcoming CCAR *machzor*. We are not creating a book, per se, so much as a sacred tool that is part of the solution to a problem (or set of problems). Therefore, before any decisions could be made concerning the book itself, we needed to make sure we accurately defined the problem. After all, as the late Stephen Covey used to teach, it doesn't matter how efficient you are chopping down trees if you are actually in the wrong forest.

The desire to make sure we were addressing the right challenge led us to create a vision statement before we began producing the *machzor*. This statement not only reflects the solution we would be proposing in the form of a sacred book but also the challenges such a book would seek to address, with the understanding that the book itself could only be a part of a larger assemblage of sacred worship tools.

At the end of the article is the full vision statement we produced. In this article I want to focus on the central bullet points of the statement and include some personal commentary. For the sake of clarity I am putting into italics the key terms that are featured in the commentary. These italics do not appear in the actual vision statement.

Bullet Points of Vision Statement

We envision a twenty-first-century *machzor* that . . .

- provides meaningful liturgy to those who pray regularly, and welcomes those who are new to Jewish spirituality and practice;
- *inspires Reform Jews* to participate in the multifaceted experience of the *Yamim Noraim*—from feelings of awe to moments of solace, from the solitude of contemplation to the solidarity of song and worship;
- draws from the deep wellsprings of Jewish liturgy, history, thought, music, interpretation, and creativity;
- guides worshipers, in accessible ways, through the journey of *t'shuvah* and *cheshbon hanefesh*;
- *values continuity and incorporates the outlook of the twenty-first-century* Reform Jewish community of North America;
- bridges the personal and the communal, the ritual and the ethical dimensions of the *Yamim Noraim*.

EDWIN C. GOLDBERG

Commentary

"Inspires Reform Jews"

In order to inspire the worshiper we must begin by defining who that worshiper is and who the worshiper is not. In this case, although we value the prayer experience of the rabbi and cantor, we are clear in our desire to fashion a prayer book for *amcha*. In other words, we are the first to admit that the book will not be the most user-friendly option out there. As with *Mishkan T'filah* it is highly likely that the clergy who use this book initially will find it less enjoyable than the congregants they serve. We know that the book will take plenty of forethought and will call upon a balance between offering directions and allowing the congregation to have their own experience. No one said that leading effective worship should be easy, and we believe that the goal is not to offer simple worship. Having said that, we want worship that is complex rather than complicated and we are striving to meet that goal as best we can.

The *machzor* is not just for *amcha* (or "Jews in the pews"); it is for specific Jews, Reform Jews. One might argue that we would be better off producing a book that we could market to all Jews. Nevertheless, our committee understands the principle that we cannot create a *kol bo machzor* for all people, so we are better off making sure the *machzor* reflects the sensibilities of Reform Jews. In our era, such a group is diverse enough to present many challenges.

"T'shuvah and Cheshbon Hanefesh"

In designing a *machzor* we find it helpful to begin with the end in mind, another useful insight from the late Stephen Covey. Specifically, what do we hope to have realized by the worshipers at the end of *N'ilah*? How will their lives have changed? What will be different? The simple answer is to suggest that *t'shuvah* will have occurred, but what does this mean? Certainly it seems impossible to measure the inner life of a person, so would we even know if we had succeeded? Such is the work of rabbis that we will never know for sure if the experiences we provide lead to the results we desire. Nevertheless, even if we cannot know for certain where people end up, we most assuredly should design the best "map" possible. Hence our *machzor* will be designed to lead the worshiper through a process that we label the "i-axis," in which the various services build up to a climax where painful truths are realized, change is considered and adopted, and the individual leaves with a plan for self-improvement.

A little more explanation of the "i-axis": If you imagine a graph with an x-axis and a y-axis, representing horizontal and vertical points, one can also speak of the actual flow-line of the graph, which ends up in a different place from where it starts. We are designing the *machzor* with a vision in mind in which the worshiper will end up in a different place on Yom Kippur afternoon than where one began on Rosh HaShanah eve (or better yet, on Rosh Chodesh Elul). We hope that an inner-process of *t'shuvah* will have occurred, including the difficult work of examining oneself, finding faults, and beginning to correct such faults.

This i-axis manifests itself in the selection of *Avinu Malkeinu* verses and *Al Cheit* confessions we choose for various parts of the service, as well as the decision to focus in particular on Musar material for Yom Kippur afternoon. By that point in the Days of Awe we hope that *amcha* is ready for "building themselves back up" through Musar meditation and learning, as well as prayer, in order to greet the end of the day with not only renewed hope but also a new direction.

"Values Continuity and Incorporates the Outlook of the Twenty-first Century"

During the course of our work we often consider the various Friday night services in the *Gates of Prayer* and how each one reflects a different theology. Then there is the *integrated theology* of *Mishkan T'filah*. Our approach is to build on the integrated theology while at the same time understanding that, to put it mildly, the theological stakes are higher on these Days of Awe. In other words, on a given Friday night one might very well focus on a non-dualistic image of God or perhaps the theology of human adequacy. The High Holy Days cannot be treated in the same manner. Somewhere a more traditional theology of hierarchy has to be offered if we are to be true to the essential message and tone of these days. Therefore we know the greatest challenge of the book will most likely be how to reflect this tradition while at the same time not turning off all those who cannot reconcile such views with the God in which they want to believe.

EDWIN C. GOLDBERG

I call this the "Singing in the Rain" factor. The popular song was eventually slated to be a movie. Asked about it, its future star, Gene Kelly, said he had no idea what the movie would be about but he was sure of two things: "There will be rain and I will be singing in it." We know as editors that there is going to be some form of *Untaneh Tokef* in the book, even if during our investigation we discovered how relatively minor this *piyut* (actually a *siluk*) was in its initial incarnation. In addition to the more traditional approach to God, we will offer, especially on the left side of the two-page spread, various images of God that challenge the hierarchical model, especially making use of poetry and well-chosen metaphor.

The purpose of having a two-page spread throughout most of the book is not to provide variety, per se, but rather to ensure that there are different theological positions mingling together so that each service can be—if the leaders choose—different every time, offering a mix of theologies in an effort to reflect the diversity of our God perspectives.

Conclusion

Harvard professor Clayton Christensen likes to tell the story of the fast food chain that found that about half of milkshake sales occurred in the morning. These buyers came into the restaurant by themselves, bought a milkshake and nothing else, and drove away with the milkshake rather than consuming it at the restaurant. Looking deeper, researchers learned that the buyers were commuters, and the job of the milkshake was to provide distraction on a long commute and to tide them over until lunch. For this job, the milkshake competed with bananas, donuts, breakfast bars, and coffee. Commuters bought milkshakes over the competition because milkshakes take a long time to consume, don't slosh or leave crumbs, and can be held in one hand or be put into a cup holder during the drive.

Most of us don't think of milkshakes as solution to a problem (i.e., hunger, boredom, need for convenience) but it turns out they are a solution and happy is the fast food establishment that knows the problem its product seeks to address.

Likewise, although milkshakes and the Days of Awe are not a natural pairing (*alas*) there is an important lesson: Our new *machzor* will be judged on how it looks and its content, but our visioning

THE NEW REFORM *MACHZOR* IS A SOLUTION, BUT WHAT IS THE PROBLEM?

process began from a different place: what problem should the *machzor* set out to solve, and therefore what are the challenges we must face? Our vision statement reflects our working through this question in an effort to make sure that our sacred book will not only be sacred but also relevant.

A VISION STATEMENT FOR A NEW REFORM *MACHZOR*

T'shuvah is the chief goal of the *Yamim Noraim*, and a *machzor* is our indispensable manual and guide. We aim to create a *machzor* that will serve Reform Jews as they seek repentance, new direction, and a sense of return to God and the Jewish people.

We envision a twenty-first-century *machzor* that . . .

- provides meaningful liturgy to those who pray regularly and welcomes those who are new to Jewish spirituality and practice;

- inspires Reform Jews to participate in the multifaceted experience of the *Yamim Noraim*—from feelings of awe to moments of solace, from the solitude of contemplation to the solidarity of song and worship;

- draws from the deep wellsprings of Jewish liturgy, history, thought, music, interpretation, and creativity;

- guides worshipers, in accessible ways, through the journey of *t'shuvah* and *cheshbon hanefesh*;

- values continuity and incorporates the outlook of the twenty-first-century Reform Jewish community of North America;

- bridges the personal and the communal, the ritual and the ethic

We embrace the rich liturgical voices of the Jewish past and the aspirations of our people today. Among those aspirations is the wish for a *machzor* whose words, tone, and theological range are uplifting, inviting, and challenging. We seek metaphors and images of God that will speak to our time, as the prayers of *Union Prayer Book II* and *Gates of Repentance* spoke with depth and authenticity to theirs. We seek an integration of tradition and innovation, prayer and music, speech and silence, the struggle with God and the struggle with being human.

Most important to our work are the people for whom this book is intended: the members of a dynamic, ever-changing, and diverse Reform Movement who gather in community to experience awe and forgiveness and hope. Some call themselves classical

EDWIN C. GOLDBERG

Reform; some seek to recover and reinterpret the broader Jewish heritage. Some resonate with traditional views of God; others find it hard to believe in God at all. One can hardly overstate the challenge before us, as we strive for a liturgical message that illuminates and inspires.

We are open to exploring the use of early *piyutim* and modern poetry, visual art used as text, commentary that is intellectually engaging and spiritually provocative, music that we already cherish as well as musical innovation. We will attempt to frame with sensitivity texts that are painful or disturbing. Translations and original materials must be beautiful and evocative, conveying to worshipers an appreciation of our inherited liturgical tradition, as well as Judaism's relevance to their lives. We seek a balance between the creative retrieval of classical texts and the present-day sensibilities of Reform Jews.

Mishkan T'filah is our base text, and a great deal will flow from the structure it provides. At the same time, the historical *machzor* is central to our efforts, as it has been to Reform liturgists of the past. Our work will be informed by the various *minhagim* developed by Jews over many centuries in response to their circumstances and their faith.

What do we mean by "base text"? *Mishkan T'filah* provides us with fundamental principles and a carefully crafted framework and design. The specific requirements of a *machzor* may lead us to expand on *Mishkan T'filah*'s paradigm, but our plan is to create a book that is a fitting companion to *Mishkan T'filah*.

Mishkan T'filah's right-side/left-side format encourages diversity, choice, and the inclusion of many "voices"; the use of counter-text; and a stimulating balance of *keva* and *kavanah*. It allows for midrashic creativity and the presentation of different ideas about God, in order to reflect contemporary realities of Reform Judaism and the Jewish world. The dialogue—or confrontation—between the two facing pages also seems particularly suited to the themes of *s'lichot, t'shuvah,* and *cheshbon hanefesh,* which are fundamentally relational and dynamic in nature.

We will take seriously the diverse opinions about gender language for God. Ours will be more than a superficial "He said, She said" approach; gender is far more profound and complex than substituting one noun or pronoun for another. We look forward to an exploration of gender that leads Reform Jews to encounter and experience God in interesting, meaningful ways.

The Editorial Core Team will oversee a process involving diverse working groups of rabbis (assigned to such tasks as translation, commentary, and poetry); consultation with cantors and

THE NEW REFORM *MACHZOR* IS A SOLUTION, BUT WHAT IS THE PROBLEM?

educators to assure that music and learning are integral to the book; consultation with academic experts in related fields; and responders who will evaluate our work and offer critique. Self-evaluation will be ongoing. We are committed to creating an efficient review and piloting process that will result in the timely production of the book.

We believe the Reform nature of this *machzor* will be most evident in its respectful yet fresh approach to tradition; in its unwavering commitment to the equality of men and women; in its attention to the present-day concerns, fears, and hopes of the people who will pray from its pages; in its faithfulness to the ethical dimension of Judaism; in its embrace of the universal and the particular; and, perhaps, most of all, in its effort to deal with the tension between the historical theology of the High Holy Days (God's sovereignty and judgment) and more contemporary beliefs, such as the "theology of human adequacy."

We are mindful that the High Holy Days are a time of change and challenge for each person; yet also, profoundly, a time of memory—a time when a familiar smell, sound, or *ta'am* can make all the difference for many of us; and a time when families and communities take stock and grow closer. We take seriously the feelings associated with holiness, as we envision a *machzor* that encourages and activates these significant levels of experience.

(The Vision Statement was created by Edwin Goldberg, Janet Marder, Shelly Marder, Leon Morris, Elaine Zecher, and Hara Person.)

What Happens When We Use Poetry in Our Prayer Books— and Why?

Sheldon Marder

In memory of Rabbi Scott Corngold (1962–2011)

1

One of my teachers, West African writer Kofi Awoonor, always began his poetry workshops with an enthusiastic pronouncement like this one: "Poetry is life! I could not live without it." Kofi knew better than to use the word "spirituality" in a college classroom in 1969; but thirty years later Edward Hirsch could give full expression to the true motivation behind Kofi's exuberance:

> Reading poetry is a way of connecting—through the medium of language—more deeply with yourself even as you connect more deeply with another. The poem delivers on our spiritual lives precisely because it simultaneously gives us the gift of intimacy and interiority, privacy and participation . . . I understand the relationship between the poet, the poem, and the reader not as a static entity but as a dynamic unfolding. An emerging sacramental event. A relation between an I and a You. A relational process.[1]

Hirsch unlocks my teacher's enigmatic pronouncement: poetry is life because it is "a way of connecting . . . a relational process." And, for a number of reasons, which we will explore in this essay, poetry is uniquely suited to the task of bringing the gifts of connection and "dynamic unfolding" into the Jewish worship experience.

SHELDON MARDER (NY78) is the rabbi and director of the Department of Jewish Life, Jewish Home of San Francisco.

WHAT HAPPENS WHEN WE USE POETRY IN OUR PRAYER BOOKS—AND WHY?

2

Current discussion on the use of poetry in the prayer book is indebted to years of public discourse on the subject. In 1981 Herbert Bronstein wrote a proposal entitled "Suggested Program for T. Carmi on Prayer Book Enhancement/Revision." T. Carmi (whose major anthology, *The Penguin Book of Hebrew Verse*, appeared in print that year) would be given the task of providing the CCAR with liturgical and nonliturgical Hebrew poetry—evocative texts to encourage "engagement, aspiration, quest, searching, [and] affirmation." T. Carmi's extant files include Hebrew poems related to all of the major rubrics and themes of the Shabbat liturgy, as well as some translations by members of the CCAR. The project was meant to be didactic (informing liberal Jews of our "spiritual treasury"), preservationist (saving the *piyutim* of modern Hebrew writers), and, most of all, liturgically creative (using Hebrew poems in translation to "open up or develop" the siddur's motifs and themes). T. Carmi's contribution would be noted posthumously twenty-six years later on the Acknowledgments page of *Mishkan T'filah*.[2]

Early examples of modern poetry in Reform prayer books can be seen in the CCAR's *A Passover Haggadah* (1974) and in *Gates of Prayer* (1975); in *Gates of Repentance* (1978) Chaim Stern placed the poems most prominently in *Avodah*—for example, Jacob Glatshteyn, Avraham Shlonsky, Haim Lensky, Chaim Nachman Bialik—though several poems appear elsewhere (e.g., Rainer Maria Rilke, Anthony Hecht). IMPJ's 1982 *Ha'Avodah Shebalev* made significant use of modern poetry (both Hebrew and Yiddish), inspiring a generation of creative liturgists, and laid the groundwork for the recent *Siddur Erev Shabbat* of the Tel Aviv community Beit T'filah Yisraeli (2011).

The Reconstructionist Movement made a strong statement about the value of poetry by choosing a professional poet (Joel Rosenberg) to translate the liturgy for its *Kol Haneshamah* series (1996, 1998, and 1999), which included poems by non-Jewish as well as Jewish writers.

The CCAR's *On the Doorposts of Your House* (1994) also includes non-Jewish works in its nearly forty pages of poems: pillars of English and American literature like Wordsworth, Shelley, Dickinson, and Stevens are side by side with superb Hebrew and Yiddish writers such as Abba Kovner and Kadya Molodovsky. The editorial

SHELDON MARDER

team for *Doorposts* envisioned Reform Jews enhancing their home rituals and personal spiritual practices with world-class poetry.

By the time Elyse Frishman led the CCAR's creation of *Mishkan T'filah,* decades of discourse and experimentation had laid a strong foundation for the pervasiveness of modern *piyutim* in Reform prayer books. With *MT's* publication in 2007, the poetry of Bialik, Lea Goldberg, and Yehuda Amichai was now fully at home among the works of Solomon Ibn Gabirol, Yehuda Halevi, and the Psalmists. Some rabbis expressed the fear that worshipers would prefer the twentieth-century Yehuda to his Spanish namesake.

When the Rabbinical Assembly published *Mahzor Lev Shalem* in 2010—with an A to Z (Amichai to Zelda) thoroughness, including poets as varied as Admiel Kosman and Denise Levertov—the Conservative Movement completed a trajectory that began with Jules Harlow's inclusion of poems by Nelly Sachs, Hillel Zeitlin, and other modernists in his groundbreaking 1972 *machzor.*

It is clear that all three major liberal movements have advanced the use of modern *piyutim* to reframe and reinvigorate worship along the lines foreseen by the Carmi Project. A box of T. Carmi's files now resides (temporarily) in my office: a symbol, for me, of modern poetry's importance in our spiritual lives. Further, those files encourage us to ask what kind of public dialogue should precede liturgical innovation.

3

Innovation is one of the core ideas in Jewish prayer—from the concept of *chiddush bit'filah* to the religious creativity of the great medieval poets. Why did the *payetanim* innovate in the ways they did? How does one explain the impulse to incorporate their poems in the prayer books of our people? Although these questions are beyond the scope of this essay, a few words on this subject by Jakob Petuchowski are most useful as we begin:

> Theology is compelled to rely on intimations. When we speak of something *of* which we only have hints and intimations, we can speak of it likewise only *in* hints and intimations. We can allude to it, and we can suggest it; but we can hardly formulate it in propositions which will pass muster before the bar of logical rigor. We had, therefore, best express it in the images and the nuances of poetry.[3]

WHAT HAPPENS WHEN WE USE POETRY IN OUR PRAYER BOOKS—AND WHY?

Guided by the idea that poetry—the genre of image and nuance—is the literary mode best suited to theology, I will take an essentially literary approach to the question I have posed in the title: "What happens when we use poetry in our prayer books—and why?"

4

Let's turn first to metaphor, one of the most compelling reasons why poetry "works" in a prayer book. Jorge Luis Borges provides our first example:

> There is a Persian metaphor which says that the moon is the mirror of time. In that phrase, *mirror of time* is the fragility of the moon and also its eternity. It is the contradiction of the moon, so nearly [translucent], so nearly nothing, but whose measure is eternity. To say *moon* or to say *mirror of time* are two aesthetic events, except that the latter is the work of a second stage, because *mirror of time* is composed of two unities, while *moon* give us, perhaps more effectively, the word, the concept of the moon. Each word is a poetic work.[4]

Think of the word "moon" as the faithful translation of a Hebrew prayer in our *machzor*. And think of the beautiful Persian metaphor "mirror of time" as a poem on the opposite page. How does the poetic "mirror of time" function in relation to the original prayer, "moon"? What does it accomplish?

For the sake of argument, imagine that, inexplicably, we have lost all reason to pay attention to the moon—the way Jews sometimes lose their appetite for God, angels, and messiah. The metaphor "mirror of time" invites us to reconsider the moon and ponder its place in our lives from a fresh, new perspective: its dynamic and visible relationship to time. So, too, evocative poetry, with interesting and surprising metaphors for God, can wake up our theological reflection.

Or consider a metaphor spoken by novelist David Grossman in a newspaper interview in 2010:

> [Grossman's] younger son, Uri, was killed in combat in the final hours of the 2006 Lebanon War . . . "You have to understand," he said, a photo of Uri—uniformed, eyes laughing behind glasses—on a shelf to his right, "that when something like this happens to you, you feel exiled from every part of your life. Nothing is home again, not even your body."[5]

SHELDON MARDER

Grossman's metaphor says that losing a child is an extreme form of *galut* in which feeling "at home" is no longer possible; for this bereaved father, the emotional reality of home no longer exists as it did before his son's death. Could a Jewish writer have chosen a more poignant, transformational metaphor to describe the death of a son? Metaphor has worked its mysterious alchemy: since the death of his son Grossman is not the same anymore; and, having read his words, neither are we.

5

Philosopher Ted Cohen presents metaphor as an effective way to cultivate and achieve intimacy.[6] Cohen's insight is remarkable and eye-opening. Let's use Grossman's metaphor to illustrate Cohen's idea. Notice, for example, how the metaphor instantly draws us into Grossman's inner life and shows us how it feels to be a grief-stricken father. Through one word, "exile," we feel close to a man we have met only through a newspaper interview. How does this happen? Edward Hirsch, excited by the poetic implications of Cohen's idea, describes it this way:

> Cohen argues . . . that the maker and the appreciator of a metaphor are brought into deeper relationship with one another. That's because the speaker issues a concealed invitation through metaphor which the listener makes a special effort to accept and interpret. Such a "transaction constitutes the acknowledgment of a community." This notion perfectly describes how the poet enlists the reader's intellectual and emotive involvement and how the reader actively participates in making meaning in poetry. Through this dynamic and creative exchange the poem ultimately engages us in something deeper than intellect and emotion. And through this ongoing process the reader becomes more deeply initiated into the sacred mysteries of poetry.[7]

Nothing proves Ted Cohen's point better than the poetry of Yehuda Amichai. In "My Mother on Her Sickbed" Amichai invites us into his mother's room, where we find ourselves face to face with a dying woman he loves. She has "the lightness and hollowness of a person/Who has already said goodbye at the airport/In the beautiful and quiet area/Between parting and takeoff."[8]

Now consider the following words, which the poet spoke to an interviewer: "The impulse to compare your inner world to the world around you is very natural, and this is how a metaphor is born . . . The right metaphor is the core of my poem."[9] Following his impulse, Amichai discovers in his mother's illness a connection between the airport's "quiet area" (where the passengers have stepped beyond our reach) and the liminal state of a loved one who is actively dying—in transition and inaccessible to her family. The two things linked in this metaphor resonate like notes in a musical chord; and, in the making of metaphor, Amichai had perfect pitch.

Again, we hear the resonance when the poet likens his tallis to a wedding canopy, a parachute, the cocoon of a butterfly—and, in the end, in Hirsch's words, "engages us in something deeper than intellect and emotion":

> Whoever has put on a tallis will never forget.
> When he comes out of a swimming pool or the sea,
> he wraps himself in a large towel, spreads it out again
> over his head and again snuggles into it close and slow,
> still shivering a little, and he laughs and blesses.[10]

That "something deeper" is the spiritual core of our lives. And I suggest that the poet gives us a spiritual thrill in this poem by means of a complex metaphor in which he invites us to join him not only in the act of wrapping a tallis, but also in the religious experience of immersion (*mikveh*). I think, perhaps, Amichai laughs between the shiver and the blessing because of the dizzying beauty of the image he has wrought.

Our tradition is rich in beautiful metaphors for God. The use of modern poetry does not trump the value of an arresting phrase like *Atik Yomin* or the High Holy Days' defining metaphor, *Avinu Malkeinu*. Tradition is the heartbeat of our liturgy. At the same time, the metaphors we discover in nonliturgical sources matter a great deal for reasons we have now put forth: metaphor awakens and refreshes perception; it cultivates intimacy by encouraging connection, community, and "a relational process"; it opens the door to a poet's inner world—and therefore can encourage us to open the doors to our inner worlds.

6

But those doors do not open easily. Religious language—prayer language—can be a barrier. For Diaspora Jews, that includes the

SHELDON MARDER

additional barrier posed by Hebrew. As we think about offering the Reform Movement a new *machzor* that speaks to our many constituencies at once (including those who do not know Hebrew, and especially those who struggle—or worse, have stopped struggling—with belief in God), we need to build bridges across the many streams of twenty-first-century liberal Judaism. Poetry can be a bridge.

In making a case for the use of poems in pastoral care, theologian Donald Capps speaks of the affinity between poets and pastors:

> The tendency of poets to be explorative, questioning, and tentative, though not spineless or without conviction and a passion for truth, has a natural fit with the kinds of human experience that have been of greatest concern to pastoral care, and with the ways that pastors, in confronting these situations, have found themselves responding to them.[11]

We learn from Capps that poems are helpful in pastoral settings because they raise more questions than they answer. Poems do not preach or dictate to us—they are not dogmatic; rather, they are suggestive, evocative, and open-ended. A poem can turn a statement of belief into a question for our consideration. Writing about one of Robert Frost's most evocative lines ("And miles to go before I sleep"), Jorge Luis Borges writes:

> Anything suggested is far more effective than anything laid down. Perhaps the human mind has a tendency to deny a statement . . . But when something is merely said or—better still— hinted at, there is a kind of hospitality in our imagination. We are ready to accept it.[12]

These qualities, which make poetry useful to the pastoral caregiver, also make it a bridge between traditional liturgical language and a worshiper for whom that language is a barrier to prayer because it has the sound of unyielding, dogmatic truth. Poetry in the prayer book can make our liturgies more pastoral, more inviting, and more intimate.

7

In her poem *"Panim"* Israeli poet Sivan Har-Shefi shows us how modern verse can function as modern *piyut*: a bridge between a challenging biblical/liturgical image and contemporary life.

WHAT HAPPENS WHEN WE USE POETRY IN OUR PRAYER BOOKS—AND WHY?

Though a faithful translation of *Birkat Kohanim* need not (perhaps should not) include the word "face," we cannot deny that the word *panav* refers literally to God's face—illumined and lifted up in blessing. Consider what this poem might add when juxtaposed to the priestly benediction.

Face[13]

Your face, from finery
from miracles that do not stop one's breath
from moist darkness in the niches of all creatures
from the ash of humanity stirred up in the winds
with great mercy I will gather

Your face, from constant kindnesses
from the man who envelops me at night
from my daughter falling asleep at the shore of the milk river
I'll seek

Your face,
for the face of the soldier has become distorted
the face of my father has dispersed
and my face is an idol in my sack

but You exist as does Your face

פָּנִים

אֶת פָּנֶיךָ, מְסֻרְקִית
מִנִּסִּים שֶׁאֵינָם עוֹצְרִים נְשִׁימָה
מֵחֲשֵׁכָה לַחָה בְּגֻמְחוֹת הַבְּרוּאִים
מֵאֵפֶר אָדָם נִטְרָד בָּרוּחוֹת
בְּרַחֲמִים גְּדוֹלִים אֲקַבֵּץ

אֶת פָּנֶיךָ, מֵחֲסָדִים קְבוּעִים
מֵאִישׁ עוֹטֵף לִי בַּלַּיְלָה
מִבִּתִּי נִרְדְּמָה עַל שְׂפַת נְהַר הֶחָלָב
אֲבַקֵּשׁ

אֶת פָּנֶיךָ,
כִּי פְּנֵי הַחַיָּל הִתְעַוְּתוּ
פְּנֵי אָבִי הִתְפַּזְּרוּ
וּפָנַי תְּרָפִים בְּאַמְתַּחְתִּי

וְאַתָּה הוּא וּפָנֶיךָ

Machzor: Challenge and Change

In Donald Capps's terms, this is a poem for a pastoral encounter: "explorative though not without conviction." It is, as well, a poem for our liturgy because, in the right circumstances, the pastoral texture and ambiance of a modern poem can give theological language a human face, as it were.

A seeker of God's face, Har-Shefi knows well the Psalmist's cry, "How long will You hide Your face from me?" (Ps. 13:2). Here she first describes the experience of seeing God's face almost everywhere: in fine clothing and acts of kindness, in the ordinary "miracles" of daily life, in her husband's embrace, and in her daughter nursing at her breast. She gathers these "sightings" together as though creating a composite sketch of God's multifaceted presence. But then we hear urgent echoes of Psalm 13 as the poet notes the places where she has felt threats to God and perhaps even God's absence: the face of war, the face of a parent no longer available to her, her own face (that is, vanity and the modern cult of self-worship). In the end, like the author of Psalm 13, the poet affirms the truth of her experience: God exists and God's face exists—both the idea of God and, more important, the living reality of God in the world: source of protection, grace, and peace.

What's more, by exploring the word *panecha* in a very personal way, and with disarming simplicity and honesty, Har-Shefi (an Orthodox Israeli) might even make non-Hebrew readers curious about the wording of the original prayer and pry open the Hebrew text to those for whom it would otherwise be a barrier or, at least, a mystery.

8

Is a poem like "Face" too confusing for worshipers? Writes Yochanan Muffs:

> Every poem is a challenge to our total being: our senses, our intelligence, and our soul. We are afraid to confront the poem head-on (or at all) because we may be found lacking in the balance. Poems are written in a special language, and even though we instinctively know this, to defend ourselves, we dismiss poems as "only poetry." Thus, most people act in one of two ways: they either reject poems as silly or they read them literally. However, to read them literally is to overlook the fact that every poetic statement is a compromise between what is seen and what can be said in the limit of words.[14]

"Face" may well be a challenging poem for many worshipers. But is it any harder to decode than, say, the familiar words "*ya-eir Adonai panav eilecha vichuneka*"? What does that sentence actually mean? There are a great many things in our prayer books that require enormous effort to explain or defend; but often we allow the claims and assertions of our liturgy to wash over us without giving them the thought they deserve.

I suggest that poetry in the prayer book is an invitation to greater mindfulness—thought, reflection, and contemplation. But, most of all, a poem invites us to join the poet in the act of imagining and wondering. For example, what might the image "God's face" mean? What does it suggest to us, as a Jewish idea or on a personal level? "Every poem," says Muffs, "is a challenge to our total being." Instead of fearing that our interpretation of a poem will be wrong or inadequate, we can learn from poets to be playful and inventive—discovering in metaphor, rhyme, and alliteration ways to expand the territory between what we see and what we are able to say with words. That territory, it seems to me, is the very place where we experience what we call spirituality and God.

9

I can look
At my body
As an old friend
Who needs my help,
Or an enemy
Who frustrates me
In every way
With its frailty
And inability to cope.
Old friend,
I shall try
To be of comfort to you
To the end.[15]

I think about the prayer *Asher Yatzar* as I read these lines by May Sarton. Their brevity encourages us to slow down and focus closely on each word or phrase: the sweetness of "old friend"; the harshness of "enemy"; the soft, slant rhyme of "help" and "cope"; the modesty of "I shall try"; the poignancy of "to the end." The prayer, too, is a "close reading" of the body, suggesting that we focus and

SHELDON MARDER

reflect on every wondrous detail of our physicality: the openings, the arteries, the organs.[16]

The prayer *Asher Yatzar* views the human body with wonder, appreciation, and gratitude. The poet sets forth a view of the aging body that is marked by tenderness, compassion, and forgiveness. Each work, in its own way, presents a countercultural perspective that challenges the message we receive from the secular world— that beauty resides only in the youthful and "perfect" body.

The poem, of course, differs from the prayer in a most significant way: the poet addresses her body, not God. And yet Sarton's poem strikes a deeply spiritual chord as she considers the choice that is entirely hers to make—and then makes it with humility and dignity. The prayer attributes the body's grandeur to its Divine Maker. The poem emphasizes, instead, the crucial function of human attitudes and perceptions in determining our view of the body. Thus it honors the idea of human adequacy and initiative that is a counterweight to the traditional theology of Jewish prayer.[17] Both *Asher Yatzar* and the poem offer, in the words of poet Seamus Heaney, "a glimpsed alternative, a revelation of potential that is denied or constantly threatened by circumstances."[18]

Sarton's poem puts human flesh on the theological bones of *Asher Yatzar*. In a sense, this is a central task of all poetry in the prayer book: to help us make the language of prayer, which can be abstract, alienating, and remote, into something concrete, inviting, and deeply personal. The Torah promises that God's teaching is "not too baffling for you, nor is it beyond reach . . . No, the thing is very close to you, in your mouth and in your heart, to observe it" (Deut. 30:11, 14). Poetry can bring the teachings of Jewish tradition close to us. Through compelling, evocative language that is "experience-near," the right poem helps us open our hearts to the ineffable.[19]

What's more, poetry offers us an opportunity for *tikkun* (an act of healing, repair, and perhaps even transformation). May Sarton's words show us a woman, entering her ninth decade of life, who is powerfully resisting the social forces that tell her that old age is an enemy and her body a source of frustration. Here she beautifully exemplifies Wallace Stevens's famous definition of poetry as "a violence from within that protects us from a violence without." Seamus Heaney elaborates: "It is the imagination pressing back against the pressure of reality." It is the power of the imagination, says Heaney, that provides the "redress of poetry"—its ability to heal and make whole, "to place a counter-reality in the scales—a reality which may only be imagined, but which nevertheless has weight."[20]

Writers like Sarton, Amichai, Har-Shefi, and Grossman show us how *tikkun* happens in real life—not suddenly and not perfectly, but as a result of thoughtful reflection, choice, the force of imagination, and will. At its best, poetry celebrates the gift that allows human beings to see things differently, to remake the world and reinterpret received ideas and traditions. This "glimpsed alternative" can be poetry's greatest contribution to our Jewish books of prayer.

Notes

1. Edward Hirsch, *How to Read a Poem* (New York: Harcourt Brace, 1999), 4–5.

2. Elyse D. Frishman, ed., *Mishkan T'filah* (New York: CCAR, 2007), xiii.

3. Jakob J. Petuchowski, *Theology and Poetry: Studies in the Medieval Piyyut* (London: Routledge & Kegan Paul, 1978), 3.

4. Jorge Luis Borges, "Poetry," *Seven Nights*, trans. Eliot Weinberger (New York: New Directions, 1984), 78.

5. Ethan Bronner, *The New York Times*, November 17, 2010.

6. Ted Cohen, "Metaphor and the Cultivation of Intimacy," *Critical Inquiry* 5, no. 1 (Special Issue on Metaphor, Autumn 1978), 3–12.

7. Hirsch, *How to Read a Poem*, 15.

8. Yehuda Amichai, *Yehuda Amichai: A Life of Poetry 1948–1994*, selected and trans. Benjamin and Barbara Harshav (New York: HarperPerennial, 1995), 368.

9. Esther Fuchs, *Encounters with Israeli Authors* (Marblehead, MA: Micah Publications, 1982), 88.

10. Yehuda Amichai, *Open Closed Open*, trans. Chana Bloch and Chana Kronfeld (New York: Harcourt, 2000), 44.

11. Donald Capps, *The Poet's Gift: Toward the Renewal of Pastoral Care* (Louisville: Westminster/John Knox, 1993), 3.

12. Jorge Luis Borges, *This Craft of Verse*, ed. Calin-Andrei Mihailescu (Cambridge, MA: Harvard University, 2000), 31.

13. Sivan Har-Shefi, *Galut Halivyatan* (Tel Aviv: Hakibbutz Hameuchad, 2005), 78. Translation: David C. Jacobson, *Beyond Political Messianism: The Poetry of Second Generation Religious Zionist Settlers* (Brighton, MA: Academic Studies Press, 2011), 133–34.

14. Yochanan Muffs, *The Personhood of God: Biblical Theology, Human Faith and the Divine Image* (Woodstock, VT: Jewish Lights, 2005), 106–107.

SHELDON MARDER

15. May Sarton, "Friend or Enemy," *Coming into Eighty: Poems* (New York: Norton, 1994).

16. From the translation of the prayer *Asher Yatzar* in *Machzor Lev Shalem*, ed. Edward Feld (New York: The Rabbinical Assembly, 2010), 35.

17. See David Hartman, *A Living Covenant: The Innovative Spirit in Traditional Judaism* (Woodstock, VT: Jewish Lights, 1997).

18. Seamus Heaney, *The Redress of Poetry* (New York: The Noonday Press—Farrar, Straus and Giroux, 1995), 4.

19. The phrase "experience-near" is from Capps, *The Poet's Gift*, 3.

20. Heaney, *Redress of Poetry*, 1, 3–4, which includes the statement from Wallace Stevens's essay "The Noble Rider and the Sounds of Words."

The End of Liturgical Reform as We Know It: Creative Retrieval as a New Paradigm

Leon A. Morris

Prayer book reform was always one of the most significant and defining features of Reform Judaism in both Europe and America. While some reforms of the liturgy were driven by practical concerns, such as abbreviating the service or removing passages that were deemed to be inconsistent with the practice of most Reform Jews, most major reforms of traditional Jewish liturgy were ideologically based. Liturgical reform overwhelmingly was grounded in the notion that our prayers should be consistent with our theology. Reforms of this type are reflected in the deletion of phrases that reference a return to Zion, the resurrection of the dead, and the desire to rebuild the Temple in Jerusalem (and even phrases recalling that we once *did* offer sacrifices there). As Jakob Petuchowski wrote, "Prayer, it was argued, demands absolute honesty; and the corollary was understood to imply that the prayerbook can contain only such statements as are factually correct, literally true, and historically verifiable."[1]

Such criteria seem out of place in twenty-first-century religious life. Does our prayer book really need to be consistent with our theology? Must we believe literally the words we recite? Is our prayer book intended to be a catechism of Jewish belief? A new generation's answers to these questions may differ sharply from those who wrote or edited *The Union Prayer Book, Gates of Prayer,* and even *Mishkan T'filah.*

Our Reform forbearers had a posture of certainty, both about what God is and what God is not, about what God can do and what God cannot. In contrast, our theological perspective tends

LEON A. MORRIS (NY97) is the rabbi at Temple Adas Israel in Sag Harbor, New York.

LEON A. MORRIS

to be marked by great uncertainty. We are suspect of almost all absolute truth claims, including those that emanate from our own denominational camp. For many of us, contemporary Jewish theology is less about what we know with certainty to be true and much more about religious ways of organizing and conceiving the world. If medieval and modern Jewish theology were prose, ours is a theology of poetry. So, the expectation that any prayer book, itself an anthology of texts reflecting multiple theological positions, must be in line with our own contemporary theology now seems inappropriate, unachievable, and outdated.

In addition, our comfort with "text study" and its centrality in our religious lives has changed dramatically, and such changes impact directly on how we relate to the words of the prayer book. For the past twenty years, there has been a renaissance of Jewish learning that has impacted the entire American Jewish community, including our Reform Movement. The phrase "lifelong learning" has become standard. There are increased opportunities for serious text study in our synagogues, on retreats, and at institutions solely devoted to Jewish learning. Events like Limmud have proliferated to most major cities, and numerous online offerings are available to anyone with a computer.

There is today, inside and outside of Reform synagogues, a strong interest and deep love for primary Jewish texts and the rich and varied conversations that emerge from a meaningful encounter with them. Among these primary Jewish texts are surely the classic siddur and the classic *machzor*. Widespread positive experiences with text study have resulted in an appreciation even for texts that are difficult and challenging in light of contemporary attitudes. Increasingly, twenty-first-century American Jews value opportunities to confront such texts directly and to play a role in trying to derive relevance and meaning from them. The history of reforming the prayer book embraced an approach that assumed that laity would be put off by such texts or simply would not know what to do with them. Such passivity regarding the texts was part of a wider context for Reform worship in which worshipers were largely observers in a service that was mostly read to them by their rabbis. In contrast, today's Reform Jews would privilege interpretation over revision. They would want to struggle with, and make meaning from, the classic words themselves, rather than have it done for them by others.

THE END OF LITURGICAL REFORM AS WE KNOW IT

Influenced, consciously or not, by the postmodern turn and deconstruction, contemporary Jews are comfortable reading on several levels simultaneously. They intuit that reading is a generative process and are less concerned about authorial intention: "And so one can state that the meaning of a text—if it is a great text—not just occasionally but always escapes its author: that is why understanding is not simply a reproductive attitude but is always a productive one."[2]

Contemporary American Jews know that the words of the siddur and the *machzor* are poetry and metaphor. They could not conceive of taking its words literally. More than reforming its words, they would desire the tools to help them appreciate the multi-vocality of the text, with commentary that speaks to the intellect as well as to the soul. While it might be argued that study and worship are entirely different modes, learning as a spiritual practice and meaningful prayer experiences share much in common.

In many ways, then, the age of liturgical reform as previously understood and implemented is over. The guiding principle of a twenty-first-century Reform prayer book must now be the notion of "creative retrieval." I first encountered this term in this journal by our colleague, Herbert Bronstein. He defined it as "the retrieval from our own traditional sources and our own roots, from the design of our own liturgy, of meaningful elements relevant to our own time."[3] In the same article, he also borrowed the term "ressourcement" from the Nouvelle Theologie, a mid-twentieth-century school of Catholic theology. "Ressourcement" refers to a return to the sources, in their case to Scriptures and writings of the church fathers. Creative retrieval or ressourcement represents an approach to Reform liturgy that is committed to mine the classic words of our sources to see how they might be used or transformed for our own context. Applying this approach to the writing and editing of a prayer book would require each prayer book to begin with the classic text itself as the primary referent and touchstone. Yes, the liturgical decisions of previous generations of Reform Jews may be noteworthy, but each generation needs for its own response to come directly from the inherited texts of our tradition. The sacred task of shaping Reform liturgy must never be seen as creating a prayer experience from scratch, any more than it is our task to write a new Torah or a new Talmud. A commitment to the project of creative retrieval means that the class prayer book

LEON A. MORRIS

is seen not as the "Orthodox" prayer book, but as our own, to draw from, to explain, and to adapt.

While such an approach may seem somewhat radical in Reform Judaism, similar ideas were expressed over a century ago in the Reform synagogue by Rabbi Judah L. Magnes. In a Passover sermon delivered in Manhattan's Temple Emanu-El in 1910, Magnes urged the abandonment of the *Union Prayer Book*:

> Far be it from me to underestimate the struggles endured in the creation of this book of prayer and the benefits that a modernized, uniform service has conferred upon numerous congregations. But I cannot be blind to the fact that the Union Prayer Book, as at present constituted, has done its work and has lived out its day. The one prayer book that can ever be the Book of Common Prayer for the Jewish people is the traditional Jewish prayer book, hallowed by the sufferings and the hopes and the religious yearnings of countless generations of our ancestors.[4]

Creative retrieval requires of us a shift from a "hermeneutic of suspicion" to a "hermeneutic of embrace." We are well aware that the prayer book is a compilation over many centuries. We know that it is the work of human beings who in many cases were responding to the issues of their time. At the same time, a hermeneutic of embrace urges us to see the classic siddur and *machzor* as the poetry of the Jewish People. A hermeneutic of embrace begins with a love for the classic liturgy and a firm belief that it can be mined for contemporary meaning and relevance. A hermeneutic of embrace is rooted in the idea that the classic text has a great deal to teach us and that our primary task is to realize how it might be reframed, explained, or translated in such a way as to allow it to live in our Reform synagogues.

Of course, there will be parts of the liturgy that will cause pain or offend and that even the most robust commentary will not be able to rescue. In these cases, the best choice may indeed be to remove it from our prayers. But such instances are few and far between, and liturgical reforms such as these represent a miniscule number of changes Reform has made to the prayer book. As Richard Rubenstein wrote in 1966:

> Our attitude in approaching the liturgy ought to be one of extreme conservatism, not for the sake of conservatism, but rather because the harm we can do by making the wrong decision af-

THE END OF LITURGICAL REFORM AS WE KNOW IT

fects the continuity of Jewish history and of Jewish religious sentiment itself. There is nothing necessarily sacred about any given liturgical form. What is impressive, however, is the extent to which both conscious and unconscious themes tend to intersect creatively in any liturgical mode.[5]

A hermeneutic of embrace rejects claims that "we Reform Jews don't say this," or that "this is the authoritative Reform *nusach.*" Such closed determinism has no place in a twenty-first-century approach to liberal liturgy. Equally important, a hermeneutic of embrace shifts the burden of proof away from the classic prayer needing to argue its worthiness for inclusion, to we who must defend why a prayer was not included, why we changed the words, or why we chose to translate it metaphorically. A hermeneutic of embrace argues against apologizing for wanting to restore the traditional text if it can be restored in ways that allow it to inspire, to teach, and or elicit creative interpretations.

Finally, a hermeneutic of embrace raises the bar for the work of liberal liturgy. It is much easier to delete and to change than to explain, to "translate" (understood narrowly and broadly), or to use in new ways. The growing phenomenon of groups reviving *piyut* through song and study, here and in Israel, and the number of new recordings of medieval *piyutim* by contemporary Israeli musicians present us with paradigms of allowing old texts to live and flourish in new ways.

A hermeneutic of embrace with respect to liturgy urges us to expand our understanding of prayer as *avodah.* Most commonly, we explain that prayer is *avodah* because it is a form of service, *avodah sh'balev* (service of the heart). However, the understanding of *avodah* as "work" might be apt as well when we consider the interpretive labor required of us when trying our best to bridge the gap between the inherited words of the classic siddur and our contemporary lives. It is hard work to make meaning from these words.[6] Simultaneously, such work is a privilege, a blessing, and an opportunity for connection and continuity.

Notes

1. Jakob J. Petuchowski, *Prayerbook Reform in Europe: The Liturgy of European Liberal and Reform Judaism* (New York: World Union for Progressive Judaism, 1968), 353.

2. Marc-Alain Ouaknin, *The Burnt Book: Reading the Talmud* (Princeton, NJ: Princeton University Press, 1995), 59.

3. Herbert Bronstein, "Yom Kippur Worship: A Missing Center?" *CCAR Journal* (Summer 2004): 7–15.

4. Arthur A. Goren, ed., *Dissenter in Zion: From the Writings of Judah L. Magnes* (Cambridge, MA: Harvard University Press, 1982), 113.

5. Richard L. Rubenstein, *After Auschwitz: Radical Theology and Contemporary Judaism* (Indianapolis: 1966), 108.

6. This notion of *avodah* as "work" as it relates to the interpretative process of making meaning from the words of the siddur is that of Dr. Elie Holzer, assistant professor of education at Bar Ilan University.

Section Two: From Professors of Liturgy at HUC-JIR

"Lu Yehi": High Holy Day Liturgy and Experience in Israel

Dalia Marx

Our cups of coffee were almost empty. Galit, an Israeli rabbinical student, and Amnon, a student in our prayer leaders course, sat in my living room to prepare for their High Holy Day student pulpits. They felt that they were almost ready. We went over *Kavvanat HaLev*, the Israeli Reform *machzor*, and discussed the different considerations when leading services in a young congregation of people who have very little liturgical background. They were a bit anxious but also very excited. They were filled with a sense of the mission of making the services meaningful and accessible to people who normally shy away from any kind of organized religious activity in the city of Holon.

After going through the bulk of the service, we reached the end of the *N'ilah* service. The question we weighed was how to conclude the day. We discussed the importance of the concluding note. How should the worshipers, most of whom are not regular shul goers, leave the service? Galit and Amnon decided to end with "HaTikvah," the Israeli national anthem, which appears at the end of our *machzor*. But then what should introduce the shofar blowing? We had a few ideas but none of them seemed to be the right fit. We paused for a moment, closed our eyes, and tried to think about the essence of the day. And then, from afar, an old and beloved tune trickled into my mind: Naomi Shemer's "Lu Yehi." One of us began softly humming the tune, and all of us immediately said:

RABBI DALIA MARX, Ph.D. (J&C03) is associate professor of Liturgy and Midrash at the Jerusalem campus of HUC-JIR. She has been teaching in HUC-JIR since 2002. She thanks Rabbi David Ariel-Joel, Rabbi Naamah Kelman, and Ms. Julie Mendelson for their helpful comments on this article.

DALIA MARX

"That's it." Both Amnon, who was drafted to the army shortly after this song was composed, and Galit, who was not yet born then, thought that it would be perfect pitch!

What was there in the song that made it the "right" ending note for the service? "Lu Yehi" is a sublime expression of Israeli concerns and hopes. It talks about the personal but also about the national home; it talks about the comfort in simplicity and normality; and it is a song about redemption: *"od yesh mifrash lavan ba'ofek mul anan shachor kaved"* (there is still a white sail in the horizon facing a heavy black cloud). It is so Israeli and at the same time it is universal. The song expresses the idea that every human being has similar wishes and fears regarding the safety of loved ones and the yearnings of the heart.[1] Naomi Shemer (1930–2004), a beloved musician and songwriter, said that initially she decided to write an Israeli version of "Let It Be" to the Beatles' tune shortly before the Yom Kippur War (1973).[2] When the war broke out, Shemer actually sat down to compose the Hebrew lyrics for her friend, the singer Chava Alberstein. It was during the days of the terrible shock and trauma caused by the war, the days between Yom Kippur and Sukkot. Shemer understood that this was going to be a fierce and harsh war, and the fears of these days are reflected in the words of "Lu Yehi." She explained that when her husband returned home from the war and heard the song, he urged her to compose her own music to it. And so she did.

"Lu Yehi" to Shemer's tune was played again and again during those difficult days. I was seven years old during the war, and like many of my friends, I still feel a chill down my spine whenever I hear it. In a way it not only became a symbol of the Yom Kippur War, but it offered the experience of the solemnity of the day to Israelis not necessarily sitting in synagogue. Only when I spend the High Holy Days outside of Israel do I realize that there is something unique and incomparable in the way they are experienced back home—especially in the case of Yom Kippur. If you ask Israelis for the first thought that pops into their minds when they hear the words "Yom Kippur," I believe that many of them will say without hesitation: *Milchemet Yom Kippur* (the Yom Kippur War). Even now, four decades later, the war, which began with the surprise attack coordinated by Egypt and Syria on the afternoon of Shabbat Yom Hakippurim, October 6, 1973, remains a painful remainder of the fragility of the young State of Israel.[3]

"LU YEHI"

For many Israelis, there is no clear-cut division between the mental, spiritual, and emotional demands of the Day of Atonement and the social and national ones that arise from memory of the Yom Kippur War. In both cases the day is an invitation for *cheshbon nefesh* (personal and communal soul searching). It is so evident to us in Israel that we actually feel it only when we are away from home, spending the Holy Day with fellow Jews for whom Yom Hakippurim is something similar and yet so different. Apart from memories of the war, there are some other matters that inform the special situation of non-Orthodox Israeli experience of the High Holy Days and its liturgy. Here is a list, which is by no means an exhaustive one, of the unique Israel experience:

1. Not unlike many North American Jews, the so called "secular" Israelis are insufficiently acquainted with the liturgy. Yet their feeling of inadequacy may be even more disturbing than that of their siblings in the Diaspora. I am referring to the fact that the language of the prayers is also our vernacular (albeit in a higher register).[4] Israeli worshipers recite the prayers "as they are." They cannot use an ideologically adequate translation as a coping device with difficult theological and ideological issues; this cannot be done in Israel because they understand the actual words of the liturgy, which are always challenging, and during the High Holy Days even more so.

2. Regardless of their liturgical proficiency, Israelis have a readymade organized High Holy Day experience: unsatisfactory as it may be, the kindergartens and the school system expose children to the holidays, and the media offers holiday programs. In a way, the entire country pauses and honors the holiday, especially Yom Kippur. When I served in a small North American community as a student rabbi, my biggest surprise was the daily city rush that did not stop when I opened the temple gates and went out to the street. Whether Israelis desire it or not, the car-free streets and the dramatic quality of Yom Kippur's stillness create an incomparable atmosphere for the High Holy Days. You do not need to enter a synagogue to experience the solemn nature of these days. This public structure and atmosphere allows people to bypass the liturgy and the synagogue. It absolves them of the

DALIA MARX

need to take the time to seriously respond to the challenges these days pose in a personal, cognizant manner.

3. It is not only the difficult content of the *machzor* that causes Israelis to shy away from the synagogue, but also their discontentment with Orthodox and ultra-Orthodox religious coercion. In the eyes of many, religion, in and of itself, is connected with the way the religious establishment requires people to submit to a stringent and outdated form of religiosity. It is a well-known fact that the ultra-Orthodox minority in Israel has much greater power than their share in the population, and at the same time, their contribution to economic and social life in Israel is, at best, insufficient. This situation drives many people away from synagogue, any synagogue. Indeed, it is quite common that people allow themselves to experience meaningful Jewish experiences only when they are outside Israel, where prayer and religion are not associated with extremism and inequality. What a paradox—you need to leave the Jewish state in order to be actively Jewish!

4. Surprisingly there is still a suspicious sentiment toward non-Orthodox forms of religiosity in Israel, albeit less than in the past. Many still maintain an "all or nothing" attitude and will tell you that if you do it, do it "properly" or do not do it at all. The Reform and Conservative movements, as well as other Jewish renewal organizations, are viewed by the majority of Israelis as a foreign implant—they do not seem local and native. This is changing though; Israeli society today is much more open to different forms of religiosity and to different expressions of our Jewishness. The Reform Movement, now in its second and third generation, has become more native and local. It is our task to provide valid and sustainable models of liberal religiosity and prayer that will overcome the initial suspicious attitude of Israelis toward anything that has a scent of religion. Therefore, the High Holy Days is an opportunity during the year when people seem to be more receptive to prayers and synagogue experience.

5. When thinking about prayer in Israel, one can detect a rather surprising phenomenon: The most serious treatment of the religious experience, questions of faith, and a true search for transcendence takes place in the last century in Israeli Hebrew "secular" literature, and especially in its poetry.[5] Israelis

"LU YEHI"

encounter questions regarding God, peoplehood, and the search for holiness through poetry in a natural and direct (yet unthreatening) manner. This observation takes us back to Naomi Shemer's "Lu Yehi." Her popular song not only encapsulated the yearnings and hopes of the Israelis during one of their most painful trials but also became the genuine expression of an entire generation. Like the classical prayers that made their way into our prayer books, it, along with a growing list of similar songs-poems-prayers, transcends its concrete context. The Israeli Reform Movement was always aware of this: poems and songs by Leah Goldberg, Natan Zach, Yehudah Amichai, and many others, entered our siddur and *machzor*. The committee creating a new Israeli Reform Machzor for the Festivals has made a deliberate effort to incorporate as many of these texts as possible.

Due to increasing religious coercion and aggressive religious institutionalization, there are more and more Israelis who are committed to grappling with their Jewishness on their own terms. They are no longer willing to consume any kind of readymade Judaism. Prayer is an important part of these somewhat subterranean efforts; it emerges in some less expected places, such as Holon, where Galit and Amnon led the *T'filah* this year. I believe that in the near future we will see more and more fascinating and genuine forms of prayer emerging from Zion. *Lu yehi!*

Notes

1. For the lyrics of the "Lu Yehi" online, see http://shironet.mako.co.il/artist?type=lyrics&lang=1&prfid=4608&wrkid=1895.
2. Shemer told this story in an interview marking thirty years of the Yom Kippur War in 2003, shortly before her death. See http://www.ynet.co.il/articles/0,7340,L-2937862,00.html.
3. See Dalia Marx, "*Untaneh Tokef* through Israeli Eyes," in *Who by Water, Who by Fire: Untaneh Tokef*, ed. Lawrence Hoffman (Woodstock, VT: Jewish Lights, 2010), 117–21.
4. See Dalia Marx, "When *L'shon HaKodesh* Is Also the Vernacular: The Development of Israeli Reform Liturgy," *CCAR Journal* (Fall 2009): 31–62.
5. See A. Hirschfeld, "God's Place in Hebrew Poetry in the Contemporary Generation," in *The Full Wagon*, ed. Y. Bartal (Jerusalem: Magnes, 2002) [in Hebrew], 165–76.

Machzor: The Poetry of Truly Awe-Inspiring Days

Richard S. Sarason

I have always found the *Yamim Noraim* (the Awe-Inspiring Days) to be deeply meaningful at a personal level. Some of this clearly has to do with childhood memories of being surrounded by a sense of solemnity and of learning to take "I'm sorry" seriously on these days. (And now further memories of one generation down: how Yom Kippur, for one of our sons as a young child, was "My Sorry Day.") Much more of it has to do with the music of the High Holy Days, first learned in religious school and Intermediate Choir at Temple Emanuel in Oak Park, Michigan; then in Hillel Choir for Reform services at Brandeis University and in a traditional synagogue choir in Chicago with my college roommate; conducting the choir at Kehillat Kedem in Tel Aviv, learning High Holy Day *nusach* and trope for my first student pulpit in Newark, Ohio, forty years ago; and conducting services most years thereafter.

Still more has to do with the themes of the High Holy Days expressed in the liturgy, which, for me, are the great existential themes of life, death, and ultimate meaning: Yom HaDin as (in the rendering of Karen Armstrong) "the moment of truth," when each of us must acknowledge our finitude and mortality, our limits and vulnerability: that, in the end, we are not in charge, as much as that hurts our vanity, and that, so many times, we fall short and miss the mark, whether or not we choose to call that "sin." But the possibility of turning and returning, of repentance and renewal (of *t'shuvah*) is always there when we reach out or when we allow ourselves to be touched by the Hand that reaches out to us (*Atah notein yad*).

RABBI RICHARD S. SARASON (C74) is Professor of Rabbinic Literature and Thought, HUC-JIR/Cincinnati. He has taught Jewish liturgy at HUC-JIR annually for twenty years and sporadically for thirteen years before that.

MACHZOR

As a musician and a wordsmith, I have always been attuned to the musicality of words, to the music *inside* the text. As a lover of theater, opera, film, and narrative, I have always viewed the *machzor* as the script for a profound sacred drama that we enact both together and separately in the synagogue. Liturgical texts are essentially poetic—they are meant to be declaimed, heard, and internalized. I find myself always responding to the music of the words and to their deeper meaning—the intense yearning (*hitgaaga-ut*) that they both encapsulate and enact.[1]

Unlike some of my friends and colleagues, I don't have a huge theological problem with most of these texts. I relate to their imagery on the symbolic, rather than the literal, level—and am very much aware of the distance between my own stance in this regard and a more traditional one that gives them literal assent. The imagery of *Untaneh Tokef*, for example, does not upset or offend me; instead it brings me up short and forces me to confront my own mortality ("Repent one day before your death" [*Mishnah Avot* 2:15]). I find that I have a capacity for deep empathy with these texts (an important trait, to be sure, for someone who has devoted his adult life to their study). I know these feelings and yearnings: they are my own—even if I am less certain that Someone is out there listening or that the Universe cares about me or anyone else. But the "human, all too human" feelings, the gut responses, the aspirations and yearnings are intensely genuine and honest. I know why my ancestors wept while chanting this poem, and I sometimes find myself tearing over as well.

I respond powerfully to the imagery and the emotions in these texts without getting tied up in knots by their literal meaning. Given that *all* God-talk is figurative—how can anyone talk literally about that which is, by definition, ineffable?—I am content not to get stuck on the analogies, but simply to respond to their affective roots.

I am aware, however, that much of what I have written above pertains to my appreciation of, and association with, the *Hebrew* text of the *machzor*. This derives, at base, from a personal, visceral identification as a Jew with the inherited rituals and liturgical texts of my people and with the religiosity that they embody—an identification that was nourished by two and a half years of formative study in Jerusalem (through Brandeis and HUC) and that motivated my decision to devote my professional and personal life

RICHARD S. SARASON

(there is no dichotomy) to the interpretation of, and engagement with, Jewish religious texts and culture. There is certainly a strong Kaplanian undercurrent here.

As a Reform Jew by upbringing and choice, I choose not to enact the entire traditional liturgy of the *machzor*, but to abbreviate (since for me, at least, less indeed is more) and—more crucially—to reinterpret. To take the imagery of the *machzor* figuratively, in the manner that I have described above, is certainly, at one level, to reinterpret. At another level, however, it is to assert that the larger human processes of taking responsibility for our actions and their consequences, of struggling to make meaning and to transcend limit and mortality *in fact* underlie that imagery—so there is nothing forced or disingenuous about my stance. Even though it might be theologically conflicted, it is not (for me) affectively reductive.

Which brings me to the issue of prayer in the vernacular, of the English text in the *machzor*. Reading poetry (or the *Tanach*) in translation has famously been likened to kissing your bride through a veil: something—perhaps even the very essence—inevitably gets lost.[2] Since Jewish liturgical speech, too, is poetic, the same can be said about praying Hebrew prayers in English. Prayers and other religious speech in the English language inevitably carry connotations of Protestant Christianity (the King James Bible, the Book of Common Prayer—these books, after all, were landmarks in the development of the English language). English is also our language of secular communication; there is nothing "holy" or "other" about it. The danger of prose prayers in English is that we automatically construe such texts literally unless the content is conveyed in poetic form, in somewhat heightened and figurative speech, with words that lift us up rather than weighing us down or infelicitously calling attention to themselves by being too colloquial or prosaic or syntactically awkward.[3]

Most members of Reform congregations do not understand Hebrew (although Hebrew prayer, for that very reason, may hold for them a powerfully numinous, symbolic quality). Therefore, it is crucially important for me that our English renderings—translations and paraphrases (both, I believe, are necessary)—attempt to convey a comparable numinosity through their style and poetic quality that may help congregants to get past the "literal" meaning of the texts

MACHZOR

and to perceive their figurative and allusive qualities. Religious speech by its very nature is allusive, not denotative. It is a kind of verbal gesture, used to allude or point to something beyond itself. There is no need, on the one hand, to over-specify that something. (This is the main reason why I am inherently suspicious of too much God-talk: better to talk less and, with humility and reverence for the mystery of our lives in the world, do more. *L'chah dumiah t'hilah* [Ps. 65:2], in the rendering of Maimonides: "For You, silence is praise.") But our paraphrases must also be careful not to completely reduce or deflate the traditional metaphors and figures; then we become "literalists" again and move from poetry to prose. I do not wish to pray either to "humanity" or to a philosophical concept. And that is the unavoidable dilemma of praying in the vernacular. How do we navigate between the extremes of prosaic reductionism (like Horton the elephant's "I meant what I said and I said what I meant") and poetic figures that stick in many people's craws when they are taken literally? For me, an answer (since there is no "the" answer) lies with clearly poetic rhetoric that is both allusive and elevating, and that possesses its own aesthetic value. This is why it is so important, to my mind, that the new CCAR *machzor* include well-crafted translations and paraphrases as well as suggestive reinterpretations, all literary work of high quality, on both the right-hand and the left-hand pages. And, of course, the more texts are sung, or are accompanied by music, the more layers of affective meaning they acquire.

To return to the beginning: The themes, images, and figures of the *machzor*, when enacted and accompanied by plaintive and stirring musical renditions, by the sights, colors, sounds, gestures, and community of the High Holy Days that we have inherited as part of our personal and communal histories force me to confront my own limitations, failings, inadequacies, and mortality in a realistic but hopeful way. *T'shuvah* and renewal are possible. The *machzor* teaches us that we have some control over the course of our lives and, with intentionality and attentive hard work, can make amends and changes in the way we live. And as for those things over which we have no control—most powerfully, our own deaths—Jewish tradition and community, as embodied in the work we are enjoined to do through the rituals of the High Holy Days, give us rich resources to acknowledge them without succumbing to despair. Rather, we must face them with hope and with

RICHARD S. SARASON

affirmation of the abiding worth of our lives, that something of us will not be lost.

Han'shamah lach . . .

Notes

1. Catherine Madsen has written eloquently—and forcefully—on this topic. See her book, *The Bones Reassemble: Reconstituting Liturgical Speech* (Aurora, CO: Davies Group, 2005), as well as her articles "Kitsch and Liturgy," *Tikkun* 16, no. 2 (March/April 2001):41-47; and "The Common Word: Recovering Liturgical Speech," *Cross-Currents* 54, no. 3 (2004), both available at http://catherine-madsen.com/Essays.html.

2. The saying has been attributed to Chaim Nachman Bialik in various forms: ללמד תרגום זה כמו לנשק את הכלה דרך צעיף ("To study a translation is like kissing the bride through a veil") or, in a literary Hebrew more akin to Bialik's own style, תרגום דומה לנשיקה מבעד לצעיף ("Translation is like a kiss through a veil"). Amos Oz has often repeated this dictum. I have not (yet?) seen the source in Bialik's writings. The Welsh poet R.S. Thomas also is reputed to have said that reading poetry in translation is like kissing through a handkerchief.

3. Once again, the writings of Catherine Madsen listed in note 1 are germane. While a principled supporter of gender-neutrality in English prayer, I am painfully aware that the avoidance of gendered pronouns creates a huge stylistic pressure on English syntax. Psalm translations are a particular challenge in this regard.

A Tale of Three *Machzorim*

Richard N. Levy

I grew up at Temple Israel of New Rochelle (NY) in the 1940s and 1950s, where of course the *machzor* (though we didn't use the Hebrew name) was the *Union Prayer Book*, Newly Revised Edition, Volume II, which I also used wher̄ ̇ed services as a rabbinic student and a newly minted rabbi in the early to mid 1960s. When I came to teach at the Hebrew Union College in 1999, I helped students find their way through *Gates of Repentance,* and I have participated in several pilotings of the new Reform High Holy Day *machzor*. Though derived from the same basic traditional text, the books are very different, and so I thought as we work our way toward the publication of the new *machzor*, it might be instructive to reflect on the three of them.

It is significant that since the beginning of the discussion of the new volume, it has been referred to as a *machzor* and not as a High Holy Day prayer book. The word, from the root *ch-z-r,* meaning to repeat, conveys the important reminder that this is a book of prayers for a unique time of the year that will repeat itself, like the seasons themselves, every year. It thus sets itself apart from a siddur, a word meaning the order of prayers, used for daily and Shabbat worship. But it was understood that the traditional *machzor* followed the same *matbeah hat'filah* ("coinage" or outline of prayer) as the siddur, only enhanced by special prayers used only at festival or High Holy Day time. There is, therefore, in its very name a tension between the recurring and the unique, between the new and the old. In some ways this tension helps to illumine the significance of the changes we

RICHARD N. LEVY is the rabbi of the synagogue and director of spiritual growth at the Jack H. Skirball (Los Angeles) campus of HUC-JIR. He was the director of the School of Rabbinic Studies at the LA Campus for ten years and was president of the CCAR from 1997–1999, where he shepherded passage of the 1999 Statement of Principles for Reform Judaism (the Pittsburgh Principles). He is the author of *A Vision of Holiness: The Future of Reform Judaism* (URJ Press, 2005) and editor of *On Wings of Awe: A High Holyday Machzor* (Hillel and KTAV, 1985, 2011).

RICHARD N. LEVY

have seen since the *Union Prayer Book* was last put on the shelf (though there are a couple of congregations in the United States that still use it, or a revision of it) and as we await the publication of the new (as yet untitled) *machzor*.

Reviewing the *Union Prayer Book* for this essay, I was struck by how intimate a book it is. It's small, its leatherette cover has a wonderful tactile feel, and its text is very personal:

> Unto Thee, O Lord my God, I open my heart at this time in the turn of the year. As I review my conduct during months that are passed, I am deeply conscious of my shortcomings . . . Lead me and guide me, for my times are in Thy hand. Amen. (Silent prayer after *Amidah*, p. 27)

> O merciful Father! May I find tranquility for my troubled soul. Help me to look into mine own heart and thus come to know myself . . . May I seek to be reconciled, O Lord, with my fellow-men and with Thee . . . Hear my prayer, and in Thy mercy answer me. Amen. (Meditation before Yom Kippur Morning Service, p. 168)

But it also offered some majestic passages:

> . . . though we cherish and revere the place where stood the cradle of our people, the land where Israel grew up as a tender plant, and the knowledge of Thee rose like the morning-dawn, our longings and aspirations reach out toward a still higher goal. The morning-dawn shall yet brighten into a radiant noonday; the tender sprout shall yet become a heaven-aspiring tree beneath which all the families of the earth will find shelter. (Yom Kippur Afternoon Service, p. 273)

While the themes are the themes of the High Holy Days, the voice is the voice of the familiar book used every Shabbat. Indeed, one might argue that both the intimacy and the majesty were greatly aided by the Thee/Thou archaisms that provided a different word for addressing God from that used to address human beings. The prayers common to the High Holy Days and Shabbat were used mostly without revision, so the book was familiar to Shabbat worshipers at the same time as it invited people to start coming to Shabbat worship with the assurance that they would find a similar experience.

The passage quoted above from the Yom Kippur Afternoon Service represented another aspect of constancy: the recurrence of classic Reform beliefs, in this case the belief in the coming of the messianic age. The Rosh HaShanah Morning Service concluded with the stirring hymn "All the World Shall Come to Serve Thee," and the various Torah services are introduced with messianic passages from the Prophets, establishing the belief that our mission is to bring Torah to all the nations of the earth. Other passages evoke the classic Reform belief that Israel is to be a priest people, pure in spirit, dedicated to bringing the nations to God's service. The *Union Prayer Book* was clearly a Reform prayer book, reflecting the beliefs of the Columbus Platform of 1937, whose main author, Samuel Cohon, was also one of the major writers of the Newly Revised *UPB*.

This tight integration of Shabbat and High Holy Days, prayer book and theology, began to loosen as the 1960s dawned. Protestants eliminated archaic English in their new Bible translations and in their liturgy, and Reform Jews began to grow restless with language that seemed now to distance people from God rather than drawing them close. Many leaders in the Reform Movement wished to restore some of the traditional prayers that had been cast out of both the Shabbat and High Holy Day liturgy, to provide roadmaps of the structure of the service as it was being prayed, and to introduce more Hebrew as the authentic language of closeness to God. As the Movement grew, and grew more diverse, the prayer book was seen as a vehicle to celebrate this diversity. The *UPB* had laid the groundwork: there were five Shabbat Evening services and five introductions to the Shabbat Morning Service. *Gates of Prayer* offered a total of eleven evening services and a variety of other services as well, most of them geared to a particular theme, which reflected many aspects of Reform theology.

How could a companion High Holy Day prayer book echo these changes? It could—and did—restore some prayers that *UPB* II either omitted (a full version of the text of *Kol Nidrei*) or buried (*Untaneh Tokef*, hidden in the Yom Kippur Afternoon Service without the final paragraph outlining the life and death decrees of Judgment Day), and it increased the amount of Hebrew in the book (though, like *Gates of Prayer*, because of an embarrassment at offering transliteration—lest it appear to others that Reform Jews did not know Hebrew—it buried the transliteration at the back of

RICHARD N. LEVY

the book). Like *Gates of Prayer*, *Gates of Repentance* identified the names of prayers to help worshipers find their way. But the major innovation of *Gates of Prayer*, the multitude of services with their diverse themes, a *machzor*—used once a year—could not replicate. Evocations of the messianic age continue ("There will come a time when morning will bring no word of war or famine or anguish"— *Hashkiveinu*, p. 29), though the priest people had faded out of Reform liturgy.

But while the Gates series provided an integrated, authoritative liturgy for the Reform Movement, some elements were lost. Its publication made us realize belatedly how beautiful *UPB* English was, and since most of Reform worship is conducted in the vernacular, the new books made it hard for the service to soar. While Hebrew is properly the language of intimacy, because so many Reform Jews do not really know Hebrew, its sound often provokes nostalgia for one's own or one's ancestors' past rather than an immediate encounter with the God who created the world with it. And while transliteration enables one to pray with Hebrew sounds, it doesn't look like Hebrew, and so for some people transliteration only emphasizes the gap between language and the God to whom it is addressed. Because some rabbis felt that *UPB* language was too personal, many of its intimate prayers were not carried over into *Gates of Repentance*, and where there are prayers in the first person (e.g., the Silent Confession on Yom Kippur morning, p. 325) they often read more like a meditation than like a direct address to God. There are sections of *GOR* that contain what my wife Carol calls "a wall of words"—most notoriously in the Memorial Service (pp. 477–94). Yet where the traditional *Yizkor* Service offers individual *Yizkor* prayers for each category of person one is remembering, encouraging a person to spend time with specific memories of one's beloved, *GOR* has only one generic *Yizkor* prayer (p. 491). Even the *UPB* offered an English memorial for each category of family member or friend (pp. 319–21).

What are we to say about the pilot editions of the new *machzor*? Because we do not know what the *machzor* will look like in its final form, it may be most useful to express some hopes of what it will enable us to do on the High Holy Days. First of all, I would hope that the new *machzor* will provide significant continuity with *Mishkan T'filah*—not necessarily in appearance, but in language and theology. We have had an "authoritative" liturgy now for a

A TALE OF THREE *MACHZORIM*

decade; I would hope that the *machzor* reflects that fact. *Mishkan T'filah* made some important liturgical choices that have helped guide our prayer: restoring the third paragraph of the *Sh'ma* (tz-itzit) to the morning but not the evening service; continuing the elimination of the second paragraph of the *Sh'ma* but offering an English interpretation of it (p. 67); continuing the emphasis on a messianic age rather than a single Davidic messiah; restoring prayers from older traditions of the siddur (e.g., the prayer before offering the *Sh'ma* on p. 227—the equivalent in the *machzor* might be the restoration of some *piyutim*, not for the sake of restoring archaic prayers but for the sake of uplifting our prayer with invigorating themes). While the left hand pages in *Mishkan T'filah* have been faithful and creative extensions of the diverse services in *Gates of Prayer*, the need for variety is less in a *machzor* used only once a year. If the new *machzor* does include interpretive passages, I would hope that they would be in the service of reflecting diverse Reform understandings of specific High Holy Day themes, rather than introducing variety for its own sake.

I would also hope that the *machzor* is, as *Mishkan T'filah* proclaims itself, "a Reform *machzor*." I hope it includes uplifting English prayers, as well as evocations of the messianic age, of the prophets as inspirations for our actions, and of the vision of Israel bringing the nations closer to God. I would hope that it does not only restore traditional prayers like *Untaneh Tokef*, but offers interpretations that speak to the diverse theologies of Reform Jews. I would hope that while it encourages rapprochement with and understanding of other streams of Judaism, it affirms the value of maintaining and strengthening the diverse streams and nurtures our determination to continue the remarkable creativity of Reform worship. Would that the coming of the messianic time and the realization of God's sovereignty be deepened by the diversity of all the movements' liturgical attempts to draw close to the Holy One. I hope that it will take on the challenge of responding to the theme of God's *malchut*—helping us understand what it means for a liberal movement to affirm and live by the principles of the sovereignty of God.

Intimacy and majesty: as these polar experiences of God have marked the best of our liturgical endeavors over a century and a half, so do they encompass our understanding of the God we Reform Jews seek every day, every Shabbat, and, in a unique fashion once a year, on the Days of Awe.

Doing It Right or Doing It Well?

Lawrence A. Hoffman

At the *chavurah* that I have attended over the years, liturgy is done well. A telling example is the Yom Kippur afternoon service, "From Creation to Redemption." In many congregations, it is treated as a throwaway, an afternoon opportunity to delegate several pages of reading to lay volunteers, while the officiating clergy rest up for the *N'ilah* finale. But "From Creation to Redemption" was composed as a liturgical highlight: a modern version of the traditional *Avodah*, updated with exquisite Reform sensitivity to the nature of sacred history for our time. The *chavurah* pays attention to this potential, outfitting the text with music and choosing readers well in advance, who then practice their parts and speak them from many foci in the room. The resulting liturgy becomes a multimedia dramatic script that engages the entire congregation in the experience of moving through Jewish history, encountering its voices of the past, and reliving the highs and lows that have brought us to where we are.

It is not, technically, a service, because it has no *Amidah*—no official status whatever, in fact, since it deviates so widely from the *Avodah* on which it is based. That is probably why most officiating clergy overlook it as secondary. It is also why it has such potential: it need not answer to halachic standards; it can be newly composed, imaginatively configured, and matched with music and with mood to carry the congregation to a climactic recognition of the eternities suggested by Jewish peoplehood through time.

I think, by analogy, of another free creation for which no adequate model existed, and which, therefore, depended entirely on the creative inspiration of its composers: the *Kabbalat Shabbat* Service that the kabbalists largely invented in the sixteenth century.

RABBI LAWRENCE A. HOFFMAN, Ph.D. (NY69), author or editor of some three dozen books and a two-time winner of the National Jewish Book Award, serves on the faculty of HUC-JIR and is cofounder of Synagogue 3000—Next *Dor*. He consults with synagogues and lectures widely across North America.

DOING IT RIGHT OR DOING IT WELL?

Descriptions of the way *Kabbalat Shabbat* was done—whole communities dressed in white while watching the setting sun and reciting psalms with symbolic double entendres, leading up to *L'chah Dodi* (itself a poetic work of genius)—suggest a liturgy brimming with the possibility of encountering a moment of transcendence, the certainty of God, and the surety that life could matter. Whether our ancestors attended worship with these specific goals in mind we cannot know. We do know of ourselves, however, that transcendence, God, and meaning are issues highly to be sought. The liturgy for the High Holy Days should provide them. "From Creation to Redemption" inevitably did, at my *chavurah* experience of Yom Kippur year after year.

By contrast I think back to my initial year as a rabbinic student, when, for the very first time, I was dispatched to lead High Holy Day services: traditional davening in a nursing home, from a hefty *machzor* that I had never seen before. There was no Israel program yet (so I knew almost no Hebrew), but back home in Canada, my local shul had been Orthodox, so the College figured I would manage somehow. Besides, the people were elderly, they explained; an hour and a half would do it.

Ten minutes into the service, it became clear that the gaggle of worshiping seniors knew more than I did. One man particularly— call him Schwartz—uttered audible sighs of discontent at each of my several errors, mumbling grotesquely at the prayers I skipped and the inauthentic tunes I invented. Like most of the worshipers in attendance, Schwartz had been deposited at the home against his will with no option to leave. He would have driven me out of town on a rail, but hadn't the power.

"How did it go?" the director of the home inquired as I left the next day.

"Not so well," I admitted, "One man especially was pretty upset."

"That would be Schwartz," she confirmed. "Don't worry, he'll get used to you by Yom Kippur."

Indeed, I arrived on Yom Kippur to find Schwartz waiting at the door to greet me. "How good to see you, Rabbi," he acknowledged. "Glad you are back." I can only imagine what dire threat the director must have leveled upon him in the interim.

Throughout services that night and the next day, Schwartz sat as he had for Rosh HaShanah, but in silence, despite the fact that

LAWRENCE A. HOFFMAN

my ignorance of the massive Yom Kippur liturgy knew no bounds. Despite copious notes drawn from a close reading of Max Arzt's classic *Justice and Mercy*, I forgot or botched one thing after another, culminating in my somehow skipping the afternoon haftarah. As I moved instead to the later parts of the service, there arose from the crowd a swelling wave of antagonism, culminating in the chant, "yoinah, YOINAH, *YOINAH !!*" I didn't get it right away, but just as it dawned on me what the unhappy congregants were saying, Schwartz raised himself up from his front-row seat to turn and face my detractors. "Shah!!" he bellowed, "*He* is the rabbi; not *you*. What *he* says goes."

I have thought frequently of that unlikely introduction to liturgy, once just a personal trauma, but now a symbol of what is problematic about the Jewish approach to prayer: the assumed question over which the battle was fought was whether I had done the service *right*—not *well*, but *right*. My *chavurah* experience, by contrast, is all about doing the liturgy *well*. *Rightness* is a function of following the rules; it responds to external standards of liturgical form and content and the technicalities associated with them. *Wellness* focuses on the worshipers; while rules remain relevant, they become secondary to the experience of worship that they either further or impede.

This obsession with doing things *right* is a consequence of living with a liturgical tradition, a tradition, that is, that treasures a canon of required readings, melodies, actions, and dress, all governed by strictures of order, style, and performance. All ritual is scripted, but rituals in liturgical traditions are closed-scripted—that is, they over-determine things to the point where performers of it are trained above all not to sing, say, or do something wrong. Non-liturgical traditions are relatively open-scripted; performers get largely to make them up. They have their own challenges: planning everything from scratch, for example. Our problem, however, is that we are constantly being judged (and judging ourselves) by criteria of rightness. Doing it right is what counts for success.

The "right doing" of liturgy has become a fetish. Rabbi Eliezer taught, "If your *Amidah* is *keva* it can hardly be *tachanunim*" (*Mishnah B'rachot* 4:4), advice grasped admirably by Bertinoro, whose accompanying commentary describes *keva* as those occasions when "the *Amidah* feels like a burden . . . a fixed duty to say the *Amidah* and be quit of responsibility." In tannaitic times, *keva* could hardly

DOING IT RIGHT OR DOING IT WELL?

have been rote recitation of a siddur or *machzor*—not in an oral era when no written prayer books were possible and when *sh'lichei tzibbur* improvised wording around a fixed liturgical structure that determined just the order of topics (*seder avodah*, taken over into Christianity as the *ordo*, the same idea). But by Bertinoro's time (1455–1520), wording had been set, codes were established, *nusach* was fixed, and rules had multiplied. A student recently asked me (trembling as she did so) whether she might conceivable omit the *k'dushat hayom* from a Yom Kippur *Amidah*. We still, apparently, judge our liturgical labor by the extent to which we have done it all, and done it all *right*.

It took several centuries for this fixation on rule-centered rightness to set in. Originally, local *custom* determined much of liturgical practice—and custom, not being written down, is flexible over time. But the codes and the printing press changed all that. The first great gaon, Yehudai, initiated an attack on Palestinian custom, only to be told that "custom trumps halachah" (*minhag m'vatel halachah*). Amram was more successful, if not in his own time, then at least later, when scribes copied his prayer book as the model for all of Europe.[1] Local custom remained critical well into the Middle Ages, however, as we see from *rishonic* works like Abraham ben Nathan's *Sefer Hamanhig*, which surveys custom throughout France, Provence, Spain, and elsewhere, in the thirteenth century. The final victory of halachah came only with the codifiers, Maimonides, Asher ben Yechiel (the Rosh), Jacob ben Asher (his son), and Joseph Caro, because, says Ruth Langer:

> In the wake of persecutions, [they had] emigrated to countries where their wisdom and knowledge brought them recognition and leadership positions, but where the dominant *minhag* was quite different from that of their birthplaces . . . Unable to be fully invested in their original customs and unwilling to adapt fully to the *minhag hamakom*, they tended to devalue the halakhic weight of *minhag* as a category and enhance the status of the strict theoretical *halakhah* in their rulings . . . Their pronouncements were turning points in the history and development of Jewish liturgy.[2]

The rhetoric of authoritarian control thus became normative, as the following centuries fixed this wording rather than that, one custom rather than another, these additions but not those, and in this way but not that one.

LAWRENCE A. HOFFMAN

Printing solidified these choices—with horrible consequences. Communities refused to pray together, over trivial differences. Worshipers watched and judged, while *sh'lichei tzibbur* quaked in fear of doing the wrong thing. It is noteworthy that *Kabbalat Shabbat*, the last great positive example of all-out creativity, came on the eve of the printing revolution. On the one hand, the printing press allowed kabbalistic teaching—and liturgy—to sweep through Europe in record time; on the other, it became captured in print and was treated canonically ever after. Further creativity on that scale died until Reform Judaism recaptured its momentum. Until then, and in traditionalist circles still today, getting it all done right became the be-all and the end-all. Langer's study of this halachic victory over free-floating *minhag* is aptly entitled, *To Worship God Properly* [!].

Robert Nisbet's classic account, *Conservatism*, demonstrates how absolutely conservative this is. Rightness implies an objective standard of judgment, and conservatives see that standard in models from the past; these alone lend our actions "legitimacy." The classic liberal tradition of the age of reason valued individuals—the inalienable rights of John Locke and Thomas Jefferson, for whom the present is "the beginning of the future," not just "the latest point reached by the past." Conservatives, by contrast, rejected a future rooted only in the vagaries of today's reason; they enshrined instead the steady accumulation of the past, in what was called *character*. "Nations have character," Disraeli proclaimed. From a nation's character, one inherits prejudice, a term of opprobrium for liberals, but for conservatives, the proper appreciation of reasoning that flows from feelings, emotion, and experience of the people, the social group, and history. Individual reason, said Burke, is "soulless [and] icy." As to change, therefore, thought Falkland, "When it is not necessary to change, it is necessary not to change." Not that change is necessarily bad, but when it comes, it tends (for conservatives) to be additive; one improves matters just by altering the accumulation of the past, and by doing so as little as possible.[3]

Critical for modern conservatives has been the twin concepts of authenticity and legitimacy. Authentic—and, therefore, legitimate—alternatives are rooted outside the individual self. Authenticity, in our time, has experienced a radical change in meaning: We value an autonomous and authentic self in search of self-realization[4]—exactly what the conservatives feared. It is

DOING IT RIGHT OR DOING IT WELL?

precisely against this notion of rampant individualism that conservatives espoused the prejudice of tradition—the experienced wisdom of the centuries, which, alone, can balance individual whim. It takes little imagination to see that if any of the authorities whom Nisbet cites had been practicing Jews, they would have championed halachic rightness, purely out of conservative principle.

I do not mean to demonize these conservatives, who operated with admirable thoughtfulness and with laudable intentions. Falkland supported King Charles I because he feared the populist attack on the rule by bishops of the church. Burke lived in proper dread of the extremes taken by the French revolution. Disraeli is a particularly good example, because despite his conservative credentials as Tory Prime Minister, he initiated policies to support the urban poor and sought valiantly to make his conservative party responsive to the far-reaching social changes that accompanied the industrial revolution. He opposed Gladstone's liberals because he thought an enlightened aristocracy the best bet for ameliorating poverty while retaining the nobility of England's past.

The issue, then, is not good guys who change and bad guys who don't. The question is an elemental gut-level judgment on who and what to trust: the mantle of history, tradition, and the past (which is to say group prejudice, positively conceived) or the reasoned imagination of an uncharted future (meaning the self-determining individual). Which one threatens us more?

Whatever else they did, the Reformers made history by answering that question differently. The intensity of Jewish assimilation among Jews who found no way to harmonize Judaism with modernity convinced the Reformers that the devil most to be feared was tradition. By modern standards, these pioneer rabbis were not liberal, if by liberal, we mean laissez-faire, anything-goes, live-and-let-live. They knew tradition exceptionally well, and valued it; but they knew also how the printed liturgy and its codified regulations had spun out of control to become a liturgical tail wagging the would-be worshiping dog.

I said before that our obsession with propriety depended on twin felons, the printing press and the codes. Reformers transformed the printing press into an ally. Technological advances from 1814 (the steam-powered press) to the 1860s (the substitution of wood pulp for rags, making paper abundantly available) made new prayer books economically feasible. And they used the

LAWRENCE A. HOFFMAN

science of Judaism to free themselves of slavish adherence to the codes. Seeing Jewish law as evolutionary and mastering the art of historical reconstruction, they could reject the end of the codifying process while substituting the "healthier" (as they saw it) stages of liturgical history that they discovered in the early years of rabbinic conceptualization.

This citing of the past to justify a future is a tried and true strategy for reformers. In his short monograph on tradition, Jaroslov Pelikan recalls both Martin Luther and Thomas Jefferson "summoning their contemporaries to move beyond tradition or behind tradition to authenticity. Tradition was relative and had been conditioned by its history. Truth was absolute and had been preserved from historical corruption."[5] So too with these nineteenth-century Jewish Reformers, who, having scientific history at their disposal, could make truth claims in ways not available to Luther or Jefferson. Tradition was an evolutionary composite with layers that could be peeled back to arrive at a critical core. The core would be kept. Nothing important would be lost, even though the worship would finally be truncated rather than expanded.

There was still, therefore, an absolutely right way to go about doing things. Only the *standard* of rightness had changed: from halachic to historical fiat, what I have elsewhere called the triumph of truth over limits—in this case, the truth of history, which became probative. Reform standards depended also on two other sources of truth: theological acceptability and elitist aesthetics, a commitment to a standard of beauty that might build refined moral character (*Bildung*).[6] As much as Reform changed the rules of the game, therefore, it did not abandon the game altogether: it simply replaced the limits of halachah with the truths of history, theology, and aesthetics, which were no less constraining than law. To take but one instance (from America), Orthodox Jewish men were not allowed to pray without *kippot*; Reform Jews in the synagogue across the street were not allowed to pray with them.

Nonetheless, the Reformers got two things right. From the perspective of halachah, the liturgy is comprised of the regular statutory prayers altered and augmented to fit the Shabbat or holiday in question. From the perspective of worshipers, however, timely additions like *Kol Nidrei, Untaneh Tokef,* and *Yizkor* stand out as infinitely more important; one attends High Holy Day services with special anticipation of hearing *them*, not the standard prayers into which they are inserted (and which are often, at best, just tolerated). The Reformers faced up to the fact that unlike their pre-Enlightenment forebears, nineteenth-century German Jews no longer had to attend services to remain comfortably Jewish, and, in fact, were hardly likely to continue doing so if the service was not changed to satisfy their newly acquired standards of aesthetics and spirituality. The Reformers therefore broke new ground by looking at liturgy from the perspective of the congregants in the pews.

That meant accenting special prayers at the expense of the regular ones, the best example being the memorial liturgy which (as they inherited it) comprised just three necessary compositions (*Yizkor Elohim, Av HaRachamim*, and *El Malei Rachamim*) inserted at the end of *Shacharit*. Knowing that people came specifically for them, the Reformers extracted them as their own liturgical unit, added prayers in the vernacular, and relabeled them the Memorial Service. They did the same thing regarding the shofar. While tradition divided the blowing of the shofar between the period following the reading of Torah (*t'kiyot m'yushav*) and *Musaf* (*t'kiyot m'umad*) the Reformers combined them into a single Shofar Service, thereby giving them prominence. Thus was born the strategy of liturgical *highlighting*, a practice we follow successfully to this very day. We are most successful when we decide what makes a day's liturgy unique and then highlight it as a separate unit that people can anticipate and appreciate as a liturgical moment that epitomizes the holiday ambience, ethos, or message.

Simultaneously, the Reformers' commitment to keeping the service small and manageable led them to reverse the age-old process of adding but never subtracting to the liturgical corpus. Even as they highlighted holiday staples, they pared away the usual prayers, excluding a whole service (*Musaf*) for example, and truncating the *Amidah*. Their criteria for keeping or rejecting any given paragraph are not as important as the fact that they adopted criteria and did the cutting in the first place. Here, then, was the second major contribution: liturgical *editing*.

These two principles, *highlighting* and *editing*, should guide us. "From Creation to Redemption" is a superb example of highlighting; but the highlighting stands out because the editors of *Gates of Repentance* also edited the liturgy down to make room for the highlighted segment without having to squeeze it into an already

LAWRENCE A. HOFFMAN

overcrowded day in which its uniqueness would be swallowed up by page after page of meaningless verbiage. Our own worship will depend on how successfully we too highlight, on one hand, and edit, on the other.

How well are we doing? We do quite well at highlighting. Not so well at editing. Our ancestors edited the liturgy dramatically, omitting or shortening standard prayers that the codes demanded but that people would find offensive or just plain boring. I worry that we lack their courage. We do not take seriously enough our own mandate to save a progressive form of Judaism for our time. Unlike our Reform forebears, we no longer have to worry about people seeking baptism—the great Christian era is over. But the threat of Jewish meaninglessness is ubiquitous. Doing it *well* (rather than just *right*) is what will matter, and we cannot do it *well* if we insist on including all the statutory prayers just because it is our habit to do so or because the codes say we should.

Whatever book we end up with as our next *machzor*, the worship that results will depend on how judiciously it is used. Editing is not just the prerogative of prayer book compilers; it is also the requirement of prayer book users. Presiding rabbis and cantors will need to cut the service to a manageable size by highlighting the prayers that are most meaningful and omitting some staples that are hugely redundant.

Let me be specific. I have been at *Kabbalat Shabbat* services where the congregation sings its heart out, builds to a crescendo at *L'chah Dodi*, and is ready to return home with the good Shabbat angel shouting a heartfelt *Amen* in their ears—only to be forced back into the usual soporific boredom for *Maariv*. Why don't we jump directly from *L'chah Dodi* to a few highlighted English readings so beautiful that the angel might have written them herself; include, perhaps, *Hashkiveinu*, for the sake of invoking *sukkat shalom aleinu*, and conclude with *Aleinu, Kaddish* and a final song?

By extension, our Rosh HaShanah and Yom Kippur worship should highlight the traditional prayers and selective modern material that express the deep themes of the High Holy Day season: human sinfulness and nobility, for example, and the promise of life affirmed and renewed. Simultaneously we should drop great gobs of the standard material that we now drone through. We should even do away with the *Amidah* on occasion (editing) while retaining some of its holiday insertions—*Uv'chein,* for example, duly

DOING IT RIGHT OR DOING IT WELL?

enlarged with modern readings that emphasize its ultimate faith in universalism (highlighting). As things stand, *Uv'chein* is swallowed up by the usual *Amidah* verbiage that renders it practically invisible. No one even realizes it is there—let alone the reason why.

Another good example is *N'ilah*, a brilliantly conceived service whose theme is the discovery that when all is said and done, *atah notein yad laposhim*, God extends a hand, regardless of where sin has taken us, no matter how low we have fallen, irrespective of how our life has unraveled. What a concept! What if worshipers really went home convinced that they are not, after all, alone! That they can start again! Imagine a service shaped around that theological insight, fashioned, that is to say, not by the canons of halachah (doing it all right) but the impact of the message (doing it well).

We don't do that because we are afraid to—the failure of nerve I mentioned above. But equally important is the "elite factor"—the fact that seminary education and clergy culture together make rabbis and cantors into an educated elite. We study the subtleties of liturgical form and content and then want to perpetuate them. We may even like sitting endlessly throughout all of Yom Kippur in order to feel renewed when its final blast announces life after death. But we are not the norm. The worshipers around us don't yell "yoinah, YOINAH, *YOINAH !!*" anymore. They don't yell anything at all. They have no idea what to yell in the first place; and they care too little to find out. Already, they don't come in droves the way they used to; and they may soon stop coming altogether. We are becoming a two-class system: the elite who love the liturgy and the "plebeians" who some day may never hear it.

The predictable conservative response (against which we should be on guard) is to reaffirm the value of the inherited liturgy as it is; then to offer the "masses" educational opportunities to raise themselves up to "acceptable" standards; and finally, to blame the people who don't take advantage of the opportunity.

But this self-righteous outcry may be masking rabbinic self-interest. Our claim to our own authenticity lies in popular acceptance of the cultural heritage that we claim to guard. Unlike our congregants, the "culture users," we are the "culture creators" whom sociologist Herbert Gans studied all the way back in 1974:

[Culture creators] make culture their work, whereas users do not, and can rarely have as much interest or ego involvement in a

LAWRENCE A. HOFFMAN

cultural product as a person who created it. For creators, culture is often the organizing principle of their lives, whereas users are more likely to treat it as a tool for information or enjoyment.[7]

Producers of culture develop expertise; they revel in each other's company, sharing a technical competence and vocabulary that explains, appreciates, and celebrates the culture they produce. Their productivity derives from the historical past: from tradition, which has its own justification in their eyes. They charge the user culture of the masses with failing to understand tradition, wanting only untutored satisfaction and enjoyment.

Producers thus critique users, but interestingly enough, "the critique has appeared when intellectuals [that is, the producers] have lost power and the status that goes with it."[8] All of this should make us wary of our own evaluation of tradition, authenticity, and the high art (for that is what it is) of the High Holy Day liturgy that we so carefully guard. Are we not the intellectuals, the producers, the very elite that Gans describes, and are we not, at this very moment, losing power and the status that goes with it?

Whatever our new *machzor* becomes, it will have to be a script that elevates doing it well over doing it right, and doing it well is an aesthetic judgment: aesthetics as a general category of experience, however, not a particular aesthetic that yet another elite judges higher, and, therefore, "righter." I mean simply the consideration of how the worship affects the worshiper, as opposed to how the worshiper abides by (and sometimes just "abides") the worship. Let us establish the axiom that worship belongs to the people. The least we can do is deliver a liturgy that makes a difference in the people's lives without demanding that they first become experts in order to feel the difference.

Our age of spirituality is nothing, if not a manifesto of the masses demanding that religion point the way to what matters—or cease mattering itself, if it cannot do that. Religion is slowly losing its grasp on North Americans. To miss this obvious long-term trend, says sociologist Mark Chaves, is like missing the reality of global warming.[9] If religion cannot deliver worship that is spiritual to its core, it will die.

People once came anyway. Less and less are they doing that. No one willingly submits to boredom anymore. People with advanced degrees in everything but religion know enough to expect

DOING IT RIGHT OR DOING IT WELL?

that religion should speak to their lives without their having to feel stupid because they took a Ph.D. in physics or a masters degree in economics, instead of a seminary degree in the way the liturgy works. If we insist on playing the role of defender of the faith, we will end up defending it as an historical curiosity, set in synagogues as museums, with the liturgy under glass.

Freed from the burden of defending tradition, we can ask such questions as: What are the real liturgical messages of the *machzor*? What gets in our way of delivering them? What must we sacrifice by editing and what must we create by highlighting in order to do that delivering? Zero-based budgeting insists on justifying expenditures every year, rather than automatically replicating them just because they have always been there. Zero-based programming urges synagogues to reevaluate programming that way: to drop programs that are barely limping along and to program intentionally, so as to achieve their visionary goals; zero-based liturgy requires looking anew at the prayers we do by habit and asking ourselves what would happen if we changed or got rid of them:

- It will be objected that the liturgy is rich; that sitting for hours has a positive cumulative effect; that we cannot get the impact we want if we take a scalpel to tradition. But that is a judgment of the elite; our own view that may be irrelevant to everyone except us.
- Others will ask, "Who are we to make such far-reaching reforms?" But whoever we are, we are all we have; and we are either up to the task or not.
- Some will say that doing it right is the properly Jewish way. But that is only partly true. Think of the *payetanim*, think of Musar, think of elemental Chasidism, think of Reform.
- Still others will fear that by radicalizing our critique, we will lose what we abandon forever. But classical Reform saved Judaism for the majority of moderns by being radical. When the time came to reclaim what had been temporarily set aside, we managed to do it.

Some Reformers acted in excess, we now may say, and some of us will too, but all great movements—science, art, politics, everything—depend on radical freedom whereby wrong turns and dead ends by some are eventually eclipsed by lasting innovations by others. *Et laasot l'adonai*. It is time to act boldly, bravely,

LAWRENCE A. HOFFMAN

and decisively. We must risk all lest we lose all. For if we do not risk enough, we will lose everything.

Notes

1. See Lawrence A. Hoffman, *The Canonization of the Synagogue Service* (South Bend, IN: University of Notre Dame Press, 1979).

2. Ruth Langer, *To Worship God Properly* (Cincinnati: HUC Press, 1998), 248.

3. Robert Nisbet, *Conservatism* (Minneapolis: University of Minnesota Press, 1986), 23–27. Quotations above are from Disraeli, Burke, and Falkland.

4. See Charles Taylor, *The Ethics of Authenticity* (Cambridge, MA: Harvard University Press, 1991).

5. Jaroslav Pelikan, *The Vindication of Tradition* (New Haven: Yale University Press, 1984), 44.

6. See Michael Meyer, "'How Awesome Is This Place!' The Reconceptualization of the Synagogue in Nineteenth-Century Germany," *Leo Baeck Yearbook* 41 (1996): 51–63.

7. Herbert J. Gans, *Popular Culture and High Culture* (New York: Basic Books, 1974), 25.

8. Ibid.

9. See Mark Chaves, *American Religion: Contemporary Trends* (Princeton: Princeton University Press, 2011). Reference to global warming is from Chandra Swanson, "Q and A With Mark Chaves," *The Chronicle: The Independent Daily at Duke University*, October 31, 2011.

Section Three: From Our Colleagues

When I Hear the Shofar I Taste Chocolate: Seeking the Synesthetic on the High Holy Days

Evan Kent

An Introduction to Synesthesia

It's a glorious night at the symphony. Michael is listening to the Los Angeles Philharmonic play a Mozart violin concerto. The opening movement in G major is a longtime favorite of his and as he listens his mouth is filled with an overwhelming taste of chocolate. Not just any chocolate, but a slightly bitter Belgian chocolate. Sitting a few rows away at the same concert, Rosalie is enjoying the opening phrases of the concerto and as she listens red bars and green circles float in front of her as the soloist begins to play. Robert, sitting toward the back of the orchestra, glances down at this evening's program. As he reads the program notes, all the letters and numbers have different colors. For Robert, the number seven appears red, three is green, nine is black, and each letter of the alphabet has a corresponding color as well.

Michael, Rosalie, and Robert are not only symphony subscribers; these concert goers are also synesthetes: persons with a neurological condition in which two senses are physiologically coupled. These sensory matchings are not the same for every synesthete and no two people experience the exact same form of synesthesia.

EVAN KENT is the cantor at Temple Isaiah in Los Angeles and is also the cantor for the synagogue on the Los Angeles campus of HUC-JIR. Evan is also a doctoral candidate at Boston University, where he is researching how music at Jewish summer camp helps to create Jewish identity.

EVAN KENT

For example, one individual with musical-taste synesthesia may taste chocolate when they hear a musical composition in the key of D major. Another might experience the taste of wild blueberries when a middle C on the piano is played. An individual with grapheme-color synesthesia associates certain numbers or letters with colors. Whatever form the synesthesia takes, it is an involuntary action and cannot be turned on or off at will.

Estimates vary on how many people are synesthetic. Oliver Sacks in *Musicophilia*[1] approximated that one in two thousand persons exhibit true synesthesia. But these numbers are a mere estimate as many synesthetes refuse to self-identify for fear of social ostracization. Many fear if they reveal their condition to others they might be labeled "strange" or "crazy" or will be accused of fabricating their observations. Other synesthetes move through life aware they perceive the world differently, but never identify it as synesthesia—only because they do not have a name for their condition. Synesthetes, according to Veronica Gross of Emmanuel College in Boston, often do not know that anything is "wrong." In fact, many synesthetes are often silent about their condition until they hear about it on a television program, a radio broadcast, or read an article in a newspaper and only then realize that they are neither mentally ill nor alone in their observations and perceptions.

Cultural Synesthesia

There is another variety of synesthetic experiences that are also intersensory experiences but without the medical or neurological basis of the synesthesia as described above. This cultural or social synesthesia is a fusing of the senses through events that deeply implant within individuals specific events, experiences, or rituals. According to Professor Steve Odin, these synesthetic moments are so profound "that the boundaries of the senses actually merge, and the multivariate sense qualities—colors, sounds, flavors, tactile and thermal sensations—all seem to melt into a continuum of feeling."[2]

Odin employs the Japanese tea ceremony to illustrate this form of synesthesia. The tea ceremony includes visual elements (the various vessels and pots used for making and holding the tea), aural stimulus (the sound of water boiling in the kettle), scent

WHEN I HEAR THE SHOFAR I TASTE CHOCOLATE

(incense burning), and even touch (the asymmetry of the *raku* tea cup). Events such as this tea ceremony are described as a synesthesia forged through the "simultaneity and harmony of multivariate sense-impulses" with the end result being a gathering "of diverse sense impulses within a physiological sensorium."[3] This synesthesia is one in which the senses are not joined together but rather the "multivariate sensations of color, sound, scent, and flavor interpenetrate in profound unity while simultaneously retaining their unique qualitative natures."[4]

The synesthetic is possible in even more everyday events. Theologian Don Saliers in *Music and Theology* presented the example of his young daughters and neighborhood friends learning jump rope songs. The fusion of words, music, and communal dancing produced a multisensory form of embodied ritual that also enhanced community. According to Saliers, these children participated in a form of synesthetic matrix as they sang and jumped to "Miss Mary Mack Mack Mack . . ." This union of activity produced "a simultaneous blending or convergence of two or more senses, hence a condition of heightened perception."[5] According to Saliers, this synesthesia not only heightens our awareness, but assists in encoding memory and creating long-lasting associations.

Ethnomusicologist Steven Feld expands this notion by stating, "As places are sensed, senses are placed, and as places make sense, senses make place."[6] Our senses provide us with an appreciation and awareness of not only the event itself but the event's location, participants, and emotions and feelings associated with the event.

Although many synesthetic occurrences take place in the secular realm, the environment of sacred ritual is an opportune setting for the synesthetic. Rituals and liturgies that invite the participation of all the senses not only serve to create deeper and richer memory and help to form cultural religious and ethnic identity, but also "have the capacity to give value and meaning to the life of those who perform them."[7]

The Synesthetic in Jewish Tradition:
Sinai, Seder, Summer Camp

One of the most famous synesthetic events occurs after the Israelites are presented with the Ten Commandments. In Exodus 20:15 we read:

EVAN KENT

Now all of the people were seeing
the thunder sounds
the flashing torches
the shofar sound
and the mountain smoking;
when the people saw,
they faltered
and stood far off. (Exod. 20:15)[8]

According to the Torah, a communal synesthetic experience was present at Sinai: The multitude *saw* the sound of thunder; the Israelites *saw* the sound of the shofar. So powerful was the moment of revelation that the boundaries between sight and sound momentarily vanished and the synesthetic occurred.

The Passover seder is another ritual experience offering opportunities for the synesthetic. Like the tea ceremony, the seder involves all the senses. We read the Haggadah; we sing blessings and songs; we smell the soup heating on the stove and the brisket roasting in the oven; we taste the symbolic foods around the seder; we touch the decorative and sacred objects on the table; we reach out and hug and kiss family and friends gathered for the evening's celebration. All of this total body engagement contributes to the synesthesia of the event. A variety of senses are employed as part of the seder and this creates a sense-rich layering that in turn triggers other sensual memories and awareness.

Seder is not recalled in sequence or as a series of atomistic moments, but rather in its totality. The Haggadah's brilliance is that it leads us through an ancient ceremony, shuttling us back and forth between the historic and the contemporary: One moment we are slaves in Egypt, the next moment we are twenty-first-century Jews tasting *charoset*. The didactic nature of the Haggadah is enhanced through the use of story, song, food, and ritual. We not only learn the story of the Exodus, but the experience of seder becomes physically embodied. Leach describes this type of synesthetic event as one of condensation and fusion.[9] By the end of the evening, all of the multiple and multi-channeled elements of the ritual are combined and condensed into a single, memorable experience we call "seder."

My own research and analysis of the Shabbat experience at residential Jewish summer camp revealed Shabbat to be a synesthetic experience as well. When campers spoke of Shabbat, it was presented as a swirl of memory with the senses intermingled. Campers spoke glowingly of a Shabbat filled with songs, swaying with arms wrapped around each other as they sang "Shalom Rav," the scent of sycamore trees, the sound of the ocean's waves, the gleam of hundreds of campers wearing white shirts, the dining room filled with the scent of freshly baked challah and roasted chicken, and a joyous song session filling the dining hall. Those interviewed vividly recalled Shabbat at camp and considered it to be one of the most salient and long-enduring memories of their total camp experience. The multisensory summer camp Shabbat celebration enables a synesthesia that permits this experience to remain within the body and mind and acts as a focus of profound, long-lasting, and rich memories. Vibrant recollections of Shabbat at camp remain with the camper for years after the camp experience has ended. Because the initial experience was so profound, even isolated elements from the camp experience (the scent of baking challah, a favorite melody from the after-dinner song session, for example) can serve as a mental trigger that kindles a remembering of the camp Shabbat experience even though it initially took place many years before.

Opportunities for Synesthesia in the High Holy Days

There is no doubt that Rosh HaShanah and Yom Kippur create significant memories for congregants. The remembrances are forged from the sheer emotion, sacred importance, and the liturgical depth of these Days of Awe. Music and communal song undoubtedly play a large role in the creation of memories, especially the stirring melodies of *Kol Nidrei* and *Avinu Malkeinu*. But, I wonder, can the High Holy Days become more sensorially integrated like the Jewish summer camp Shabbat and the Passover Seder and thus ultimately provide the congregation with an experience that is not only synesthetic in nature but is also more memorable and thus creating a deeper connection to community and to the sacred.

Synesthetic opportunities are possible through the development of those senses not normally part of the liturgical experience: taste, smell, and touch.

Taste and Smell

The High Holy Days are filled with speech, song, and written word, but they lack the elements of touch and taste. Sephardic and

EVAN KENT

Mizrahi Jews have a tradition of an Erev Rosh HaShanah seder-like ceremony with Talmudic roots (*Horayot* 12a) in which a variety of fruits and vegetables are used to represent aspirations for the New Year. Congregants should be made aware of this custom to share with guests around the Erev Rosh HaShanah dining table, but it is also possible to bring this Rosh HaShanah seder into the synagogue. Imagine how delighted the community would be to see tables laden not only with the requisite apples and honey but with festive fruits and vegetables accompanied by blessings and explanations available to be tasted as part of a prelude to Erev Rosh HaShanah.

The ubiquitous honey cake could also enable an enhanced Rosh HaShanah synesthesia. Honey cakes baking in the synagogue kitchen and then served at the end of services as part of an *oneg* could help to enhance the relationship of scent and taste to the holidays. Like Proust's *madeleine,* the aroma and taste of honey cake could become associated with myriad memories connected with the joy of Rosh HaShanah.

Touch

The sound of the shofar is one of the most ancient sounds present in the synagogue's musical repertory and when the *baal t'kiah* raises the shofar and the calls of *t'kiah-t'ruah-sh'varim* resound through the sanctuary, the ancient world meets modernity. The most ancient of musical instruments could be used to create a synesthetic matrix featuring not only sound, but sight and touch as well.

The new CCAR *machzor*'s repositioning of the three rubrics for the sounding of shofar (*Malchuyot, Zichronot, Shofarot*) throughout the service rather than having them appear sequentially as is common in traditional High Holy Day prayer books is a first step in highlighting the shofar as elemental in the ritual of the *Yamim Noraim*. However, more can be done to enhance the shofar's power. For example, in lieu of just one shofar blower on the synagogue's bimah, a more dramatic approach with potential for greater impact would the organization of a shofar "choir" comprised of multiple *baalei t'kiah* lining the aisles of the synagogue. This choir of shofarot would present greater visual impact, surround the congregation with the clarion call of the ram's horn, and present worshipers with a vibrational and tactile energy from the shofarot. A singular shofar provides incredible impact; a shofar ensemble would be an unforgettable addition to the Rosh HaShanah liturgy.

Other opportunities for enhancing touch exist within the liturgy. During the chanting or singing of *Mi Shebeirach* congregants could be asked to hold hands or put their arms on each other's shoulders. As the cantor recites the Priestly Blessing or a final benediction, all those wearing tallitot could be asked to share their tallit with those around them and feel enveloped not only by the tallit but by the community as well.

We should also encourage congregants to experience the power of full prostration during the Great *Aleinu*. The physical act of falling to one's knees in the presence of God is not only humbling but a physical representation of full emotional and spiritual supplication before the Almighty in which we physically declare, "We surrender. Please help us, God. Protect us. Guide us." There are no words in the liturgy that can fully express this moment of physical prayer; no text in the *machzor* can adequately describe the moment of the Great *Aleinu*.

Tasting Chocolate

When we are part of synesthetic events, these experiences become encoded and implanted within us. We hold onto these memories and reflect upon them as years pass. When ritual is deeply embodied and synesthetic (like the experiences of summer camp Shabbat and the Passover seder) not only are our feelings and beliefs enhanced, but the participation in these rituals joins us to a larger, broader, Jewish collective. The new *machzor* will surely enhance the experience of prayer for a new generation of Jews. But that experience can be greatly enhanced if we make a concerted effort to move beyond the pages of the prayer book. We need to present our congregants (and I dare say clergy as well) with ritual moving beyond music and spoken or read text that permits worshipers to experience prayer with all their senses and moves our worship— and indeed ourselves as worshipers—to a higher spiritual plane. Creating synesthetic worship may transform the High Holy Day liturgy from beautiful and emotional words to life-altering fully embodied ritual. Don Saliers reminds us, "If we only take in the literal surface of what we hear in words and song, the awakening of the deeper dimensions of reality and of the soul are prevented.

EVAN KENT

When the singing and the hearing allow us to 'taste and see,' we come to 'hear' more. The soul is awakened to a humanity stretched more deeply before the mystery and the glory of God."[10]

May our prayer be guided not only by words of our mouth and the meditations of our heart, but the tastes and scents of the seasons, the reverberation of the shofar, the healing touch of our neighbors, and the communal embrace of our fellow worshipers.

Notes

1. Oliver Sacks, *Musicophilia* (New York: Alfred A. Knopf, 2007).
2. Steve Odin, "Blossom Scents Take Up the Ringing: Synaesthesia in Japanese and Western Aesthetics," *Soundings* 69, no. 3 (Fall 1986): 256.
3. Ibid., 259.
4. Ibid., 270.
5. Don E. Saliers, *Music and Theology* (Kindle ed.) (Nashville: Abingdon Press, 2007), Kindle location 171.
6. Steven Feld, "Waterfalls of Song," in *Senses of Place*, ed. Steven Feld and Keith H. Basso (Santa Fe, NM: School of American Research Press, 1996), 91.
7. Paul Connerton, *How Societies Remember* (Cambridge: Cambridge University Press, 1989), 45.
8. Translation from Everett Fox, *The Five Books of Moses* (New York: Schocken Books, 1983).
9. Edmund Leach, *Culture and Communication* (Cambridge: Cambridge University Press, 1976).
10. Saliers, *Music and Theology*, Kindle location 301.

Love, Liturgy, Leadership

Elyse D. Frishman

Sh'ma koleinu, Adonai Eloheinu, chus v'racheim aleinu. Does God hear us? How would we know that we have been heard?

Hear our prayer: not just listen, but comprehend, understand us. If God truly understands, God will listen with compassion and mercy (*chus v'racheim*), because despite our failings, God knows that we are desperate to become more.

Hear *our* voice: The plural reveals the power and essentiality of communal prayer. The individual voice gains not only in volume but also in measurable importance when offered in community: man, woman, child, lay leader, cantor, rabbi.

Hear our *voice*: because our voices' voice is one, opened in anguish to the exigencies of life. Prayer emerges in humility, facing existential desperation, hoping for understanding and embrace. That desire for embrace cries out, *"Racheim, have mercy!"* Since *racheim* is linked to the womb (*rechem*), it is as though we are pleading, "As once we were protected, nourished, and grown, so embrace us now."

Does God hear? Our liturgy affirms this with the priestly blessing. Moments after *Sh'ma Koleinu* is offered, the *kohanim* or clergy raise their hands to bless the people, and the people are assured: God hears.

But the priestly figure is the agent of that blessing, and how that blessing is communicated says a great deal about who God is, and where God is in that moment.

The *machzor*, magnificent script for our deepest hopes and dreams, must communicate consistently that God is present and that our voices are heard. But Larry Hoffman has taught that a prayer book remains a tool, as effective as its wielder: "No new

---

ELYSE D. FRISHMAN (NY81) is the editor of *Mishkan T'filah: A Reform Siddur.* She is the senior rabbi at The Barnert Temple in Franklin Lakes, New Jersey. She is married to Rabbi Daniel Freelander, and they have three children, Adam, Jonah, and Devra.

ELYSE D. FRISHMAN

book *alone* will solve the problem . . . The problem is . . . systemic."[1] We have learned that successful worship requires attention to many additional components: environment, music, sermon, clergy, lay leaders, the people. The responsibility of clergy is *to inspire* the system, and to manage the *machzor* in the context of the whole. The implications are huge, not just for our worship experience, but because that experience will communicate a great deal about God's identity and God's accessibility. *We* demonstrate the ethic of inclusivity. Most importantly, we demonstrate the presence of *love.*

A Community of Strangers

A reflection on Shabbat worship and its application to the *Yamim Noraim*: In many Shabbat morning Reform sanctuaries, the worshipers constitute a "community of strangers"—gathered for *b'nei mitzvah,* often from "elsewhere," often not knowing each other. Yet, for that period of prayer, study, and celebration, it is an opportunity to link them to each other, to open the gates of prayer to them. They haven't necessarily come to pray; often their attire and attitude speak of enduring the service. Yet, it doesn't take much to open their hearts by *taking note of who they are that day.* To trust them to be present. To welcome the teens warmly and sincerely. To know and respect what matters to each person, each soul present.

Before worship begins, these should be strangers no more. Then, we will know which prayers will resonate: English? Hebrew? The right or left side? *Mishkan T'filah* allows the opportunity to choose in the midst of the service. Worshipers may be insecure about prayer. They might not want others to hear them pray or sing. They might feel Jewishly illiterate or lost in unfamiliar music. Perhaps there are complicated family dynamics; is this a *sanctuary* for them? How do we help create that safe environment that can open every person, every age, to matters of the heart? These are the questions that guide the content of our prayer books, *and the way in which we use them.* Group worship relies on trust of each other as well as with God. Relationships are being shaped during worship.

On Rosh HaShanah and Yom Kippur, our worshiping community shifts yet again. Blended are Shabbat regulars, High Holy Day guests, and High Holy Day regulars. The latter are as much a

LOVE, LITURGY, LEADERSHIP

community of regulars as on Shabbat. They enter and look to see whom they know. They often sit where they did last year, with the same people. They rely on comfort and familiarity; and then they may be open to spiritual growth, to character refinement, to God.

How people discern God varies by personality. Different personality types are drawn to different spiritual expressions.[2] Individuals are hard-wired spiritually. Some resonate to action (community service or social justice) while others are drawn to meditation and mysticism. This should inform the development of our *machzor*—and the prayer choices we clergy make during worship. All spiritual types could be present; do we recognize them? Is every worshiper certain that *we* are listening?

The *machzor* itself must include feelings *and* thoughts. Different poetic *styles* matter as much as the content. The two-page spread allows for this variety. As in *Mishkan T'filah*:

> Theologically, the liturgy needs to include many perceptions of God: the transcendent, the naturalist, the mysterious, the partner, the evolving God . . . An integrated theology communicates that the community is greater than the sum of its parts. While individuals matter deeply, particularly in the sense of our emotional and spiritual needs and in the certainty that we are not invisible, that security should be a stepping stone to the higher value of community, privilege and obligation. We join together in prayer because together, we are stronger and more apt to commit to the values of our heritage . . . Prayer must move us beyond ourselves. (*Mishkan T'filah*, ix)

The contents of the *machzor* inform and propel *us* as well as our congregants. We are reminded, too, of the diversity of our community. As in *Mishkan T'filah*, the *machzor* will uphold the ethic of inclusivity, and the "awareness of and obligation to others rather than mere self-fulfillment." To be personally included and to serve others should be possible simultaneously.

Leadership from Love

The worship experience of the clergy is different than the person-in-the-pew. We attend to the people. Yet that attention need not distract from personal prayer; it may deepen it. Serving others is a form of *avodah*, serving God. How might we serve most effectively during the High Holy Days?

ELYSE D. FRISHMAN

Humility and Love:
Levi Yitzchak of Berditchev cautions, "There is a danger that the performance of God's *mitzvot* could cause a *sin*, that sin being one's smugness about having performed even a single *mitzvah*. Such smugness is spiritual arrogance. Any Jew who considers himself 'a somebody,' as a result of having performed *mitzvot* instead of having acquired a more profound sense of humility, has failed to absorb basic lessons of Judaism. That person forgets or forgot that even the strength, physical and moral, to perform these *mitzvot,* was something granted to us by the Creator; it is not something 'homegrown' . . . We should be careful lest we acquire any notion of superiority, because if we were to do this, what was meant to be a blessing could turn into a curse due to our arrogance."[3]

Offering *Hineini* at the outset of the High Holy Days reminds us that we are bound to one another, clergy and community. We pray that our congregation will not falter on our account, nor we on theirs. *Hineini* downsizes us so that we can remember before whom we stand. We clergy stand before God *and everyone* humbly, so that *we can see our people, we can hear them, we can take note of and be with them.*

If we utilize the *machzor* to see into our people's lives, to hear their voices, we will be serving them. Service deepens humility. Humility opens the door for us to pay attention and to serve. To serve with love furthers humility, which opens our own hearts to personal prayer—and again to service.

The Sages describe the importance of *love* during the offering of the Priestly Blessing. First, the priest must face the people. "R. Isaac said, 'Let respect for the community always be with you, for you will note that (while blessing the worshippers), the priests' faces were turned towards the people and their backs were towards the Presence'" (*Sotah* 40a). By looking into the eyes of the community, of the people, the individuals before us, we see into their eyes and hearts. We don't stand before the people; we stand *amidst* them.

The priestly blessing brought God into the people's midst. So the priest needed to bless the people through *chesed* (*Zohar Naso* 145b).[4] As agents of that blessing, *we* emanate *chesed*. We love our people. Especially during the *Yamim Noraim,* standing before the congregation, looking into the eyes of individuals, we radiate care

LOVE, LITURGY, LEADERSHIP

for each and every one of them. No matter what has taken place between us, we reveal *chesed*; we love them.

The *Zohar* also teaches that while the priest must love the people, *they must love him*:

> On one occasion, when a priest went up and spread forth his hands, before he completed the blessing he turned into a heap of bones. This happened because there was no love between him and the people. Then another priest went up and pronounced the blessing, and so the day passed without harm. A priest who loves not the people, nor whom they love not, may not pronounce the blessing. (*Zohar Naso* 147b)[5]

It is dangerous to pretend love. The hidden wisdom here is that while the priest must learn how to love, the people must also learn to love. We are all in need. On the *Yamim Noraim*, we come together to be reassured that we are seen, we are heard, we are loved.

Certainly, though, as clergy, there may be an obstacle to our love for the people, and theirs for us. Will we work to overcome this before we join in this sacred endeavor?

We learn from Esau, in Genesis 33, about forgiveness. After years of separation, Jacob and Esau must face each other. Jacob is afraid; it is their first encounter since Jacob's primal thefts from Esau and Esau's threat to kill him. Esau, too, is worried; what might his brother wrest from him now? Yet as they draw close, Esau observes, physically and spiritually, that Jacob is no longer dangerous: He bears no weapon and he appears humble. Can Esau be sure? No. Yet, he takes a risk. As Jacob arrives, Esau runs to embrace him, perhaps showering him with kisses. (There are several diacritical marks above *va'yishakeihu* suggesting an image of multiple kisses.) Esau's offers *chesed*, and then Jacob offers gifts.

> Esau said: "I have plenty, my brother; let what is yours remain yours." Yaakov said: "No, I pray! Pray, if I have found favor in your eyes, then take this gift from my hand. For I have, after all, seen your face, as one sees the face of God, and you have been gracious to me."[6]

Esau had become secure in his own life, so he could forgive Jacob. What might we clergy learn about forgiveness from Esau—the so-called enemy? About looking into the eyes of the other and finding

ELYSE D. FRISHMAN

chesed (love)? How can our own encounter at the High Holy Days bring a reunion of brothers and sisters?

In the system that is worship, how worshipers position themselves physically can impact the sense of God's Presence and where God is found. A *baraita* in *B'rachot* 30a teaches:

> One who stands outside of Israel should direct his heart towards *Eretz Yisrael*, as it says, "And they will pray to you by way of their land," (I Kings 8:48). One who stands in *Eretz Yisrael* should direct his heart towards Jerusalem, as it says, "And they will pray to God by way of the city which You have chosen," (I Kings 8:44). One who stands in Jerusalem should direct his heart towards the Temple, as it says, "And they will pray towards this House," (II Chronicles 6:32). One who stands in the Temple should direct his heart towards the Holy of Holies, as it says, "And they will pray towards this place." (I Kings 8:35) . . . Thus, one who stands: in the east—turns his face towards the west; in the west—turns his face towards the east; in the south—turns his face towards the north; in the north—turns his face towards the south. Thus, all of Israel directs their hearts to one place.

If worshipers around the world all look towards the Temple, we face each other. Seeking God, and with no Temple blocking the way, we find one another.

A sanctuary is traditionally designed to face the Holy of Holies. Within our sanctuaries, worshipers face the ark—and clergy. We are elevated by the bimah. This architectural design creates a spiritual impression that we are "higher up." Rather, let it impress upon us the *opportunity* to see into the eyes and hearts of our people.

And when we join together vocally in prayer, rather than "leading" most of the liturgy, we may be more apt to listen to the voices of others. The experience of sharing the prayers aloud may bring a deeper awareness of the other. Then, what might we hear?

Let's return to the priestly blessing. *Zohar Naso* 146a explains that the offering of *Yivarech'cha* connects the upper and lower worlds; it leads to completion. To effect this, the priest must *understand* this. "R. Judah said, 'If a priest is ignorant of this inward significance of the blessing and does not know whom he blesses or what his blessing connotes, his blessing is naught.'"[7]

In 147b, R. Judah continues: "Indeed, we find that a real blessing is associated with the opening of the eye. Thus it is written, 'Open

LOVE, LITURGY, LEADERSHIP

Your eyes,' (Daniel 9:18), that is, in order to bless."[8] "Open"—not *p'tach*, but *pokeiach* (take note). The verse references God taking note, but R. Judah infers that the priest must open *his* eyes and *take note*. To take note of the people in blessing them mirrors the empathy of God taking note of Sarah, hearkening to not merely her prayer, but her deep need. When Sarah was acknowledged, she became fruit-full (fruitful). Often negative emotions and behavior are the weeds of an untended spirit. A barren spirit, even more so, is parched for attention. *Taking note* therefore leads to fruit-bearing, positive action. Our people, as do we, need recognition and acknowledgment in the deepest sense. Consider the fuller context of the Daniel verse:

> Now, our God, hear the prayers and petitions of your servant. For your sake, Eternal, look with favor on your desolate sanctuary. Give ear our God, and hear; open your eyes and see the desolation of the city that bears Your Name. We do not make requests of You because we are righteous, but because of Your great mercy.

Daniel beseeches God to act from mercy and not judgment. So, too, our people want to be seen and understood through eyes of mercy and not judgment. *Sh'ma koleinu, Adonai Eloheinu, chus v'racheim aleinu.* Our challenge, in both sermon and liturgy, is not to preach but *to teach to action*. Where is God? Where action is inspired by *chesed* and love.

We need each other. *We clergy* need our *community*:

> And let them make me a sanctuary, that I may dwell among them, (Exodus 25:8). That is, any sanctuary whatever, in that any synagogue, wherever situated, is called *sanctuary*, and the *Shechinah* hastens to the synagogue (even before the worshippers arrive). Happy is the one who is of the first ten to enter the synagogue, since they form something complete, and are the first to be sanctified by the *Shechinah*. (*Zohar Naso* 126a).[9]

Ten people are necessary for a group to worship. Rabbi Zalman Shachter-Shalomi[10] teaches that each kabbalistic *s'firah* is an attribute of God. Each of the ten *s'firot* is emphasized in a different person. That is, each individual is a vessel for one *s'firah* in particular: wisdom, intuition, judgment, endurance, etc. We need each other, and we need community, because we bring different aspects

ELYSE D. FRISHMAN

of God together. When all ten of the attributes are present through ten different people, God is fully present. Technically, a minyan could accomplish this. Yet, likely it will take many more than ten people, since the distribution of these *s'firot* is so spread out. *Who knows which final person entering the sanctuary will complete us all?*

Continuing the discussion about a minyan, the *Zohar* teaches:

> For inasmuch as the single members are not together there is no complete body . . . Observe that the moment the body is made complete here below a supernal holiness comes and enters that body, and so the lower world is in truth transformed after the pattern of the upper world. *Thus it is incumbent on all not to open their mouths to talk of worldly matters,* seeing that Israel then are at their most complete and holiest. (*Zohar Naso* 126a)[11]

As people enter the synagogue environment, what would be considered "worldly matters"? Is ordinary schmoozing and greeting people out of place? No, for this renews relationships, and good relationships deepen spirituality. What matters would be deemed ordinary? Transaction of business, phone calls, texting—any action that distracts us from the *makom hakodesh.*

What might we do to encourage spiritual engagement before High Holy Day worship arrives? What training will our leaders need? What preparation might we provide our congregants? Considering again the reunion of Esau and Jacob: What will be the arena for wrestling before we greet one another? Preparing each and every person, congregant and guest, will deepen the experience of the entire community, and us. Skill and insight acquired by one impact all.

Our guidance of the community begins well before the commencement of worship. What occurs on the entire property matters, outside in the parking lot, into the building, in the lobby. The transition from profane to sacred is in the details. Imagine: patient, smiling parking attendants; warm greeters from all cohorts of the community, so one is likely to recognize and welcome each congregant; *and clergy who are ready to receive.*

Where are the clergy as people enter? If we are readying ourselves—rehearsing Torah readers, choir members, lay leaders, one another—then we do not model readiness to others. We must be fully present, all-ready for our people in the *makom hakodesh.*

LOVE, LITURGY, LEADERSHIP

And truly, *where are we?* What is our frame of mind? *The frame of our soul?* As we facilitate worship, no matter what, we must model the offering of *chesed* (of forgiveness and love).

How will we guide the ordinary to blend gently into the holy? Until suddenly each person will realize, *"Achein, yesh Adonai bama-kom hazeh, vaanochi lo yadati?"* (Surely God is in this Place, yet I, I did not know?) (Gen. 28:16).

The experience of worship on the High Holy Days is unique to the season. The *machzor* varies from the siddur not only in tradi-tional liturgy, but also in the choices of contemporary poetry. Will the *machzor* preach, or will it inspire? Will *we* preach or inspire?

Worship opens us to transformation of the self and of the com-munity. If we don't transform ourselves, we won't be able to guide our congregants—or the world around us.

On the *Yamim Noraim*, we join together to be heard and loved and inspired to serve anew. Clergy and laity alike are uncertain, insecure, afraid, still searching for the Promised Land. Even Moses was unsure at times; he, too, needed the people as they needed him. The vision is extraordinary. The journey must be shared.

For we, too, must cry out, "I, I did not know." Weeping for the pride that has distracted us, praying for the humility that might save us, and listening to the hearts that surround us, we will offer: *Sh'ma koleinu.* And God will be there.

Notes

1. Lawrence A. Hoffman, *The Art of Public Prayer* (Washington, DC: The Pastoral Press, 1988), 44.
2. Consider four areas of distinct application:
    1) Concrete engagement through reciting Hebrew, chant-ing, singing, touching Torah, imagining the stories of our tradition;
    2) Meaningful symbolic language, and music that is deep, prayer-centering;
    3) Study and reflection, theological inquiry, existential thought-fulness; and
    4) Socializing, being surrounded with friends, talking, sharing amidst worship.

    Cf. Timothy Noxon, "Myers-Briggs Type Indicator (MBTI) and Christian Spirituality," http://thenoxfactor.com/files/Noxon-Myers-Briggs.pdf; Charles J. Keating, *Who We Are Is How We Pray* (Mystic, CT: Twenty-Third Publications, 1987); Roberta Louis

ELYSE D. FRISHMAN

Goodman and Sherry H. Blumberg, eds., *Teaching about God and Spirituality: A Resource for Jewish Settings*, Denver: A.R.E. Publishing, 2002).

3. Eliyahu Munk, *Kedushat Levi*, vol. 3 (New York: Lambda Publishers, 2009), 756–57; Levi Yitzchak, *Sefer Kedushat Levi Hashalem, Parshat Re'eh* (Jerusalem: Mishur Publishing), 89.

4. Harry Sperling and Maurice Simon, trans., *The Zohar*, vol. 5 (London: The Soncino Press, 1984), *Naso*, 192b.

5. Ibid., 198.

6. Translation from Everett Fox, *The Five Books of Moses* (New York: Schocken Books, 1983), 159.

7. Sperling and Simon, *Zohar*, 194.

8. Ibid., 198.

9. Ibid., 184.

10. Zalman Meshullam Schachter-Shalomi, *Spiritual Intimacy: A Study of Counseling in Hasidism* (Rowman & Littlefield, 1990).

11. Sperling and Simon, *Zohar*, 184–85

The *Yamim Noraim*: Concentric Circles of Liturgy and Relation

Lawrence A. Englander

I do not understand
the book in my hand.

Who will teach me to return?
Loss of custom, ruin of will,
a memory of a memory
thinner than a vein.
Who will teach us to return?

To whom nothing speaks
Not shofar, not song, not homily. . . .

Suppose even God
turned out to be a god?

We do not want to come back.
We do not know where we are.
Not knowing where we are, how can we know
      where we should go?

This poem by Cynthia Ozick may capture the mood of many congregants who come to synagogue over the High Holy Days. Especially for those who attend only at this time, it is ironic that they confront the most complex liturgy of the entire year. As they attempt to reacquaint themselves with the prayers, they find that the *machzor* is replete with medieval *piytim*, originally composed by and for scholars, whose meanings can often be obscure. As they seek dialogue with a God who can make sense to them, these congregants find that the hierarchical images of Ruler and Judge

LAWRENCE A. ENGLANDER is rabbi of Solel Congregation of Mississauga, Ontario, Canada, and is a former editor of the *CCAR Journal*.

LAWRENCE A. ENGLANDER

dominate the text. And as they struggle to reconcile the ancient stories of the Bible with contemporary values, the first Torah portion they encounter is the tale of a father attempting to slaughter a son—at God's command, no less!

On the other hand, there are aspects of the liturgy that are more majestic than at any other time of year. The stark content of *Kol Nidrei* and *Untaneh Tokef* is mitigated by their awe-inspiring musical settings. The blast of the shofar touches us in a spot that even the greatest symphonies cannot reach. The prevalence of white—from Torah mantles to floral arrangements to clergy attire—radiates a sense of purity and innocence.

In the midst of all these phenomena, rabbis, cantors, and service leaders face a challenge: how can we manage to perform a "makeover" on parts of the liturgy that have become unintelligible to many—even obstacles to prayer—while at the same time maintaining the richness of the traditions we encounter at this time of Year? This challenge will be especially acute for any group—such as the CCAR at present—who plans to produce a new *machzor layamim nora'im.* Although there is no single solution, I shall concentrate on one approach. Rather than a wholesale deletion of material currently found in *Gates of Repentance,*[1] my recommendation is to add liturgy that will provide a balance of perspective for the contemporary Reform Jew. I see this process operating within three concentric circles of Jewish life, each of which we shall consider in turn.

The Inner Circle: The Self

If we were to ask the average thoughtful Jew, "What are you thinking about during services on the High Holy Days?" I believe we would often receive the following reply: "I'm thinking about my life: my behavior during the past year, my relationships and how I can improve them." The liturgy of Yom Kippur inspires us—and ideally helps us—to perform the difficult task of *cheshbon hanefesh.* The *Vidui* takes us through a range of attitudes and actions in which we have fallen short of the ideal, from conduct in business

עַל חטא שחטאנו לפניך בנשך ובמרבית
For the sin we have committed against You by financial exploitation.[2]

to intimate interpersonal relationships

THE *YAMIM NORAIM*

עַל חֵטָא שֶׁחָטָאנוּ לְפָנֶיךָ בְּגִלּוּי עֲרָיוֹת

For the sin we committed against You by sexual immorality.[3]

to social justice.

For keeping the poor in chains of poverty.[4]

While the traditional *Vidui* is phrased in the first person plural, a moving passage in *GOR* (pp. 325–26) provides an opportunity for silent, individual introspection as well.

These confessions certainly provoke us toward *t'shuvah*; yet they also suffer a common drawback. They all deal with the negative side of our behviour. One the one hand, we acknowledge that the Rabbis, in their wisdom, instruct us to beat our breasts during the *Vidui* in order to give us a sense of humility before the Holy Blessed One—all the more necessary in our current culture of self-entitlement. On the other hand, should there not also be an opportunity to celebrate our accomplishments during the past year, to identify those moments when we came closer to realizing our better selves? Is there a way to engage in a balanced self-evaluation without replacing the fist on the chest with a pat on the back?

To help achieve this balance, I recommended, in another publication,[5] the following addition to our liturgy. Along with the traditional recitaiton of the *Al Cheit*, we might insert another list that begins with the phrase:

עַל תִּקּוּן שֶׁתִּקַּנּוּ לְפָנֶיךָ.

The word *tikkun* is difficult to translate, but in this context it would have the following sense: "For all our efforts, in Your presence, to work toward completion."[6] The intent of this language is to portray *tikkun* as a process rather than an accomplished feat. Then, as a counterpoint to *V'al Kulam*, this section might end as follows: "May all these efforts, O God of mercy, be recorded for belssing in our Book of Life for the coming year."[7]

The Middle Circle: Jewish Community

Another motivation for Jews to attend High Holy Day services—in fact, the overriding motivation for many—is to reconnect with

LAWRENCE A. ENGLANDER

their Jewish community. Electronic media and social networking have added new dimensions to our sense of self; and yet, as our identities become more diffuse, we run the risk of becoming fragmented into pieces of a pie without a uniform filling. It is therefore comforting to "return to the well" once in a while and draw from our Jewish source. For example, I especially enjoy watching the young adults of our congregation during the *Yamim Noraim*. Returning from school or work that has taken them around the world, they mingle in the aisles of the sanctuary to catch up with each other and exchange contact information.

There are many congregations that excel in bringing this sense of community to their people. For example, special groups (Board and committee members, teachers, etc.) are called up for collective *aliyot*. Some congregations hold up a *tallit* or chuppah on the *bimah* for people to gather during the prayer for healing.[8] It is interesting to note that these are choreographical strategies that go *beyond the liturgy*. How do we capture this feeling of communal closeness within the pages of the *machzor* itself?

I wish to suggest a couple of texts that may enable us to do so. In BT *B'rachot* 58a we find this statement: "The Rabbis teach: Whenever one sees a large gathering of Jews, one should say, 'Praised is the One wise in discerning secrets.' For no one is like another, either in mind or appearance." At the very beginning of the service for Rosh HaShanah, the following blessing could be recited:

ברוך אתה יי אלהינו מלד העולם, חכם הרזים.

Although many non-Jews will be present in our congregations, I believe that they will understand the import of this blessing and may also feel embraced by the community. For those uncomfortable with its ethnocentricity, there is the blessing found in the morning liturgy:

ברוך אתה יי מקדש את שמו ברבים
We praise You, Eternal One, whose Name is sanctified within assemblies.

Without doubt, creative *sh'lichei tzibur* will develop the choreography to accompany these liturgical words, in order to give expression to the reaching out that we all do at this holy time of year.

THE *YAMIM NORAIM*

The Outer Circle: Relating to God

The dominant image of God on the *Yamim Noraim* is that of a ruler, modelled after an ancient potentate, who sits in judgment of our deeds. This image is perhaps the most difficult of all for many congregants (and, I dare say, for many Jewish professionals). Although the English tries to soften the metaphor, many are still troubled by its hierarchical nature.

This matter has been addressed in a previous issue of this journal.[9] Yoel Kahn refers to High Holy Day liturgy as reflecting "the theological assertion of God's absolute power and our human smallness and powerlessness,"[10] and yearns for "a prayer life that is authentic and honest, a prayer language whose metaphors and images are both comfortable and provocative, a prayer experience that reaches deep within and deep beyond the self."[11] Margaret Wenig analyzes the content of *Untaneh Tokef* and suggests alternative ways of understanding this prayer that invoke human initiative and partnership with God.[12] Nevertheless, she acknowledges that these renderings bring no consolation to people who find the prayer hurtful and offensive. How, then, are we to bridge the growing gap between those worshipers who resonate to the ancient imagery of the *machzor* and those who seek other metaphors in relating to God? Especially within Reform and Progressive congregations, the wide spectrum of theologies may necessitate an equally vast array of liturgy.

To address this question, it might be helpful to understand that this is not a new problem. The scholar Joseph Weiss noted that, even within Chasidic communities that we assume to have been homogeneous, we witness some serious theological differences.[13] Taking only two schools, the mystical contemplation of the Mezeritchers and the pietistic faith of the Bratzlavers, Weiss depictcs two very divergent relationships with God. By understanding these two approaches, we may find some means of addressing the variety of divine-human relationships among our own congregants.

The Bratzlaver school is closer to what we may consider to be classical Jewish theology. God is perceived to be "personal and voluntaristic."[14] Ruling from beyond the world, God intervenes in history to bring humanity toward redemption. For the Mezeritchers, however, God is not personal but is rather a "'divine essence' (*chiyyut*), that 'divine spark' (*nitzotz elohi*) which dwell[s] in all worlds and in all beings."[15] Today we might describe this view as

LAWRENCE A. ENGLANDER

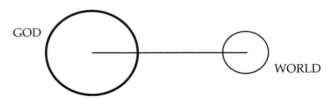

GOD

WORLD

Figure 1

panentheistic: God embraces the entirety of the universe but is also greater than it—in other words, the universe is a subset of God.[16]

These two views result in two distinct attitudes toward prayer. For the Bratzlav school, since God is separate from the universe, there must be some bridge to connect the two (see Figure 1). When the direction goes from God to the world, we call it revelation. When it goes in the opposite direction, we call this prayer. Thus for the followers of Rabbi Nachman of Bratzlav, prayer is dialogue with a Being who transcends them and who is reached through faith (*emunah*).

The process is entirely different for the school of Dov Baer of Mezeritch. Since God's presence permeates the world, God is immanent rather than transcendent. The bridge thus performs a different function (see Figure 2). The direction from God to the world is not a bridge across a gap but rather an *acknowledgment* of our inhering within God. We attain this state through the mystical exercise of *devekut* (clinging to God), which results in *bitul ha-yesh* (an extinction of the ego) so that we apprehend the divine organism of which we are a part.

It seems clear how the traditional High Holy Day liturgy would work for the Bratzlavers, since the images of ruler and judge stress

GOD (outer)

WORLD (inner)

Figure 2

THE *YAMIM NORAIM*

God's transcendence. But how did the Mezeritchers deal with these metaphors? We know that they davened the same liturgy as the Bratzlavers, since no Chasidic school would arrogate to themselves the power of changing it. In order to reconcile the liturgy with his theology, Dov Baer taught the following approach to prayer:

> When one needs to request anything from the Creator, one should imagine that one's soul is a limb of the Shekhinah, as it were, like a drop of water in the sea. If one makes the request on behalf of the Shekhinah, in that a particular thing is lacking in her, then one will certainly possess the spiritual power to act beyond the Shekhinah. Only if one clings properly to the Shekhinah will the overflow spread upon one.
>
> (*Magid Devarav LeYa'akov*, #32)

The disciples of Dov Baer would pray with this *kavanah* in mind in order to receive the *shefa* of God who is both within and beyond.

We can therefore understand how the challenge of multiple theologies within any congregation is not a new one. However, there is also a significant difference between the Chasidic communities and our own. If a Chasid in the eighteenth or nineteenth century did not subscribe to the theology of the Tzaddik, that individual could migrate to another Chasidic court. Yet in our Progressive congregations today, we welcome individual differences and seek to cast a net wide enough to accommodate everyone who comes to us. In order to make the liturgy meaningful to such a broad variety of people, we have two options—neither of which excludes the other. First, as previous prayer books have done, we can add commentaries that explain how a prayer might be understood within a different theological context. Second, unlike the Chasidim, we do have the option of adding new prayers or of amending the old liturgy to yield new meanings. It is this second option, practiced by generations of Reform liturgists, that I now wish to explore in more detail.

Fusing the Circles: a Recommendation
for High Holy Day Liturgy

If we examine the liturgical additions that we currently find in many progressive *machzorim*, I believe that we can identify the following major categories of style:

LAWRENCE A. ENGLANDER

1. Commentaries in the margins or at the bottom of the page, often designed to reinterpret the liturgy to appeal to contemporary outlooks. These selections are normally meant to be studied rather than prayed.
2. Readings that mention neither prayer nor God directly. These often deal with ethical matters and sometimes quote from *Tanach*.[17]
3. Selections that "read" as prayer but do not mention God.[18]
4. Readings that mention God in the third person.[19]
5. Selections that address God indirectly.[20]
6. Direct address to God. Most of the traditional liturgy belongs to this category, along with many English readings.

Within each of these style rubrics, it is possible to reflect a range of theologies. Here are but a few examples[21]:

1. The "classical" view of an omnipotent, omniscient God who acts in the world to bring justice and goodness. Emil Fackenheim and Abraham Joshua Heschel are two examples of this view.
2. The "naturalist" view of a God who is a force within nature. The theologies of Mordecai Kaplan and Marcia Falk would fall into this broad category.
3. The "mystical" God, who is made manifest through nature and Torah. Contemporary advocates of this view are Lawrence Kushner and Arthur Green.
4. The "humanist" view in which God is perceived as an inner voice of conscience. Erich Fromm is one example.
5. The "non-absolute" or "evolving" god who leads the world toward perfection by influencing human action. Proponents of this view include Milton Steinberg, Henry Slonimsky, and Harold Kushner.

Now here's the rub: it seems clear that the traditional liturgy reflects view #1 most accurately. As we go further along the list, holders of these views are faced with reinterpreting metaphors to such a degree that they may no longer hold up. What is to be done, then? With all the different styles of liturgy (first list), and all the theologies (second list) that they need to reflect, how do we construct a meaningful prayer experience for an entire

THE *YAMIM NORAIM*

congregation? How can all these permutations be contained between two covers of a book? Moreover, if the *machzor* provides so many choices for the worshiper to pray, how do we preserve the dynamic between individual and community that is so important for *t'filah b'tzibur*?

This brings me to my final recommendation, which is not original with me but rather has been under discussion for some time. Thanks to the computer and word processing programmes, the *written* word today has become as fluid as the *oral* word was to our Rabbinic ancestors. We know that it took many generations for the Oral Torah to be canonized into written form; and even now, we often wish that some of those principles and laws had been left to develop beyond the printed page.

In order to prevent a premature canonization of the liturgical word, we can use this technology to our advantage. In addition to publishing a printed *machzor*, the CCAR could instead compile a vast digital array of prayers and readings, in Hebrew and English, reflecting the liturgical styles and the theologies outlined above, along with explanatory notes to guide *sh'lichei tzibur*. This content could be combined with the attractive layouts that have been produced through Visual *T'filah*. There is also a bolder alternative to consider: rather than purchasing a *machzor*, communities would purchase the rights to use a compilation of electronic material along with whatever *machzor* they currently use. As well as keeping the liturgical content fluid, this approach has the added advantage of lifting people's eyes off the printed page to look up at a screen, at the *bimah* and, most importantly, at each other.

Once this project is launched, a reportage system could be set up to determine how the materials are being used in various communities, what successes and failures are encountered along the way, and what new suggestions people may have to fine-tune the project. In this way, more and more professionals and congregants can become drawn into the process and feel that they have a stake in its outcome.

I wish to stress that I do not view this approach as a compromise to publishing a printed *machzor*. On the contrary, I see it as a way to open more doors to our exploration of liturgical content and method. After all, if our words to God are among the most important we can say, is it not worth the time and effort to examine them carefully?

LAWRENCE A. ENGLANDER

Notes

1. Published by CCAR, 1978, hereinafter referred to as *GOR*.
2. *GOR*, p. 334, my translation.
3. *GOR*, p. 330.
4. *GOR*, p. 328, among other selections under the title "Failures of Justice."
5. "We Can't Really Be That Evil!" in Lawrence A. Hoffman, ed., *We Have Sinned: Sin and Confession in Judaism* (Woodstock VT: Jewish Lights, 2012). See, in particular, p. 159.
6. Below are a few examples of how we might complete this sentence:
   - by dedicating ourselves to lifelong Jewish study (Torah)
   - by taking time to give thanks for our many blessings (*Avodah*)
   - by treating the elderly with dignity (*G'milut Chasadim*)
   The liturgy might even provide an opportunity for worshipers to add their own achievements to the list.
7. I understand that the *Machzor* Editorial Committee of CCAR is planning to insert such a prayer and I applaud their efforts.
8. Some congregations have introduced the practice of calling up those who are facing a new challenge during the coming year, such as moving to a new home, beginning a new job, or sending a child to university.
9. *CCAR Journal*, Spring 2009.
10. Y. Kahn, "Wrestling with God's Image in the High Holy Day Liturgy," ibid., 28.
11. Ibid., p. 36.
12. M. Wenig, "The Poetry and Power of Paradox," ibid., 52–74.
13. Joseph Weiss, "Contemplative Mysticism and 'Faith' in Hasidic Piety," *Studies in East European Jewish Mysticism and Hasidism* (London and Portland: Littman Library of Jewish Civilization, 1997), pp. 43–55.
14. Ibid., 45.
15. Ibid., 46.
16. This is reminiscent of the midrash (*B'reshit Rabbah* 65:9 and elsewhere) that comments on the divine name *HaMakom* by remarking: "God is the place of the world, but the world is not God's place."
17. One of many examples can be found in *GOR*, p. 27.
18. E.g., *GOR*, pp. 51–52 and 283–84.
19. E.g. GOR, pp. 102, 103, and 118.
20. Here I have in mind the original formula of Marcia Falk: נְבָרֵךְ אֶת עֵין הַחַיִּים וְכֹה נִתְבָּרֵךְ. See *The Book of Blessings* (San Francisco: Harper, 1996). This formula is Falk's means of connecting

THE *YAMIM NORAIM*

with a God immanent in the world. A rough equivalent can be found in *GOR*, pp. 363–65.

21. Readers of this Journal can easily think of several more theological outlooks. In this list, I have chosen those which, in my opinion, would have significant representation among our congregants.

The Calves of Our Lips:
The Inescapable Connections
between Prayer and Sacrifice

Leon A. Morris

The notion of sacrificial offerings was an anathema in the shaping of a modern Jewish life. Since the earliest days of Reform Judaism, those most ancient forms of divine service were understood as primitive and outmoded.[1] Although the classic, traditional liturgy continued to reference the ancient sacrificial service that predated it, the very first nineteenth-century liturgical reforms removed most of the references to the Temple, and to the sacrifices that had been offered there.

There are many examples of this in both Reform liturgy and ritual. The wording for *Birkat Avodah (r'tzei Adonai Eloheinu)*, the seventeenth blessing of the *Amidah* on weekdays, and the fifth blessing of the Shabbat and festival *Amidah*, was altered to remove the references to sacrificial offerings.[2] *Musaf*, a service specifically recalling the additional sacrifice on Shabbat and festivals, was either altered or eliminated altogether.[3] The *maftir* reading for special Sabbaths, particularly those that recalled the specific offerings of that festival day, were eliminated.[4] The Torah reading for Yom Kippur morning from Leviticus 16, describing the sacrificial service to be performed by Aaron and his sons—the original observance of Yom Kippur—was also eliminated and a different selection was chosen.[5] Likewise, the most distinctive liturgical rubric of the classic Yom Kippur liturgy, *Seder HaAvodah* was either radically altered or excised altogether. Even the piyut *Ein Keloheinu* had the final line excised in order to avoid referencing that "our ancestors offered fragrant incense."

This deliberate distancing from the sacrificial service, and from memories of the ancient Temple, extended well beyond the prayer

---

LEON A. MORRIS is the rabbi at Temple Adas Israel in Sag Harbor, New York.

THE CALVES OF OUR LIPS

book into daily ritual life. The washing of the hands prior to eating bread with its accompanying blessing recalls the priests who washed prior to eating from the sacrifices. This practice was by and large eliminated. Similarly, the salting of bread recalling the salting of the sacrifices was no longer encouraged.[6] These reforms extended to the Hebrew calendar itself. Tishah B'Av, the anniversary of the Temples' destructions, has generally not been marked in the majority of Reform congregations, and even the newest American Reform prayer book has no liturgy to mark the day.[7]

To the sensibilities of modern Jews attempting to shape a nineteenth- and twentieth-century Judaism, the primitive nature of animal and grain sacrifices seemed to offer little by way of inspiration or critical ideas. The burning of animals in service to God seemed cruel. The idea that God was to be found in one central place, and the land of Israel in particular, was highly objectionable to Jews eager to demonstrate their loyalty to the countries in which they lived.

What was to be gained by this elimination of references to the sacrificial service? The most prevalent justification is rooted in a rejection of the hope for the rebuilding of the Temple and the reestablishment of sacrifice. In fact, many of the early Reformers seemed to assume a necessary and inseparable connection between referencing the centrality of sacrifices in our past and the undying hope for the Temple to be rebuilt and for sacrifices to be restored in our future.

The linking of those two ideas has continued to our time. For example, in an article almost a decade ago in this journal about the centrality of the *Avodah* service, Herbert Bronstein writes:

> The elimination of the Musaf service from Reform Jewish worship as early as the late nineteenth century is, of course, understandable in the light of Reform's constant and consistent opposition, from its beginnings, to prayers for the future restoration of the priestly sacrificial cult of the Jerusalem Temple.[8]

Does such a link have to be made at all? Certainly, there could be a recollection of the central role that sacrifices played in the past without any hope for their future restoration.

Indeed, even if deemed desirable, it would be impossible to entirely eliminate the memory of sacrifice from contemporary Jewish

LEON A. MORRIS

life. References to the Temple and to sacrifice are unavoidable in classical Jewish sources. Indeed, they are ubiquitous as a reference point, as metaphor, and as symbol. Specifically with regard to prayer, references to sacrifices are indispensible. The sacrificial offerings are the very basis for our having morning and afternoon services. The names of the services themselves bear the name of those daily sacrifices.

The early Reformers assumed that what was most needed for a meaningful and relevant Jewish life was a severing of the connection between prayer and sacrifice. However, severing the link between prayer and the sacrificial system may have subverted that goal. More was lost from dropping the connection between them than was gained. There is much to be learned from the sacrificial system that has the potential of deepening our experience of prayer. These ancient practices present notions of relationship, closeness and distance, gift giving, and mystery.[9] Our age opens us up to new possibilities of meaning that such connections can provide for us. Texts about the ancient sacrifices call upon us to develop approaches and methods of interpretation that can treat such texts seriously. To do so, we need to more clearly understand the relationship between sacrifice and prayer.

Sacrifice, Study, and Prayer: Replacement or Substitution?

Once the Temple was destroyed, and sacrifice was no longer being performed, an expanded notion of the sacred space and sacred service was required. Upon resolving to build the Temple, Solomon sent a message to King Huram of Tyre requesting wood and additional craftsmen. He writes:

> See, I intend to build a House for the name of the Eternal my God; I will dedicate it to God for making incense offering of sweet spices in God's honor, for the regular rows of bread, and for the morning and evening burnt offerings on Sabbaths, new moons, and festivals, *as is Israel's duty forever.* (II Chron. 2:3)

הִנֵּה אֲנִי בוֹנֶה־בַּיִת לְשֵׁם ה' אֱלֹהַי לְהַקְדִּישׁ לוֹ לְהַקְטִיר לְפָנָיו קְטֹרֶת־סַמִּים וּמַעֲרֶכֶת תָּמִיד וְעֹלוֹת לַבֹּקֶר וְלָעֶרֶב לַשַּׁבָּתוֹת וְלֶחֳדָשִׁים וּלְמוֹעֲדֵי ה' אֱלֹהֵינוּ לְעוֹלָם זֹאת עַל־יִשְׂרָאֵל:

THE CALVES OF OUR LIPS

Nothing lasts forever; not the Temple, nor its offerings. The Rabbis, living in the aftermath of the Temple's destruction, are faced with the challenge of explaining what is meant by "Israel's duty forever." This interpretive and symbolic challenge is expressed in BT *M'nachot* 110a:

> Rav Gidel said in the name of Rav: This refers to the altar built [in heaven], and Michael, the great ministering angel stands and offers a sacrifice upon it. Rabbi Yochanan said: These are the students who engage in studying the laws of sacrifice. The verse regards them *as though* the Temple were built in their days.

> א״ר גידל אמר רב: זה מזבח בנוי ומיכאל שר הגדול עומד ומקריב
> עליו קרבן; ורבי יוחנן אמר: אלו תלמידי חכמים העסוקין בהלכות
> עבודה, מעלה עליהם הכתוב כאילו נבנה מקדש בימיהם.

In many ways, the disagreement between Rav Gidel and Rabbi Yochanan is about what constitutes *avodah* (the sacrificial service) in their day, and by extension, in ours.

Rav Gidel posits a "virtual" temple in heaven in which the ancient rites of the Temple continue unabated. In contrast, Rabbi Yochanan claims that the very meaning of *avodah* has changed in the aftermath of the Temple's destruction. The place of *avodah* has shifted from the *Beit HaMikdash* (Temple) to the *beit hamidrash* (study hall). All post-exilic Jewish communities, both Orthodox and Reform, are in many ways an extension of Rabbi Yochanan's reasoning. The form of divine service has changed.

Rabbi Yochanan's boldly adaptive interpretation is representative of the Rabbinic project in which the human-God encounter shifts from the Temple to the study hall. Sacrifice lived on, not as performance but rather in memory, language, and imagination. Study is redefined as a religious act, not simply learning in order to do, but as a performance itself.

Following the debate between Rav Gidel and Rabbi Yochanan, on the very same Talmudic page we read the opinions of Rava, Resh Lakish, and Rabbi Yitzchak. Their voices cover a spectrum of opinions regarding the relationship between study and sacrifice.

> Resh Lakish said: What is meant by the verse, "This is the teaching [*Torat*] of the burnt offering, the meal offering, the sin offering, the

LEON A. MORRIS

guilt offering . . ."? (Leviticus 7:37) Anyone who engages in [the study of] Torah, it is as though they sacrificed a burnt offering, a meal offering, a sin offering and a guilt offering. Rava [objected] saying: This [verse] says *for* the burnt offering, *for* the meal offering. [According to Resh Lakish's opinion] it should have said the burnt offering *and* the meal offering . . . Rava said: Anyone who engages in [the study of] Torah does not need a burnt offering, nor a meal offering, nor a sin offering, nor a guilt offering. [The repetitive use of the prefix *lamed* here is interpreted as meaning *lo*, "no."]

Rabbi Yitzchak said: Why is it written, "This is the teaching [*Torat*] of the burnt offering, the meal offering, the sin offering, the guilt offering . . ."? [In order to teach that] anyone who engages in the study of the sin offering is regarded as though he sacrificed a sin offering; anyone who engages in the study of the guilt offering is regarded as though he sacrificed a guilt offering. (*M'nachot* 110a)

אמר ריש לקיש, מאי דכתיב: (ויקרא ז') זאת התורה לעולה למנחה
ולחטאת ולאשם? כל העוסק בתורה, כאילו הקריב עולה מנחה
חטאת ואשם. אמר רבא: האי לעולה למנחה, עולה ומנחה מיבעי
ליה אלא אמר רבא: כל העוסק בתורה, אינו צריך לא עולה
(ולא חטאת) ולא מנחה ולא אשם. אמר רבי יצחק, מאי דכתיב:
(ויקרא ו') זאת תורת החטאת וזאת תורת האשם? כל העוסק
בתורת חטאת כאילו הקריב חטאת, וכל העוסק בתורת אשם כאילו
הקריב אשם.

On one end of the spectrum, Rabbi Yitzchak suggests that study of a particular type of sacrifice is the equivalent of offering that specific sacrifice. For him, study and sacrifice are most closely linked when study parallels the sacrifices for which it serves as a substitute. On the other end of the spectrum, Rava suggests that there is no need to measure study against sacrifice—ours is a whole new world, and the study of Torah, regardless of its subject, replaces sacrifices and precludes a need for engaging with the memory of the sacrificial system at all.

While this particular *sugya* deals with the relationship between sacrifice and study, it nonetheless presents us with two conceptual frameworks that are equally helpful to us as we consider the relationship between sacrifice and prayer: prayer as replacement for sacrifice and prayer as substitution for sacrifice.

THE CALVES OF OUR LIPS

By replacement, I mean to suggest that prayer or study obviates the need for sacrifice and takes on the same value sacrifice once had. This replacement model completely severs the connection between sacrifice and prayer. Like Rava's position above, prayer in itself replaces sacrifices and is not reliant upon liturgical recollections of the sacrificial system.

One Talmudic example of this approach might be found in the rhetorical question posed in *Taanit* 2a, "What is the *avodah* of the heart?" דתניא לאהבה את ה' אלהיכם ולעבדו בכל לבבכם, איזו היא עבודה שהיא בלב-הוי אומר זו תפלה.
Drawing upon the words of the *Sh'ma's* second paragraph, "If, then, you obey the commandments that I enjoin upon you this day, loving the Lord your God and serving Him with all your heart . . ." (Deut. 11:13) the Talmud states that it is prayer that is now the service of heart.

In contrast, by substitution I mean to suggest that prayer or study evokes the sacrifices themselves and reminds us that these words recall and represent the sacrificial service that can no longer be performed. These prayers or study texts serve as substitutes for the sacrifices themselves. This approach is demonstrated in BT *B'rachot* 26b:

> It has been taught also in accordance with R. Joshua b. Levi: Why did they say that the morning Tefillah could be said till midday? Because the regular morning sacrifice could be brought up to midday. R. Judah, however, says that it may be said up to the fourth hour because the regular morning sacrifice may be brought up to the fourth hour. And why did they say that the afternoon Tefillah can be said up to the evening? Because the regular afternoon offering can be brought up to the evening.

ותניא כוותיה דרבי יהושע בן לוי: מפני מה אמרו תפלת השחר עד חצות - שהרי תמיד של שחר קרב והולך עד חצות ורבי יהודה אומר: עד ארבע שעות, שהרי תמיד של שחר קרב והולך עד ארבע שעות. ומפני מה אמרו תפלת המנחה עד הערב - שהרי תמיד של בין הערבים קרב והולך עד הערב

When trying to delineate Rabbinic sources about prayer and sacrifice along this conceptual framework of replacement and substitution there is a great deal of ambiguity. Indeed, this is the case with the Rabbinic interpretations of one of the most widely cited

LEON A. MORRIS

texts about the relationship between sacrifice and prayer, Hosea 14:3:

> Take words with you and return to the Eternal. Say to God: For-give all guilt and accept what is good; *we will pay the calves of our lips.*

קְחוּ עִמָּכֶם דְּבָרִים וְשׁוּבוּ אֶל־ה' אִמְרוּ אֵלָיו כָּל־תִּשָּׂא עָוֹן וְקַח־טוֹב
וּנְשַׁלְּמָה פָרִים שְׂפָתֵינוּ׃

The end of this verse, *un'shalmah farim sefateinu*, which JPS translates as "instead of bulls, we will pay [the offering of] our lips," notes that the meaning of Hebrew is uncertain. There are subtle differences in interpretation found in various midrashim that could be understood to be reflective of our conceptual framework—prayer as substitution or as replacement. In *P'sikta D'Rav Kahana, Shuva* 24, Rabbi Akiba asks, "Who pays for those calves that were of-fered before You? Our lips in the prayers that we pray before You."
(א"ר אבהו מי משלם אותם הפרים שהיינו מקריבים לפניך, שפתינו,
The midrash asserts that our words (.בתפילה שאנו מתפללים לפניך)
and prayers are the equivalent of our offerings of old. They are now the equivalent of the calves that had been offered. Alterna-tively, in *Shir HaShirim Rabbah* 4:9, the midrash states, "What shall we pay *in place of* the calves and *in place of* the scapegoat? Our lips."
(מה נשלם תחת פרים ותחת שעיר המשתלח שפתינו) Our words will serve as substitutions in place of the calves and other sacrifices that were once offered. They will be our offerings. In *P'sikta D'Rav Ka-hana,* our words *are* our offerings. They are a replacement. In *Shir HaShirim Rabbah,* our words are offered *in place of* those offerings. They are a substitution.

The *Musaf* Model

Our early Reform heritage already presents us with some mod-els of how this "substitution model" might take hold in a post-modern context. Jakob Petuchowski demonstrated the complex relationship that has existed with regard to the *Musaf* Service and Reform liturgies.[10] While most of the European rituals retained some form of the *Musaf* Service, the liturgy needed to be adjusted to make it theologically in line with Reform sensibilities. Part of

THE CALVES OF OUR LIPS

the compelling reasons to maintain it had to do with the fact that, as with many traditional congregations, a critical mass of the congregation does not attend the earlier part of the service.

As religious reform in Europe began to take on the forms of a movement, the discussion of how to treat *Musaf* arises. In the 1884 Frankfort conference, an appointed Commission on Liturgy found themselves unable to decide decisively on whether or not to retain the *Musaf* Service.

One of the supporters of retaining the *Musaf* Service with references to the sacrifices was Abraham Adler, whom Petuchowski notes was regarded as a "radical reformer." Responding to the notion that the idea of sacrifice had become obsolete, Adler responds (as cited by Petuchowski),

> The idea of sacrifice must be an eternally true one, since we cannot and must not assume that, throughout the millennia, Judaism has retained a lie. There is a confusion between the idea itself and the form in which that idea was outwardly expressed. The idea of sacrifice is one of devotion, of the union of the finite individual with the Infinite, the submersion of the transitory in the eternal Source. As long as man himself still stood on the level of externality, he was in need of the external act, through which alone he achieved self-consciousness . . . Only when Judaism transcended the level of externality, did sacrifice become something abstractly external, and only then did the Prophets begin to fulminate against it. The idea then created for itself a new and more appropriate form, that of prayer. In that sense we must understand the Talmudic passage, *tephilloth keneged temidin tiqqenu* (the sacrifices found their counterpart in the prayers). [11]

Adler concludes with a statement that could serve as a basis for a twenty-first-century "substitution model" of prayers about sacrifice.

> *We cannot, therefore, become indifferent to the sacrificial cult, since, in it, we possess the original form of devotion. I, therefore, demand the retention of those liturgical passages which refer to the sacrificial cult—as a reminiscence.* On the other hand, the prayers for its restoration, about which we cannot be serious, are to be omitted.[12] (emphasis mine)

Petuchowski notes that Adler's recommendations for liturgical practice were adopted.

Petuchowski shows how these various Reform *Musaf* liturgies shift from preserving a memory of the sacrifices to those that deliberately sever such connections. Early nineteenth-century Reform liturgies include a *Musaf* Service that is contextualized as a *substitution* for the sacrifices they recalled. This is reflected in Adler's perspective above and became the prevalent approach to *Musaf* prayers. However, Geiger's prayer book of 1870 includes *Musaf* but shapes the liturgy in ways that see it as a *replacement*. The *Musaf* Service continued to be included, but once the theoretical basis had been eliminated from the prayer itself, it was only a matter of time before *Musaf* itself would be eliminated.

Apart from *Musaf*, one can find in earlier Reform prayer books other examples of the "substitution model" at play. In Einhorn's *Olat Tamid*, as in *Gates of Repentance*, a reference to the sacrificial element of Yom Kippur is unavoidable. Here we see ways in which the ancient rites can be unapologetically referenced and used as a metaphorical application to our own lives:

> Like this priest of old, we, too are called to this duty; our priestly service demandeth that we, to the fullest extent of our ability and opportunity, bring the tidings of peace and reconciliation unto all. We, too, must lead back upon the right path those that have gone astray, and honor Thee by keeping alive and deepening the consciousness that all the children of Abraham are bound together by the ties of the common responsibility to sanctify Thy name in the eyes of the world.[13]

Preserving the Power of the Sacrifice

In Reform liturgy, barring the exceptions noted above, we have almost entirely approached prayer as *replacement* for sacrifice rather than *substitution*. In doing so, the centrality of sacrifice has been muted and its memory deemed insignificant. In contrast, by embracing a model of substitution rather than replacement we open up a symbolic universe that greatly increases the significance of prayer.

The "post-modern turn" has renewed an interest in symbols and ritual. There is a greater openness toward the very experiences that were dismissed by previous generations as "primitive." There is a recognition that reason is the not the sole criteria for determining what can have religious meaning for us:

THE CALVES OF OUR LIPS

Obviously modern Jews can do as they please with the prayer-book without fear of sanction, but it is important that, if they make any changes, they do so for reasons which are very good indeed. Simply to remove the sacrificial readings because of a conception of "higher" and "lower" religion, which will not stand the test of scrutiny, is an injustice not only to one generation but to the generations which are heir to the fruits of this misconception.[14]

Approaching liturgy as a *substitution* for sacrifice, rather than a *replacement*, keeps the memory and symbolism of sacrifice alive. That memory and symbolism, in turn, expands the meaning and significance of our prayer life. The notion that prayer is *avodah sh'balev* (the sacrificial service of the heart) is only meaningful so far as one continues to understand what *avodah* itself once was. Once that connection is severed, the effect is a diminishment of the significance of prayer, a narrowing of the wide spectrum of meaning that prayer can have.

If a connection between sacrifice and prayer is maintained or reestablished, it offers vital ideas that can revive our spiritual lives. Prayer becomes an offering, a gift, something we deeply long to be received. The language of sacrifice in the context of prayer also reminds us that ours is a communal relationship with God, and that prayer too is not just about the individual, but about the collective. Furthermore, a connection between prayer and the ancient *korbanot* underscores the enormous gap that exists between ourselves and God, a needed counterpoint for us in a spiritual climate in which God is increasingly presented exclusively as "our friend" or "our conscience." When we see our prayers as a substitution for sacrifice—on the *Yamim Noraim* and throughout the year—we assert that every home and every synagogue is a Temple, and that each Jew is a priest.

Once we construct prayer as a *replacement*, rather than as a *substitution* for sacrifice, we diminish our spiritual vocabulary, lose central frames of reference, and allow a locus of Jewish memory throughout the ages to disappear. Restoring this connection allows such words and memories to contribute a myriad of ideas we need in our prayer life now more than ever before.

Notes

1. Paragraph 5 of the Pittsburgh Platform states: "We consider ourselves no longer a nation, but a religious community, and therefore

LEON A. MORRIS

expect neither a return to Palestine, nor a sacrificial worship under the sons of Aaron, nor the restoration of any of the laws concerning the Jewish state."

2. The traditional wording includes the words, "Restore the service to Your most holy House, and accept in love and favor the fire-offerings of Israel and their prayer." Jonathan Sacks, *The Koren Siddur* (Jerusalem: Koren Publishing, 2009). Compare with *Mishkan T'filah* (and previous Reform prayer books), where the words *v'hashev et haavodah lid'vir beitecha v'ishei Yisrael* are omitted, but creatively, the words remaining are joined to make one coherent statement.

3. The diverse approaches to *Musaf* in Reform liturgies are explored below.

4. For example, Num. 28:9–15 for Shabbat Rosh Chodesh; Num. 29:1–6 for Rosh HaShanah morning; Num. 29:7–11 for Yom Kippur morning; Num. 29, selected verses for each day of Sukkot; Num. 28, selected verses for each day of Passover, and for Shavuot.

5. *Union Prayer Book II* and *Gates of Repentance* substitute selected verses from *Parashat Nitzavim*, Deut. 29:9–30:20.

6. For the absence of ritual hand-washing and salting of bread, see *On the Doorposts of Your House* (New York: CCAR, 2010), 62. In *Gates of Shabbat* (New York: CCAR, 1991), 28–29, although the ritual blessings are not included in the liturgy itself, both the mitzvah of hand-washing and the custom of salting bread are explained and presented as an option.

7. The only official American Reform liturgy exclusively for Tishah B'Av is the work of Herbert Bronstein, in *The Five Scrolls* (New York: CCAR, 1984). *Gates of Prayer: The New Union Prayer Book* (New York: CCAR, 1975) includes a liturgy that can be used interchangeably for Yom HaShoah or Tishah B'Av.

8. Herbert Bronstein, "Yom Kippur Worship: A Missing Center?" *CCAR Journal* (Summer 2004): 7–15.

9. See Moshe Halbertal, *On Sacrifice* (Princeton: Princeton University Press, 2012).

10. Jakob Petuchowski, *Prayerbook Reform in Europe: The Liturgy of European Liberal and Reform Judaism* (New York: World Union for Progressive Judaism, 1968). See chapter 9, "Reform of the Musaph Service."

11. Ibid., page 243-244. Petuchowski cites *Protokolle und Aktenstrücke der zweiten Rabbiner-Versammlung*, p. 382.

12. Ibid.

13. David Einhorn, *Olat Tamid: Book of Prayers for Jewish Congregations* (1913). "Services for the New Year's Day and The Day of Atonement," p. 185..

14. Richard Rubenstein, *After Auschwitz: Radical Theology and Contemporary Judaism* (New York: Macmillan, 1966), 108.

"*Baavur Sheani Noder Tzedakah Baado*"

Margaret Moers Wenig

Thoughts about *Yizkor* and mourning, *Yizkor* and memory, *Yizkor* and mortality, *Yizkor* and the living, *Yizkor* and Yom Kippur, and *Yizkor* and God.

Mourning

Mournful music is common during *Yizkor* services, at least in Reform synagogues, where *Yizkor* also often ends with or includes the recitation of Mourners' *Kaddish*.

A mournful tone to *Yizkor* rings true for many for whom mourning does not end, even years after a loved one has died. As attested by these mourners, the pain from some losses never fully heals: I have learned one has "to honor the part of oneself that's irreparable. Not to apologize for it, disguise it, not to try to mend it in any seamless way."[1] "The break from now on is an inescapable part of who I am, perhaps the inescapable part. Hasn't it become my essential definition, my central fact: I loved a man who died?"[2] "If you ask me whether this . . . [feels] like closure, I'll tell you what I've come to believe: Closure is bullshit."[3]

A mournful tone to *Yizkor* rings true to be sure. But do those who still mourn *need Yizkor* to afford them an opportunity to express their grief? I think not. I think for most who are still grieving it is a fairly private process for which no ritual prompting is needed.

Memory

We call *Yizkor* the "Memorial Service." What does it mean to remember those who have died? What does it mean to remember?

MARGARET MOERS WENIG (NY84) is instructor in Liturgy and Homiletics at HUC-JIC/New York since 1985 and rabbi emerita of Beth Am, The People's Temple, New York. She thanks Helen Blumenthal, Daniel Fleshler, Rabbi Lawrence A. Hoffman, Ph.D., Marion Marx, Elizabeth Lorris Ritter, Steven Rosenberg, Liba Rubenstein, Monica Saez, Ph.D., and Rabbi Elaine Zecher for feedback to, and in some cases, trenchant criticism of, an earlier draft.

MARGARET MOERS WENIG

Neurologists, who study the effects of trauma or neglect on the development of children, argue that "early influences can literally leave imprints on the brain that last a lifetime."[4] "Memories make us. . . . What we experience first filters what comes afterwards."[5] Even people whom we have known later in life, even people whose effect was wholly positive, may leave indelible impressions on us. Some people we'll never forget.

> My friends are dying [wrote Grace Paley *z"l*]
> well we're old   it's natural
> . . . but this is not what I meant to
> tell you   I wanted to say that
> my friends were dying but have now
> become absent   the word dead is correct
> but inappropriate
> I have not taken their names out of
> conversation gossip   political argument
> my telephone book or card index in
> whatever alphabetical or contextual
> organizer I can stop any evening of
> the lonesome week at Claiborne   Bercovici
> Vernarelli   Deming and rest a moment
> on their seriousness as artists   workers
> their excitement as political actors in the
> streets of our cities or in their workplaces
> the vigiling   fasting   praying in or out
> of jail   their lightheartedness which floated
> above the year's despair
> their courageous sometime hilarious
> disobedience before the state's official
> servants   their fidelity to the idea that
> it is possible with only a little extra anguish
> to live in this world   at an absolute minimum
> loving brainy sexual energetic redeemed[6]

I, for one, light two *Yizkor* candles for my parents, but those two candles already stand for, and will one day stand for, even more of the dozen who have helped to shape me, including teachers and members of the congregation I served,[7] some dead and some, thank God, still living. I think of the older synagogue member, who never had children of her own, quietly cradling and soothing every baby wheeled in through the doors. I think of the young man,

"BAAVUR SHEANI NODER TZEDAKAH BAADO"

whose parents were long dead, who visited every hospitalized or homebound elderly member. I think of the mentoring I received from the first president with whom I worked. They continue to affect me to this day. I think of the social studies teacher who, in 1967, suspended her curriculum to explain to us the war in the Middle East and melt the ice that had frozen relationships between the Syrian, Lebanese, and Jewish members of our class.[8] I think of the high school math teacher[9] who testified to me about the love of Jesus, impelling me to search for God's love in Judaism that was always there but never discussed. I think of the college history professor who taught us to ask of every secondary source: "How do you know?"[10] I think of the rabbinical school sage who taught his students to test every theological proposition against "the toughest case."[11] I think of my spouse who regularly interrupted my intense concentration on whatever I was cooking to take me in her arms and, singing, dance with me around the kitchen floor. In addition to my parents, these people have also left their imprints on my brain. They, too, have shaped the person I've become and will remain. If they have died, their legacy did not die with them and when the others die, their legacies will not die when their bodies give out.

And yet remembering those who have affected us is not simply a process of opening a window and looking through it back in time. For memory doesn't simply "equal events plus time. . . . Time doesn't act as a fixative, rather as a solvent."[12] "Narrative memory is not simply a videotape of experiences that can be replayed with accuracy."[13] We "cut and splice the magnetic tape on which our lives are recorded."[14] Yes "memories make us" but "we make memories."[15] "What we feel now can influence what we recall from the past. When we retrieve a memory from where it is stored in the brain, just as when we open a Word file, we automatically open it to 'edit' and when we 'save' the memory again and place it back into storage, we may well have modified it."[16]

Yizkor, then, cannot be about simply remembering people who have died. For the act of remembering is more complicated than that.

The Living

Memories come to us. We may be unconsciously driven by them as we are driven by a *yetzer hatov* or a *yetzer hara.* And yet, we are held

MARGARET MOERS WENIG

accountable as if we had free will. *T'shuvah* is, in part, a process of gaining, little by little, greater mastery over our inclinations, including those present inclinations driven by memories of the ways in which people have treated us in the past.

How can we even begin to gain such mastery? It took me six months to clean out my parents' house after my mother died: many trips to the library to donate books, many trips to Goodwill to donate clothes, many trips to the town dump to unload recyclables, an auctioneer to buy furniture, a moving company to put things in storage, and eight dumpsters to fill with things that simply crumbled in my hands. And boxes of things to save: personal papers from seventy years of life and even from previous generations—many I'd never seen—with great emotional and/or historical significance; and a large envelope with the words "For Maggie only" written in my mother's hand.

Cleaning the house, painting it, and readying it for rental and eventual sale was a monumental task, a part-time job for six months. When the job was finished and I'd handed over the keys to the tenants, I came home and fell, satisfied, into a deep sleep. That very night my mother appeared in my dream, irate. "Now that you have rented my house," she complained, "where am I supposed to live?" In a moment, my pride in a difficult job well done was deflated.

In life, I don't recall ever arguing with my mother's relentless criticisms of me. But in the dream I talked back, saying: "But, Mom, you've been dead for six months. How was I supposed to know that you would come back and need a place to live?"

My mother was not warm or affectionate, at least not after tragedy had hardened her. When I was very young, however, she used to read to me at bedtime. And I remember well the books she read. Among them: *Winnie the Pooh.* Last year, missing her terribly, I looked for recordings of Pooh. I found one in which Judy Dench plays the narrator! Now, I sometimes listen to the recording in bed at night as if the loving part of my mother is once again reading me to sleep.

During *Yizkor*, we do not have time to compose long eulogies in our heads. If we give ourselves over to memories, they are by necessity brief: sound bites, excerpts, fragments. Not dissimilar to the ways in which we must memorialize our loved ones when we choose what to inscribe on their tombstones. With what final words do we choose to remember a loved one whose body has been returned to dust?

In Eastern Europe there was a custom of engraving a symbol of the deceased's trade on his tombstone, or, if the deceased had been a *kohein*, two hands in the position of priestly blessing might have been engraved. Hundreds of years following a person's death, those symbols may be the only way he or she is remembered.

My father was many things, a labor lawyer, an arbitrator, a teacher of labor law, a less than admirable husband, a father whose parenting was hampered by depression, but who, when well, made us laugh. Sailing was his greatest pleasure and source of peace. On his tombstone we chose to engrave his own drawing of a sailboat. My grandmother was a tyrant as a mother, a bitter wife, a doting grandmother, and a serious painter. Before we gave up her apartment, we found all of her paint brushes, many of them decades old and well used, as clean as the day she purchased them, and dozens of rolled-up tubes of paint carefully organized in her art closet. On her headstone we engraved my daughter's drawing of three of my grandmother's own paint brushes and a half-used tube of her oil paint. My mother was a pioneer in her field of law. And we mentioned that on her stone. But she cared a great deal about her home and, while she never fulfilled her dream of creating a loving and safe home for her family, she always filled her home with fresh flowers that she arranged herself. When my daughter was young, she made a sketch of a cut glass vase my mother had just filled with flowers. And for over ten years my mother kept that sketch taped to her bathroom mirror. It was that sketch that we engraved on my mother's stone.

Memories make us. And we make memories. *Yizkor*, I believe, is about making memories.

Mortality

For some, burying a loved one, erecting a tombstone, reciting *Yizkor*, focuses their attention on their own mortality, a feared or even a welcomed fate, as suggested by this widow's engraving on her husband's stone:

> Mrs. Beranek . . . had engraved on the monument not only Mr. Beranek's name and dates but her own name and birth date, followed by an eloquent hyphen waiting in the stone like a held breath.[17]

MARGARET MOERS WENIG

Is *Yizkor* on Yom Kippur a time for the living to focus our attention on our own mortality? Some *machzorim* have chosen to fill their Yom Kippur *Yizkor* liturgies with words such as these from the *Gates of Repentance*:

> We are feeble. We live always on the brink of death. Scarcely ushered into life, we begin our journey to the grave . . . our fondest hopes are buried with us.[18]

> The number of our days may be many or few; yet vain toil fills their span, for it is soon ended, and we fly away.[19]

Even Lewandowski's musical setting of *Enosh*, which opens many a Reform *Yizkor* service, concludes *not* with "*Chesed Adonai mei olam v'ad olam*," that text's final promise of God's everlasting love, but rather with a reprise of the text's *opening* words: "Our days are like grass. We shoot up like flowers that fade and die as the chill wind passes over them. And they are no more. *V'lo yakirenu od.* [Not to be remembered ever again.]" [20] sounded with notes of doom. The music is sublime, but is "*Lo yakirenu od*" the right note to sound for *Yizkor*?[21]

There is a time and a place for our expressions of humility, for acknowledgments of our minuteness in the grand scheme of things, our relative powerlessness, the futility of some of our schemes. But is *Yizkor* on Yom Kippur that time? Isn't *Yizkor* precisely the time in which we consider the *lasting impact* people have had on us, the significance of their lives, the legacy they have left behind? Should *Yizkor* liturgies express the notion that our lives are futile because they end in death? I think not.

On many a Jewish gravestone you'll see carved an open book. It's *Sefer HaChayim*. On Rosh HaShanah and Yom Kippur we pray to be inscribed "*b'sefer chayim b'rachah v'shalom, ufarnasah tovah.*"[22] That's clearly a reference to an earthly life in which we have to earn *parnasah*. But some use the term *Sefer Chayim* to refer to the Book of Eternal Life, a book from which no one's name is omitted; a book we don't have to plead to be inscribed in because we ourselves inscribe our own names on its pages. "*V'tiftach et sefer hazichronot umei eilav yikarei v'chotam yad kol adam bo.*" [God will open the Book of Memories and from its pages will be read the signature of every human being.][23] We

"BAAVUR SHEANI NODER TZEDAKAH BAADO"

inscribe our legacy in *Sefer HaZichronot* with our own words and our own deeds *as others have inscribed their words and deeds, on our very brains.*

Is *Yizkor* about the futility of human endeavors, all of which evaporate with death? I think not. I think *Yizkor* is, rather, about what remains.

Yom Kippur

Yizkor is about what remains. But what remains of the dead is not fixed and unchanging, as what is embodied by the living is, hopefully, not fixed and unchanging.

Yizkor is original to Yom Kippur. Some say we call this day Yom Hakkipurim, in the plural, because both the living and the dead are in need of *kapara*, not infrequently from each other.

Maimonides is clear that the living may need absolution, even if those we have wronged have since died:

> If you sin against another and he dies before you have had a chance to repay him and ask his forgiveness, you bring ten Israelites to the dead person's grave as witnesses and say before them: I have sinned in such and such a way against so and so. If the deceased has heirs, you pay your debt to the heirs. If the deceased has no heirs, you pay your debt to the *bet din* and confess.[24]

A Chasidic tale imagines the other side of the dynamic in which a dead husband seeks forgiveness from his surviving spouse (or his widow *needs* to forgive her deceased husband):

> In the night after the seven day mourning for Reb Abraham the Angel, his wife had a dream. She saw a vast hall and in it thrones, set in a semicircle. On each throne sat one of the great. A door opened, and . . . Abraham, her husband, entered. "Friends, my wife is angry with me because in my earthly life I lived apart from her. She is right and therefor I must obtain her forgiveness." His wife cried out: "With all my heart, I forgive you." And [she] awoke comforted.[25]

Note, in both cases, these acts of confession or pleas for forgiveness are made in public before a minyan, a *beit din*, or an angelic court. That I believe is, or should be, the purpose of a reciting *Yizkor*, in a *kahal,* on Yom Kippur: to make a public pledge to do *tzedakah* on behalf of the deceased, for the *kapara* of the deceased or for our own *kapara.*

Thus many *Yizkor* formulas begin: "*Yizkor Elohim et nishmat* _____ *baavur sheani noder/noderet tzedakah baado/baadah . . .*"[26] Why was this phrase omitted from some *Yizkor* liturgies? Out of discomfort with the notion that a person may face judgment following death and that the verdict could possibly be improved by deeds the living perform on the deceased's behalf. I am not uncomfortable with those notions. But even if you are, consider this: Did not our relationship with those who raised us, and with partners who loved and/or deserted us, not shape, to a large extent, the ways in which we can, do, or cannot relate to others to this day? Do not even deceased parents or spouses, or the loss of children continue to influence us for good and for bad, in complicated and often unconscious ways?

Yom Kippur is the cathartic climax to (though not the final end of) a long period of repentance, during which we examine our words, our thoughts, and our deeds and endeavor to change them for the better, if only incrementally. We work to improve our relationships with our peers, with those who depend on us and with those upon whom we depend, including, I believe, the dead. For, isn't it often difficult to separate our relationships with the living from our relationships with the dead?

Earlier American *Yizkor* liturgies were more affirmative about the continued presence of the dead even in their absence, the ongoing connection between the dead and the living. Perhaps this is what Moses meant when he said to the Israelites, "*Atem nitzavim hayom kulchem*" [You are all standing here this day], even "*et asher einenu po imanu hayom*" [those who are not present with us this day].[27] People can be physically absent but still very much present. These earlier liturgies, some in German, included prayers *addressed directly to the deceased,*[28] prayers of gratitude, prayers asking for the deceased to continue to look out and care—even intercede—for the living,[29] prayers looking forward to being reunited with the deceased,[30] petitions for forgiveness from the deceased,[31] prayers hoping to live a life worthy of the values imparted or examples set by the deceased.

If today we recite, "*Yizkor Elohim et nishmat* _____ *baavur sheani noderet tzedakah baadah,*" we might mean:

"BAAVUR SHEANI NODER TZEDAKAH BAADO"

May God take note of _____ for whom I pledge _____ so that her sins may be diminished and her merits magnified.
Or . . . for whom I pledge ____ so that *my* sins may be diminished and my merits magnified.
Or . . . for whom I pledge _____ as an expression of gratitude for all that she has taught me.
Or . . . for whom I pledge _____ so that their deaths not be entirely in vain.
Or . . . for whom I pledge ____ so that I may be worthy of the gift they have bequeathed to me.

And if we are able, we might add:

I hereby forgive _____ for the sin he/she committed against me.
I hereby ask _____ to forgive me for the sin I committed against him/her.

I think that reciting *Yizkor* on Yom Kippur is less about mourning, mortality, or memory and more about connection, continuity, and change.

God

Is *Yizkor* addressed to God, or, as some liturgies render it, are we, in effect, saying: "I remember . . ."? It is, I believe, an intersection of the two.

When we recite *"Yizkor Elohim et nishmat _____"* are we uttering a petition? *"May* God remember (or notice) the soul of_____"? Does the God we imagine ever *forget* what's written in *Sefer HaZichronot*? Archival photo prints last "forever." But "forever," in this case, means for two hundred years. Two hundred years is not a long time compared with the durability of other works of art and artifacts, manuscripts, engravings, and inscriptions in pottery or stone. And two hundred years is but a moment in God's sight. What's written by a person in *Sefer HaZichronot* is not written in ink that fades or on paper that deteriorates with time. *Yizkor Elohim* can't be a petition, *May* God remember, may God take note,[32] *unless* we are asking God to take note of something that hasn't happened yet: namely, a *change* in our relationship with the deceased, a change in the deceased, a change in ourselves that we are about to attempt to bring about; for example, "By pledging and then doing this act of *tzedakah*, I hope to extend the reach of my mother's

MARGARET MOERS WENIG

legacy. By pledging and doing this act of *tzedakah*, I hope to open my grandmother's heart a little more in forgiveness. By pledging and doing this act of *tzedakah*, I hope to add to my father's merit to tip the scales a bit from his bad deeds to his good deeds. By pledging and doing this act of *tzedakah*, I hope to resurrect in my life a person from whom I have been estranged. By pledging and doing this act of *tzedakah*, I hope, little by little, to externalize and thus internalize my lost one's love and, perhaps, feel her presence more and more and grieve her absence less and less."

"*Yizkor Elohim et nishmat* _____*baavur sheani noderet tzedakah baadah* . . .*"* May God notice how the soul or the legacy *of the deceased* will change, if ever so slightly, through this act of *tzedakah*; and may God notice how *my* own soul, my inner life, and my outer life will change, if ever so slightly, through this act of *tzedakah*. For with this pledge and act of *tzedakah*, I open the files inscribed and stored in my brain and *edit* them before resaving them."

Yizkor on Yom Kippur is, I believe, not about human frailty or the futility of human endeavors. *Yizkor* on Yom Kippur is about the power of others to affect us, about our power to affect others, about the power of the dead and the living to continue to affect each other. *Yizkor* on Yom Kippur is, I believe, not simply about remembering the dead, but about attempting to affect *change* in our relationships with the dead and thus to affect change in ourselves and in our relationships with those who are still among the living.

Notes

1. Mark Doty, *Heaven's Coast: A Memoir* (New York: Harper Perennial, 1996), 287. (Note: Thank you to my spouse, Rabbi Sharon Kleinbaum, for giving me this book while we were staying in Provincetown.)
2. Ibid., 286.
3. Elizabeth McCracken, *An Exact Replica of a Figment of My Imagination: A Memoir* (New York: Little Brown and Company, 2008), 103.
4. Bruce D. Perry and Maia Szalavitz, *The Boy Who Was Raised as a Dog: And Other Stories from a Child Psychiatrist's Notebook: What Traumatized Children Can Teach Us About Loss, Love and Healing* (New York: Basic Books, 2006),19, citing the work of Dr. Seymour Levine, neuroendocrinologist, who "conducted pioneering work on the impact of stress during early life on the development of the brain."
5. Ibid., 156.

"*BAAVUR SHEANI NODER TZEDAKAH BAADO*"

6. Grace Paley, from the poem "Sisters" in the collection of poems entitled *Fidelity* (New York: Farrar, Straus and Giroux, 2008), 78–79.

7. Beth Am, The People's Temple in New York, New York, where I served as rabbi from 1984–2000 and where, since 2002, I have returned as rabbi for the High Holy Days and now for a few Shabbatot a year.

8. Mrs. Sylvia Gordon at the United Nations International School.

9. Mr. Alan Jolly at Staples High School in Westport, Connecticut

10. Professor Jacob Neusner, Brown University.

11. Professor Eugene Borowitz, HUC-JIR/New York.

12. Julian Barnes, *The Sense of an Ending* (New York: Knopf, 2001), 69.

13. Perry and Szalavitz, *Boy Who Was Raised as a Dog*, 156.

14. Barnes, *Sense of an Ending*, 143.

15. Perry and Szalavitz, *Boy Who Was Raised as a Dog*, 156.

16. This quotation has been excerpted from a longer passage in ibid.

17. Patricia Hampl, *I Could Tell You Stories: Sojourns in the Land of Memory* (New York: WW Norton and Co.,1999), 69. (Note: Thank you to Rabbi Stacy Offner for recommending this book to me.)

18. *The Gates of Repentance*, 479–80.

19. Ibid., 482

20. Text in ibid., 477.

21. Interestingly, *Gates of Repentance* does not translate these Hebrew words into English. But worshipers who understand the Hebrew know what they mean. Other examples of this expression of futility and emphasis on mortality abound: Look at what *Gates of Repentance* has included and what it has omitted from Psalm 8: Included:"When I behold Your heavens, the work of Your fingers, the moon and stars that You have established, what are we that You are mindful of us, what are we mortals that You consider us?" (p. 479) Omitted: "But You have made . . . [mortal man] *m'at mei-Elohim* [little less than divine] and adorned him with *kavod v'hadar* [glory and majesty]." *Yizkor* in *Gates of Repentance* includes these words that appear elsewhere in the *machzor*: "All the heroes are as nothing in Your sight. The men of renown as though they never existed. The wise as though without knowledge. The intelligent as though they lacked insight. Most of their actions are worthless in Thy sight. Their entire life is a fleeting breath. Man is not far above beast, for all is vanity. But when those same words appear in *N'ilah*, they are immediately followed by: "*Ata hivdalta enosh meirosh . . .*" [But, from the first you singled out mortal man and considered him worthy to stand in Your presence . . .]. Philip Birnbaum, trans., *High Holiday Prayer Book* (New York: Hebrew Publishing Company, 1951), 1005; *Gates of Repentance*, 520–21.

MARGARET MOERS WENIG

22. This petition is inserted in the final blessing of every *Amidah* for all of Rosh HaShanah and Yom Kippur.

23. From the *piyut Untaneh Tokef*, recited, in the Reform tradition, during the morning *Amidah* and in other Ashkenazi traditions, during the Reader's Repetition of the *Musaf Amidah*.

24. Maimonides, *Mishneh Torah, The Laws of Repentance*, 2:11.

25. Buber, *Tales of the Hasidim,* vol. 1, 117, quoted in Simcha Paull Raphael, *Jewish Views of the Afterlife* (Northvale, NJ: Jason Aronson Inc., 1994), 353.

26. Birnbaum, *High Holiday Prayer Book*, 731. "*Baavur . . .*" is also included in the *Yizkor* formula that's recited at the end of each of the three Festivals. There the pledge is understood to echo the offerings Ancient Israelites brought to the Temple on each of those Festivals.

27. From the Torah reading for Yom Kippur morning according to Reform *minhag*.

28. "What is perhaps most surprising of all is that the climactic private prayers in the vernacular, German, or English, were as a rule addressed to the departed themselves." Eric L. Friedland, *Were Our Mouths Filled With Song: Studies in Liberal Jewish Liturgy* (Cincinnati: Hebrew Union College Press, 1997),147; e.g., in the High Holy Day prayer books edited by Leo Merzbacher (ibid., 148), David Einhorn (ibid., 151), Isaac Meyer Wise (ibid., 156), Adolph Huebsch (ibid., 159), J. Leonard Levy (ibid., 170).

29. Ibid., 160, 161, 163.

30. Ibid., 151, 158, 160.

31. Ibid., 161.

32. *ZCHR* [remember] and *PKD* [take note of] are sometimes used interchangeably. See Lawrence A. Hoffman, "Does God Remember? A Liturgical Theology of Memory" (unpublished manuscript).

Visions for a New/Old Reform *Yizkor* Service

Donald B. Rossoff

If there are any holidays that bring Jews to synagogue more than any others, they are Rosh HaShanah and Yom Kippur. And if there is any one element during these Awesome Days that engages more Jews during this sacred season, it is the *Yizkor*/Memorial Service for Yom Kippur. The question that our temple office is asked the most in the days before Yom Kippur is: "What time does *Yizkor* begin?" From the beginning of the Yom Kippur Afternoon Service to its end, the number of filled seats in our synagogue nearly doubles. And in the minutes following *Yizkor*, the number of occupied seats more than halves. For reasons known perhaps only to theologians, sociologists, psychiatrists, and thanatologists, the *Yizkor* Service is a Jewish/spiritual/psychological magnet of the highest order.

Having lost both of my parents as a young child, I have attended more than my share of *Yizkor* services. It is no surprise, then, that this service as historically and currently observed within Reform Judaism would be of heightened interest to this particular orphan. I wanted to have a better sense of where this service came from, how it has developed within the tradition and within our own movement, and what its theological, spiritual, and emotional underpinnings were. Were there elements of the service as they have been or might be that might inform and deepen our experience of remembering, honoring, and sanctifying the memories of our dear departed, regardless of the particular liturgy we used?

My initial sense of *Yizkor* was based on my experiences with the *Yizkor* services in the *Union Prayerbook II, Gates of Prayer, Gates of Repentance,* and, to a smaller degree in *Mishkan T'filah.* That understanding was expanded through study of the *Yizkor/Hazkarat*

DONALD B. ROSSOFF has been a rabbi at Temple B'nai Or in Morristown, New Jersey, since 1990. He is the author of *The Perfect Prayer* (URJ) and composer (with Cantor Bruce Benson) of "Adonai Li" (Transcontinental Music).

DONALD B. ROSSOFF

HaN'shamot Service in both its traditional expression[1] as well as in earlier Reform iterations. And, of course, my appreciation of *Yizkor* has been illumined by years of being with and learning from family, friends, and congregants who have faced the most profound of losses.

More and more, I saw the power the *Yizkor* Memorial Service has to be deeply meaningful, comforting, consoling, cathartic, healing, and perhaps even transformative. Trying to think creatively, I began to explore a flow of a service and modalities of worship that, regardless of whatever liturgies we use, might provide for the worshiping community a coherent and meaningful "journey." These ideas are rooted in practices and concepts from our tradition, which includes our rich Reform tradition, which, more than any other Jewish expression, has taken the *Yizkor* moment and the opportunities it offers most seriously and creatively.

I. Background on Reform *Yizkor* Services

Although special memorial prayers, such as *Yizkor, Av Harachamim,* and *Hazkarat HaN'shamot,* have long been part of the traditional liturgy for the Festivals and Yom Kippur, the expanded *Yizkor* service as experienced by most North American Jews (Reform, Conservative, modern Orthodox) is, in large part, a creation of Reform Judaism. As Prof. Larry Hoffman points out:

> The Memorial Service is distinctively ours . . . Though rooted in memorial prayers that reach back a few centuries, "*Yizkor*" (as it was known) was at best a tiny interlude at the end of the Morning Service, by the time the Reform Movement was born. But Reform Jews were convinced of the merit of a deeper experience of memorializing the dead on Yom Kippur. So they granted the Memorial Service its own structural autonomy, an idea that has since been adopted by Conservative and Orthodox Jews as well.[2]

The first such liturgy was found in the first *Gebetbuch* of the first Reform Temple in Hamburg in 1819.[3] While the historic trend in our movement has been to shorten the traditional liturgy to fit our needs and proclivities, this trend was reversed when it came to the Memorial Service for Yom Kippur. When compared with the "bare-bone" traditional *Yizkor/Hazkarat HaN'shamot* Service following the Torah reading on Yom Kippur morning, Reform

VISIONS FOR A NEW/OLD REFORM *YIZKOR* SERVICE

Yizkor services (known by various names), in their European and especially American expressions, have incorporated many more prayers, traditional and original, as well as medieval *piyutim*, and an expanded cantorial/choral repertoire.[4] By and large, each of these services built on those that proceeded, while addressing the historical experience and perceived needs of their particular generation.[5]

What this said to me was that the Reform *Yizkor* Service, both in content, and to a large degree, structure, presents a wide open field in which we have the opportunity to reenvision a meaningful and beautiful worship experience that will speak to our own historical and personal experience and needs.

II. Possible Elements

As we have received it, there are certain elements typically found in Reform *Yizkor* services for Yom Kippur. These include:

- Readings on the universality and inevitability of death
- Presentation, either through the spoken word or through musical renditions, of particular psalms, including Psalms 23, 121, and 90
- Remembrance of Jewish martyrs
- Individual remembrance of one's family members who have passed on, minimally using the actual *Yizkor* prayer
- Public reading of the names of those who have died during the past year
- Recitation or chanting of the *El Malei* (although this has varied from community to community)
- Recitation of *Kaddish* (not a part of the traditional *Yizkor* liturgy)

There are, however, other concepts and thematic elements undergirding or embedded within *Yizkor* that could be explored more deeply and perhaps reimagined in a way that might speak to our own generation and those that follow. These include:

1. Belief in immortality
2. The dead need *kaparah*
3. Pledging צדקה\גמילות חסדים in memory of the dead
4. Readings addressed to the departed
5. *Yizkor* as catharsis

DONALD B. ROSSOFF

6. Learning history through the martyrs
7. Jewish transcendence

1. Belief in Immortality

The cornerstone of the traditional memorial prayers, *Yizkor, Haz-karat HaN'shamot, Av HaRachamim,* and *El Malei,* is the presumption of the "soul's" continued existence after the death of the body. While it is possible to read any of these prayers in a less literal, more metaphoric way, it would be like swimming upstream in the face of a powerful opposing current, generated both by the words themselves as well as by the desire by many of our worshipers in that moment to believe that there is something still existent that God can remember and bind up in the bonds of (eternal) life.

Luckily, Reform Judaism enables us to swim with, not against, the current, and affirm the "eternality" or immortality of the soul. Irrespective of any individual rabbi's personal beliefs, CCAR platforms, from Pittsburgh to Pittsburgh, have consistently affirmed, in differing ways, that "the spirit within us is eternal" (1999) (i.e., that there is some sort of continued existence beyond death). Yet as consistently as our platforms have affirmed the concept of immortality, this affirmation has inconsistently, hesitantly, and only sporadically been given expression in our liturgical publications, the literature in which our theology is most effectively embodied and promulgated.

I think this approach needs to be rethought, especially as we contemplate creating the one worship moment when memory and hope most naturally converge. In the *Yizkor* moment, we have an opportunity to express what we say we believe in ways that will bring a modicum of understanding, comfort, and hope. Inquiring minds and hurting souls want to know. It may be enough to say that we believe that there is something, not nothing; and perhaps that, in its simplest form, is all we can say. Even though we already affirm in our liturgies that "the world to come . . . is our sure inheritance and our everlasting portion,"[6] we admit that "beyond the gate . . . all is darkness to our mortal sight,"[7] "hidden . . . by an impenetrable veil."[8] But there are poems and readings—a small number of which are scattered in our various liturgies—that express this understanding in ways that are affirmative, beautiful, and comforting. Some of these writings are learned and lofty (as those just quoted), while others use concrete image and metaphor to give the concept a warm overcoat.[9]

VISIONS FOR A NEW/OLD REFORM *YIZKOR* SERVICE

And since there is no unanimity as to what "immortality of the soul" means, and since worshipers think, feel, conceptualize, and believe in so many different ways, the use of a *Mishkan T'filah*–like, multi-option format could be very effective in presenting alternative ways through which we can affirm something, not nothing.

2. The Dead Need *Kaparah*

The belief that the dead are in need of *kaparah* (atonement/forgiveness/absolution), while largely foreign to our sensibility, is in fact the major linchpin that connects the recitation of the *Yizkor/Hazkarat HaN'shamot* prayers with *Yom HaKippurim*. One of the traditional interpretations of the plural form of *Yom HaKippurim* (lit. Day of Atonements) is that the Holy Day atones for both the living and for the dead.[10]

כַּפֵּר לְעַמְּךָ יִשְׂרָאֵל אֲשֶׁר־פָּדִיתָ—דברים כא:ח
כַּפֵּר לְעַמְּךָ: אֵלּוּ הַחַיִּים.
אֲשֶׁר פָּדִיתָ: אֵלּוּ הַמֵּתִים מְלַמֵּד שֶׁהַמֵּתִי׳ צְרִיכִי׳ כַּפָּרָה
— סִפְרֵי פָּרָשַׁת שׁוֹפְטִים פִּיסְקָא סז

Absolve Your people Israel whom You have redeemed.

(Deut. 21:8)

Absolve Your people Israel: these are the living . . .
Whom You have redeemed: these are the dead, which teaches that the dead need atonement.

(*Sifrei, Shoftim* 67)

I doubt that any of us would advocate belief in an after-life system in which the souls of the departed are being punished or simply not enjoying the heavenly bliss they otherwise might have and are thus in need of postmortem forgiveness via vicarious atonement. However, I believe that there are ways in which these concepts could be fruitfully utilized. First, there is the tradition of making ongoing commitments in memory of the dead, as discussed below in section 3. Second, and addressing the concept of *kaparah* more directly, we recognize that there are many among us for whom the forgiving of and reconciling with departed dear ones—not by God but by us—might be desirable and even possible. But this requires providing for moments of intimate connection between the mourner and the mourned, as discussed in section 4.

DONALD B. ROSSOFF

3. Pledging צדקה\גמילות חסדים in Memory of the Dead

From a traditional point of view, one of the ways in which the dead can earn *kaparah* and better their portion in the next world is by having the living perform *mitzvot* on their behalf, specifically *tzedakah* and *g'milut chasadim*. This is why some of the traditional prayers include a pledge (בלי נדר) made in memory of the deceased to advance the cause of their soul in עולם הבא.

נהגו לידור צדקות ביוה"כ בעד המתים
ומזכירין נשמותיהם דהמתי ג"כ יש להם כפרה ביה"כ (מרדכי):
— שלחן ערוך אורח חיים סימן תרכא:ו

> "It was customary to contribute charity on Yom Kippur on behalf of the departed" [Isserles, quoting the Mordechai, adds the comment,] "And we make mention of the names of the departed souls, since they also obtain atonement [absolution?] on the Day of Atonement."
>
> (*Shulchan Aruch, Orech Chaim,* 621:6)

Making—and then fulfilling—a pledge to do a *mitzvah* in memory of the departed is but one way that our dear ones live on in the immortality of their influence in our lives and, through us, in the world. We do have elements of this in our liturgy already (e.g., how we aspire to live "as, in their higher moments, they themselves wished to live").[11] But beyond whatever wishes they might have had in those precious higher moments, we could take a cue from the tradition and, creatively and prayerfully, point our people in a more concrete direction (e.g., giving *tzedakah* in memory of their dear one).[12] Acts of *tzedakah* and *g'milut chasadim*, while perhaps not atoning for the dead, keep their memory and their influence alive. We may have a different understanding than our traditionally believing coreligionists of how צדקה תציל ממות, but I think we believe it with equal conviction.

4. Readings Addressed to the Departed

In 1855, Rabbi Leo Merzbacher introduced a new concept into the Memorial Service in his *Order of Prayer:* private readings in which the worshiper "spoke," not *about* their dear departed but *to* them. Prayers addressed "To my beloved father," "to my

VISIONS FOR A NEW/OLD REFORM *YIZKOR* SERVICE

beloved mother" or "spouse" or "child," gave voice to feelings of loss, longing, and gratitude and provided moments when, for many, worshipers felt that they were in the presence of, perhaps even in dialogue with, deceased loved ones. Such readings were also part of subsequent American Reform *Yizkor* services, including the *Todtenfeier* in Rabbi David Einhorn's *Olath Tamid* (1858), the *Seelenfeier* in Rabbi Isaac M. Wise's *Minhag Amerika* (1866), and in the Memorial services of the various editions of the *Union Prayerbook II*.[13]

Such readings were not included in *Gates of Repentance*. Perhaps sensing that something important was missing, many congregations such as ours brought back this personalized element through supplemental readings.

Reintroducing such personalized readings in which departed relations are addressed in the second person presents certain challenges, but offers unique opportunities as well. One of the challenges is to offer readings that are meaningful and respectful, understanding that, while most people had a fairly good (though not perfect) relationship with, let's say, parents, many did not. Often there is pain, anger, brokenness, and unfinished business between the worshiper and the deceased upon who she or he is focusing. But within the challenge such hurt and brokenness present lie opportunities to heal broken hearts and bind open wounds. While we cannot account for every family constellation, I believe we can find and/or compose any number of personalized readings through which our people would reconnect with their loved ones in honesty, sincerity, and love. Done skillfully and sensitively, such prayers would lead the worshiper through a spiritual process by which understanding, forgiveness, and emotional reconciliation might be experienced, granting, in a sense, *kaparah* for the dead. *Yizkor* can provide the opportunity for worshipers to mourn the loss, not only of that which was and can never be again, but of that which might have been and should have been, but was not and, perhaps, could not have been. And this just might set the stage for reconciliation with, perhaps even forgiveness of, those from whose memories we might have hitherto been estranged. Such opportunities might enable and empower us to מחיה מתים (resurrect our relationships) ברחמים רבים (by means of our increased compassion, understanding, and love).

DONALD B. ROSSOFF

5. *Yizkor* as Catharsis

But can a *Yizkor* Service serve in this way, as a therapeutic cathartic, a means through which unresolved feelings vis-à-vis past relationships can find resolution and guilt can be addressed and perhaps cleansed? Historically, the answer may very well have been yes, suggesting that it can again. In his examination of the development of American Memorial Service liturgies, Eric L. Friedland suggests that some of these liturgies were meant to do just that, to provide a cathartic relief of guilt, the mixed feelings experienced by more than one generation of immigrants who left behind (abandoned) the older generation and their graves.

> A swift comparison between the nineteenth-century American prayerbooks and their European correlates shows the former by and large to be on a somewhat grander scale, and more involved and imposing. The suggestion might be ventured that the elaborateness of the American *Yizkor* Service stems from an implicit wish to ward off or cleanse oneself of guilt, [satisfying] a felt need for a *kippur* or *kapparah* between the generations . . . The role of the Yom Kippur *Yizkor* Service as an occasion for catharsis was to last a fairly long time, if not at least an entire century, chiefly because of the two major waves of immigration and their overlap.[14]

While the guilt presumed to be felt by the immigrant generations has long since passed, worshipers of subsequent generations often feel their own specific guilt, also stemming from trans-generational relationships. Through the use of well-crafted "second-person" readings, a Reform *Yizkor* Service has the potential to address these issues and on some level move the worshiper closer to resolution and reconciliation.

6. Learning History through the Martyrs

From its inception, the theme of martyrdom has been a seminal focus within Jewish Memorial services. Through the centuries, Jews have felt a sacred obligation to pay due homage to those who died *al kiddush Hashem,* and in doing so, we have maintained a relationship with the martyrs and their convictions. By and large, today's Jew in the pew has little or no grasp of the historic experience of the Jewish people and sparse knowledge of the martyrs of the past, save for those souls lost during the Shoah, as victims of terrorism, and in defense of the State of Israel. While we cannot teach the entirety of Jewish history on one foot, nor should we perpetuate the lachrymose theory of Jewish history, the *Yizkor* moment offers an opportunity to help our people become more aware of those of every age who have found something in Judaism worth dying for.

7. Jewish Transcendence

The *Yizkor* Service provides a unique opportunity to build upon the sense of obligation and/or connectedness that brought the worshiper to the service in the first place, by fostering a feeling of greater connectedness with or obligation to his or her extended meta-family (i.e., the Jewish People). Moments of transformative spirituality are often born when one experiences on a deep level the sense that he or she is part of something that transcends the self and connects with something greater and of ultimate meaning. For both the "regular" and the "*Yizkor*-only" Jew, this service has the potential to help one feel that one is a part of and a needed conduit of the legacy, both of his or her own family as well as that of the Jewish People. The hope would be, of course, that a *Yizkor* service would motivate a higher level of Jewish engagement, especially those for whom the *Yizkor* service is their primarily, perhaps sole, engagement with synagogue life.

III. Suggestion on Putting It Together

Were the concepts and thematic elements presented above to be included in a new *Yizkor*/Memorial liturgy, a thematic flow might look something like this:[15]

1. Human frailty and finitude
2. Reference to *Yizkor* as rooted in martyrdom as a transition to
3. Readings regarding martyrs of the past
4. Transition to present day "history," leading into
5. Reading names of the year's deceased
6. Extended time of private reading/prayer, perhaps with directed musical background:
   a. Readings/poems/psalms relating to immortality
   b. Readings/poems/personalized prayers—in the second or third person—relating to specific relatives (e.g., parent, spouse, child). These might also consist of guided meditations.[16]

DONALD B. ROSSOFF

    c. Readings/poems/psalms relating to perpetuating the "immortality of influence," through *tzedakah* and acts of kindness in memory of . . .

    d. Recitation of personalized *"Yizkor Elohim . . .,"* as well as *Yizkor* prayers relating to martyrs and the fallen soldiers of our particular countries and the IDF

7. Communal *"El Malei"*

8. Reading(s) on Jewish transcendence, referring to the history of the martyrs and the connection with one's own families, and helping the worshipers see themselves as those who are privileged and tasked to carry on the Jewish legacy of their individual families as well as that of the meta-*mishpachah* of the Jewish People[17]

9. Communal recitation of *Kaddish*

10. A final moment of comfort and continued closeness with God, such as the reading and/or singing of *Shiviti*

When contemplating a new Reform *Yizkor* Service, my hope is that we will be able to create liturgical moments that will most effectively, most personally, most spiritually, and most beautifully enable individuals and communities to look into the mirror of the past, link memory and hope, and connect deeply and personally with those who are no more with us in *haolam hazeh*—those to whom we owe so much. I pray that this article will add to and enrich that sacred enterprise.

Notes

1. A fine source is Daniel Goldschmidt, *Machzor l'Yamim HaNora-im* (Jerusalem: Koren, 1970).

2. Lawrence A. Hoffman, *Gates of Understanding 2: Appreciating the Days of Awe* (New York: CCAR, 1984), 147.

3. Ibid., 149.

4. The *Yizkor* Service found in MARAM's *Avodah Shebalev* also continues this tradition with poems and readings from modern Israeli poets and authors.

5. Eric L. Friedland, "The Atonement Memorial Service in the American Mahzor," *Hebrew Union College Annual* 55 (1984): 243–82.

6. *Rabbi's Manual* (New York: CCAR, 1988), 159.

7. *Gates of Repentance*, 483.

8. *Gates of Prayer*, 548.

VISIONS FOR A NEW/OLD REFORM *YIZKOR* SERVICE

9. For example, Henry Van Dyke's "Parable of Immortality (A ship leaves . . .)."

10. Jeffrey M. Cohen, *Understanding the High Holyday Services* (London: Routledge & Kegan Paul, 1983), 155.

11. *Gates of Prayer for Weekdays and at a House of Mourning*, 43.

12. This is actually embodied in the *Yizkor* booklets that congregations prepare that lists names of family members in whose memory a donation has been made to the synagogue.

13. Friedland, "The Atonement," 245.

14. Ibid., 277.

15. My thanks to Gail Lalk, grief therapist, for her help in this.

16. I am grateful to Rabbi Mary Zamore for the suggestion of guided meditations within the quiet, personalized readings. Perhaps this might be in the form of open paragraphs or paragraphs with brief guided readings, directing the worshiper then to "fill in the blank"; for example:

    I remember . . .
    I am grateful . . .
    I regret . . .
    I mourn . . .
    I forgive . . .
    I resolve . . .

17. In this context, inclusive consideration should be given to persons of other faith backgrounds in our congregations, those who are not Jewish and/or those whose honored departed were of other faiths.

We, the *Avaryanim,*
Chant *Kol Nidrei*

Donald P. Cashman

A powerful mystique surrounds *Kol Nidrei,* derived from the combined elements of the drama of the ceremony: the seasonal white of the *parochet,* the Torahs' mantles, and on the officiants themselves; the removal of many, if not all, of the scrolls from the ark, to be held by congregational leaders or elders; the proclamation of the unique formula *"biyshivah shel malah . . ."* before the chanting; and the larger than usual crowd for the service, garbed uniquely for the evening service in tallitot, all contribute to the drama of the moment.

Then there is *Kol Nidrei* itself, with its unique words, unlike anything else in our usual liturgy. And, of course, we have the Ashkenazic melody, which is many hundreds of years old. Made up of melodic fragments strung together, it is unlike either the patterns of *nusach* or biblical cantillation on one hand, nor like the chorus and verses style of later song on the other. By virtue of its words and music, not to mention the great solemnity of the occasion, *Kol Nidrei* is a piece for the well-trained, or at least the well-practiced. Aramaic legalese coupled with runs and leaps join to make the chanting of *Kol Nidrei* one of the most advanced synagogue skills— one customarily reserved for a professional.

As with virtually every other Jewish ceremony, the *Kol Nidrei* ritual has evolved over time and place. Every epoch in Jewish history has contributed to the evolution of the *Kol Nidrei* ceremony as we have it today. The story begins with the Torah's statements about obligation to fulfill one's vows (e.g., Deut. 23:22–24, Num. 30:3). Other biblical literature gives examples of the length to which people went to keep their vows, perhaps most dramatically the story of Jephthah (Judges 11:30-40). Yet while the Bible does

---

RABBI DONALD P. CASHMAN (NY83) is the spiritual leader of B'nai Sholom Reform Congregation in Albany, New York.

WE, THE *AVARYANIM*, CHANT *KOL NIDREI*

not allow for the nullification of vows and oaths,[1] the desirability of being able to extricate oneself from them if necessary was readily apparent. By the Second Temple period, Josephus stated that "some were of the opinion that they should disregard those oaths as having been sworn under the sway of passion, without reflexion or judgement . . . and that perjuries were not grave or hazardous when they were prompted by necessity, but only when rashly committed with malicious intent."[2] Philo took a different tack, expressing in *Hypothetica* 7:5 that priests were empowered by God to accept or reject dedicated property and thus can release someone from a vow to dedicate property.

While the Mishnah, *Tosefta,* and Gemara contain tractates on vows and on oaths, the issue of nullification is ascertained in *Mishnah Chagigah* 1:8 to have no biblical basis. The *Tosefta* on that passage adds that "a sage may nullify by means of his wisdom" (*Tosefta Chagigah* 1:9), which may mean that he has the skill to determine how the vow was in fact not valid to start with. It has also been suggested that dissolution of vows may in fact be "a power vested in the Rabbis" that is "an outgrowth of the role of priest and sage as Temple functionary."[3] The Rabbinic literature therefore includes the particulars required for dissolving or nullifying vows.[4]

Eventually, a formula for the dissolution of vows appears in the liturgy for Yom Kippur in *Seder Rav Amram*.[5] Various *geonim*[6] and *rishonim*[7] are linked to the text, changes in the text, establishing the ritual around the text, and discussions of its limits. But the established fact is that *Kol Nidrei*, whether referring to vows of the recently concluded year, or of the newly begun year, became part of the Yom Kippur liturgy.

The old paradigm behind *Kol Nidrei*, indeed, behind much of Rabbinic Judaism, is of halachic responsibility: How do we deal with unfulfilled vows, which are supposedly inviolable? Our newer paradigm is one of meaning: How do we derive meaning from our performance of the *Kol Nidrei* ceremony?

As we are poised on the threshold of creating a new *machzor* for North American Reform Judaism, we are wondering what to do with some pieces of the liturgy for the Days of Awe. We ponder retention, rejection, modification, addition; we equivocate, we gloss over, or we leave untranslated. We want a *machzor* that has integrity as both a Jewish prayer book for the Days of Awe as well as having integrity as a Reform Jewish prayer book.

DONALD P. CASHMAN

To be sure, Reform Judaism has struggled with *Kol Nidrei* for two hundred years. Our *machzorim* have changed the words, substituted Psalms, and left it out. We have omitted the words and played instrumental versions instead.[8] In 1978, the words appeared in *Shaarei T'shuvah/Gates of Repentance* after an accidental appearance in the first edition of the *Union Prayer Book II, Newly Revised* (1945).[9]

In the twenty-seven years I have served my congregation, we have tried a variety of approaches to bring meaning to *Kol Nidrei.* Still emerging out of classical Reform in the late 1980s, an organ accompanied our vocal soloist. When the organist retired, we moved to harp accompaniment for the Days of Awe, a dignified and formal sound, with biblical antecedent. Those who heard the organ and thought "church" as well as those who heard no accompaniment and thought "Orthodox" were pacified, as were those who felt guitar too colloquial. Twice we began the service with the Bruch cello composition using the piano reduction, not an orchestra, with musicians from the outside. The first time was a disaster because no one thought to make sure that the beautiful Steinway in the sanctuary was tuned. Several years later we tried again, but I did not find the ten or twelve minutes particularly moving, even with a tuned piano and a better cellist. Perhaps a decade ago a past president serving on the regional URJ board brought to the ritual committee the idea of calling up all the past presidents for *Kol Nidrei.* This certainly adds a measure of formality and uniqueness to the service.

In 2010, it was brought to my attention that one of these past presidents, a fiddler in a klezmer band, wanted to play *Kol Nidrei.* There's a tradition, first cited in *Machzor Vitry,*[10] about *Kol Nidrei* being done three times; the instrumental could be the first, the soloist and harp would be another. What could a third, *different* version be?

In 2010, the *avaryanim* (all the sinners) sang *Kol Nidrei:* We had a congregational sing-along. It provided a sense of ownership and opened up a text for people in a way like never before. We began with the instrumental version of the tune on violin, followed it up with the sing-along, and concluded with our soloist and harp.

Fortunately, the congregation loves to sing, and is willing to learn new pieces, even in the midst of the solemnity of services during the Days of Awe. Within the last few years we've introduced the responsive chanting of *Ashamnu, Bagadnu*, with them repeating each word after me—no transliteration involved! The following year, they were receptive to the congregational responses during the "Chasidic" Full *Kaddish* written by Jacob "Yankl der Heizeriker" Gottlieb (1852–1900) during *N'ilah*, a piece often associated with the great *chazan* Yossele Rosenblatt (1882–1933). A year later, following a moving few days learning and performing an arrangement of Israel Goldfarb's "B'sefer Chayyim" at the North American Jewish Choral Festival, I crafted a sermon around this text, noting that it may be the essence of our prayers, and taught it during Rosh HaShanah; we've continued with it ever since.

The sing-along was carefully planned and rehearsed. There were two elements to the single-page handout the ushers distributed with the *machzorim*: sheet music and the words. I took a simple version of the Lewandowski arrangement,[11] and using Finale Notepad (musical notation software)[12] input it, making a few changes, including transliteration into Sephardic Hebrew. This software, available as a free download, permits key changes with a mouse click. The arrangement has a vocal range of an octave + a fifth, identical to the notoriously difficult to sing American national anthem, "The Star Spangled Banner." Thus, finding a key that would be good for me as well as conducive to group singing was paramount. I decided on E minor, with a range from G2 to D4 (the women, of course, sang in their register an octave higher), which gave me the slightest clearance on the highs just above middle C and wasn't too low for most congregants. The lowest and highest notes are only touched upon twice.

The handout also included four columns in tabular form. From left to right they were the measure number corresponding to the sheet music; the transliterated word or words that would be sung at one time; a translation of the word or phrase; and the actual Aramaic or Hebrew text. For example:

| 23 | *l'tovah* | for good | לטובה |
| | *kulhon* | all of them | כלהון |

The two elements on the handout allowed the music readers to have pitches, rhythms, and words, while the nonreaders would simply go down the column of words and repeat each phrase after me.

DONALD P. CASHMAN

I began with brief introductory remarks about the source of the power of *Kol Nidrei*. Is it the day? The ritual? The text? The melody? *The Jazz Singer* complex, where the day is saved because the hero can sing *Kol Nidrei*?[13] Probably, I mused, it is a combination of all of these. After a tiny bit of historical information, I explained what we would be doing.

First, we listened to the melody on violin. Then, with our sheets in hand, I had them repeat after me each word, or a short phrase such as *"mi Yom Kippurim zeh."* We then drilled four especially challenging musical phrases (measures 9–11, 34–37, 45–48, and 52–54). With the words and the most difficult passages already experienced, we began from the top.

Phrase by phrase I sang, and the congregation repeated: full-voiced, a full sound from a full sanctuary. I could sense the excitement as we worked our way through this significant piece, and I could see the joy on their faces as we accomplished what we had set out to do: everyone sang *Kol Nidrei.*

Then we invited up the past presidents as a group, not by name as in the past so as not to interrupt too much the power of the moment. The congregation rose, the Ark was opened, the scrolls removed, and our vocalist chanted *Kol Nidrei* with the harp accompaniment. The scrolls were returned, and only then, as has been our practice, did we turn back a few pages to light the candles to establish the start of Yom Kippur proper.

I debriefed our experiment with a short sermon about the empowerment of Jewish competency. If they could chant *Kol Nidrei,* an advanced skill, how simple should it be to accomplish a wide variety of other Jewish behaviors.

Programmatically, the sing-along was a huge success. Congregants were genuinely pleased not only with what they had done, but with the entire scripting and drama of the evening: descriptive introduction, melodic prelude, working through of the words and melody, the communal singing, the rendering of it by soloist and harp, and the follow-up sermon. We all felt empowered to do the serious work of atonement that lay ahead of us in the rest of the day.

Could this be replicated? Should it be? Should we make it congregational *minhag*? Might we suggest to others to try this? Was it even a good idea to begin with?

Who should sing *Kol Nidrei*? The extent of possibilities of any piece of the traditional liturgy is limited: a particular prayer may

WE, THE *AVARYANIM*, CHANT *KOL NIDREI*

be recited either by the prayer leader (*sh'liach tzibur*), by the congregation, by all, or by one then the other. *Kol Nidrei* is a *sh'liach tzibur* prayer, recited by the prayer leader. Or, are there other possibilities?

The *Shulchan Aruch* (*Orach Chaim* 619) tells us the *sh'liach tzibur* recites this. The Rema uses the verb in the plural: "afterwards we pray the evening prayer, and we customarily say *Kol Nidrei* on that day, and [the *sh'liach tzibur*] continues with tunes (*nigunim*) until night, and says it three times, each time the voice raised more loudly than the first." One could try to make a case from the plural verb that this signifies that it is the congregation reciting *Kol Nidrei*, but the return to the singular "the [*sh'liach tzibur*] continues" and "the voice," would very much seem to negate that.

Before the *Shulchan Aruch*, however, Yaakov ben Moshe haLevi Moellin, the Maharil (1365–1427), stated that "it is meritorious that everyone recite *Kol Nidrei* with the prayer leader quietly [דניחא *d'nicha*]."[14] The notion that everyone should actively recite along with the *sh'liach tzibur*, rather than passively listen or even just follow along, is a nugget that surfaces through later traditions, although is practically invisible in the Ashkenazic liturgy. Perhaps the development of the Ashkenazic melody, along with the rise of the virtuoso cantorate, held back the Ashkenazic masses.

In the Sephardic world, however, it seems as if communal recitation, albeit quietly, is the norm in many communities. Ya'akov Chaim ben Yitzhak Baruch Sofer (b. Baghdad 1870, d. Jerusalem 1939), in *Kaf HaChaim*, a 1905 commentary to the *Shulchan Aruch*, states that "all the congregation will recite it quietly [בנחת *b'nachat*] with the *sh'liach tzibur*."[15] Shem Tov Gaguine (b. 1884 Jerusalem, d. Manchester, England 1953), scion of a Moroccan rabbinic dynasty and who served as a *dayan* in Egypt, authored *Keter Shem Tov* (published 1934–1953) where he similarly stated that *Kol Nidrei* is recited quietly (בנחת *b'nachat*) with the *sh'liach tzibur*.[16]

Sephardic *machzorim* give similar instructions. *Machzor Rinat Yisrael* has the *sh'liach tzibur* say *Kol Nidrei* three times "and the congregation says it with him silently [בלחש *b'lachash*]."[17] *The Complete ArtScroll Machzor, Yom Kippur, Nusach Sefard* informs us in an introduction that "it is customary, therefore, for everyone to recite it quietly with the chazzan."[18] Above *Kol Nidrei*, itself, the instruction is "the congregation recites along with him in an undertone."[19]

DONALD P. CASHMAN

Other sources reveal even more active congregational participation. In the *machzor* of Congregation Shearith Israel in New York, edited by David de Sola Pool, "the Rabbi intones the formula of Kal[20] Nidre" from the opening words until "from the preceding Day of Atonement unto this Day of Atonement (may it come upon us in peace)." At this point the congregation answers with the remainder of the passage; about 40 percent of the text is recited by the congregation and not by the prayer leader.[21]

The Syrian Jews chant the *Kal Nidrei* prayer twice in unison, and only the third time is it sung by the rabbi or *chazan*.[22] The Moroccan Jews have three *chazanim*, each taking a turn chanting *Kal Nidrei*.[23]

While the well-circulated American Ashkenazic Orthodox *machzorim* (i.e., those edited by A. Philips [1931], P. Birnbaum [1951], and H. Adler, [1959]) do not have any such instruction, at least one did. In this volume[24] above *Kol Nidrei* the English instructs that "the Congregation join in prayer softly." Above that, in Rashi script, the instructions say that "each person says it silently and with great concentration יאמרנו בלחש ובכוונה גדולה (*yomruno b'lachash uv'chavanah g'dolah*) with the *sh'liach tzibur*."

Who recites *Kol Nidrei*? In most of our earliest records since *Seder Rav Amram*, it has been the *sh'liach tzibur*. The *ArtScroll Machzor* refers to the *chazan*, while De Sola Pool places it in the mouth of the rabbi (החכם *hechacham*). In De Sola Pool's historic synagogue, Congregation Shearith Israel, the rabbi was considered the *chazan* (the prayer leader), while someone like the Amsterdam-born Rev. Abraham Lopes Cardozo (1914–2006), who served as its *chazan* from 1946–1984, was titularly the "assistant hazzan." Cardozo himself wrote: "In many Sephardic congregations the *hakham* or the rabbi also not infrequently acts as reader."[25]

In Orthodox and Conservative synagogues, where the liturgy is chanted, the chanter may or may not be the rabbi. In Reform congregations, however, we have a more pronounced bifurcation of the roles of rabbi and cantor: the rabbi reads, and the cantor sings. In the Spanish-Portuguese synagogue, "apparently . . . the rabbi can feel free to take the juicier liturgical items for himself, including the main plum of the year, *Kol Nidre*."[26] Do we diminish the impact of *Kol Nidrei* by transforming a solo rendering into a triptych such as I have suggested of instrumental/congregational/solo? Do we diminish the honor and prestige of the cantorate with this?

WE, THE *AVARYANIM*, CHANT *KOL NIDREI*

To both of these questions I must not only say "no," but I must say that we are perhaps doing just the opposite.

By highlighting *Kol Nidrei* in three different ways, we call added attention to it. It is not just another piece of music in an un-understood language to which the congregation will listen. Rather, by putting their mouths around every single geonic and Rabbenu Tam-ic word, worshipers will have a greater appreciation of the text, and of the musical phrases that make up this unique work. Also, our cantors and other musical professionals, indeed all those synagogue functionaries who practice before they get up in public—*baalei k'riyah, baalei t'kiah*, soloists, instrumentalists, and yes, rabbis—make their tasks look easy. They have spent weeks, months, and years practicing their lines, learning their skills, honing their crafts. If the Jew in the pew is given an opportunity to try something, he or she will realize that it is not as simple as the person on the bimah makes it seem.

Moreover, in the suggested scenario, we build up to the solo recitation of *Kol Nidrei* by the congregation's chosen *sh'liach tzibur*. "In matters of holiness, we only increase, we do not decrease."[27] From this point at the beginning of Yom Kippur, we increase our repentance, hoping to reach a personal pinnacle before the gates close.

Notes

1. Except for a woman's vows in Numbers 30, which can be nullified by her father or husband.
2. *Antiquities of the Jews*, 5:2:12 (=5:169) .
3. Moshe Benovitz, *Kol Nidre: Studies in the Development of Rabbinic Votive Institutions* (Atlanta: Scholars Press, 1998), 152, 164.
4. For full discussions of the texts and history of *hatarat n'darim* and *Kol Nidrei*, see Stuart Weinberg Gershon, *Kol Nidrei: Its Origin, Development, and Significance* (Northvale, NJ: Jason Aronson, 1994), and the Benovitz study cited in note 3 above. See also Eliezer Diamond, "*Kol Nidre*: A Halakhic History and Analysis" and Daniel Landes, "Choice, Commitment, Cancellation: Vows and Oaths in Jewish Law," in *All These Vows: Kol Nidre*, ed. Lawrence A. Hoffman (Woodstock, VT: Jewish Lights, 2011).
5. *Seder Rav Amram* (Warsaw, 1865), 47, www.hebrewbooks.org/pdfpager.aspx?req=42696&st=&pgnum=101.
6. Lawrence A. Hoffman, "Morality, Meaning, and the Ritual Search for the Sacred," in Hoffman, *All These Vows*, especially 7–19, a summary of the early history.
7. See Gershon, *Kol Nidrei*, chap. 9.

DONALD P. CASHMAN

8. A thorough presentation of the treatment of *Kol Nidrei* in Reform Judaism is Annette M. Boeckler, "The Magic of the Moment: *Kol Nidre* in Progressive Judaism," in Hoffman, *All These Vows*, 39.

9. Lawrence A. Hoffman, "*Kol Nidre* from the *Union Prayer Book* to *Gates of Repentance*," in Hoffman, *All These Vows*, 99. I am pleased to own one of these 1945 first editions with the full text of *Kol Nidrei*.

10. S. Hurwitz, ed., *Machzor Vitry* (Nurnburg, 1923), 388.

11. See, e.g., Gershon, *Kol Nidrei*, 155; Nathan Ausabel, *A Treasury of Jewish Folklore* (New York: Crown, 1948), 710; A.Z. Idelsohn, *Jewish Music* (NY: Schocken, 1967), 155; *Shirei T'shuvah/Songs of Repentance* (New York: Transcontinental, 2000), 263.

12. http://www.finalemusic.com/notepad.

13. *The Jazz Singer* versions include 1927 (Al Jolson), 1940 (Moyshe Oysher, "Overture to Glory"), 1952 (Danny Thomas), 1959 (a live television version with Jerry Lewis), and 1980 (Neil Diamond).

14. *Sefer Maharil* (Warsaw, 1875); *Hilchot Leil Yom Kippur*, 45, http://hebrewbooks.org/pdfpager.aspx?req=14721&st=&pgnum=89.

15. *Kaf HaChaim*, vol. 8 (Jerusalem, 1965), *Orach Chaim* 619:18, p. 120, http://hebrewbooks.org/14425.

16. *Keter Shem Tov*, vol. 6 (London, 1955), 323, http://hebrewbooks.org/14391.

17. S. Tal, ed., *Machzor Rinat Yisrael L'Yom Kippur, Nusach S'fard* (Elon Sh'vut: Yad Shapira, 1979), 40.

18. *The Complete ArtScroll Machzor, Yom Kippur, Nusach Sefard* (New York: Mesorah Publications, 1986), 63.

19. Ibid., 66.

20. "*Kal*" is the pronunciation within the Sephardic community. See S. Morag, "Pronunciations of Hebrew," in *Encyclopedia Judaica* (1972), 13:1136.

21. David de Sola Pool, ed., *Prayers for the Day of Atonement according to the Custom of the Spanish and Portuguese Jews*, 2nd ed. (New York: Union of Sephardic Congregations, 1939), 26.

22. Herbert C. Dobrinsky, *A Treasury of Sephardic Laws and Customs* (New York: Ktav/Yeshiva Univ. Press, 1986), 334.

23. Ibid., 340.

24. *The Form of Prayers for the Day of Atonement according to the Custom of the German and Polish Jews*, with an English translation, carefully revised by Samuel Summer (New York: I. M. Alter, 1934). Printed on both the Hebrew and English Title pages is "Made in Austria," which is overstamped with "Made in Germany."

25. Mark Slobin, *Chosen Voices: The Story of the American Cantorate* (Urbana and Chicago: University of Illinois, 2002), 207.

26. Ibid.

27. E.g., BT *B'rachot* 28a, BT *Yoma* 20b.

The *Untaneh Tokef* Prayer—
Sealing Our Faith, Not Our Fate

Y. Lindsey bat Joseph

וּנְתַנֶּה תֹּקֶף קְדוּשַׁת הַיּוֹם . . .

Let us proclaim the sacred power of this day; it is awesome and
  full of dread . . .
On Rosh HaShanah it is written, on Yom Kippur it is sealed;
How many shall pass on, how many shall come to be;
Who shall live and who shall die;
Who shall see ripe age and who shall not;
Who shall perish by fire and who by water;
Who by sword and who by beast;
Who by hunger and who by thirst;
Who by earthquake and who by plague;
Who by strangling and who by stoning;
Who shall be secure and who shall be driven;
Who shall be tranquil and who shall be troubled;
Who shall be poor and who shall be rich;
Who shall be humbled and who exalted.
But repentance, prayer and charity temper judgment's decree.[1]

In the *Untaneh Tokef* prayer we are confronted with the classic *Yamim Noraim* theme of the Holy One sitting in judgment and sealing
the fate of every soul for the coming year, which seems at odds
with our contemporary worldview. We often tell our congregants
to read the prayer metaphorically, but without providing a metaphorical framework, that advice seems to be little more than code
for "don't read it literally." And if we are not going to read and

RABBI Y. LINDSEY BAT JOSEPH (C96) is the director of the Sol Mark Centre for
Jewish Excellence, an outreach program to unaffiliated Jews in Western Canada. She has been involved with small Jewish communities in various locations
throughout British Columbia as well as teaching and studying in the Greater Van-
couver Region. She has been awarded the Alberta Centennial Medal for community service and was a contributing writer to the Jewish Lights' *Women's Haftarah
Commentary*

Y. LINDSEY BAT JOSEPH

understand it literally, then how do we understand it? Can this prayer speak to our contemporary circumstances and sensibilities?

The God of the "Big Bang" and of particle physics is an impersonal God; the God of the *machzor* and the Torah is not. We seldom think of God as being intimately involved with our day-to-day lives the way our ancestors did, and many doubt whether the God of our science-based worldview is the author of human history either. In this article I examine the *Untaneh Tokef* prayer within its historical context and that of the *Yamim Noraim* prayer services and consider the question of whether or not this prayer belongs in a modern *machzor.* In recasting the poem within the context of contemporary philosophical debate and emerging physical science, I argue that the seeming discordance between the text and our contemporary worldview is not as pronounced as it first appears. Lastly, I offer a new approach to interpreting this text that can, perhaps, speak more appropriately to our experience and our lives.

Untaneh Tokef in its Historical and Liturgical Context

According to tradition, the *Untaneh Tokef* prayer was written by Rabbi Amnon of Mainz, Germany, in the eleventh century. Documentary evidence, however, establishes that this poem was most likely composed in Israel at least five hundred years prior to the time of R. Amnon.[2] Moreover there are Italian liturgical traditions that allude to this poem well before the time of R. Amnon. Nevertheless, for us the prayer is tied to the story of his martyrdom, which is known primarily from the account preserved in the *Or Zarua* (thirteenth century) by Rabbi Isaac of Vienna.[3] R. Isaac's account cites an earlier chronicle by Rabbi Ephraim of Bonn.[4]

The standard versions of this tale, which are often found in the commentary of traditional *machzorim,* describe R. Amnon of Mainz as an affluent and respected Jew who was being pressured by the local bishop to convert to Christianity. At one point, the rabbi tries to forestall the badgering by requesting three days to meditate upon the question. Subsequently the rabbi feels terribly grieved for even hinting that he might seriously consider abandoning Judaism and he fails to show up for his appointment with the bishop. His failure to appear before the bishop was punished by having his hands and legs amputated, joint by joint. At various stages during this torture, he is again asked if he would be willing to convert, but

THE *UNTANEH TOKEF* PRAYER—SEALING OUR FAITH, NOT OUR FATE

the rabbi declines. Then the bishop orders that he and his amputated body parts be carried home.[5]

Rosh HaShanah arrived a few days later and R. Amnon asked to be placed on the bimah of the synagogue, along with his dismembered limbs, prior to the chanting of the *K'dushah* of the *Musaf* Service. As the story goes, R. Amnon recited the *Untaneh Tokef* and then died. The legend continues three days after his death when he reportedly appeared in a dream to Rabbi Kalonymos ben Meshullam, to whom he taught the text of the *Untaneh Tokef* and asked him to send it throughout the Jewish world.

The harsh and complex realities of Jewish medieval life are the backdrop of this story of suffering and sacrifice. Its portrayal of the strained relations between Jews and the non-Jewish dominant culture (in this case medieval Christianity) that culminates in martyrdom is a story that was often repeated in Jewish history, from the days of Babylonian and Roman emperors to Christian and Muslim medieval Europe, to the brutality of the Shoah. It is hardly surprising that it resonated so strongly with our ancestors or with the generation that survived the concentration camps. These were the generations who lived firsthand the horrors of oppression. In addition to recalling R. Amnon within the context of the *Untaneh Tokef* recitation, their stories, along with those of martyrs from the Rabbinic Era, are woven into the Yom Kippur *Minchah* liturgy as part of a remembrance of Jewish martyrs throughout our history.[6]

Within the context of his own personal tragedy, R. Amnon's actions constituted a supreme statement of surrender to divine justice—a justice that is as enigmatic as it is unpredictable. By reciting the poem as a prelude to the *K'dushah*, the central theme of which is God's holiness, R. Amnon transformed the meaning of the *K'dushah* from a prophetic vision of an angelic declaration of God's holiness to a meditation on the human sanctification of God's Name that is measured by our willingness to suffer martyrdom for the sake of our faith.[7]

However, these are the contexts that seem to resonate poorly with many contemporary Jews. Sixty years plus after the establishment of the modern State of Israel, we are hesitant to see ourselves as victims. We are *victors* who have survived the vicissitudes of Jewish history and continue to struggle for Judaism and for Israel. Even though today that struggle still sometimes results in death, we resist seeing ourselves as victims and martyrs—we are much more comfortable with that being part of our past.

Free Will, Determinism, and Contemporary Physics

The *Untaneh Tokef* reminds us that our ultimate destiny does not lie entirely in our own hands. The future is not something we can contemplate with absolute certainty, but as I noted at the beginning of this discussion, this is not out of step with our contemporary science-based understanding of the world. For centuries philosophers and theologians alike have debated the notions of free will, determinism, and human fate. In the determinist worldview, whatever we do depends on our choices, decisions, and wants, and that whatever those choices may be they were determined by the circumstances that preceded them. Determinism does not claim that we can predict what will happen in the future—there are too many unknown factors involved and, unlike God, we can never have perfect knowledge of all the conditions that lead up to a given decision—but there are laws of nature and everything that happens in the world is governed by those laws, in accordance with which the circumstances before any action will determine its outcome and rule out any other possibility. In other words, all our choices are inevitable and free will is a myth.[8]

Critics of determinism question how it is possible to be held morally accountable for our actions if we are not ultimately responsible for our choices. If everything is determined, then morality doesn't seem to be possible and yet we do want to hold one another accountable for our actions. Those who argue in favor of free will often cite the unpredictable nature of particles at the quantum level as proof that the world is not quite as determined as some might suppose. However, our rapidly evolving understanding of physics only adds more complexity to the debate about the nature of human existence and the possibility or impossibility of free will. On the one hand, much of what goes on at the quantum level is indeterminate. It is largely unpredictable, which would suggest a certain amount of freedom in the universe. On the other hand, our empirical observations of the physical world is that it is filled with objects and systems that seem, for all practical purposes, to be quite deterministic, which suggests a certain lack of freedom. Compatibilists argue that it is possible to have free will in a largely

THE *UNTANEH TOKEF* PRAYER—SEALING OUR FAITH, NOT OUR FATE

deterministic universe, which would make moral accountability still possible.[9] Philosophically, this claim is not without its difficulties and yet, as our emerging new physics clearly demonstrates, despite the randomness of quantum particles and the predictability of the macro (physical) world, the two levels manage to coexist. So perhaps the entire universe is "compatibilist."

Free Will, Jewish Tradition, and Human Suffering

The intersection between free will and determinism occurs early in Jewish tradition. In the story of the expulsion from Eden, the chain of events that leads to humanity's exile from paradise begins with the Tree of Knowledge being placed in the middle of the Garden and the divine admonition to Adam and Eve that they should not eat from it. In some ways, it seems a foregone conclusion that that is precisely what they are "destined" to do. In a state of innocence where we do not know the difference between good and bad, good and bad technically do not exist. It is not until we acquire the capacity for moral discrimination that humanity becomes capable of committing sin. Without the capacity to commit sin, there would be no need for the mitzvot. So, while on the "quantum level" Adam and Eve choose to disobey and eat the fruit, on the "macro level" of the physical world this all seems to be part of a grander plan that God has set into place.[10]

In *Parashat Nitzavim*, a portion of which is read in Reform synagogues on Yom Kippur, the notion of choice is affirmed for Israel: "I have set before you life or death, blessing or curse; choose life, therefore, that you and your descendants may live" (Deut. 30:19).[11] There is always the possibility that one could reject entirely the inheritance from our ancestors, indeed the medieval commentator Isaac Abarbanel considered this very question but asserted that Israel would not and could not ever do such a thing. Our history has demonstrated that we continue to choose to cling to the covenant.[12] And it is to the future that this revelation is also directed. When God addresses the entire nation of Israel, the covenant is made "not with you alone, but with those who are standing here with us this day before the Eternal our God and with those who are not with us here this day" (Deut. 30:13–14).[13] The covenant is extended to future generations, which makes sense in terms of guaranteeing the continuity of Torah, but there is a philosophical/

Y. LINDSEY BAT JOSEPH

theological component in this unfolding drama. As Rabbi Plaut explains: "That the present can and does commit the future to some extent is unquestionable. We are who we are because of our ancestors and their achievements and failures."[14] On the personal or quantum level, each of us, individually, decides how we connect with the covenant and our obligation to follow the mitzvot, but at the macro level, we, as a people, are bound by the decisions and actions of our ancestors; so in some sense our choices are also already determined.

Returning to the legend of R. Amnon, we can see more than a meditation on human suffering through the lens of martyrdom and the seemingly capricious nature of divine judgment. The *Untaneh Tokef* is the nexus where the notions of free will and determinism and the personal versus the impersonal God come together. Like R. Amnon and our ancestors, many of us crave the intimacy of a relationship with a personal God, but at times we feel that the separation between us and God is a chasm that cannot be bridged. God and divine judgment remain inscrutable, our future remains hidden, yet it remains within our power to choose. Recall that R. Amnon's spiritual crisis was of his own making. He is wracked by guilt for having given the impression that he would even consider abandoning his faith—that is the sin for which he seeks to make *t'shuvah* at Rosh HaShanah. His treatment at the hands of the bishop is the result of his actions. Recast in this light, his recitation of the *Untaneh Tokef* can be understood as an acknowledgment of his moral failings, his acceptance of responsibility for them, and a reaffirmation of the faith to which he was bound by the choices of our ancestors. His death may be understood as inevitable given the nature of his injuries, or it may be interpreted as an act of divine mercy that relieves him from both his spiritual suffering and his physical pain, but the rabbi's anguished spiritual struggle for redemption and forgiveness mirrors our own.

The *Untaneh Tokef* in the Twenty-First Century and Beyond

I noted above that reading a text metaphorically without understanding or knowing the metaphorical framework is ultimately self-defeating. It leaves the text devoid of meaning. Similarly to simply advise worshipers to not take it literally doesn't offer much theologically or spiritually unless we also provide another way

THE *UNTANEH TOKEF* PRAYER—SEALING OUR FAITH, NOT OUR FATE

of understanding the text. I believe it is possible to employ the traditional imagery of the *Yamim Noraim*—that of God taking an account of every soul within God's dominion, passing judgment, and sealing that judgment in the Book of Life—and reinterpret it in such a way that the original beauty of the text need not be sacrificed to bring it into accord with our contemporary sensibilities.

First, an anecdote that provides the background for my rethinking of this prayer: The day after Yom Kippur, 1998, my eldest daughter was hit by a car on her way to school.[15] In the immediate aftermath of the accident, the *Untaneh Tokef* prayer came back to me in a most haunting way, not because I took it literally, but because it was clearly troubling so many of those around me. As congregants poured into the hospital to offer support, I repeatedly heard the refrain, "the day after Yom Kippur, the day after Yom Kippur!" I couldn't think much about it then, but I knew that ultimately I would have to find a way to reconcile "on Rosh HaShanah it is written, on Yom Kippur it is sealed" and the fact that this accident happened *the day after Yom Kippur*! I had a full year to reflect on the words of this prayer and on the following Yom Kippur I was finally able to articulate how I understand it in light of my life's experiences and my theology.

The *Untaneh Tokef* poem enumerates various tragedies that can befall us, none of which are strictly limited to bygone days. There are a myriad of reasons why people live and die and why some seem to lead charmed lives while others struggle daily just to survive. To lay the blame for all of this squarely at God's feet is a very simplistic, counterintuitive theology that is ultimately devoid of meaning for most of us. While some things are clearly beyond our control, the fact of our lives is that we make choices every day and those choices affect others as well as ourselves. It behooves us, then, to be diligent in our decisions. Whether we choose to provide funding for education, health care, and other social services, or cut it back; whether we choose to protect the environment or only exploit it; whether we choose to drive too fast or too recklessly or choose to obey the rules of the road; whether we drink too much or indulge in illicit drug use or choose a life of sobriety; whether we choose to respond quickly to natural disasters or not; whether we choose to wage war or not—with all these choices we affect our lives and the lives of potentially many others. That is the intersection of both the micro and macro worlds—individual

Y. LINDSEY BAT JOSEPH

choices affect the larger, overall picture for everyone. This is the case whether we envision a personal God or not.

This raises the question of whether or not there is a role for God in all of this. I believe so. Returning to the traditional imagery of God and the Book of Life, the liturgy describes God as writing and sealing the events of our lives, but if we are the ones making the choices, then what is it that God "writes and seals"? The only rational answer, for me, is that God seals the outcomes of our choices. If we approach Rosh HaShanah with the notion of the Book of Life being opened up and turned to a new page for the new year, then God is placing the pen *in our hands*. We write on the pages and God seals the outcomes—some immediate, some long term; some good, some bad, and some neutral—of *our* decisions. That is the blessing and curse of having the right to choose. The question to ask as we look forward is: What will we write? Will we write pages of kindness, of love, of reconciliation with each other and with God? Or, will we write pages of cruelty, neglect, hatred, and ignorance?

The *Untaneh Tokef* is a stark reminder that we cannot control everything that happens to us and sometimes the choices we make lead to completely unanticipated consequences. The legend of R. Amnon and the other martyrs recalled on Yom Kippur remind us that what we can control is how we handle the challenges and tragedies that befall us. We should, therefore, strive to make the best choices we can in thos situations where we do have a measure of freedom and control over the outcome so that when Yom Kippur concludes, we will hand the pen back to God to close the book, and seal ourselves for blessing rather than sorrow.

לשנה טובה וגמר חתימה טובה

Notes

1. Chaim Stern, ed., *Gates of Repentance*, rev. ed. (New York: CCAR, 1996), 107–9.
2. Eliezer Segal, "Legend and Liturgy: the Elusive Tale of the Unatanneh Tokef," *The Jewish Free Press* (Calgary), September 29, 2005, 26, http:// people.ucalgary.ca/~elsegal/Shokel/050929_RabbiAmnon. html.
3. According to Segal there is also some scholarly debate as to whether or not R. Amnon actually existed.

THE *UNTANEH TOKEF* PRAYER—SEALING OUR FAITH, NOT OUR FATE

4. A reference to this story appears in the prelude to the recitation of *Untaneh Tokef* in the Rosh HaShanah *Shacharit* Service in *Gates of Repentance*, 106.

5. Noson Scherman, *The Complete Artscroll Machzor for Yom Kippur, Nusach Sefard*, ed. Meir Zlotowitz and Avie Gold (New York: Mesorah Publications, 1986), 560.

6. See the *"Eleh Ezkerah"* section of the Yom Kippur *Minchah* Service in *Gates of Repentance*, 429–449; especially the section beginning on page 432, which recalls the Ten Martyrs from the time of Emperor Hadrian.

7. Segal, "Legend and Liturgy."

8. See John Hospers, "What Means This Freedom," in *Determinism and Freedom in the Age of Modern Science*, ed. Sidney Hook (New York: Collier, 1961); Thomas Nagel, *What Does It All Mean?* (New York: Oxford University Press, 1987).

9. See W. T. Stace, *Religion and the Modern Mind* (New York: Harper-Collins, 1952); Harry Frankfurt, "Freedom of the Will and the Concept of a Person," *Journal of Philosophy* 68, no. 1 (January 14, 1971): 5–20. Both of these philosophers view psychological states as the locus of freedom of the will, although they both acknowledge there are constraints on that will.

10. W. Gunther Plaut, ed., "Expulsion from Eden," *The Torah: A Modern Commentary*, rev. ed. (New York: URJ Press, 2005), 37–39.

11. *Gates of Repentance*, 345.

12. Plaut, "Commitment for the Future" in *The Torah: A Modern Commentary*, 1378.

13. Plaut, *The Torah: A Modern Commentary*.

14. Plaut, "Commitment for the Future."

15. My daughter made a full recovery and has grown into a beautiful independent woman in her own right who has also brought another generation of Jews into the world.

Viewing *Untaneh Tokef* through a New Lens

Amy Scheinerman

Let us now relate the power of this day's holiness . . . Behold, it is the Day of Judgment . . . Who will live and who will die, who will die at his predestined time and who before his time?

These words from *Untaneh Tokef* danced hauntingly through my mind twenty-two years ago, just at the time Jews in synagogues all around me were chanting *Kol Nidrei*. Tears welled in my eyes. The surgeon looked down at me and said, "You will be alright." I fell into anaesthetized slumber.

I had started bleeding that morning. How would I fit in an un-scheduled trip to the OB/GYN the morning before Yom Kippur? But the doctor said: "You have an ectopic pregnancy. You have one hour to get to the hospital." By the time I was wheeled into the operating room, the sun was dipping below the horizon. At a time when I sought comfort, the Yom Kippur liturgy delivered cold judgment. In the place of assurance, it delivered guilt. Or so it seemed. I had not yet found a theological fit that permitted me to understand *Untaneh Tokef* as anything more than an artifact of an ancient theology to which I didn't subscribe.

The tears that spilled out in the operating room were not for me or for my husband; we were exceedingly blessed to already have three healthy children. I knew my children, who had been cam-paigning for another sibling, would be sorely disappointed, but we would try again. My tears were not for them either. My tears were for all the people who suffer real tragedies, far greater losses, genuine adversity and calamity, and come to synagogue on the High Holy Days to hear *Untaneh Tokef* tell them that their suffering is God's just judgment.

RABBI AMY SCHEINERMAN (NY84) does Jewish hospice, chaplaincy, teaching, writing, and public speaking. She is president of the Baltimore Board of Rabbis and the Greater Carolinas Association of Rabbis.

VIEWING *UNTANEH TOKEF* THROUGH A NEW LENS

Untaneh Tokef paints a picture of God as a Being who controls and manages the world, abrogates the laws of physics, and determines the length and quality of our lives. It is far from the only prayer that reflects a theology of judgment and retribution; it is merely the most graphic.

In *The Foreskin's Lament*, Shalom Auslander, who grew up in Monsey, New York, writes:

> When I was a child my parents and teachers told me about a man who was very strong. They told me he could destroy the whole world. They told me he could lift mountains. They told me he could part the sea. It was important to keep the man happy. When we obeyed what the man had commanded, the man liked us. But when we didn't obey what he had commanded, he didn't like us. He hated us. Some days he hated us so much, he killed us; other days, he let other people kill us . . . We called these days "holidays" . . . The people of Monsey were terrified of God, and they taught me to be terrified of Him, too . . . And so, in early autumn, when the leaves choked, turned colors, and fell to their deaths, the people of Monsey gathered together in synagogues across the town and wondered aloud and in unison, how God was going to kill them:—Who will live and who will die, they prayed—who at his predestined time and who before his time, who by water and who by fire, who by sword, who by beast, who by famine, who by thirst, who by storm, who by plague, who by strangulation and who by stoning.

Auslander describes how this theology can shape the soul of a child and instill fear and guilt. In fact, it eventually drove him out of Monsey, and far from his family of origin. Those of us raised in far different Jewish communities, if we had any Jewish education growing up, were probably exposed to a similar theology: God is omnipotent and omniscient, controlling and commanding. God loves and rewards, to be sure, but also becomes enraged and punishes. Auslander missed the loving and rewarding side of God and absorbed only the angry and punishing messages. On the High Holy Days, with *Untaneh Tokef* taking liturgical center stage, we might too.

Structurally, *Untaneh Tokef* is comprised of three parts:

1. The prayer opens with the assertion that each year we all stand trial for our deeds and failures to act in the past year. Will we be judged worthy to live another year, or will we be

AMY SCHEINERMAN

found to lack merit? In the courtroom on high, so much is at stake that even the heavenly angels are gripped by fear and trembling. God, the cosmic Shepherd, herds us all before the divine throne for review; not a single one of us can escape judgment. God is Judge, Prosecutor, Witness, and Jury. (But aren't shepherds supposed to protect, not judge? And in what sense is a court where Judge, Prosecutor, Witness, and Jury are all the same "just?")

Then the terrifying litany begins: "How many shall leave this world and how many shall be born into it, who shall live and who shall die, who shall live out the limit of his days and who shall not, who shall perish by fire and who by water, who by sword and who by beast, who by hunger and who by thirst. . . ." Were this prayer being penned today, perhaps it would say, "Who by Hurricane Katrina or the Indian Ocean earthquake, tsunami, and floods? Who at the hands of terrorists in Israel or Mumbai? Who by violent car crashes on our highways? Who by brain cancer? Who by heart disease? Who by depression that drives them to suicide?"

The prayer continues: "Who shall rest and who shall wander, who shall be at peace and who shall be tormented, who shall be poor and who shall be rich, who shall be humbled and who shall be exalted?" Perhaps our twenty-first-century version might say, "Who will enjoy job security and who will be unexpectedly unemployed mid-career? Who will prosper and who will watch the bottom drop out of their 401(k)? Who will retain peace of mind, and who will suffer unending anxiety?"

2. The climax and turning point comes when we say, "*U't'shuvah u't'filah u'tzedakah maavirin et roa hag'zeirah*" ("repentance, prayer, and righteousness temper the severity of the decree"). In the ancient world, royal decrees were irrevocable. King Ahasuerus cannot retract the decree Haman issues with his imprimatur authorizing the wholesale slaughter of the Jews of Persia; at best he can issue an additional decree permitting the Jews to defend themselves. Given this understanding, what does it mean that we can *temper* the divine decree?

3. *Untaneh Tokef* finishes with the assertion that God does not want to slam a guilty verdict down on us and consign us to the rubbish heap of history. God wants us to repent and

VIEWING *UNTANEH TOKEF* THROUGH A NEW LENS

merit life. Yet the rock bottom reality is that we are ephemeral, mortal creatures. However long our lives, they are limited because we are like "fragile clay vessels, withering grass, fading flowers, passing shadows, fleeting clouds, vanishing dreams." God, in contrast, is boundless, timeless, and eternal. So the best we can do is to attach ourselves to God and ride God's coattails into eternity.

Untaneh Tokef takes us on the yearly trip into the Forest of Frustration and Confusion. If God is both omnibenevolent and omnipotent, why is there such evil in the world? Why doesn't God prevent it? And if God is omniscient and omnipotent, in what sense can we say that God is good? Suffering is not reserved only for those who are "deserving." What is more, living in the twenty-first century, we are grounded in science: the laws of physics, biological processes of disease, and consequences of human choice. *Untaneh Tokef*, long a theological conundrum, strikes the twenty-first-century mind steeped in science and rationalism minimally as straining credulity, generally as archaic and meaningless, and maximally as cruel and sadistic.[1]

What if we read the prayer not through the lens of rabbinic theology, but through the lens of process thought, as a process theology? Process theology is built on the foundation of Alfred North Whitehead's Process-Relationship Philosophy.[2] Alfred North Whitehead was a British mathematician and philosopher. After finishing *Principia Mathematica*, he turned to philosophy, seeking a cogent and comprehensive philosophy based on the one thing we know to be real: our experience. In the last analysis, it is all we "know." Whitehead sought to formulate a philosophical framework that is not at odds with science and, in particular, the revolutionary new ideas emerging from quantum theory about the nature of the universe and matter and their implications for human perception and experience. In a sense, Whitehead crafted a metaphysics of quantum physics. Whitehead believed that philosophy, and by extension theology, should work in concert with the discoveries of science to explain our universe and help us make meaning of our lives. Even more, he believed that his philosophical framework should be able to accommodate future scientific discoveries and "truths" without having to wholly revamp its notion of God and human existence.

AMY SCHEINERMAN

The terms "process theology" or "process relational theology" first came into usage in 1950s in the Protestant world. They emerged from a debate between "Biblical-religious" thinkers and philosophical theologians. The former emphasized that the God of the Bible interacts with his creatures. The latter held that God is unchanging, absolute, and unconditioned, and hence unaffected by the universe. Whitehead, along with Charles Hartshorne, a theologian from the University of Chicago, sought a third way. Classical medieval theology, taking its cue from ancient Greece, saw the world as composed of forms and substances. Under the influence of quantum mechanics, Whitehead and Hartshorne described the world as composed of *events* and *processes*: occasions of experience. Our lives are a composite of experiences; when strung together we see that our lives are not static, but rather processes. We are not "beings," which are static and unchanging, but rather "becomings," continuously changing and evolving.

Process theology is panentheism: The world is in God, and God is in everything in the world. As *B'reishit Rabbah* 68:9, commenting on Psalm 90:1, expresses it: "God is the dwelling place of the world, but the world is not God's dwelling place." Put another way: Everything in the universe is part of the "body" of God, but God is also beyond the universe. God saturates and interpenetrates every part of the natural universe. God is the sum total of all of our experiences, and the experiences of the entire universe, but God is also beyond the universe.[3] God, who encompasses the entire universe, experiences all that we experience, including our pain and suffering. When we suffer, God suffers. This is not a God who judges and metes out punishment; this is God suffering with us, sharing our pain. *This* is the God I needed to meet in the operating room that Yom Kippur eve; this is the God I need in my life.

With this in mind, imagine for a moment that God is not as Shalom Auslander was taught: not a powerful, commanding, coercive, punishing Being who waits for us to slip up. Imagine that God is not a being at all, but rather that everything is contained within God and God is also beyond the universe. God is not immutable, unchanging, and wholly separate from our world but rather continuously changing and becoming because the universe is always in flux, always changing. God is as near and as intimate as our breath, our cells, the DNA that animates us and makes us who we are, the divine spark in each of us that makes us little lower than

VIEWING *UNTANEH TOKEF* THROUGH A NEW LENS

the angels. We, who are saturated with God are the hands, feet, eyes, ears, and mouths of God: We are the body of God. God cannot be omnipotent, because then we would be utterly powerless. God is not omniscient, knowing what we will choose before we decide, because then we would not have free will. Rather, God is the ethical lure that draws us to make the right choices, but does not force or coerce our choices. God is present at every decision and offers us the best choice, but we are completely free to decide. Because God is *within* us, as well as *beyond* us, God changes because we change. Perhaps it might help to think of God as the cosmic mind of the universe—always in flux, dynamic, rippling, changing. God knows each of us as we are—every decision we have made and how it is affecting the universe—but does not direct, control, reward, or punish. It is we who place that layer of interpretation on our experience of the world and ascribe it to God.

For the process theologian, rather than seeking to direct, control, reward, or punish us, God seeks to engage with us and empower us to align our lives with God and recognize the unity of all being and our place in the universe.

Through this lens, *Untaneh Tokef* conveys a wholly different message. It is not about judgment, condemnation, and punishment, as Shalom Auslander hears it. Rather:

1. *Untaneh Tokef* reflects the frightening and stark reality that our lives are finite may end prematurely. Our ancestors imagined that there is a God separate from the universe who is in charge. For a process theologian, the universe is in God, and only in that sense does God bring floods, earthquakes, and disease: They are part of the natural world. In the words of science fiction writer Robert Heinlein, "The supreme irony of life is that hardly anyone gets out of it alive."[4] But it is more than the knowledge of our mortality that haunts us. Novelist and essayist Joan Didion watched her husband die of a heart attack one evening at dinner. In her memoir of the year following his sudden and tragic death, *A Year of Magical Thinking*, she wrote, "Life changes fast. Life changes in the instant. You sit down to dinner and life as you know it ends."[5] Even if our lives do not end in sudden violence or illness, they will end because we are by nature, "like withering grass, a fading flower, a passing shadow, a fugitive cloud. . . . " It is only

AMY SCHEINERMAN

when we stand in the stark, blinding light of our mortality that we can fully appreciate the immeasurable, incalculable *value* of our own lives. When we come to that realization—as Rosh HaShanah invites us to stop and do each year—we are faced with questions, the very asking of which can open doors to immense change for the better: **What am I doing with my life? How am I using my time? How am I spending my love? This is the power of** *Untaneh Tokef.*

2. *Sefer HaZichronot* (the Book of Remembrance) is indeed written with our deeds. It is the totality of our universe—all that has ever been and all that is. Our decisions and actions have had their effect on the world, and in that sense *Sefer HaZichronot* is signed and sealed with our deeds. *Untaneh Tokef* reminds us—at the moment we feel *most* vulnerable and powerless, and perhaps even inconsequential—that we have *genuine power.* We cannot change the fact of mortality and we cannot always avoid misfortune. But we can *temper its severity.* Consider our effect on the environment and how we have changed the landscape of our world. Consider how our decisions, individually, and nationally, affect the lives of people suffering in our backyard and around the world. Consider how your behavior—your attitude, your mood, your willingness to give and receive love—affects those nearest you on a day-by-day basis. *Untaneh Tokef* **reminds us that we have real and meaningful power and must therefore use it with caution and in the cause of good. This is the power of** *Untaneh Tokef.*

3. *U't'shuvah u't'filah u'tzedakah maavirin et roa hag'zeirah* ("repentance, prayer, and righteousness temper the severity of the decree") is the climactic statement and turning point of the prayer. As *Untaneh Tokef* is the lynchpin of the High Holy Day liturgy, *u't'shuvah, u't'filah u'tzedakah* is the lynchpin of *Untaneh Tokef.* While it may be the case that King Ahasuerus's decree is immutable, in God's real universe the future does not exist because it hasn't happened yet. The laws of nature limit the possibilities, and the past suggests probabilities, but we are not automatons responding to innate programming. We are more than our biology, more than massively complex chemical factories. We are not slaves to our instincts. We are endowed with free will, a divine spark, and the capacity to

VIEWING *UNTANEH TOKEF* THROUGH A NEW LENS

cultivate our thoughts, choose our words, and make moral choices: Repentance is about our thoughts and intentions. Prayer is about our words. *Tzedakah* is about our deeds. Repentance, prayer, and righteousness are the avenues by which we exert our constructive will and influence on the world. They are how we *"maavirin et roa hag'zeirah,"* how we influence the direction of our lives and the life of the world. Where there is choice, there is hope and possibility. At every moment, God meets us and offers us a moral choice and the freedom to choose. **Untaneh Tokef reminds us to use our freedom purposefully, carefully, and deliberately. This is the power of Untaneh Tokef.**

Untaneh Tokef reminds us where our immortality lies. Not in biology, but in having lived, learned, loved, and left our footprint on this world. Everything we do brings change to the world—and to God. Everything we do sends ripples out into the universe that continue to be felt by others—and by God. We are part of the cosmic mind of the universe, forever part of God. Therein lies our immortality, and it is indeed meaningful. As *Untaneh Tokef* expresses it: "Your years have no limit. Your days have no end. Your mysterious name is beyond explanation. . . . And You have linked our name with Yours."

Interpreted through a process theology lens, *Untaneh Tokef* is deeply comforting. Rather than imparting an ancient warning from a coercive, commanding, punishing God, it says: While there is much that is entirely beyond my control, and mortality is a reality I must face, I am not powerless: vulnerable yes, powerless no. The facts are the facts, but how I *respond* to them is entirely up to me. In every moment, with every breath, I have the opportunity to make choices that nurture life and cause goodness and righteousness to flow into the world. *Untaneh Tokef* is a reality check that empowers us to live our lives with greater integrity and courage. What better message to hear on the High Holy Days?

Viktor Frankl was a neurologist and psychiatrist in Vienna when Hitler came to power. In 1942 he was deported to Theresienstadt along with his wife and parents. In Theresienstadt, Frankl treated both the medical and psychological needs of inmates overcome with shock and grief. He worked alongside Rabbis Leo Baeck and Regina Jonas. Frankl's wife was transferred to Bergen-Belsen and

AMY SCHEINERMAN

his parents were sent to Auschwitz. All three perished. Frankl survived the war, and from his experiences and observations he crafted the psychological theory of Logotherapy. In his pioneering book, *Man's Search for Meaning*, published in 1946, Frankl wrote, "We who lived in concentration camps can remember the men who walked through the huts comforting others, giving away their last piece of bread. They may have been few in number, but they offer sufficient proof that everything can be taken from a man but one thing: the last of the human freedoms—to choose one's attitude in any given set of circumstances, to choose one's own way."[6]

Untaneh Tokef reminds us, when we feel powerless in the face of our mortality, that we have enormous strength: First, an inner power to ascribe meaning to our experiences and to decide for ourselves the purpose of our lives. Second, moral power to take charge of our lives and respond to the ethical lure God holds out to us by making the right choices. And third, a power that comes from knowing that as we do, we are changing the world and leaving our mark on it for all time. *U'sh'meinu karata vish'mecha.* (You have linked our name with Yours.)

Notes

1. The inverse problem also exists. Those for whom God is altogether absent resonate to the words of the Psalmist in the psalm of repentance recited from Rosh Chodesh Elul through Sh'mini Atzeret: *"Et panecha Adonai avakeish. Al tasteir panecha mimeni."* (O Lord I seek You. Do not hide from me.) (Ps. 27:9).

2. An excellent introduction to process theology was published in these pages last year, authored by Rabbi Toba Spitzer: "Why We Need Process Theology," *CCAR Journal* (Winter 2012): 84–95.

3. Process theologians describe that differently. For some, it is *existence* itself: the very possibility of existence (which we usually take for granted). Ralph Waldo Emerson spoke of the Oversoul. Alfred North Whitehead himself described God as the Ultimate Source of possibility and potentiality in the universe. Torah describes God as *"Ehyeh-Asher-Ehyeh"* (I will become what I will become) (Exod. 3:14)—God is also becoming.

4. Robert A. Heinlein , *Job: A Comedy of Justice* (New York: Ballantine Books, 1984), 93.

5. Joan Didion, *A Year of Magical Thinking* (New York: Alfred A. Knopf, 2006), 3.

6. Viktor Frankl, *Man's Search for Meaning* (Boston: Beacon Press, 2006), 65–66.

Mystical Journeys and Magical Letters: The *Y'rushalmi's* Cosmology in the *Machzor*

Judith Z. Abrams

So much of Judaism is clearly put together by contentious committees that it can be difficult to discern any coherent theology underlying it all. For example, our calendar is clearly a compromise between the solar and lunar factions, which led to the unwieldy nineteen-year, solar-lunar cycle we have today. Such negotiations, and their results, can be seen throughout our texts and traditions, including our prayer book and *machzor*. Both are pastiches of different schools of worship, and to understand them we must untangle the interwoven "genetic" strands so that we can see what different groups of Jews contributed to our worship. Then we can consider what is important to us and emphasize those elements.

Of course, we have at least two schools duking it out: the scribes and the priests. The scribes' voice is heard in the recitation of the *Sh'ma* and Its Blessings with the "choreographical" element of wearing *t'fillin*. If you think about it, there is nothing terribly prayerful about the recitation of the *Sh'ma* itself unless it is simply to proclaim one's love of the text.

The priests managed to get their prayer in as well: the *Amidah*, which replaces the sacrifices and gives almost no airtime to the scribes. Once we are into the body of the weekday *Amidah* and we pass the personal petitions, we have a step-by-step plan of action for the restoration of the Temple cult: God will return, punish the wicked, reward the righteous, and rebuild Jerusalem and the Temple and the sacrifices—normal, thanksgiving, and peace offerings—will begin again. (It is telling that in the *Y'rushalmi's* version of the weekday

RABBI JUDITH Z. ABRAMS, Ph.D. (C85) is founder of Maqom: A School for Adult Talmud Study (www.maqom.com) and is the author of many books and liturgies.

JUDITH Z. ABRAMS

Amidah [JT *B'rachot* 2:4], the House of David is not mentioned. Apparently the priests felt no great love for the political leaders that caused their business to crash.)

Now, if there are three crowns—the crowns of the priesthood, the Torah (scribes), and royalty (*Avot* 4:13)—where do we find the prayers of the kings in the prayer book? It seems unlikely that their voice would be silenced altogether. So where is it? It is in the prayers of *Heichalot* mysticism, created in the land of Israel between 70 and 500 C.E. Royalty is there; it's just changed its address. Earthly kings had failed the Jewish people too many times. Only God could be king. But a heavenly king must have a palace, guards, retinues, and court procedures, just as an earthly one did. To come before a king was a risky business on earth; all the more so, approaching one in heaven.

Let us imagine making a journey to meet our closest approximation to a king: the president. One doesn't simply knock on the White House door and say, "Yoo hoo, I'm here!" You have to make the journey to Washington, going through airport security, which might stop you from getting on your plane. Once in Washington, you'd have to petition your congressman or some other official to get you an audience with the president. You'd encounter roadblocks, inspections, and unhelpful guardians during that process. Then you'd have your background thoroughly checked by the Secret Service. There is a gatehouse before you can approach the White House. There is another guard inside who would wand you and there are further Secret Service agents ready to arrest you should you even sneeze incorrectly. There is an undersecretary who might block your approach to an actual secretary, who might block you before you get to an actual presidential aide, who might inform you that, unfortunately, the president is busy today and won't be able to see you and that you'll have to come back tomorrow. And if you actually met the president, you'd probably sing *Hallel* for actually having made it—or at least taken out your iphone and have your picture taken with the president to prove you'd actually visited the Oval Office. Afterward, you might jump up and down and grin, saying, "Wow! That was cool!" The prayers that embody this experience are the prayers of the *Heichalot* mystics, and they are part of our standard prayer service, too. In this essay, we'll explore parts of our weekly and High Holy Day prayers from this school.

MYSTICAL JOURNEYS AND MAGICAL LETTERS

Early Mysticism in the Land of Israel

When the Temple was destroyed, the place for our direct connection with God, our private line, so to speak, vanished. But the corresponding "telephone" still existed in the place it had always been—in heaven. The Sages of Israel sought to rebuild the connection to heaven, untethered to one physical location. That meant that the worshiper, instead of using the Temple's "direct line," would have to make the trip to meet God in heaven. But how could we go and visit God in heaven without staying there permanently? The journey would be almost unimaginably long and arduous and we would have no guarantee of a safe return to our world. So the Sages outlined the journey, and its dangers, by casting it as a trek through seven heavenly halls in early mystical works (70–500 C.E.) such as *Maaseh Merkavah* and *Heichalot Rabbati*.

Rhythmic Prayers and *Kaddish*

Prayers from these schools of worship have their own unique rhythms and rules of composition. So, for example, we learn that: "Second and third-person, imperfect hitpa'el verbs praising God are used as a form of opening for prayers . . . The accumulation of such verbs in series is . . . a feature of Heikhalot hymnology."[1]

Kaddish, of course, in all its permutations, would be the parade example of this sort of prayer. Each word, therefore, is a step up a steep ladder to meet God. Each set of steps (i.e., each new recitation of *Kaddish* throughout the service) signals us that we are moving higher and closer to God. This renders repetition of *Kaddish* meaningful instead of boring.[2] By the time we reach the Mourner's *Kaddish*, then, we are not only in God's presence, we are in the presence of our deceased relatives, who, presumably, are in heaven. (The video of Gershwin's "I'll Build a Stairway to Paradise" from *An American in Paris* can be an effective teaching tool here. As each stair lights up as he ascends, so each word of *Kaddish* is a step that leads us higher and higher.)

The rhythm of the *Kaddish* also can induce a meditative state, as can other *Heichalot* prayers that find voice in the *machzor*, for example, this acrostic:

Excellence and faithfulness—are His who lives forever.
Understanding and blessing—are His who lives forever.

JUDITH Z. ABRAMS

Grandeur and greatness—are His who lives forever.
Cognition and expression—are His who lives forever.
Magnificence and majesty—are His who lives forever.
Counsel and strength—are His who lives forever.
Luster and brilliance—are His who lives forever.
Grace and benevolence—are His who lives forever.
Purity and goodness—are His who lives forever.
Unity and honor—are His who lives forever.
Crown and glory—are His who lives forever.
Precept and practice—are His who lives forever.
Sovereignty and rule—are His who lives forever.
Adornment and permanence—are His who lives forever.
Mystery and wisdom—are His who lives forever.
Might and meekness—are His who lives forever.
Splendor and wonder—are His who lives forever.
Righteousness and honor—are His who lives forever.
Invocation and holiness—are His who lives forever.
Exultation and nobility—are His who lives forever.
Song and hymn—are His who lives forever.
Praise and glory—are His who lives forever.[3]

The rhythmic, repeated descriptions of God, as well as the acrostic form are forerunners to the *piyutim* that mark so much of the High Holy Day liturgy.

The King

While earthly kings come and go, and even dynasties arise and fade, God as King in the *Heichalot* literature is untethered to history. In this literature, we enter a realm outside of history, even fictional history. If we think of Israel at this time, this is logical. Human history for the Jews in Israel from 70 to 500 C.E. is tough at best and tragic at worst. The kings are Roman emperors who, unlike their Persian predecessors, do not allow the Temple to be rebuilt. It is no accident, then, that these mystics sought out a different sort of king.[4]

For the High Holy Days, prayers systematically draw attention to God as King; whether it be in the *K'dushah* (. . . *hamelech hakadosh*) or in *Avinu Malkeinu*, changes in the liturgy for the High Holy Days emphasize God's kingly aspect. This is another feature of *Heichalot* mysticism. "The repetition of the word *melekh,* 'King' followed by an adjective or noun as a construct pair forms the basis for several hymns found in Heikhalot literature, particularly in Heikhalot Rabbati."[5] Thus, whenever we refer to God as King in the *machzor*, we can direct worshipers to experience this as a step upward in their spiritual quest to come as close to God as possible.

Unfriendly Spirits

On the High Holy Days, our sins and merits are marshaled as prosecuting and defending witnesses against us or in our behalf. Our sins loom large as we see them assembled in full. God remembers, counts, and weighs all our sins, and they pile up to the heavens. When taken in their aggregate, they form threatening, monstrous obstacles to the gates of redemption. This sense of impending danger is the counterpoint to the *Heichalot*'s experience of ecstatic union with God and it, too, is given voice in the *machzor*. In *Heichalot* mysticism, obstacles guard the seven levels of heaven. For example, each gate into the palace is defended by eight guards:

> At the gate of the seventh palace, the guards stand angry and war-like, strong, harsh, fearful, terrifying, taller than mountains and sharper than peaks. Their bows are strung and stand before them . . . Their swords are sharpened and in their hands. Bolts of lightning flow and issue forth from the balls of their eyes, and balls of fire [issue] from their nostrils, and torches of fiery coals from their mouths. They are equipped with helmets and with coats of mail, and javelins and spears are hung from their arms. (*Pirkei Heichalot* 17:8)

These are "killer angels" in the most literal sense. They have all the violence that is the hallmark of the Big Bang. They may also be echoes of the guards that were likely to be in an earthly court, surrounding the king. (A visual aid here might be the Terra Cotta warriors guarding the king's tomb.)

It is no accident, then, that when the journeyer finally reaches the seventh heavenly hall, and stands before God's footstool, s/he says, "*Alai l'shabeiach la-Adon hakol.*" The origin of the *Aleinu* is this early mysticism and we place it at the end of our services not to signal that we're mopping up, but to signal final, ecstatic union with the Divine. And it is an individual achievement, not a team effort, in this liturgy.

JUDITH Z. ABRAMS

Counting as Mystical Practice

Another feature of this kind of mysticism is its penchant for counting as a way to comprehend God's vastness and one's own smallness. So, here, we see how long and dangerous the journey to heaven is:

> Rabbi Yishmael said: I asked Rabbi Akiba: What is the distance between one bridge and another? He said to me: Between one bridge and another [the distance] is 12,000 parsangs. At their ascent 12,000 myriad parsangs and their descent 12,000 parsangs.
> Between the rivers of fire and the rivers of awe 21,000 parsangs
> Between the rivers of awe and the rivers of fear are 22,000 parsangs.
> Between the rivers of hail and the rivers of darkness there are 36,000 parsangs.
> Between the chambers of thunder and the cloud of consolation there are 42,000 parsangs.
> Between the clouds of consolation and the Merkavah there are 84,000 parsangs.
> Between the cherubim and the Ofanim there are 24,000 parsangs.
> Between the Ofanim and the chamber of chambers there are 24 myriad parsangs.
> Between the chambers of chambers and the Holy Creatures there are 4,000,000 parsangs.
> Between one wing and another there are 12,000 parsangs, and such was their width.
> Between the Holy Camps and the Throne of Glory to the place where the Holy, high and exalted King, God of Israel is seated upon it there are 40,000 parsangs and his Great name is sanctified there. (*Maaseh Merkavah* para. 559, p. 234)[6]

The distance to the goal *increases*, rather than decreases, as the journey wears on. This is one of the counterintuitive truths of the spiritual quest: the more you learn, the less you know.

Counting and measuring all sorts of things is a feature of this school of mysticism. For example, Shiur Koma measures God's physical form. Obviously, the actual measurement of God is not the point; the point is contemplating numbers so large that they make us aware of our own Lilliputian dimensions.

The *K'dushah* as an Organizing Principle Underlying Services

Part of the liturgy that marks the seeker's progress through the heavenly halls is the *K'dushah*. The third blessing of the *Amidah* is

MYSTICAL JOURNEYS AND MAGICAL LETTERS

a simple form of the prayer that is recited during the silent saying of the *Amidah*. It is not automatically logical that it should change into the *K'dushah* in the *Amidah's* repetition. So why is it there? It is a post marker along "heaven's highway" through the seven heavenly halls. As you progress through the heavenly halls, the *K'dushah* is recited:

> In the first Hekhal, Merkavot of fire say: Holy, Holy, Holy is the Lord of Hosts, the whole earth is His glory and their flames spread out and gather together to the second Hekhal and say, "Holy, holy, holy . . ." (Maaseh Merkavah, 232)

The *K'dushah* is repeated in various ways until, in the seventh *heichal*, they say:

> Blessed be the King of Kings, Adonai, Lord of all power.
> Who is like God, great and enduring?
> His praise is in the heaven's heaven,
> The holiness of His Majesty in the highest heaven,
> His might is in the inner chambers,
> From this one, "holy" and from that one "holy"
> And they present song perpetually pronouncing the name . . .
> and say, "Blessed be the name of His majesty's Glory forever and ever from the place of His Shekhinah." (*Maaseh Merkavah*, 232–33)

If you think about the number of *K'dushahs* in a standard (non-Reform) Shabbat service you have a total of seven (including the *K'dushahs* in the *Amidahs* as repeated).[7] Thus, we see that the journey through the seven heavenly halls and the seven heavens underlies our liturgy.

Other Mystical Heroes and Democratizing Heaven

We are used to thinking of Rabbi Akiba as the mystical journeyer par excellence. However, the *Y'rushalmi* emphasizes Rabbi Elazar ben Arach's spiritual acumen. When Rabbi Elazar ben Arach and Rabban Yochanan ben Zakkai learn the works of the chariot together:

> Fire fell from heaven and surrounded them, and the ministering angels skipped before them like wedding guests rejoicing before the bridegroom. An angel answered from the midst of the fire

and said: According to your words, Elazar ben Arach, is the Work of the Chariot. (JT *Chagigah* 2:1, 77aV)

In other words, though some occupants of the heavenly halls mean the journeyer harm, there are also some who rejoice when we successfully make the trek.

Rabbi Elazar is joined in his spiritual excellence by Rabbi Yose haCohen and Rabbi Shimon ben Netanel:

Rabbi Yose the priest and Rabbi Shimon ben Natanel . . . began to discourse on the Work of the Chariot. They said: it was a day in the summer season, and the earth shook and a rainbow appeared in the cloud. And a heavenly voice (*bat kol*) came forth and said to them: "Behold the place is vacant for you and the dining couches laid out for you. You and your disciples are destined for the third heaven." This corresponds to what is said, "In Your presence there is fullness of joy (Psalm 16:11)." There are *seven* classes of righteous in the time to come. (JT *Chagigah* 2:1, 77aV)

This passage lends a democratizing bent to the spiritual quest. We need not be great sages to attain a place in the heavenly spheres. There is room in these halls for seven whole classes of souls with sufficient righteousness.[8]

Heavenly Gates and a Midrash on Jonah

The idea of gates to each heavenly hall is a memory and reflection of the gates within the Temple compound. In this "midrash" on the story of Jonah, the mystics tell us that the Temple gates were also miraculous (and the heavenly ones, all the more so):

Miracles occurred to Nikanor's doors and he was remembered with praise. He was bringing them to Israel on a ship to Israel and a great storm came upon them on the Mediterranean Sea.

They threw one of his doors overboard, then they sought to throw the second door overboard, too. But Nikanor hugged the door and said to them: If you throw this door into the sea, you will have to throw me overboard with it. The storm subsided but Nikanor continued crying and mourning for the door that was lost until they landed in Jaffa. And some say a giant sea creature swallowed the door and spit it up onto the land at Jaffa port.

Once they docked in Jaffa, the door popped up from under the boat.

MYSTICAL JOURNEYS AND MAGICAL LETTERS

And this is what we learn (in *Mishnah Midot* 2:3): All the gates were changed from copper to gold except for Nikanor's gates because a miracle occurred with them.

And some say that their copper shone so brightly that they looked like gold.

And it was taught in Rabbi Eliezer's name that the copper shone and was more beautiful than gold [so there was no need to change these doors to gold]. (*Tosefta Yoma* 2:4; JT *Yoma* 3:8, 25a2; BT *Yoma* 38a)

Nikanor's gates in the Second Temple were in a central place, figuratively and literally. They were the gates through which worshipers passed from the waiting area to the place where they offered their sacrifices. It would have been before these gates that people would wait and through these gates that atonement and salvation awaited via the sacrifices. In a very real sense, they were the physical gates of prayer to which the Reform Movement so often referred metaphorically.

Even the Letters of the Alphabet Give Us Courage

This democratization of heaven is even built into the letters that recount the creation of the world:

אֵלֶּה תוֹלְדוֹת הַשָּׁמַיִם וְהָאָרֶץ בְּהִבָּרְאָם בְּיוֹם עֲשׂוֹת יְהוָה אֱלֹהִים אֶרֶץ וְשָׁמָיִם:
Two worlds were created with two letters—with the yud and the hey—this world and the world-to-come. From where do we know this? "Trust in the Lord for ever and ever, for in Yah you have an everlasting rock. (Isaiah 26:4)"

בִּטְחוּ בַיהוָה עֲדֵי־עַד כִּי בְּיָהּ יְהוָה צוּר עוֹלָמִים:
But from this verse we still do not know which of the two was created with the yud and which with the hey. However, we know what is written, "These are the generations of the heaven and of the earth *b'hibaram*, i.e., with a hey and a yud they were created. (Genesis 2:4)"

"With hey He created them." This world was created with the hey and the next was created with the yud. As the hey is open be-

JUDITH Z. ABRAMS

neath, this indicates that all the inhabitants of the world shall go down to Sheol. As the *hey* has an upward projection, after they have gone down to Sheol they shall go up [to heaven]. As *hey* is open on every side, so a door is open to all who repent. As the *yud* is bent, so all the inhabitants of the world shall be bent low [with shame], as it is written, "All faces are bent low with pallor. (Jeremiah 30:6)"

When David saw the significance of the letters, he began praising the Holy One, blessed be He, with the two letters, with the *yud* and with the *hey*, as it is written, "Halleluyah! Praise God in His sanctuary. . . . Let every thing that has breath praise Yah. Halleluyah (Psalm 150:1, 6)" (JT *Chagigah* 2:1; *P'sikta Rabbati Piska* 21:20; *B'reishit Rabbah* 12:10)[9]

In the *Y'rushalmi*, this midrash immediately follows the story of Elisha ben Abuya who won't repent because he is sure he will never be forgiven. So this playful midrash is a counterbalance to that story. The implication is that *everyone* is forgiven in the end.

Conclusion

We can think of our prayer services as living, breathing entities. Beneath the "skin" are layers of muscle and fascia, organ systems, and circulation mechanisms. And underlying all of these is the skeleton. One important part of that skeleton, which gives structure to our prayers, is *Heichalot* mysticism, which leads us higher and higher. Through the imaginings of mystical journeys, fanciful midrash, counting and meditative prayer, our services form a great, rising arc toward holiness.

Notes

1. Michael D. Swartz, *Mystical Prayer in Ancient Judaism: An Analysis of Ma'aseh Merkavah* (Tübingen: Mohr, 1992), 201.
2. "The composers of Ma'aseh Merkavah were evidently not content to sublimate their longing for the direct presence of God in this manner. They wished to experience the heavenly worship directly. To this purpose, they marshaled the affective powers of prayer and incantation." Ibid., 223.
3. *Pirkei Heichalot* 28:1; David R. Blumenthal, *Understanding Jewish Mysticism: The Merkabah Tradition and the Zoharic Tradition*, trans. Lauren Grodner (Jersey City, NJ: KTAV, 1978), 86.
4. "In *Heichalot* literature, historical allusions of any kind, accurate or fictional, are rare." Swartz, *Mystical Prayer*, 216.

MYSTICAL JOURNEYS AND MAGICAL LETTERS

5. Ibid., 205.

6. See BT *Chagigah* 12b–13a for more on the contents of the seven levels of heaven. "From the earth until the first heaven is a 500-year journey. And from one heaven to another is a 500-year journey. And the thickness of a heaven is a 500-year journey. And the same is true of each and every heaven . . . Even to traverse the hooves of the Chayyot [heavenly beings] is a 515-year journey . . . equal to the numerical value of the word yesharah [shall dwell, covering, straight, or unified; see Ezek. 1:7]. See how high God is above His world, yet when a person enters into a meetinghouse (beit k'neset) and stands behind the pillar and prays in a whisper, the Holy One, blessed be He, listens to his prayer." BT *Chagigah* 12b.

7. *P'sukei D'zimrah, Yotzer, Amidah* (2), Torah Service, *Musaf* (2).

8. A parallel text tells us about the organization of the righteous in heaven: "In Your presence is fullness of joy, at Your right hand there are pleasures for evermore." Ps. 16:11. "The companies of the righteous will be arrayed in the form of the candlestick of the Temple . . . Which of these companies is the most excellent and best loved? The one standing upon the right side of the Holy One blessed be He." Midrash Psalms 16:11.

9. In *P'sikta Rabbati* this midrash is part of a commentary on the Ten Commandments.

The *Machzor* before the *Machzor*: Interpreting the High Holy Days during the Second Temple Period

Aaron D. Panken

The little-known Second Temple period (586 B.C.E. to 70 C.E.) represents one of the most exciting periods of literary development in the early phases of our people's history. Heady interactions with Persian, Greek, Roman, and other external cultures created a potent brew of intellectual foment that resulted in experiments with new forms of writing, the potential for broad reinterpretation of extant literature, and the expansion of the activities of the literate class in highly creative ways. While there was certainly no authoritative, written assemblage of prayer texts (let alone a developed *machzor*) in this pre-Rabbinic era, much fascinating activity took place that shaped the course of later developments during the Rabbinic period, influencing far later impressions of the High Holy Days. Best of all, many of the issues that pervade the literature around the High Holy Days from this period are remarkably parallel to our own situation in contemporary North America. In this article, I hope to provide a glimpse into just a few of the uniquely creative interpretive developments of this period and briefly consider what lessons it might have for *machzor* reform in our own time.

Philo

Philo Judaeus of Alexandria (c. 10 B.C.E. to 45 C.E.) provides us with the High Holy Day phenomenological standout of his time. His *De Specialibus Legibus* (*The Special Laws*) takes on the momentous task of explaining the manifold laws and customs that make

RABBI AARON D. PANKEN, Ph.D. (NY91) has served as dean and vice president of HUC-JIR and has taught Rabbinic and Second Temple Literature at HUC-JIR/ New York since 1996. He thanks the students in his Advanced Second Temple Literature class at HUC-JIR/New York of Fall 2011 for their helpful insights and musings on these texts as they studied them.

THE *MACHZOR* BEFORE THE *MACHZOR*

Judaism different from other religious systems. In his discussion on Yom Kippur, we find words describing the situation in first-century Egypt that feel as if they were written yesterday:

> On the tenth day [of the seventh month] is the fast, which is carefully observed not only by the zealous for piety and holiness, but also by those who never act religiously in the rest of their life. For all stand in awe, overcome by the sanctity of the day, and for the moment the worse vie with the better in self-denial and virtue. The high dignity of this day has two aspects, one as a festival, the other as a time of purification and escape from sins, for which indemnity is granted by the bounties of the gracious God Who has given to repentance the same honour as to innocence from sin.[1]

Here, Philo grapples with themes still prevalent in contemporary *machzorim* and the congregations reading them: bringing close those normally distant from religious practice and piety, the uniquely universal feeling of awe Yom Kippur evinces, and the tension between the experience of the "worse" sinners and once-a-year attendees who stand right next to the "better" regulars among the multitudes swelling a normally smaller congregation. The two overall aspects Philo delineates (festival versus purification) also parallel our own experience. Our observance is so often a mélange of binary oppositions: haute couture versus humility; the festive dinner before *Kol Nidrei* and the sumptuous post-*N'ilah* breakfast versus the headaches, halitosis, and hunger of the day's purification; the unified duality of *avinu* (the loving, celebrating parent) versus *malkeinu* (the harsh, judging sovereign); and so on. Notably, in this definitively pre-Christian document, Philo also presents a Jewish concept of salvation by grace—God does not forgive us because we are worthy of forgiveness, rather it is God's gracious equating of repentance with innocence that creates even the possibility that we might be forgiven. Such eschewing of God's harsh judgment and concomitant privileging of divine mercy recurs regularly in the words of the *machzor*.[2]

Earlier in this same work, Philo offers an imaginative reinterpretation of the Temple ritual on Yom Kippur. Beginning with a physical description of the Temple precincts in Jerusalem, he explains:

> Right in the very middle stands the sanctuary itself with a beauty baffling description, to judge from what is exposed to view. For

all inside is unseen except by the high priest alone, and indeed he, though charged with the duty of entering once a year, gets no view of anything. For he takes with him a brazier full of lighted coals and incense, and the great quantity of vapour which this naturally gives forth covers everything around it, beclouds the eyesight and prevents it from being able to penetrate to any distance.[3]

Amidst the sublime beauty of the most sacred place of Jewish worship, Philo implies that it is not actually the physical surroundings that make High Holy Day worship especially sacred. In fact, it is the unseen, unknowable reality that exists just beyond our eyes, inaccessible even to the High Priest, which elevates us beyond the mundane. This is so often the case at the High Holy Days: the unseen—long-past deeds and long-gone loved ones and those with whom we interact infrequently—loom somehow larger as we muster and number and consider on this sacred day. Likewise, God's presence seems enlarged and fortified not because of any particular physical space, but because of our special sense of focus. Cloaked in invisibility there exists a *mysterium tremendum*, a powerful, unknowable presence that bespeaks, in Rudolf Otto's felicitous terms, "awfulness," "overpoweringness," and "urgency."[4] Long before modernity, Philo's outlook anticipates this important concept of the power of the unseen at Yom Kippur.

The Book of Jubilees

Beyond Philo's evocative descriptions of contemporary celebrations and celebrants, much of the additional creative output of the Second Temple period turns its gaze toward the past, building upon a firm foundation of biblical texts to imbue the High Holy Days with innovative meanings. Second Temple authors often chose to link Rosh HaShanah and Yom Kippur back to various biblical characters and occurrences, reconstructing these holy days into annual commemorations of specific pivotal occasions in the lives of revered ancestors. This served two purposes: first, it rooted the observance of these holidays more firmly into our people's cherished folk history. Second, it allowed later authors to reshape the valence of particular elements of the holidays to stress the values and ideals they held dear, allowing for the redirection of tradition in new and continuously relevant ways.

THE *MACHZOR* BEFORE THE *MACHZOR*

We find some fine examples in the Book of Jubilees, an early interpretive parallel to the Book of Genesis, likely written in Hebrew during the second century B.C.E. in Palestine. While it often follows Genesis quite closely, it reinterprets and adds freely to the biblical tradition, opening a fascinating entrée for understanding the exegetical and improvisational trends of this period. In Jubilees, the date of Rosh HaShanah is set alternately against a backdrop of activity by Noah and Abraham. In Noah's case, Jubilees defines the first day of the seventh month (Tishrei) as the moment when "the mouths of the abysses of the earth were opened, and the waters began to descend into them."[5] That is to say, God's primordial Flood began to drain away from the earth on the day of Rosh HaShanah, a potent reminder that though those who engage in injustice will face God's penalty, the punishment meted out will not be arbitrary or endless: rather, only the righteous will be saved by God. Linking Noah with Rosh HaShanah in this manner reinforced *midat hadin* (the judgmental aspect of the holiday), crafting it as a time when the righteous (read: Noah and his family) will choose to abandon their sins, even as they watch the sinners (read: everyone else) pay dearly for their sinful actions. Jubilees, then, marshals the Flood story as an impetus toward *t'shuvah*, goading those who can act righteously to do so and raising the specter of horrid punishments to bring the sinner back in line.

Contrast this punishing reminder of judgment with Jubilees' longer depiction of Rosh HaShanah as a signpost along the way on Abraham's journey to monotheism:

> Abram sat up during the night on the first of the seventh month,
> so that he might observe the stars from evening until daybreak,
> so that he might see what the nature of the year would be with respect to rain. And he was sitting alone and making observations;
> and a word came into his heart saying: "All of the signs of the stars, and the signs of the sun and the moon are all in the hand of God. Why am I seeking?
>
> If God desires, God will make it rain morning and evening,
> and if God desires, God will not send [it] down;
> and everything is in God's hand."
>
> And he prayed on that night, saying:
> "My God, the Most High God, you alone are God to me,

AARON D. PANKEN

And You created everything,
And everything which is was the work of Your hands,
And You and Your sovereignty I have chosen.
Save me from the hands of evil spirits,
Which rule over the heart of humanity,
And do not let them lead me astray from following you, O my God,
But establish me and my seed forever,
And let us not go astray henceforth and forever."[6]

Jubilees provides, here, a very early explicit linkage between Abram and Rosh HaShanah, one that will eventuate in the reading of the *Akeidah* as one of the Rosh HaShanah Torah portions many years later. It also anticipates the various annual judgments of agriculture we find later in *Mishnah Rosh HaShanah* 1:1. At a deeper level, for Jubilees' Abram, Rosh HaShanah was his first day of repentance and change—the moment when he ceased to see the world through idolatrous eyes and acknowledged, instead, God's providence and ultimate control of the world. This realization led him to leave his pagan homeland and family and begin the famous trek described in Genesis 12 to a new land and the founding of a new people. Read thus, Rosh HaShanah becomes the initial point for the personal spiritual journey from that which is prohibited—idolatry and the worship of stars and constellations—to that which is endorsed—the proper worship of the one God behind it all. Rosh HaShanah stands as an opportunity for each of us to walk in the footsteps of our ancestor Abram—to journey to a better place through the abandonment of misplaced personal religious faith and the taking on of more appropriate belief and practice. Such actions have the potential to build the future of our people in powerful, meaningful and long-lasting ways, as they once did for Abram.[7]

Read together, Jubilees' utilization of Noah and Abram encourages a useful combination of carrot and stick. The connection to Noah's Flood reminds readers of the punishment that awaits sinners as a stick that will inspire the unmotivated penitent to action (not unlike God's withholding inscription in the Book of Life or some of the scarier death sentences so prominent in *Untaneh Tokef*). The more self-motivated penitent may simply look to Abram's carrot, the compelling prospect of many offspring and a life well-lived in service to God and the Jewish people.

THE *MACHZOR* BEFORE THE *MACHZOR*

Jubilees' author proceeds to create new understandings of Yom Kippur as well. Jubilees reorients the background for Yom Kippur by tying it to the ongoing strife between Joseph and his brothers. After paraphrasing Genesis 37, in which Joseph's brothers throw him into a pit and sell him to passing Ishmaelites, Jubilees states:

> And the sons of Jacob slaughtered a kid and dipped Joseph's garment into the blood and sent (it) to Jacob, their father, on the tenth of the seventh month. And he lamented all of that night, because they had brought it to him in the evening. And he became feverish in lamenting his death, and said that, "A cruel beast has eaten Joseph." And all of the men of his house lamented with him on that day. And it happened as they were mourning and lamenting with him all that day that his sons and his daughter rose up to comfort him but he was not comforted concerning his son.[8]

On Yom Kippur, Jubilees suggests, Jacob received the bloodied clothing of his beloved Joseph, along with the fabricated story of Joseph's jealous brothers, and he commenced intense mourning without any possibility of being comforted. One could certainly read this as a plea for honesty and integrity to other human beings. After all, nearly the entire family knew that Joseph's death had been faked and that Jacob's grief was unnecessary at best, or misdirected at worst. This primordial moment of mourning sets the scene for Jubilees' next interpretive act, which reads Yom Kippur as a communal day of mourning:

> Therefore it is decreed for the children of Israel that they mourn on the tenth [day] of the seventh month—on the day when that which caused him to weep for Joseph came to Jacob, his father—so that they might atone for them[selves] with a young kid on the tenth [day] of the seventh month, once a year, on account of their sin because they caused the affection of their father to grieve for Joseph, his son. And this day is decreed so that they might mourn on it on account of their sins and on account of all their transgressions and on account of all their errors in order to purify themselves on this day, once a year.[9]

This represents a significant excursion from the text of Genesis 37, which certainly never ties Yom Kippur to this incident. While this sort of insertion is not unusual for the Book of Jubilees, one has to ask what provoked the editor to make such an addition? A

AARON D. PANKEN

few possibilities come to mind. First, since the Jewish people are defined initially as children of Jacob (*B'nei Yisrael*), their actions in this story represent the first significant *communal* sin for which they can be held accountable as a corporate body. Such communal sin makes this incident well-suited for introducing the concept of the Day of Atonement for *all* the people of Israel.

Second, the appearance in Genesis 37:31 of the term *seir izim* (he-goat) creates a compelling intertext with identical language to the two goats of the Yom Kippur ceremony in Leviticus 16. There, the entire Israelite community provided two male goats for the Yom Kippur observance. Aaron (the High Priest) offered one goat, selected by lot, as a sin offering, ensuring its immediate death. Aaron then confessed the communal sins of the Israelites over the other goat, now designated the "scapegoat," and drove this sin-bearing goat out to the wilderness, to carry away the people's sins and make expiation for them.[10] Such an uncanny and uncomfortable resemblance with the story of Joseph (designated for God, and sent to his death) and his brothers (carrying sin, but living on) is hardly an accident. Jubilees reengineers the symbolic goats of Yom Kippur into reminders and atonement vessels not only for the community's current sins, but also for its earliest sin, assuaging leftover communal guilt from this troubling piece of our ancestral story. Tying Yom Kippur to these behaviors holds a mirror up to the brothers and demands their repentance, even as it warns future generations to avoid such cruelty.

The Dead Sea Scrolls

An obscure text from the Dead Sea Scrolls known as the Words of Moses (1Q22), likewise, proffers an interesting reinterpretation of biblical precedent with respect to Yom Kippur. This short work parallels parts of Deuteronomy and is preserved on thirty-two small fragments found at Qumran.[11] Unfortunately, the extant text is quite fragmentary, as can be observed in this excerpt about Yom Kippur:

Column III
7 [Go]d will bless you, forgiving you your] sin[s...] ...
8 [...] in the year [...] of the month of
9 [...] ... [...] on this day [... For] your [father]s wandered
10 [in the wilderness] until the [te]nth day of the month{the [...on

THE *MACHZOR* BEFORE THE *MACHZOR*

the te]nth [day] of the month}
11 [You shall] refrain [from all work]. And on the te[nth] day [of the] month, atonement shall be made...

Column IV
1 in the congregation of the gods [and in the council of the ho]ly ones and in their [..., in favour of the sons of Isra]el and on behalf of the la[nd]
2 [And] ta[ke] from [its blood and] pour (it) on the earth [...] ... [...]
3 [and atone]ment [shall be made] for them by it...[12]

If we accept the reconstructions in brackets above, we find, unsurprisingly, the standard trope of Yom Kippur as day of atonement. Yet Yom Kippur is also aligned with a variety of notable moments in our people's mythic history. Yom Kippur comes, this Qumran text posits, at the time of the cessation of our people's wanderings (column III, lines 9–10). That is to say, our people stops their nomadic way of life and becomes settled in their land (presumably the land of Israel, though the text is not explicit) specifically on the day we celebrate Yom Kippur. Further, in column IV, line 1, when atonement is made, it is not only for the *people* of Israel, but for the *land* as well.[13] Atonement, then, becomes an act linked with landedness—a time of proper settling when one finds one's rightful, righteous place in this world. Yom Kippur represents the time of coming into a new and better home and keeping that home properly ordered and free of sin.

Intriguing, as well, is the reference in the same line to "the congregation of the gods [and in the council of the ho]ly ones," which certainly causes the mind to drift to thoughts of the introductory lines of *Kol Nidrei*, where both the *yeshivah shel maalah* and *yeshivah shel matah* participate in the courtroom setting established for the purpose of judging sinners. These words have preceded *Kol Nidrei* only since the thirteenth century, when they were added by Rabbi Meir of Rothenburg (1215–1293), but the ideas they express have a much older provenance, based in divine councils of the Ancient Near East[14] and echoed here in the Dead Sea Scrolls.

Another text from the unique genre of Qumranic *pesharim* constructs Yom Kippur as the day of a critical battle between the representatives of good and evil. Similar to midrash, but earlier and less developed, a *pesher* is a "type of biblical interpretation found in the

AARON D. PANKEN

Qumran scrolls in which selected biblical texts are applied to the contemporary sectarian setting by means of various literary devices."[15] *Pesharim* begin with a *lemma* (a biblical statement quoted verbatim) from the book at hand[16] and follow it with an interpretation that is specific to the contemporary situation of the sectarians. This allows *pesharim* to apply older biblical texts to the present-day, retrojecting interpretations to create biblical support for the ideology of the sect. Pesher Habakkuk, one of the first scrolls to be found at Qumran, applies this method to the Book of Habakkuk with intriguing results:

> Column XI
> 2 (Hab. 2:15) "Woe to anyone making his companion drunk, spilling out
> 3 his anger, or even making him drunk to look at their festivals."
> 4 Its interpretation concerns the Wicked Priest who
> 5 pursued the Teacher of Righteousness to consume him with the heat
> 6 of his anger in the place of his banishment. In festival time, during the rest
> 7 of the day of Atonement, he appeared to them, to consume them
> 8 and make them fall on the day of fasting, the sabbath of their rest.[17]

Pesher Habakkuk understands Habakkuk 2:15's use of the term "their festivals" (*mo'adeihem*) as referring specifically to one manifestation of Yom Kippur in its contemporary world. The festival becomes the specific occasion for attacks on the sect by the Wicked Priest, a standard Qumranic character who works against the accepted sectarian leadership. Having this evil individual act against the Teacher of Righteousness (apparently one of the sect's most revered leaders) on the most sacred day of the year creates a nexus of heinous actions, far beyond any sectarian's possible acceptance. Such a scenario further valorizes the Teacher of Righteousness as a warrior for good, even as it completely vilifies the Wicked Priest. The interpreter's goal seems to be to personify the battles between good and evil that take place within each of us during Yom Kippur and expand them to have greater cosmic significance as they play out on the axis of sect versus world. In this way, it structures a world in which there are two very distinct poles in a grand struggle between the righteous and the sinners. Such a structure motivates listeners to

THE *MACHZOR* BEFORE THE *MACHZOR*

consider carefully where they sit and to place themselves in the right corner through their deeds and through proper atonement.

In these few examples, we have begun to garner a sense of the active, innovative minds that were at work on our tradition during this early period of biblical interpretation and literary innovation. We noted some remarkable similarities between Philo's vision of his congregation and its rituals and those of our own time; we saw the exciting redeployment of biblical characters and scenes for new effect; and we saw how the agglomeration of ideas affiliated with Yom Kippur has served as a flexible symbol set with room enough for our people's nomadic wandering, our ancestors Noah, Abram, and Joseph, and even the battle of a Wicked Priest and Teacher of Righteousness. Such broadly meaningful symbolism was well-prepared to stand the tests of time and supplied useful precedents for themes that inhabit our *machzorim* still centuries later.

A Brief Closing Thought

Aside from reveling in the exciting ingenuity of these texts, there is also a meta-message to those who would engage in new acts of Jewish creativity as the editors of any new *machzor*: Second Temple texts suggest that editors not be afraid to rework, reconsider, and redirect understandings of prior material, for this is a healthy and natural part of the enduring Jewish interpretive process. Such literary creators must look to respond to the needs of the contemporary community in each new time and place, as the generations before always have. At the same time, though, they ought to note how their predecessors valued what came before them: rather than wantonly discarding challenging texts and ideas, they redeployed earlier models with sensitivity, respect, and love for their inherited tradition. That, surely, is the balance, the challenge, and the joy inherent in confronting any traditional text and remaking it for new meaning, whether before there was a *machzor* two millennia ago or before our movement's new one right now.

Notes

1. F. H. Colson, trans., *Philo*, vol. 7 (Cambridge, MA: Harvard University Press, 1937, repr. 1998), Special Laws 1:186.
2. See, for example, *Avinu Malkeinu* and the closing paragraphs of *Untaneh Tokef* for just two examples of this tension between God's mercy and God's judgment.

AARON D. PANKEN

3. Colson, *Philo*, Special Laws 1:72.

4. Rudolf Otto, *The Idea of the Holy* (London: Oxford University Press, 1923; repr. 1958), 12–30.

5. Adapted from Jubilees 6:26–27 in James H. Charlesworth, *The Old Testament Pseudepigrapha*, vol. 2 (New York: Doubleday, 1985), 68.

6. Adapted from Jubilees 12:16–20 in ibid., 81.

7. Compare, also, elements of the story in Genesis 15, when God takes Abram outside at night to count the stars and states that his offspring will be as numerous as they are. Rashi, ad loc., reads this as a call to give up his astrological speculation and see that with his new name (Abraham instead of Abram) comes an entirely revised celestial fate, also a sign of God's power over celestial happenings.

8. Jubilees 34:12–14, in Charlesworth, *Pseudepigrapha*, vol. 2, 121.

9. Jubilees 34:18–19, in ibid.

10. The Mishnah and Gemara also depict this ceremony in great detail, in chapter 4 of tractate *Yoma*.

11. Lawrence H. Schiffman and James C. VanderKam, eds., *The Encyclopedia of the Dead Sea Scrolls* (Oxford: Oxford University Press, 2000), s.v. "Moses"; Eibert J.C. Tigchelaar, "A Cave 4 Fragment of Divrei Mosheh (4QDM) and the text of 1Q22 1:7–10 and Jubilees 1:9, 14," *Dead Sea Discoveries* 12, no. 3 (2005): 303–12.

12. The English translation is from Florentino García Martinez and Eibert J.C. Tigchelaar, *The Dead Sea Scrolls Study Edition*, vol. 1 (Leiden: Brill, 1997), 62–63. The text was originally published in J.T. Millik, *Qumran Cave 1 (DJD 1*; Oxford: Clarendon Press, 1955), 91–97.

13. Some scholars locate the origins of the High Holy Days within an ancient temple purification ceremony, observed in Sumerian, Babylonian, and Assyrian cultures. For a useful bibliography see David Noel Freedman, ed., *Anchor Bible Dictionary* (New York: Doubleday, 1992), s.v. "Akitu." The biblical account of Yom Kippur in Exodus 30:10 appears to preserve the concept of an annual purification of the altar in a similar vein, and the purification of the High Priest himself is a main focus of Leviticus 16's understanding of the holy day. These factors bolster the idea presented in this text of a land- or temple-centered festival.

14. See Marc Zvi Brettler, "The Heavenly Assembly," in *All These Vows—Kol Nidre*, ed. Lawrence A. Hoffman (Woodstock, VT: Jewish Lights, 2011) for a short review of the ancient precursors to the concept of *yeshivah shel maalah*.

15. Schiffman and VanderKam, *Encyclopedia*, s.v. "Pesharim."

16. A *lemma* is not unlike the familiar *dibbur hamatchil* by which printed commentaries indicate the verse they are analyzing.

17. Martinez and Tigchelaar, *Dead Sea Scrolls*, vol. 1, 18–21.

Yom Kippur in Moab: Reflections on the Setting of the *Parashah*

Elsie R. Stern

The designation of new Torah portions for Rosh HaShanah and Yom Kippur was one of the signature innovations of the early Reform High Holy Day liturgy. Since at least the 1894 *Union Prayer Book for Jewish Worship*, Reform *machzorim* have designated Deuteronomy 29:9–14 and 30:11–20 as the Torah portion for Yom Kippur morning instead of the traditional readings from Leviticus 16 and Numbers 29:7–11. In addition, until the publication of *Gates of Repentance* in 1979, American Reform *machzorim* omitted the entire *Avodah* service.[1] When they were instituted, these liturgical innovations articulated key ideological principles of the Reform Movement. The traditional readings and the *Avodah* service promulgated both traditional Judaism's affirmation of the privileged role of the ancestral priesthood and its ongoing hope for the reestablishment of the Temple cult. The omission of these texts by the early Reformers signaled the movement's rejection of these doctrines; the choice of the Deuteronomy readings affirmed the movement's belief in "the doctrine of personal responsibility" and articulated the central Reform principle that Torah, rather than the Temple cult, was the primary tool in the quest for redemption.[2]

While their ideology may have been radical, the Reformers' choice to use the Torah service as an opportunity to express their convictions is a time-honored one. Since its origins in the Second Temple period, the ritual recitation of Scripture in the synagogue has provided an opportunity for communal leaders to articulate ideas that they feel are important for their communities. The earliest literary representation of the reading of a prophetic text in a synagogue, which appears in the New Testament in Luke 4:15–21, provides a case in point. In this scene, Jesus recites verses from

ELSIE R. STERN, Ph.D. is associate professor of Bible at the Reconstructionist Rabbinical College.

ELSIE R. STERN

a scroll of Isaiah and then explains that "today this scripture has been fulfilled in your hearing." Similarly, the lectionary readings that emerge during the Rabbinic period often articulate, in biblical language, central Rabbinic tenets and perspectives.[3] In addition, Rabbinic *p'tichtaot,* medieval *piyutim,* and medieval and modern *divrei Torah* all testify to the ways in which the texts of the Torah service have provided material and vocabulary for reflection on contemporary concerns and experiences.

Before the standardization of the liturgy, some of these Torah-inflected reflections were woven into the liturgy itself through the composition and performance of *piyutim* that were keyed to parts of the liturgy but were specific to the language and themes of the lectionary readings for a particular Shabbat or festival. For example, in a synagogue that performed Eleazar Kallir's *k'dushtaot* for the weeks following Tishah B'Av, the generic *K'dushah* would have been replaced by a poetic composition that combined elements of the *K'dushah* rubric with themes and language drawn from the week's haftarah and the midrashim associated with it. After the liturgy became standardized, however, this porousness between the lectionary and liturgy disappeared; the statutory liturgy and the lectionary readings, along with their accompanying explication or reflection, became two discrete elements in the worship service. One of the affects of this change was the creation of a contrapuntal relationship between liturgy and lectionary that allowed the Torah service to function as a thematic and experiential "change of venue" within the worship service—a time for communal engagement with, and potential immersion in, images and themes distinct from those of the surrounding liturgy.

The traditional Torah portion for Yom Kippur morning provides a powerful example of this phenomenon. With the exception of the *Avodah* service, the liturgy specific to Yom Kippur morning is saturated with royal and forensic language and imagery. The confessions and petitions all situate the worshipers as supplicants in the divine court where they confess their sins and attempt to earn acquittal, or at least a reduced sentence, from the omniscient and omnipotent divine sovereign. While the characterization of God in the Yom Kippur prayers is awesome, the construction of the human experience is quite earth-bound and naturalistic. In the imaginary courtroom of the Yom Kippur liturgy, worshipers confess their sins, proclaim their insignificance and remorse, and pray for forgiveness. The results of

YOM KIPPUR IN MOAB

these actions unfold in real time over the course of the day. If their repentance is sincere, and if God acts mercifully, by the end of the day, they will be absolved of their guilt.

This scene shifts radically during the Torah and *Avodah* services. The traditional Torah readings describe the rituals for the annual purification of the innermost shrine of the tabernacle (Lev. 16) and the offerings mandated for the day (Num. 29:7–11). The ritual described in Leviticus 16 in turn becomes a generative text for the *Avodah* service. BT *Yoma* 36b and 56b attest to the recitation of the Mishnaic tractate *Yoma*, which is a tannaitic description of the Yom Kippur ritual that took place in the Second Temple. By the Middle Ages, the *Avodah* service had developed into an extensive reflection on this ritual and its role as centerpiece in a cosmic narrative that begins with the creation of the world and continues to the present day. As a meditation on the Temple cult and a theologically charged review of cosmic history, the *Avodah* service provides the worshiper with an opportunity to take a break from the liturgical courtroom and engage with an array of ideas and images that are absent from the surrounding liturgy. The *piyutim* of the *Avodah* service invoke creation, angels, the privileges of Israel and the priests, and divine glory and grandeur. Poetically, they deploy tropes of beauty, mystery, and wonder that are absent from the confessions and petitions of the rest of the day.[4] As Lawrence Hoffman has noted, the *Avodah* service also places the issues of sin, repentance, and forgiveness, which are at the heart of the surrounding liturgy, into a cosmic perspective by identifying sin, repentance, and forgiveness as the engines that drive Israel's historical experience.[5] The traditional Torah portion then, serves as the doorway into the cosmic theater of the *Avodah* service. Reflection on the priestly ritual from Leviticus leads to reflection on the Temple and its Yom Kippur ritual and their respective roles in the geography and history of the cosmos. The worshipers' experiential sojourn in the world of the *Avodah* service has the potential to shape the surrounding work of *t'shuvah* by placing it in a cosmic perspective. The *Avodah* service potentially inflects the worshipers' experience with nostalgia for the glory of the Temple and an anxiety about the cosmic effects of its absence. At the same time, the dialogue between the surrounding liturgy and the *Avodah* service suggests that the results of the individual "trials" that are unfolding on Yom Kippur have the power to influence the history of the world.

ELSIE R. STERN

As I noted above, the Reformers used the Torah service as an opportunity to "speak their truth" through biblical texts. However, they did not exploit the potential change of venue made possible by the relationship between the new lectionary text and the liturgy. In what follows, I will take up that task. What would happen if we used the Torah portion as the gateway to a sojourn in Moab, which is the setting of Deuteronomy 29–30? Where might this imaginative journey lead and what effects could it have, at least potentially, on the Yom Kippur experience?

Unlike "Egypt," "Jerusalem," and the "land of Israel," the mythic resonances of "Moab" have not survived in Jewish culture. Whereas the invocation of "Egypt" has the power to conjure images of slavery, plagues, and the "narrow places," the invocation of Moab has far less resonance. This fact belies the size of Moab's footprint in the Pentateuch and beyond. Within the Torah alone, Moab is mentioned thirty-one times and is the subject of two discrete narrative episodes: Genesis 19 articulates a myth of origin for the Moabites and Numbers 22–24 tells the story of Balak, the king of Moab, and his attempts to get Balaam to curse the Israelites. In addition, Deuteronomy 2 and 23 refer to a prior encounter of the Israelites with the Moabites. Finally, the entire book of Deuteronomy is set in the steppes of Moab on the boundary of Canaan. Because it is the setting for Deuteronomy, in terms of pure page count, more of the Torah takes place in Moab than in any other single locale. Outside the Pentateuch but still within the *Tanach*, Moab and the Moabites continue to appear. Ruth is a Moabite and the beginning of the book of Ruth takes place in Moab; there are narratives of battles with the Moabites throughout the Deuteronomic history and oracles against the nation appear in several prophetic books.[6] Among this array of texts, a significant cluster deal with concerns about the boundaries and stability of Israelite identity—suggesting that, in the postexilic period at least, Moab and Moabites provided loci for anxiety over, and reflection on, these concerns.[7]

While communal identity is often a concern of contemporary Jewish communities, it is not the primary focus of Yom Kippur. In the context of the holiday, a different cluster of Moab texts emerges that resonate with the process of *t'shuvah*. In the spirit of the theatrical metaphor I used above, I will present these texts as different scenes that the worshiper might experience during a Yom Kippur sojourn in Moab.

YOM KIPPUR IN MOAB

Scene 1: Deuteronomy 29–30—If Only It Were So (Part 1)

[15]See, I set before you this day life and prosperity, death and adversity. [16]For I command you this day, to love the LORD your God, to walk in His ways, and to keep His commandments, His laws, and His rules, that you may thrive and increase, and that the LORD your God may bless you in the land that you are about to enter and possess. [17]But if your heart turns away and you give no heed, and are lured into the worship and service of other gods, [18]I declare to you this day that you shall certainly perish; you shall not long endure on the soil that you are crossing the Jordan to enter and possess. [19]I call heaven and earth to witness against you this day: I have put before you life and death, blessing and curse. Choose life—if you and your offspring would live— [20]by loving the LORD your God, heeding His commands, and holding fast to Him. For thereby you shall have life and shall long endure upon the soil that the LORD swore to your ancestors, Abraham, Isaac, and Jacob, to give to them. (Deut. 29:15–20)

Our first Moab text, the Torah reading for Yom Kippur morning, asserts that its hearers inhabit a world that is marked by moral clarity (v.15), free will (v.19), and clear and consistent consequence (vv.15–18). When stated so baldly, the utopian nature of this vision becomes apparent. Any worshiper engaged seriously in the work of *t'shuvah* knows that each aspect of this assertion is subject to nuance, if not outright rejection. The clarity assumed by the assertion of an accessible divine will contradicts much contemporary experience of real moral ambiguity. Similarly, the unnuanced assertion of free will resonates naively for many contemporary people. Even within its ancient Israelite context, the assertion of a clear and simple choice was part of Deuteronomy's rhetorical strategy, rather than a worldview shared by all members of its audience. In all probability, the choice to worship only *YHVH* in the central shrine in Jerusalem was not a simple one. It would have demanded the abandonment of ancient and traditional practices including the worship of other long-venerated gods as well as *YHVH* in ancient and holy shrine sites. Any thoughtful Israelite would have experienced this as a difficult choice in which the pull of tradition and traditional authority came into conflict with newer forms of authority allied to the king and Jerusalem priesthood. By describing the choice of *YHVH*-only worship as a starkly simple

ELSIE R. STERN

one, Deuteronomy denies the validity of the alternatives it outlaws and denies the complexity of the choice that it demands. Like its vision of moral clarity, the Torah portion's unequivocal assertion of free will may also strike contemporary Jews as an idealized vision, out of synch with lived experience. While many contemporary Jews still adhere to a theoretical doctrine of free will, most also recognize that our choices are rarely, if ever, unfettered. Gender, race, class, and DNA all place constraints on our freedom in ways that make the reality of choice far more complicated than Deuteronomy's clarion call admits.

Perhaps the most wishful part of Deuteronomy's worldview is its assertions that all our actions have consistent and predictable consequences. Like the doctrine of free will, the belief that human experience is an unalloyed meritocracy in which good is rewarded and bad is punished rarely sustains extensive scrutiny. Here, too, factors of power and privilege as well as luck come to bear, making it far from certain that good will be rewarded and evil punished. By spending time in Moab on Yom Kippur, worshipers can take a break from the complexities of the moral world they inhabit and both recognize and engage with the powerful fantasy of moral clarity, free choice, and consistent consequence that the Torah portion asserts. Just as the traditional Torah portion serves as a gateway into longer imaginative sojourns in the Temple, so, too, can the portion from Deuteronomy serve as a gateway to other Moab experiences that lie outside the bounds of the lectionary reading.

Scene 2: Numbers 22–24—If Only It Were So (Part 2)

And now that I have come to you, have I the power to speak freely? I can utter only the word that God puts into my mouth. (Num. 22:38)

The story of Balaam offers a fantasy that is diametrically opposed to, but equally as poignant as, that of Deuteronomy 29–30. Numbers 22–24 recounts the story of Balaam, a seer who reluctantly agrees to the king of Moab's request to curse the Israelites. Despite his eventual acquiescence, Balaam states clearly from the outset that he can only say what God wants him to say. In the ensuing scenes, Balaam repeatedly blesses the Israelites in more and more enthusiastic terms. After each oracle, Balak protests: "What have you done to me? Here I brought you to damn my enemies, and instead you have blessed

YOM KIPPUR IN MOAB

them!" Balaam repeats: "I can only repeat faithfully what the Lord puts into my mouth." Thinking that a change of venue might improve the outcome, Balak suggests that Balaam try again from a different vantage point. However, the outcome is the same. Each time Balaam opens his mouth to curse the Israelites, he ends up blessing them, in total conformity to God's will. When read in its canonical context, this story functions as a testament to God's immense power. Like the story of the hardening of Pharaoh's heart, the Balaam story asserts that God is more powerful than even the most powerful gentiles. Within the context of the Book of Numbers, this assertion of power functions ironically in light of the ability of the Israelites to repeatedly resist God's will. On Yom Kippur morning, however, the Balaam story resonates in yet another way—as a wishful counterpoint to the work of *t'shuvah*. Unlike Yom Kippur worshipers who are grappling with the consequences of human agency and the ability to make good and bad moral decisions, Balaam presents us with the fantasy of the person who has no choice but to do the right thing. No matter how many times he tries, no matter how rich the reward, no matter the change of venue, Balaam cannot do other than what God wants. While Deuteronomy 29–30 asserts that we are totally free, the story of Balaam offers us the possibility of no choice at all—the only possibility is obedience to God.

When we consider these two texts together, Moab becomes the site for the articulation of two fantasies, diametrically opposed to one another, that give voice to two of the longings that the process of *t'shuvah* can bring: On the one hand is the longing for crystalline moral clarity, unfettered free will, and clear and consistent consequences for good and bad behavior. On the other is the desire for a world in which moral behavior did not require such vigilance—a world, like that which Balaam inhabits in Numbers 23, in which we are compelled to do what is right regardless of our self-interest or the interests of people more powerful than we are.

Scene 3: Deuteronomy 2:28–29, 23:4–5—*Ashamnu,* or Maybe Not

What food I eat you will supply for money, and what water I drink you will furnish for money; just let me pass through—as the descendants of Esau who dwell in Seir did for me, and the Moabites who dwell in Ar—that I may cross the Jordan into the land that the LORD our God is giving us.

(Deut. 2:28–29)

ELSIE R. STERN

No Ammonite or Moabite shall be admitted into the congregation of the LORD; none of their descendants, even in the tenth
generation, shall ever be admitted into the congregation of the
LORD, because they did not meet you with food and water on
your journey after you left Egypt, and because they hired Balaam
son of Beor, from Pethor of Aram-naharaim, to curse you.

(Deut. 23:4–5)

Both of these references to the encounter between Israel and Moab
during the Israelites' journey to Canaan are ascribed to Moses in
his farewell addresses on the steppes of Moab. Despite their common attribution, the two versions are incompatible. The first implies that Moab did grant the Israelites safe passage; the second
asserts that they did not. From a historical perspective, these two
versions represent variant traditions about the encounter between
the Israelites and the Moabites that were circulating in ancient Israel before the redaction of the book of Deuteronomy. For reasons
that are now irretrievable, both versions made it into the textual
tradition that became the backbone for the Masoretic text. During
our Yom Kippur sojourn in Moab, however, this contradictory account provides a fruitful counter-narrative to the Deuteronomic
worldview. Whereas Deuteronomy 29–30 asserts that human experience is marked by moral clarity and clear consequence, the
conflicting accounts of the encounter with Moab offer a vision of
a much muddier human experience where not only the moral valence of our actions is unclear but where even the very facts of the
case are up in the air.

Scene 4: Deuteronomy—Remembering and Retelling

These are the words that Moses addressed to all Israel on the
other side of the Jordan.

(Deut. 1:1)

Moab is the site of the Bible's most extensive recollection. In the
beginning of the book, Moses remembers for the people what they
have experienced since they left Egypt. In comparison to the wishful portrayals of moral action in Deuteronomy 29–30 and Numbers 20–22, the act of remembering attributed to Moses feels far
more realistic. Like most memories, Moses' account is selective,
self-serving, and purposeful. He "remembers" and retells those

YOM KIPPUR IN MOAB

episodes that are relevant to the moment of remembering—his farewell to the Israelites on the brink of their entrance into the land of Canaan. He also "remembers" in a way that serves his own interests. In Numbers, Moses is forbidden from entering the land of Canaan on account of his own actions. In Moses' account, he is not allowed to enter because of the transgressions of the Israelites (Deut. 3:26). Finally, Moses' retelling is purposeful. He tells a version of the wilderness experience that testifies to God's power and to the allegiance that the Israelites owe God as a result both of their gratitude for God's saving actions and of their covenantal agreement. On Yom Kippur, this distinctively human portrayal of memory can come into conversation both with the portrayal of divine memory in the *Zichronot* section of the Rosh HaShanah liturgy as well as with the acts of memory that are necessary to the work of *t'shuvah*. On Rosh HaShanah, worshipers remind God of God's role as "remember-er" and urge God to remember those elements of the past that will work in the community's favor. On Yom Kippur, worshipers echo this act by searching their memories for the sins that they have committed and the webs of habits and circumstances that led to these misdeeds. In the *Zichronot*, God's memory is cosmic, flawless, and magisterial. Deuteronomy's portrayal of memory reminds us that ours is not. Rather the act of remembering is as personal and as purposeful as the remembered deeds with which we grapple.

A Yom Kippur sojourn in Moab then provides worshipers with the opportunity take a break from the nuts and bolts of *t'shuvah*: the cataloguing of transgressions, the work of true repentance, and the quest for alternative ways forward. Just as the sojourn in the Temple provided by the *Avodah* service situates the rest of Yom Kippur in a larger cosmic perspective, so, too, does the sojourn in Moab offer a wider perspective. Imaginative reflection on the Moab texts allows us to engage with the larger context of memory, morality, and agency that frame our understanding of our actions and their consequences. Whereas the traditional *Avodah* service might well lead participants to regard their transgressions with even greater rigor and dread and to mourn for the absent Temple with greater fervor, a sojourn in Moab has the potential to lead worshipers to do the work of *t'shuvah* with greater compassion and gentleness as it strikes poignant notes of both contrast and penitence with the experience of the day.

ELSIE R. STERN

Notes

1. *Gates of Repentance* includes an *Avodah* service that explicitly reflects a modern myth of history and does not rely on the Temple and Temple service as central or generative symbols. For an analysis of this service, see Lawrence Hoffman, *Gates of Understanding,* vol. 2 (New York: CCAR Press), 138–44.

2. Ibid., 129.

3. Elsie Stern, "Concepts of Scripture in the Synagogue Service," in *Jewish Concepts of Scripture: A Comparative Introduction,* ed. Benjamin D. Sommer (New York: NYU Press, 2012), 19-26.

4. Michael Swartz and Joseph Yahalom, *Avodah: An Anthology of Ancient Poetry for Yom Kippur* (University Park: Pennsylvania State University Press, 2005), 30–39.

5. Hoffman, *Gates of Understanding,* vol. 2, 142.

6. Isa. 15:1–16:14, 25:10–12; Jer. 48:1–47; Ezek. 25:8–11; Amos 2:1–3; Zeph. 2:8–11.

7. Deut. 23:4–5 prohibits the admission of Moabites into the congregation of *YHVH.* This prohibition is invoked in Neh. 13:1–3 as support for the radical endogamy policy of the book's protagonists. The characterization of Ruth as a Moabite in the book of Ruth is likely a polemical response to exclusionary policies like that advocated by Ezra-Nehemiah. As Regina Schwartz has observed, even Gen. 19, which ascribes Moab's origins to the incestuous union between Lot and his daughters, can be seen as part of this conversation. Regina Schwartz, *The Curse of Cain* (Chicago and London: University of Chicago Press, 1997), 99. As quintessential foreigners, Moabites symbolize forbidden exogamy; as products of incest, they also stand in for prohibited radical endogamy. Appropriate Israelite marriage resides between these two extremes. It is not surprising that Moab became a flashpoint for these concerns. Moab was a close relation to Israel: The two entities probably came into being at about the same time; their languages, material culture, and religions were similar; and parts of the territory of Moab were sporadically under the control of the kingdom of Israel. It is often similar cultures, rather than radically different ones, that spark anxiety over communal identity and boundaries.

Poetry

Stretching toward *S'lichot*

Ruth Lerner

The last angel arrived at midnight to take me home.
I did not want to go with her.

I did not want to put on my soft black ballet shoes
to begin my annual practice at the barre.

I did not want to begin the lengthy limbering up
the slow stretching of mind muscles
moving in time to ancient melodies.

I did not want to begin the sacred *pliés* or *relevés*
the well-disciplined risings and descendings of the soul
struggling to return to the Source.

I did not want to begin the silent conditioning of the body:
the bending and the bowing
the pushing and the pausing
the stretching and the searching within.

I did not want to begin peering over the past year's
lapsed practiced sessions:
the ones where I had failed completely
the ones where I had erred half-way
the ones where I had done the bare minimum
or the ones where I did more than the bare minimum,
but did them with a stony detachment.

RUTH LERNER has been writing poetry for the High Holy Days for more than twenty years. Every year her poetry is integrated into the High Holy Day services at her synagogue, Kehillat Israel in Pacific Palisades, California.

All these holy loosening-up exercises
I did not want to begin.
But it was *S'lichot* and I had no choice.

The last angel arrived at midnight to take me home.
I held her hand, clasped my black ballet shoes to my breast
and began beating them into my heart.

POETRY

Rosh HaShanah in the Pines, 2011/5772

Hara E. Person

Darkness settles, slowly, across the horizon.
The new year rises before us,
its fragile moon awaiting our embrace.

Heaven and earth entwine
in their annual dance of re-creation.
A fissure appears in the firmament tonight,
an entranceway into new beginnings.

Out beyond the swales
the sea expands and contracts,
keeping time to the thrumming of the universe.

Under this Rosh HaShanah sky
the path before us is uncertain.
All we can do is hold each other tight
as we make our way home.

RABBI HARA E. PERSON (NY98) is the publisher and director of CCAR Press and the managing editor of the *CCAR Journal*. She also serves Congregation B'nai Olam in Fire Island Pines as the High Holy Day rabbi.

POETRY

What if . . .

Donald B. Rossoff

What if each of us was like a drop of rain
forming weightless in the clouds,
having made our ascent from the great ocean below,
in ways that were us but not yet,
coming into being as separate selves,
spending our time in a great journey
back to where all are one again?

And what if some of us were soft and gentle
like the soothing showers of spring,
barely noticed
as we brought life to the earth?

And what if some of us were hard and strong
like the raging summer storms,
spending our journey midst thunderous tumult
that never finds peace?

And what if God were like that great ocean,
teeming with life and its potential
where we each begin
     and end
     and begin again
     and again?

Together we would be forever
But I would not be I
and you would not be you
but together we would be in that greater I
dancing to the rhythm
of rising and falling

DONALD B. ROSSOFF (C81) has been a rabbi at Temple B'nai Or in Morristown, New Jersey, since 1990. He is the author of *The Perfect Prayer* (URJ), the composer (with Cantor Bruce Benson) of *Adonai Li* (Transcontinental), and has contributed chapters to several books.

POETRY

dissolving and transforming
being and becoming,
never missing a step
even when we thought we had.

What if each of us was like a raindrop
and God were like the ocean
and life was the journey
of leaving and coming home?

Would my heart not still be shattered?
Would the seas not be filled with my tears?

POETRY

Kol Nidrei

Jenni Person

Kol Nidrei's streaming live
chanting
from a bedside laptop;
Game Seven
is muted on TV;
kids are nestled between us
"Sssssssh, listen to the rabbi."
They fall asleep at the mention of her name
too bad they don't do that in shul.

Now some guy is being interviewed on the tube
"Hey, he's cute, is he a Jew?"
David pulls out his iPhone Wiki app
and discovers: Jew/Half-Jew
"He did what Sandy Koufax
swore he'd never do
But never needed to
hey, I'd play Game Seven on Yom Kippur too
and I'm the seminarian!"

Because baseball is a faith.

Marlins fans meet at a third inning minyan.
And the Jew/Half-Jew in question
shares the last name
of Sandy Koufax's mom before she married.
And his grandfather lived in a house previously owned
by Hank Greenberg.
So the lineage is long

and *Kol Nidrei* is live online.

JENNI PERSON is a literary artist and the director of Next@19th, a Jewish Culture Center in Miami. She received her MFA in Interdisciplinary Arts from Goddard College.

POETRY

Yom Kippur, The Essence Does Not Change

Yehoshua November

Isn't this why, though he knew little Torah,
Sandy Koufax gave up what is unthinkable to give up?
Isn't this why, a century earlier,
young Jewish boys—
kidnapped from the *cheder* and raised
in the Russian army—
took off their shirts
at the last hour of Yom Kippur?
Revealing their whip marks, they said,
"God, we did not forget you, please bless us."

YEHOSHUA NOVEMBER is the author of *God's Optimism,* which won the MSR Poetry Book Award and was selected as a finalist for the *L.A. Times* Book Prize in Poetry. He teaches writing at Touro College and Rutgers University.

POETRY

The Ankle of the High Priest

Joseph R. Black

The cord is thick: silky soft
Belying its macabre purpose.
They tie it tight—to remind him of his holiness
And his mortality.

Once a year he crosses the threshold of that sacred, musty site.
He leaves behind his glory, his splendor, his pretense.
Accompanied by the sound of bells
He is hampered in his forward progress
By the tautness of his tether.

He limps toward the place that only he and his fathers before
    him have seen.

    A year of dust covers the altar—
        Spilling over like so many unanswered prayers—
        That someday, in a different time, will be
        Gathered together,
        Hastily scribbled, and
        Shoved between the cracks of massive stones.

He hesitates while walking—
Dragging his rope,
Hoarding the hope of his people
He knows he cannot remain silent for long
Lest those outside the entryway grow nervous.

And yet, he yearns to be still:

        To remember
        To reveal
        To rule

JOSEPH R. BLACK serves as senior rabbi of Temple Emanuel in Denver, Colorado. In addition to his work in the pulpit, he also is a poet, singer/songwriter, and author of two children's books, several CDs, videos, and a songbook.

POETRY

For what shall he ask?
Two goats have already died.
Shofars have sounded.
Souls afflicted.
What's left to do?

He carries the dreams and fears of all who wait outside:
Petitions for health and healing
For wealth and feeling
For babies to be born
And loved ones who are mourned
For enemies defeated
And lovers entreated

He is the one
Who speaks to The One

Jumbled pleas and petitions
Swirl round his head
As the knot grows tighter round his foot.
He opens his mouth in prayer:

　　　Return, O Israel, to your God
　　　Return, O God, to your Israel

We are pulled towards one other
In an ancient game of tug of war.

He falls, prostrate at the foot of the altar.
Digging in his fingers, he holds tight
Until, drawing ten straight lines in the dust,
He emerges into the light of a new day.

The Wilderness of Tishrei

Barbara AB Symons

Two goats, brothers perhaps.

One has the honor of being
sacrificed
Becomes *tahor*
postmortem.

One touched with sin
is led out to the wilderness
Becomes *tamei*
for life.

How did he choose the fate?
He, author of the Book of Life volume II
Did he see which goat was strong enough
to live with sin
to die without sin
Did he look into eyes as human as can be without being?

We are in the wilderness of Tishrei.
What does it mean to live with sin?
What does it mean to die without?

BARBARA AB SYMONS (NY94) has served congregations in New York, Connecticut, and Massachusetts and is currently serving as rabbi and director of education at Temple David in Monroeville, Pennsylvania, where she lives with her husband, Rabbi Ron Symons, and three children.

Additional Discussion Questions

Preparing for the New *Machzor* and the High Holy Days: An Integrated Approach, *Rabbi Elaine Zecher*

1. How do you care for your spiritual health?
2. How do you prepare for the High Holy Days?
3. In a prayer book, do you prefer to have alternative services, each with its own consistent theology, or to have the presence of multiple theologies within each service (what the author calls "integrated theology")? Why?
4. How does or might integrative worship look in your community?
5. What different elements would you like to see in integrative worship?

Section One: From the Editors of the New *Machzor*

The New Reform *Machzor* Is a Solution, but What Is the Problem? *Rabbi Edwin C. Goldberg*

1. Which translation of *Yamim Noraim* do you prefer—Days of Awe or Days of Fright? Why?
2. Should a High Holy Day prayer book begin with Rosh HaShanah eve or Rosh Chodesh Elul, and why? What might the latter look like?
3. The author asks on page 272, "How do we help ourselves return to our sacred path, in a world that continually seduces us away from the work

459

that we must do?" Is this *the* essential question of the High Holy Days and their liturgy, or is there another question that you consider to be more central?

4. What makes a book "sacred"? Is it form, function, or something else altogether?

5. What does it mean to be a Reform Jew in the twenty-first century?

6. The author asks on page 274, "Specifically, what do we hope to have realized by the worshipers at the end of *N'ilah*? How will their lives have changed? What will be different? . . . What does [*t'shuvah*] mean? . . . Would we even know if we had succeeded?" What are some possible answers to these essential questions? How would you measure "success" in your community regarding High Holy Day worship?

7. Exercises:

   a. Read the article's introduction only, study the editorial team's vision statement using the discussion questions provided, and then read the rest of Goldberg's article to learn some commentary on the vision statement.

      i.   Do you agree that "*t'shuvah* is the chief goal of the *Yamim Noraim*"? Why or why not? What might be (an)other chief goal(s) of the Days of Awe?

      ii. If "a *machzor* is our indispensable manual and guide," what would it look like?

      iii. Are there only two groups of prayers who attend High Holy Day services—the regular and the new? Who else might there be in our communities?

      iv. Is the new *machzor* intended for synagogue use only or in the home as well, since *t'shuvah* and *cheshbon hanefesh* are ongoing processes not limited to one space or time period?

    v.   What does "continuity" mean here? Does it refer to continuity with our Reform forebears or our biblical ancestors or somewhere in between?

    vi.   What High Holy Day texts do you consider to be painful or disturbing?

  b. Create your own vision statement for creating a new *machzor,* then compare your creation with the editorial team's vision statement. Guiding questions: What are you hoping for in the new *machzor?* What do you want to see?

What Happens When We Use Poetry in Our Prayer Books—and Why? *Rabbi Sheldon Marder*

1. How do you feel about the liturgical use of non-Jewish poetry?

2. What are your questions regarding liturgical innovation?

3. Do you agree with the author that, "Innovation is one of the core ideas in Jewish prayer" (p. 282)? Why or why not?

4. How can we encourage our communities to respond to poetry in a playful and inventive way when their initial reaction may be negative? How can we be comfortable with the mystery and that which is uncomfortable?

5. Exercises:

  a. Open to any right-hand page of *Mishkan T'filah,* without looking at the left-hand page, and write a poem or other creative reading in response to the classical liturgy.

  b. Take a secular poem and connect it to a prayer, explaining the connection. Examples of secular English and American poets:

- Emily Dickinson
- Percy Bysshe Shelley
- Wallace Stevens
- Walt Whitman
- William Wordsworth
- William Butler Yeats

The End of Liturgical Reform as We Know It, *Rabbi Leon A. Morris*

1. The author asks on page 293, "Does our prayer book really need to be consistent with our theology? Must we believe literally the words we recite? Is our prayer book intended to be a catechism of Jewish belief?" What are some possible answers to these essential questions about liturgy?
2. Why does uncertainty often make us uncomfortable?
3. Do you agree with the author that "the age of liturgical reform . . . is over" (p. 295)? Why or why not?
4. How do you understand "creative retrieval" and "ressourcement" in Reform Judaism today?
5. Exercise: Take a piece of challenging High Holy Day liturgy (such as *Avinu Malkeinu, Untaneh Tokef,* or *Kol Nidrei*) and reframe, explain, or translate it "in such a way as to allow it to live in our Reform synagogues" (p. 296).

Section Two: From Professors of Liturgy at HUC-JIR

"Lu Yehi": High Holy Day Liturgy and Experience in Israel, *Rabbi Dalia Marx*

1. Who are "the people who normally shy away from any kind of organized religious activity" in

our community (p. 299)? How can we make services meaningful and accessible for everyone?

2. What is the journey on which you want to take your community throughout High Holy Day worship, and how do musical choices impact that journey?

3. What might be a song in English that parallels "Lu Yehi" as described in this article?

4. How might the American experience of Rosh HaShanah that immediately followed 9/11 be similar to and different from the Israeli experience of the Yom Kippur War? Are there other particular High Holy Day experiences that remain in the American Jewish social psyche?

5. Have you ever experienced the High Holy Days in Israel? If so, how did they compare with similar experiences outside of Israel?

6. How can an understanding of the challenges of the Israeli experience of the High Holy Days help us to shape High Holy Day worship outside of Israel?

7. Exercise: Do a text study of "Lu Yehi" by Naomi Shemer or another modern Israeli poem or song by writers such as Leah Goldberg, Natan Zach, or Yehudah Amichai. For possible texts, see *Kavvanat HaLev*, the Israeli Reform *machzor*.

Machzor: The Poetry of Truly Awe-Inspiring Days, *Dr. Richard S. Sarason*

1. Personal reflection and introspection: How does your personal history affect your High Holy Day experience?

2. How do you relate to the existential themes of the High Holy Days described on page 304 ("life, death, and ultimate meaning . . .")?

3. Do you tend to read the *machzor* symbolically or literally? How does this method of reading the text affect your High Holy Day experience?

4. What role does the *machzor* play in reinterpreting the High Holy Day liturgy for our communities? What role do the *sh'lichei tzibur* (service leaders) play?
5. Do you prefer English liturgical readings to be written in elevated poetic language or more colloquial language? Why?
6. Communal reflection and introspection: How does the communal history affect your community's High Holy Day experience?
7. The author identifies a number of tensions inherent in the experience of High Holy Day liturgy. How do you balance each of these tensions in High Holy Day worship?
   a. Symbolism versus literalism (p. 305)
   b. English versus Hebrew (p. 306)
   c. Talking versus doing, speech vs. silence (p. 307)
   d. Poetry versus prose (p. 307)
   e. Personal versus communal (p. 307)

A Tale of Three *Machzorim,* *Rabbi Richard N. Levy*

1. If you could name the new *machzor,* what would you call it?
2. What are contemporary Reform beliefs? Can we use the platform adopted in Pittsburgh in 1999 in the same way our forebears drew upon the Columbus Platform in the creation of a new *machzor*? Why or why not?
   • Pittsburgh Platform of 1999: https://www.ccarnet.org/rabbis-speak/platforms/statement-principles-reform-judaism/
   • Columbus Platform of 1937: https://www.ccarnet.org/rabbis-speak/platforms/guiding-principles-reform-judaism/

3. Communal reflection: What is your community's history with *machzorim*? Which have you used over time and why? When a change in *machzor* was made, how and why was that decision made?

4. The author identifies a number of tensions inherent in the experience of High Holy Day liturgy. How do you balance each of these tensions in High Holy Day worship?

   a. Recurring/familiar/constant versus unique (p. 309)
   b. New versus old (p. 309)
   c. Intimacy versus majesty (p. 310)
   d. English versus Hebrew (p. 311)
   e. Formal English versus colloquial English (p. 312)
   f. Variety versus simplicity (p. 313)

Doing It Right or Doing It Well?
Dr. Lawrence A. Hoffman

1. How would you describe liturgy done well (what does or might it look like, sound like, feel like)?
2. Does your community stress doing liturgy right or well? How successful has that focus been?
3. How do we see that "custom trumps halachah" in Reform Jewish liturgy (p. 317)?
4. Who gets to decide what is authentic or legitimate in liturgy and why? How do they decide? What are their criteria?
5. When it comes to liturgy, which resonates with you more—the past or future? Why?
6. Is there "truth" in liturgy (p. 320)? If so, is there only one, or can there be multiple truths?
7. How might you utilize liturgical highlighting and editing in the creation of High Holy Day worship?

8. What is the ambience, ethos, or message of the High Holy Days?
9. What is meaningful High Holy Day worship for your community?
10. How can we use High Holy Day worship to bridge the educated elite and the "plebeians" in the pews (if they are even there)?
11. The author asks on page 325, "What are the real liturgical messages of the *machzor*? What gets in our way of delivering them? What must we sacrifice by editing and what must we create by highlighting in order to do that delivering?" What are some possible answers to these essential questions?
12. Which do you value more in High Holy Day worship: Doing it right or doing it well? Tradition or authenticity?
13. Is High Holy Day worship in your community done right or well? If the former, what changes could you implement to do it well or at least better?

Section Three: From Our Colleagues

When I Hear the Shofar I Taste Chocolate, *Cantor Evan Kent*

1. Have you ever had a synesthetic experience with ritual or liturgy? Describe that experience, identify its operating principles, and explore how you could apply those principles to High Holy Day worship.
2. What are some other ways in which we can make High Holy Day worship a multisensory/embodied/synesthetic experience?
3. How can we use the words of the *machzor* to help us in this endeavor?

Love, Liturgy, Leadership,
Rabbi Elyse D. Frishman

Exercise: The author asks many questions throughout her article. As you read her words, pause after every question and respond in writing in a journal-like fashion.

The *Yamim Noraim*: Concentric Circles of Liturgy and Relation,
Rabbi Lawrence A. Englander

1. If you were to draw your own figure of the relationship between God and the world (see p. 350), what would yours look like?

2. Among the various theologies listed on page 352, which speak(s) most to you and why? Is there a theology to which you subscribe that is not listed here?

3. What is the place of technology in worship in general and on the High Holy Days in particular? How can new technology augment the High Holy Day worship experience?

4. Can a *machzor* be manifest in more than one way?

5. Exercise: Study the poem on page 345 by Cynthia Ozick as a text. Use the following questions as a guide:

   a. Have you ever shared the sentiment expressed in the first stanza? If so, what about the book didn't you understand?

   b. In the second stanza, the narrator shifts from talking about *what* ("the book") to talking about *who* ("Who will teach . . . ?"). What does the author suggest about the nature of High Holy Day worship by this contrast?

   c. What does the narrator identify as problems with "return" (*t'shuvah*)?

d. Is this poem optimistic or pessimistic (or simply realistic)? What is its message for us?

The Calves of Our Lips: The Inescapable Connections between Prayer and Sacrifice, *Rabbi Leon A. Morris*

1. How do you understand sacrifice? What is your relationship to it?
2. What should the role of sacrifice be in the *machzor*?
3. What would liturgical language around prayer as the substitution for sacrifice look like?

"Baavur Sheani Noder Tzedakah Baado" (*Yizkor*), *Rabbi Margaret Moers Wenig*

1. Do you agree that "for most who are still grieving it is a fairly private process for which no ritual prompting is needed" (p. 367)? Why or why not? If so, what is the role of ritual in the grieving process then?
2. How can we foster the making of memories during *Yizkor*? What memories of a deceased loved one would you like to share at *Yizkor*?
3. How do you as an individual honor the dead? How can we as a community best honor the dead?
4. How has the death of a loved one (or someone you know) changed you?
5. Using this article as a guide, how would you (re)craft *Yizkor*?

Visions for a New/Old Reform *Yizkor* Service, *Rabbi Donald B. Rossoff*

1. How do you understand the concepts of immortality, soul/spirit, afterlife, and eternality?

2. Which elements of past *Yizkor* services do you want to keep? What new elements would you like to introduce?

3. How do you feel about the *Yizkor* service proposed by the author? Is anything missing? Would you add anything? Would you reorganize/reorder at all?

We, the *Avaryanim*, Chant *Kol Nidrei*, Rabbi Donald P. Cashman

1. What are the implications of "halachic responsibility" for Reform Jews today (p. 391)?

2. On page 391, the author lists Reform approaches to challenging liturgy: "We ponder retention, rejection, modification, addition; we equivocate, we gloss over, or we leave untranslated." Which of these methods are more appealing than others?

3. What has your community done in its approach to *Kol Nidrei*?

4. How could you use the questions on the top of page 394 to frame *Kol Nidrei* for your community?

5. Would the model of *Kol Nidrei* presented in this article work for your community? Why or why not? If not right now, what work could be done in your community to prepare them for such a *Kol Nidrei*?

The *Untaneh Tokef* Prayer—Sealing Our Faith, Not Our Fate, *Rabbi Y. Lindsey bat Joseph*

1. Which theology is more compelling for you: determinism or particle physics? Are these theologies and those described on the top of page 402 mutually exclusive? Why or why not? Are human beings able to hold multiple theologies at once?

2. Does it help or hinder the recitation of *Untaneh Tokef* to recall the legend of Rabbi Amnon of Mainz?

3. How do you understand "divine justice" (p. 401)? How does your understanding relate to the understanding of divine justice presented in *Untaneh Tokef*? To answer this question, refer to the English text of *Untaneh Tokef* on page 399.

4. What is an experience from your life that relates to *Untaneh Tokef's* themes of suffering and sacrifice?

Viewing *Untaneh Tokef* through a New Lens, *Rabbi Amy Scheinerman*

1. What are your reactions to Shalom Auslander's portrayal of *Untaneh Tokef* on page 409?

2. "What does it mean that we can *temper* the divine decree" (p. 410)?

3. How does process theology as described here resonate with you? How does it aid or challenge your understanding of *Untaneh Tokef*?

4. How could we apply the ideas in these two articles about *Untaneh Tokef* into meaningful worship experiences for our communities? What might these ideas look like in practical application (as opposed to the theory stated here)?

Mystical Journeys and Magical Letters, *Rabbi Judith Z. Abrams*

1. How do you relate to each of the schools of prayer described in this article: priesthood, Torah/scribes, and royalty?

2. How might this understanding of *heichalot* mysticism inform your approach to High Holy Day liturgy? How could its teachings be used to frame an experience of the *Yamim Noraim*?

The *Machzor* before the *Machzor*, Dr. Aaron D. Panken

1. How might this understanding of Second Temple literature inform your approach to the High Holy Days?
2. How could you use these Second Temple texts around High Holy Day worship and education?
3. How could we emulate the authors of this Second Temple literature and "rework, reconsider, and redirect" the High Holy Day liturgy and rituals, reinterpreting them for our contemporary audience (p. 437)?

Yom Kippur in Moab, *Dr. Elsie R. Stern*

1. Why has Reform Judaism moved away from "traditional Judaism's affirmation of the privileged role of ancestral priesthood and its ongoing hope for the reestablishment of the Temple cult" (p. 439)?
2. How is Torah a "tool in the quest for redemption" (p. 439)? What other tools might we use in this quest?
3. Should we provide High Holy Day worshipers with "a break from the complexities of the moral world they inhabit" (p. 444)? Or does this deviate from the goals of the High Holy Days?
4. Within High Holy Day worship, what is the relationship between fantasy and actual lived experience, between fiction and nonfiction?
5. What is the role of the Torah service in general and on the High Holy Days in particular?
6. If you were to choose the Torah readings for the High Holy Days, what would you pick and why? What is the message you would want these readings to convey?

7. What is the journey on which we want to take our communities over the course of the High Holy Days? How can our *machzor* enable this journey?

Poetry

Instructions for reading poetry:

1. Read these poems in tandem with Sheldon Marder's article "What Happens When We Use Poetry in Our Prayer Books—and Why?"
2. After reading each poem, ask: How could this poem be used liturgically?

Stretching toward *S'lichot, Dr. Ruth Lerner*

1. <u>Background</u>: "The last angel arrived at midnight . . ."
   a. Traditionally *S'lichot* begins at midnight.
   b. There is a controversial passage toward the end of *S'lichot* called *Machnisei Rachamim,* or "those who deliver the prayers." This text is controversial because it appeals to the angels to deliver our prayers to God on our behalf instead of appealing directly to the divine authority.
2. What are the parallels between preparing for the New Year and ballet exercises? Does this metaphor work for you? Why or why not?
3. Do we often feel burdened by the onset of the *Yamim Noraim*? Does that sense of burden continue throughout the High Holy Day season, or does it ease once our bodies get back into the rhythm?
4. How is *S'lichot* practiced in your community? How do you prepare for the New Year? What is your Elul or *S'lichot* practice?

5. "I had no choice." What does the narrator mean by this? Do you ever share this sentiment?

Rosh HaShanah in the Pines, 2011/5772, *Rabbi Hara E. Person*

1. Compare this poem with the Creation narrative found in Genesis 1. How many parallels can you find? How do these biblical parallels inform the poem?
2. Background: In the Creation story of Lurianic Kabbalah, God "expands and contracts" while creating, a process called *tzimtzum*. Another mystical concept is *d'veikut*, or cleaving to God, echoes of which might lie behind the words "All we can do is hold each other tight."
3. Why is the moon described as fragile here? What might this celestial body represent?
4. The poem ends with "home." To which home does the narrator refer? What does "home" mean? How does it change your undersanding of the poem to learn that the Hebrew for "cemetery" is literally "eternal home" (*beit olam*)?

What If . . . , *Rabbi Donald B. Rosoff*

1. "What if . . ." is the question par excellence of the *Yamim Noraim*. Before reading this poem you might expect to see a series of questions that review the past year, asking, "What if I had done X instead of Y?" This is not how the poem reads, which aligns with Jewish tradition to apologize for past mistakes and to prepare for a better year instead of dwelling on the past that we cannot change.
2. Our bodies are predominantly made of water. Water is a necessary life force, the substance that makes earth the only known inhabitable planet

(also predominantly made of water). Water is also a powerful motif associated with the *Yamim Noraim.* The most well known tradition in this regard is *Tashlich,* in which water is supposed to carry away our sins. However, if we are the water, what are the implications of this metaphor for *t'shuvah* (repentance)? If God is also the water, what are the implications of this metaphor for *s'lichah* (forgiveness)?

3. The poem also ends with "coming home." How does this poet understand home?

Kol Nidrei, *Jenni Person*

1. What real-life issues does this poem raise? What are the tensions it reveals?
2. What role does Sandy Koufax play in this poem? What does he or his character symbolize?
3. Do you agree with the narrator when she says "baseball is a faith"? Why or why not?
4. What is the "lineage" that "is long"?

Yom Kippur, The Essence Does Not Change, *Yehoshua November*

1. What is the essence of Yom Kippur that the narrator is trying to convey in this poem?
2. What contributes to a Jewish identity: Torah, commemorating Yom Kippur, or is there more?
3. What are the wounds and scars we bear for God or the Jewish people?

The Ankle of the High Priest, *Rabbi Joseph R. Black*

1. Background: In the ancient Temple, no one was allowed to enter the Holy of Holies except for the High Priest and only on Yom Kippur. Apparently there was a concern about what to do

should the High Priest die while inside. The *Zohar*, a thirteenth-century mystical Jewish commentary on the Torah written by Moses de Leon, suggests a solution to this potential problem: "R. Isaac said: A cord was tied to the feet of the High Priest before he entered the Holy of Holies, so that if he died suddenly within they should be able to draw him out" (*Soncino Zohar, Vayikra, Parashat Emor*, section 3, p. 102a).

2. What holds you back from "forward progress"?
3. What have you seen that no one else has had the privilege or burden of seeing?
4. What does this poem suggest about the role and responsibility of the Jewish people's leaders?
5. To whom do you relate most in this poem and why—the High Priest, the other priests, the people, the narrator, or another character?

The Wilderness of Tishrei, *Rabbi Barbara AB Symons*

1. Background:
   a. Leviticus 16 describes a sacrificial rite in which two goats are selected for the expiation of communal sin. Lots are cast to determine which goat will be dedicated to God and sacrificed on the altar and which goat will be destined for Azazel. The goat that receives the latter designation is sent into the wilderness alive, carrying away the community's sins.
   b. *Tahor/tamei*: pure/impure. Ritual impurity is a concept that a person or object can be in a state that prevents the person or object from having any contact with the Temple or its cult.
2. Which goat would you rather be and why?

3. Does God choose our fate, as the narrator suggests? Do we choose our fate?
4. What do you think the narrator means by "the Book of Life volume II"?
5. How would you respond to the questions posed by the narrator?

Glossary

achat: "One."

Adonai Mah Adam: "Adonai, what is humanity?" *Yizkor* rite that is a series of psalm verses from all over the Book of Psalms.

Adonai maon atah hayita lanu: "Adonai You have been our dwelling place" (Psalm 90).

aggadah: "Legend."

Akeidah: "Binding." Generally refers to the Torah text in which Abraham binds his son Isaac in preparation for sacrificing him (Genesis 22).

alav hashalom: "Peace be upon him" (plural: *aleihem hashalom*). Recited when mentioning someone who is deceased.

Al Cheit: "For (the) sin." Liturgical confession of sins recited on Yom Kippur.

amcha: "Your people." Generally refers to the folk (or "Jews in the pews") as opposed to the elite.

Amidah: "Standing." The core and main element of each of the prescribed daily services. Also known as *T'filah* and (among Ashkenazim) as *Sh'moneh Esreih* (Eighteen) because of the eighteen benedictions that it originally comprised.

Amora: A rabbi of the Talmuds (plural: Amoraim).

Ana Adonai! Chatati af aviti l'fanecha harbeh pashati ani uv'nei Aharon: "Please Adonai! I have sinned, also I have done wrong before You, greatly have I committed crimes, me and the children of Aaron" (*Seder HaAvodah*).

Apocrypha: Along with the Pseudepigrapha known in Hebrew as "hidden" works, both terms refer to collections of intertestamental literature, ca. 200 BCE to 200 CE, primarily of Jewish authorship. They are hidden by exclusion from the Hebrew canon. Books of the Apocrypha and Pseudepigrapha, like Maccabees and Judith, are included in some Christian Bibles.

aron: "Closet; ark; casket"; *aron hakodesh*: "the holy ark." Where *sifrei Torah* are stored.

Ashamnu: "We are guilty." Central prayer in High Holy Day liturgy.

Ashkenazi(c): "German." Pertaining to the Jewish community originally from Central or Eastern Europe.

Atah notein yad laposhim: "You [God] give a hand to the sinners" (*N'ilah*).

Atik Yomin: "The Ancient of Days."

Av HaRachamim: "Father of mercy." Name of liturgical unit located in the Shabbat Torah service.

Avinu Malkeinu: Literally, "Our Father Our King." One of the central liturgical rubrics of the High Holy Days.

avodah: "Service, work." The entire sacrificial system was known by this name. The liturgical section of the Yom Kippur *Musaf* service became known as *Seder HaAvodah* (the Order of the *Avodah*) because it described the most important sacrificial service of the entire year carried out by the High Priest on Yom Kippur.

avodah shebalev: "Service of the heart." The Talmudic Sages understood the biblical command "You shall serve God with your whole heart" (Deuteronomy 11:13) as an injunction regarding prayer, for "What service is performed with the heart? This is prayer" (Babylonian Talmud, *Taanit* 2a). Therefore this term refers to prayer, the form of worship that replaced sacrifice after the destruction of the Temple.

Baal HaZohar: "Master of the Zohar." Appellation for the compiler of the *Zohar*, Moses de Leon in thirteenth-century Spain, who attributed his work to Shimon bar Yochai, a second-century rabbi in the Land of Israel.

baal t'kiah: "Master of [the shofar] blast." Shofar blower (plural: *baalei t'kiah*).

Bachodesh hashvi-i b'echad lachodesh: "In the seventh month on the first [day] of the month" (Leviticus 23:24).

baraita: "Outside." A tannaitic statement cited in the Talmud but not found in (i.e., outside) the Mishnah.

Baruch shem k'vod: "Blessed is the glorious Name" (*Sh'ma*).

bashert: Yiddish word meaning "destiny" referring to one's soulmate.

Bavel: Babylonia.

Bavli: Babylonian Talmud, compiled around 600 CE in Babylonia.

bedeken: Yiddish word for the veiling ceremony prior to a Jewish wedding.

bein adam laMakom: "Between human beings and God."

bein adam l'atzmo: "Between a human being and him/herself."

bein adam l'chaveiro: "Between human beings."

Beit HaMikdash: "The Holy House." The Temple (First and Second). Also shortened to *Mikdash*.

Birkat Kohanim: "Priestly Benediction." Text found in Numbers 6:24–26.

b'meizid: "Deliberately, on purpose."

b'rachah: "Blessing" (plural: *b'rachot*). *B'rachot* is also the name of a tractate of Mishnah, *Tosefta*, and Talmud.

b'shem omro: "In the name of the one who spoke it." To cite one's source.

Chasidei Ashkenaz: "Pietists of Ashkenaz." A group of Ashkenazic medieval mystics.

chatimah: "Signature." The closing line of a blessing that expresses the overall theme of that blessing.

chayim: "Life."

chazal: Acronym for *chachamim zichronam livrachah*, meaning "sages whose memory is for a blessing."

chazan: "Cantor."

chesed: "Loving-kindness."

cheshbon hanefesh: "Accounting of the soul." Process of introspection and self-examination we are called to do throughout the *Yamim Noraim*.

chevruta: "Study partner."

chidush: "Innovation."

chotmeinu: "Seal us."

chuppah: "Wedding canopy."

darshan: "Interpreter" (plural: *darshanim*).

Diaspora: The scattering of the Jewish community across the world, beginning with the exile from the Land of Israel during the Babylonian conquest of 587 BCE.

din: "Judgment."

D'rashah: "Interpretation" (plural: *d'rashot*).

Eichah: "How." The Book of Lamentations.

Eileh Ezkerah: "These shall I remember." Yom Kippur liturgy recalling the Ten Martyrs.

Ein Kitzvah: "There is no set span." Final passage of *Untaneh Tokef*.

El Malei Rachamim: "Fully compassionate God." Prayer for the dead.

El melech yosheiv al kisei rachamim: "God King sits on a throne of mercy" (*Eileh Ezkerah*).

Elohim Eili Atah: "God, You are my God" (Psalm 63).

Elul: The sixth month of the Jewish calendar, often marked by preparation for the *Yamim Noraim*.

emtza: "Middle" (noun); *emtzai*: "middle" (adjective).

Erech apayim v'rav chesed: "Endlessly patient and full of loving-kindness" (Exodus 34:6). Element of the thirteen attributes of God.

Eretz Yisrael: "The Land of Israel."

Esa Einai: "I will lift up my eyes" (Psalm 121).

Gemara: "Learning." A word popularly applied to the Talmud as a whole or, more particularly, to the discussions and elaborations on the Mishnah by Rabbinic authorities of the third to fifth centuries CE.

gemeinde: "Community" (German).

haftarah: "Conclusion" (plural: haftarot). A section from the prophetic books of the Bible read on Shabbat and holidays after the reading of the Torah.

halachah: "The path." Collective body of Jewish ritual and ethical law, as determined by textual sources such as biblical law, Talmudic law, and later Rabbinic law codes. Also a term for "verses" in the *Tosefta*.

Han'shamah lach: "The soul is for You." One of the prayers of *S'lichot*.

Har HaBayit: "The Temple Mount."

Hashem Hashem El rachum v'chanun: "*Adonai Adonai*, gracious and compassionate God" (Exodus 34:6). Element of the thirteen attributes of God.

Hashkavah: "Laying to rest." Sephardic memorial prayer.

Havdalah: "Separation." The ceremony that marks the end of Shabbat and festivals. The *Havdalah* blessing separates the holy from the ordinary.

Hazkarat N'shamot: "Mentioning [i.e., naming] of souls." Another name for *Yizkor*.

heichalot: "Palaces." Genre of Jewish mystical literature originating in the Land of Israel between 70 and 500 CE.

Hin'ni: "Here I am." A central prayer in High Holy Day liturgy.

Holiness Code: Refers to Leviticus 17–26, a section outlining a series of ritual and ethical purity laws, seen as a discrete unit in this biblical book.

iyun t'filah: "Study of prayer." An introduction to a prayer to teach one of its themes or to set a tone for its recitation.

Jaffe, Mordecai: (ca. 1535–1612) Author of *Levush Malchut*, a ten-volume codification of Jewish law that particularly stressed the customs of the Jews of Eastern Europe.

kahal: "Congregation."

kaparah: "Forgiveness, absolution, expiation." The setting aside of charity money before sunset on the eve of Yom Kippur. Implicit in this act of *kaparah* is the idea that the charity money serves as atonement for one's sins. The concept of *kaparah* is probably based on the ancient scapegoat ritual for Yom Kippur (Leviticus 16:5–22).

kavanah: "Directed intention or intentionality" (plural: *kavanot*). The ideal state of mental concentration and devotion at prayer and during the performance of mitzvot. Also a creative supplement to the fixed liturgy.

kavod: "Honor, glory."

k'dushah: "Holiness" (plural: *k'dushot*). The Hebrew word also has the connotation of separation, setting aside.

Kiddush: "Sanctification." Prayer recited over wine to mark the holiness of Shabbat (or the Festivals).

Kiddush L'vanah: Sanctification of the new moon.

K'lal Yisrael: "The whole Jewish people."

Kodesh HaKodashim: "The Holy of Holies." The innermost chamber of the Temple, where the Ark of the Covenant was kept. The room was seen as the most holy location within the Temple complex. The Holy of Holies was only entered once a year: by the High Priest on Yom Kippur afternoon.

kohein: "Priest." A male descendant of Aaron, brother of Moses. The *kohanim* (plural) were in charge of the duties of running the Temple and its system of sacrifices. The *Kohein Gadol* was the High Priest. Among his many responsibilities was the performance of the Yom Kippur *Avodah* ritual.

kol d'mamah dakah: "Still small voice." God did not appear to Elijah in the wind, earthquake, or fire but instead as a still small voice (I Kings 19:12).

Kol Nidrei: "All Vows." A declaration of annulment of all vows that begins the evening service of Yom Kippur. See *Machzor: Challenge and Change*, volume 1, for an in-depth discussion on this liturgical subject.

korban: "Sacrifice" (plural: *korbanot*). From the Hebrew meaning "to bring close."

kotveinu: "Write us."

kotzer ruach: "Short of spirit." The spiritual version of "short of breath."

k'riat haTorah: "The Torah reading."

k'toret: "Incense."

k'vod malchuto: "Glorious is God's kingdom."

L'shanah habaah biY'rushalayim: "Next year in Jerusalem."

Maamad: "Post." A division of popular representatives deputed to accompany the daily services in the Temple with prayers, and also a corresponding division in the country towns, answering to the divisions of priests and Levites.

Maaseh Asarah Harugei Malchut: The legend of the ten sages put to death by the Romans, also called *Midrash Eileh Ezkerah*.

machloket: "Debate."

machzor: Special designated prayer book for the Festivals and the High Holy Days (plural: *machzorim*). Derived from *machzor hashanah*—the cycle of the year.

magid hamakom: "Local storyteller."

Mah anu? Meh chayeinu? Meh chasdeinu? Mah tzidkeinu?: "What are we? What are our lives? What is our kindness? What is our righteousness?" (*N'ilah*).

Maharil: Jacob ben Moses Levi Moellin (ca. 1360–1427) was a Talmudist and authority on Jewish law best known for his codification of the customs (*minhagim*) of the German Jews in *Sefer HaMaharil*.

malchut: "Sovereignty."

Malchuyot: "Sovereign Verses." The first of the three central benedictions of the Shofar Service on Rosh HaShanah morning.

mamlechet kohanim: "Kingdom of priests" (Exodus 19:6).

Mareih Kohein: "The appearance of the High Priest." Ashkenazic *piyut* chanted during *Seder HaAvodah* on Yom Kippur.

masechet: "Tractate," particularly of the Mishnah, *Tosefta*, or Talmud.

mashal: A short parable with a moral lesson or religious allegory, called a *nimshal*.

mashehu m'tzuyan: "Something exceptional."

matnat yad: "The gift of his hand" (Deuteronomy 16:17).

melech: "King, ruler."

midah: "Quality, value" (plural: *midot*).

midrash: "Interpretation" (plural: midrashim). Midrash is the method of interpreting Scripture to elucidate legal points or to bring out lessons through stories or homiletics. Midrash is also the designation of a particular genre of Rabbinic literature extending from pre-Mishnaic times to the tenth century.

Mikdash: See *Beit HaMikdash*.

Mikol chatoteichem . . . tit'haru: "From all your sins . . . you shall be cleansed" (Leviticus 16:30).

mimesis: Imitation or reproduction.

Minchah: From the verb *l'haniach*, meaning "to lay down, to place before." Refers to the afternoon prayer service, which itself is derived from the flour offering that accompanied each sacrifice in the Temple.

minhag: "Custom" (plural: *minhagim*).

Mipnei chata-einu galinu mei-artzeinu: "Because we sinned we were exiled from our land" (*Seder HaAvodah*).

Mishkan: "Tabernacle." Built in the desert by the Israelites before entering the Land of Israel, it served as the blueprint for the Temple, which would supercede it.

Mishnah: The first legal codification of basic Jewish law, arranged and redacted by Rabbi Y'hudah HaNasi about 200 CE.

mishpachah: "Family."

mitzvah: "Commandment, religious obligation" (plural: mitzvot).

M'lo chol haaretz k'vodo: "The whole earth is full of [God's] glory" (Isaiah 6:3).

M'nuchah n'chonah tachat kanfei haShechinah: "True rest under the wings of God's presence" (*Hashkavah*).

Musaf: "Additional." An additional service added after *Shacharit* on Shabbat, holidays, and Rosh Chodesh. It recalls the extra sacrifices brought to the Temple on these special days (Babylonian Talmud, *B'rachot* 26b).

nefesh: "Soul."

N'ilah: "Closing, locking (of the gates)." The concluding prayer, recited close to sunset, on Yom Kippur.

nimshal: The moral lesson or religious allegory of a *mashal*.

n'shamah y'teirah: "Additional soul." According to Rabbinic legend, an additional soul dwells in each Jew during Shabbat.

nusach: "Version." Either the style of a prayer service or the melody of the service depending on when the service is being conducted.

ol malchut shamayim: "The yoke of the kingdom of heaven."

ol mitzvot: "The yoke of obligations."

Omer: "Sheaf; wave offering." The sheaf offering of barley brought to the Temple on the sixteenth day of Nisan, and thus the name of the forty-nine-day period between the first day of Passover and Shavuot.

pasuk: "Biblical verse" (plural: *p'sukim*).

pay'tan: "*Piyut* composer" (plural: *pay'tanim*).

Pirkei Avot: "Ethics of the Ancestors." Tractate *Avot* of the Mishnah.

piyut: A liturgical poem composed in Hebrew that was inserted into the fixed liturgy of the prayer book. Poems in this liturgical genre, which includes common prayers such as *L'chah Dodi* and *Adon Olam*, are often composed as acrostics. They supplemented the liturgy as early as the first century (plural: *piyutim*).

P'sikta D'Rav Kahana: A collection of homilies on the scriptural readings in synagogues for special Shabbatot and holidays, written around the fifth century in the Land of Israel.

P'sukei D'zimrah: "Verses of song." Psalms of praise that serve as introductory warm-ups in the morning prayer service.

Rabbanim: "Rabbis."

rachamim: "Mercy."

Rosh Chodesh: "The New Moon; the New Month." The first day of the month.

sa-ir laAzazel: "Goat for Azazel" (Leviticus 16). "Scapegoat" (idiomatically).

seder: "Order, arrangement." By itself often refers to the family meal and home ritual for Passover.

Seder HaAvodah: "The Order of the *Avodah*." The liturgical section of the Yom Kippur *Musaf* service, which describes the most important sacrificial service of the entire year carried out by the High Priest on Yom Kippur.

Seder Rav Amram: The earliest compilation of the Jewish prayer book, created by Rav Amram Gaon in Babylonia ca. 870.

Sefer HaChayim: "The Book of Life."

sefer Torah: "Torah scroll" (plural: *sifrei Torah*).

Sephardi(c): "Spanish." Pertaining to the Jewish community originally from the Iberian Peninsula.

Seven Benedictions: A collection of seven blessings for the *Amidah* on Shabbat and festivals instead of the weekday eighteen.

Shechinah: The Divine Presence, from the Hebrew root meaning "to dwell."

shivah: "Seven." Seven days of mourning following a funeral.

Shiviti: "I have set" (Psalm 16).

Sh'liach tzibur: "Messenger of the community." Refers to the prayer leader, who also represents the entire community before God.

Sh'ma koleinu: From the liturgical phrase "Hear our voice, Adonai our God, have mercy and compassion on us."

Sh'ma Uvirchotecha: "*Sh'ma* [the prayer] and Her Blessings [those that precede and follow]."

Sh'moneh Esreih: "Eighteen." An Ashkenazic name for the *Amidah* because of the eighteen benedictions that it originally comprised.

Shoah: The Holocaust.

Shofar Gadol: "Great Shofar." Believed to usher in the messianic age.

Shofarot: "Shofar Verses." The last of the three central benedictions of the Shofar Service on Rosh Ha-Shanah morning.

Shulchan Aruch: "A Prepared Table." The basis for Jewish law today, by Joseph Caro (1488–1575), codifying Sephardic custom and to which was added Moses Isserles's *Mapah* (lit., "Tablecloth"), codifying Ashkneazic custom.

shuv: "Return." See also *t'shuvah*.

s'lichah: "Forgiveness."

S'lichot: Special penitential prayers that are recited during the penitential season, which begins before Rosh HaShanah and concludes with Yom Kippur. A special *S'lichot* service is recited late on the Saturday before Rosh HaShanah.

sugya: "Talmudic passage."

talmud Torah: "Study of Torah." The mitzvah of Jewish study.

tannaitic: Referring to the *Tannaim*, the rabbis of the Mishnah and *Tosefta*.

Tashlich: "You shall cast off." The custom of going to a body of water on the afternoon of Rosh HaShanah and symbolically casting off one's sins in the form of breadcrumbs or another symbol.

Theodicy: The branch of theology concerned with defending the attributes of God, particularly holiness and justice, against objections resulting from physical and moral evil.

Tisha B'Av: "Ninth of Av." A day of mourning and fasting commemorating the destruction of the First and Second Temples in Jerusalem as well as other tragic events in Jewish history.

t'filah: "Prayer" (plural: *t'filot*). Also, *T'filah*, another name for the *Amidah*.

tikkun: "Repair."

Tizku l'shanim rabbot: "May you merit many years [of life]."

Tosefta: "Addition." A collection of Rabbinic material contemporaneous with the Mishnah but not included in it.

t'shuvah: "Return." Repentance, denoting a return to God after sinning.

tzedakah: "Righteous act; charity." A gift given as an act of justice and moral behavior. *Tzedakah tatzil mimavet*: charity saves from death.

Tzion: "Zion."

Union Prayer Book: The *Union Prayer Book* (*UPB*), volume 1, was the first prayer book published by the CCAR and was meant to be suitable for all American Jews. The *UPB*, volume 2, was the first *machzor* published by the CCAR.

Untaneh Tokef: "Let us proclaim the [sacred] power [of this day]." Medieval (or earlier) *piyut* commonly ascribed to Rabbi Amnon of Mainz that precedes the High Holy Day *K'dushah*.

Ush'meinu karata vishmecha: "And our name You have linked with Your own" (*Untaneh Tokef*).

Ush'mi Adonai lo nodati lahem: "But My name *Adonai* I did not make known to them" (Exodus 6:3).

Vidui: "Confession." Confessional prayers that form a central part of the Yom Kippur and *S'lichot* liturgy.

Vidui Rabbah: "Long Confession." One type of the confessional prayers that form a central part of the Yom Kippur liturgy.

Vidui Zuta: "Short Confession." One type of the confessional prayers that form a central part of the Yom Kippur liturgy.

V'initem et nafshoteichem: "You shall afflict your souls [on Yom Kippur]" (Leviticus 16:31, 23:27). It is from this verse that the mitzvah of fasting on Yom Kippur is derived.

Yamim Noraim: "Days of Awe." The period from the first day of Rosh HaShanah until Yom Kippur, and these two days in particular.

Yizkor: "[God] shall remember." Service of remembrance for the martyrs of our people as well as for our own relatives and friends, recited on Yom Kippur (as well as the last days of Sukkot and Passover, and on Shavuot).

Yizkor Elohim nishmat _____: "God shall remember the soul of _____."

yontif: Yiddish for the Hebrew *"yom tov,"* meaning "good day" or "holiday."

yotzei (et chovato): "Fulfilled (one's obligation)."

Yovel: "Jubilee." In the Bible, a year of rest to be observed by the Israelites every fiftieth year.

Y'rushalayim: "Jerusalem."

Y'rushalmi: "Jerusalemite." Shorthand for the Jerusalem (or Palestinian) Talmud compiled around 400 CE in the Land of Israel.

z'chut avot: "Merit of [our] ancestors."

Zichronot, zikaron: "Remembrance Verses." The second of the three central benedictions of the Shofar Service on Rosh HaShanah morning.

z"l: Abbreviation for *zichrono liv'rachah,* meaning "may his memory be for a blessing."

Suggestions for Further Reading

Agnon, Shmuel Yosef. *Days of Awe: A Treasury of Jewish Wisdom for Reflection, Repentance, and Renewal on the High Holy Days.* New York: Schocken Books, 1995.

Ansky, S. *The Dybbuk and Other Writings by S. Ansky.* Edited by David G. Roskies. New Haven: Yale University Press, 2002.

Arzt, Max. *Justice and Mercy: Commentary on the Liturgy of the New Year and the Day of Atonement.* New York: Holt, Rinehart and Winston, 1963.

Bick, Ezra. *In His Mercy: Understanding the Thirteen Middot.* Translated by David Silverberg. New Milford, CT: Koren Publishers Jerusalem, 2011.

Cohen, Jeffrey M. *Understanding the High Holyday Services.* London: Routledge & Kegan Paul, 1983.

Dan, Joseph. "The Development and Purposes of the Story of the Ten Martyrs" (Hebrew). In *Simon Halkin Festschrift,* edited by Ezra Fleischer, 15–22. Jerusalem: Magnes Press, 1973.

Dan, Joseph. *The Hebrew Story in the Middle Ages.* Jerusalem: Keter, 1974.

Feld, Ed, ed. *Mahzor Lev Shalem: Rosh Hashanah and Yom Kippur.* New York: Rabbinical Assembly, 2010.

Freehof, Solomon B. "Hazkarath Neshamoth." *Hebrew Union College Annual* 36 (1965): 179–89.

Friedland, Eric L. "The Atonement Memorial Service in the American Machzor." *Hebrew Union College Annual* 55 (1984): 243–82.

Frishman, Elyse D., ed. *Mishkan T'filah: A Reform Siddur.* New York: CCAR Press, 2007.

Goldschmidt, Daniel. *Machzor l'Yamim HaNora-im.* Jerusalem: Koren, 1970.

Halbertal, Moshe. *On Sacrifice.* Princeton, NJ: Princeton University Press, 2012.

Hoffman, Lawrence A., ed. *Gates of Understanding.* 2 vols. New York: CCAR Press, 1984–1997.

Jellinek, Adolph. Bet Hamidrash (6 vols.; Leipzig: Friedrich Niese, 1853-77; reprint in 2 vols., Jerusalem: Wahrmann Books, 1967).

Kaplan, Mordecai, Eugene Kohn, and Ira Eisenstein, eds. *High Holiday Prayer Book.* New York: Jewish Reconstructionist Foundation, 1948.

Klein, Max D. *Seder Avodah: Service Book for Rosh Hashanah and Yom Kippur.* Philadelphia: Maurice Jacobs, 1960.

Levy, Richard N. *On Wings of Awe: A Fully Transliterated Machzor for Rosh Hashanah and Yom Kippur.* Rev. ed. Brooklyn: Ktav Publishing House, 2011.

Machzor: Challenge and Change, Volume 1. New York: CCAR Press, 2009.

Marcus, Ivan R. *The Jewish Life Cycle: Rites of Passage from Biblical to Modern Times.* Seattle: University of Washington Press, 2004.

Milgrom, Jacob. *Leviticus: A Book of Ritual and Ethics.* Minneapolis: Fortress Press, 2004.

Pine II, B. Joseph, and James H. Gilmore. *The Experience Economy.* Updated ed. Boston: Harvard Business School Publishing, 2011.

Reeg, Gottfried, ed. *Die Geschichte von den Zehn Martyrern / Ma'aseh Asarah Harugei Malkhut.* Tübingen: Mohr-Siebeck, 1985.

Reimer, Gail Twersky, and Judith A. Kates, eds. *Beginning Anew: A Woman's Companion to the High Holy Days.* New York: Touchstone, 1997.

Spiegel, Shalom. *The Last Trial*. Woodstock, VT: Jewish Lights Publishing, 1993.

Spitz, Elie Kaplan. *Does the Soul Survive: A Jewish Journey to Belief in Afterlife, Past Lives, and Living with Purpose*. Woodstock, VT: Jewish Lights Publishing, 2000.

Stern, Chaim, ed. *Gates of Forgiveness: The Union S'lichot Service; A Service of Preparation for the Days of Awe*. New York: CCAR Press, 1993.

Stern, Chaim, ed. *Gates of Prayer—Shaarei T'filah: The New Union Prayerbook for Weekdays, Sabbaths and Festivals*. New York: CCAR Press, 1975.

Stern, Chaim, ed. *Gates of Repentance—Shaarei Teshuva: The New Union Prayerbook for the Days of Awe*. Rev. ed. New York: CCAR Press, 1996.

Turner, Victor. *The Forest of Symbols: Aspects of Ndembu Ritual*. Ithaca, NY: Cornell University Press, 1967.